Perspectives on Judgment and Decision-Making

Edited by
Wing Hong Loke

The Scarecrow Press, Inc.
Lanham, Md., & London

SCARECROW PRESS, INC.

Published in the United States of America
by Scarecrow Press, Inc.
4720 Boston Way
Lanham, Maryland 20706

4 Pleydell Gardens, Folkestone
Kent CT20 2DN, England

British Cataloguing-in-Publication Information Available

Library of Congress Cataloging-in-Publication Data

Perspectives on judgment and decision making / edited by Wing Hong Loke.
p. cm.
Includes bibliographical references.
1. Decision-making. 2. Judgment. I. Wing Hong Loke, 1961–
BF448.P47   1995   153.8'3—dc20   92-39353   CIP

ISBN 0-8108-2642-9 (cloth : alk. paper)

Printed in the United States of America

⊖™ The paper used in this publication meets the minimum requirements of
American National Standard for Information Sciences—Permanence of
Paper for Printed Library Materials, ANSI Z39.48–1984.

Dedicated to my parents,
Loke Woh Hee and Kum Po Sheng

CONTENTS

Section C: Medical Decision Making

Section D: Decision Making in Law

PREFACE

As we move into the 1990s and into the era of management of human resources and information technology, how individuals process information will become increasingly important. Consequently, *Perspectives on Judgment and Decision Making* introduces a range of recent topics dealing with how people process information (otherwise known as judgment and decision making). There is considerable diversity in the topics addressed by the articles accepted for publication, with the following distinct categories emerging: (a) general models and applications of decision making, (b) cross-cultural factors and decision making, (c) medical decision making, (d) legal decision making, (e) group decision making, and (f) approaches to the evaluation of decision making.

Perspectives on Judgment and Decision Making consists of twenty-five articles. In the introductory section, three articles describe recent developments in the psychology of decision making in real-life situations. The interplay between theory, methodology, and application is stressed. Areas of application include consumer judgments, educational evaluations, the formation of public policy, negotiations in industrial and government settings, and perceptions of jobs.

The second section is about cross-cultural factors on decision making and comprises eight articles, with the importance of cross-cultural research in decision making being emphasized. Current research using different cultural groups such as Singaporeans, North Americans, Japanese, Australians, Chinese (from People's Republic of China), and Norwegians is examined.

The third section looks at the area of medical decision making. Of the five articles, one reviews the relationship between psychiatric disturbance and decision making. Two others discuss the use of diagnostic aids and another two deal with the attendant issues of validity and appropriate analysis in clinical decision making.

The fourth section on legal decision making consists of two articles which examine the influence of extralegal factors (e.g., gender) in decisions made by judges and jurors. Of note is that in some countries like Singapore the legal system does not include the use of jurors in court. Readers are, therefore, reminded to interpret the results with care when applied to such countries.

Group decision making is examined in the fifth section. Making decisions in a group can overcome judgmental errors that might occur because of human fallibility. On the other hand, a phenomenon known as "group-think" may prevail, resulting also in faulty judgment. In the latter's case, decision makers tend to abide by the decisions of the group, even beyond justification by the quality of information used in the decision-making process. One article focuses its discussion at the organization level and another at the committee level.

The last section in this volume examines several approaches to the evaluation of decision making. Several examples are used to illustrate the decision-making process and how to develop good decision-making methods. Finally, a decision-aiding software is suggested for all fields of behavioral science.

On a personal note, I am very grateful to Tan Wee Lee, Alvin Tan Hong Seong, and W. Keong who have spent an inordinate amount of time typing and re-typing this manuscript, using the latest desktop publishing facilities. Also, I thank all the authors who have submitted articles for publication. Regrettably, due to the overwhelming response, not all articles could be published. The enthusiastic response and support for this book suggest that interest in "judgment and decision making" is very much alive and, in particular instances, an increasingly important area of concern. I hope that the broad range of topics in this volume will prove to be useful and enjoyable reading for practitioners, researchers, and students. Given its scope, *Perspectives on Judgment and Decision Making* could be a useful supplementary text for students. And at the end of this volume is a list of recent articles which complements this book, providing an up-to-date view in this area of research.

Wing Hong **Loke**, Ph.D.
Department of Social Work and Psychology
National University of Singapore
Republic of Singapore

SECTION A
Introduction to Human Judgment and Decision Making: Models and Applications

MODELS OF JUDGMENT AND DECISION MAKING: AN OVERVIEW

Wing Hong Loke

In everyday activities, individuals make decisions which may be important for survival. For example, decisions such as those made while driving, formulating policies, in employment, the college to enroll in, and which restaurant to patronize have a direct impact on individuals' lives. These decisions may be based on an evaluation of the information available, perception of the probabilities, or influenced by external factors (e.g., attractiveness). To understand the process of decision making, two approaches are presented: one approach examines how individuals should reason (normative) and the other how they do reason (descriptive). The present review suggests that the various competing theories on decision making can also be viewed as emphasizing the many facets of decision making. Therefore, one suggested approach is to develop comprehensive yet parsimonious theories which would account for the whole process of decision making. The information integration theory is illustrated as an example. The present review concludes with some views of the current state of research and direction for further study.

The study of human judgment and decision making has evolved to a stage whereby case-by-case analyses of decisions are worthless. Instead, researchers have attempted to hypothesize rules by which similar decisions are made. The following is a discussion on some of the main models which have been proposed for the understanding of human judgment and decision making.

Definitions and Approaches to Decision Making

The two main approaches to decision making are the classical and the behavioral. The classical approach assumes that events are well controlled and certain. For example, students face a well-defined problem as to whether to take psychology as a major. The students have knowledge of all possible actions, alternatives, and their consequences. They then choose the best alternative for the particular problem. This is the ideal way of making a decision.

In practice, however, the process of making a decision is less than certain. The students, in the above example, act only in terms of what they perceive about a given situation and such perceptions are often incomplete. Instead, individuals tend to make decisions according to the behavioral approach. With limited information, individuals choose the first alternative that they perceive would give them a satisfactory solution to their problems. Hence, individuals are bounded in their ability to make decisions by their finite cognitive capacity, affective attributes, and the environment. Simon (1957) states that most human decision making tends to be concerned with the discovery and actual selection of satisfactory alternatives rather than in obtaining optimal decisions. As such, research attempts to find ways to reduce the limitations placed on individuals, thereby allowing decisions to be closer to an optimal state.

Models for understanding judgment and decision making. Many models have been derived from theories which illustrate the development of the methods and models for understanding the processes underlying judgment and decision making. In general, the two prescriptions for consistent behavior are the normative approach (logically consistent decision procedures and how individuals should decide) and descriptive approach (decisions individuals make and how they decide).

When decisions are made through comparing actual behavior with that predicted by the calculated law of probabilities, we say that the decision has been made via normative procedure (which follows the classical approach). Edwards (1962) provides an example of this in terms of an individual's ability to determine the probability of obtaining 8 blue and 4 white poker chips on 12 successive independent choices from a bag of 70 blue and 30 white poker chips. One way of calculating the probabilities in such a situation would be to use Bayes' theorem. Such an analysis assumes that there are laws of probabilities which govern behavior and that behavior and decisions are rational. However, when subjects were asked to make the decision as to the probability of the poker chips outcome, the calculated mean probability was 0.97 while the judgment was 0.75. (Edwards, 1962). The error of underestimation or conservatism was involved. So, the subjects were limited by their knowledge of probabilities, and they made decisions on a less than rational (non-normative) method.

The descriptive procedure is a different method of examining behavior. Here, the procedure does not examine whether the judgments and the decisions are correct but rather attempts to describe the underlying processes involved. This analysis allows for the consideration of the individual who is making the decision and incorporates this into the analysis. The analysis examines what individuals actually do in decision-making situations, and hence, it is a behavioral approach to decision making.

Normative Models

The models which fall under this type of decision making were used prior to the 1960s. The underlying assumption for these models is that humans act in a rational and accurate manner, and behavior occurs through a combination of formal probability and utility. So, individuals behave to maximize performance based on utility and probability. Such behavior can further be subgrouped into the decisions which are static (i.e., deterministic) and dynamic (i.e., stochastic—take into consideration the element of the subjective decision maker).

The Utility Model

One of the earliest normative models was the utility model. According to this model, when individuals are faced with a decision, they would take the action with the largest sum of product of subjective value and objective probability of payoff. For example, if individuals have a preference for a belief in truth over the belief of compassion and compassion over moral right, they would always choose truth over moral right or compassion as a rule. Such an example characterizes the process emphasized by the decision-making model—a model known as the expected utility model.

The Dynamic Model

The second subgroup of normative models is the dynamic model. An important aspect of this model is that it attempts to account for risky decision-making behavior. Such behavior would appear in gambling situations or where information is limited and the outcome is ambiguous. Here, the utility model is a subjective one. That is, the decision maker chooses the action which will give the largest sum of product of subjective value (utility) and subjective probability of payoff.

A variant of this model would be the Atkinson subjective value model. This model includes the personality variables of the decision maker. It assumes that there are two types of decision makers—those whose motivation to succeed is greater than to fail, and those whose motivation to fail is greater than to succeed. With this, the decisions which each person makes will depend on whether they would want to maximize their chances of success or failure.

Considerations of the Dynamic Model. To understand the way decisions are made, the model accounts for the individual's subjective view. One reason for the consideration is that the value of "payoff" benefits is determined solely by the decision maker. In addition, the decision relies on the subjective estimation of the decision maker on how likely a given event is to occur. The usual situation is that an estimated probability is given at the initial stages followed by subsequent estimates of probability as a result of experience.

The dynamic models are therefore a more accurate representation of the real world than static models, especially for decisions which involve a series of choices among the courses of action. Dynamic models would also be accurate in decisions for preference events which are either inconsistent or transitive. Using an above-mentioned example, an inconsistent preference event would be when truth is not always preferred over compassion. A transitive event would entail that moral right is preferred over truth, although compassion is chosen over moral right. Furthermore, dynamic models account for the variance of preferences where the variance of bets confound with the utility of the subjective expected utility model.

Aside from viewing what is a "payoff," the question of what constitutes a choice can only be seen from a subjective viewpoint. The dynamic model makes assertions about the probability between choices. As in the Luce (1959) choice axiom, the ratio of the probability of choosing an alternative A to the probability of choosing an alternative B is a constant independent of the number of alternatives in the set of choices. Specifically, if A is preferred 2:1 over B when only A and B are in the choice set, then the 2:1 ratio should be maintained even if C and D are introduced as alternative choices. If C and D are each chosen 20 percent of the time, then according to the Luce choice axiom, A should be chosen 40 percent of the time and B chosen 20 percent of the time. (Mathematically stated, the probability of choosing C, given that C is a subset of B and B is a subset of A, is the sum of the product of probabilities of C x B and B x A.) To illustrate, in choosing ice cream flavors, the probability of choosing chocolate to the probability of choosing vanilla as an alternative is a constant, independent of the number of the individual's choices. Hence, if chocolate is preferred 2:1 times over vanilla, then this should still hold even if there are other choices, like strawberry or butterscotch. Chocolate should be chosen 40 percent of the time and vanilla chosen 20 percent.

Evaluation of Normative Models

Static decision models are limited in being unable to predict real-world events. The models are developed with the support of contrived (laboratory) data or are developed with an exactness that does not allow accurate prediction given variations in real judgment and decision-making situations. In contrast, the dynamic models are preferred because they correspond closer to real judgments. Perhaps, researchers should study the development of dynamic models to describe the multi-variables that influence behavior and, whenever possible, work towards the development of static models that have greater predictive power.

In general, a limitation of the normative models is that utility and probability are insufficient to predict all decisions, e.g. in cases such as bargaining situations. In bargaining, individuals tend towards equal distribution of payoffs. This split-the-difference principle (Flood, 1954 & 1955) is observed in a three-person game where two individuals tend to seek equity by bargaining in a way as to disadvantage a third stooge player (Hoffman et al., 1954). However, not all bargaining games observed the split-the-difference principle. Scodel, Minas, Ratoosh, and Lipetz (1959) studied the prisoner's dilemma (see Luce & Raiffa, 1957) where each player seeks to obtain the optimal strategy even though the payoffs are little. Edwards (1961) concluded that free communication encourages equity and restricted communication encourages optimal strategies regardless of the importance of payoffs. Alternatively, a mixed-motive strategy is observed in employer-union negotiations. Here, the first (integrative) phase is a competitive one—where the union attempts to acquire as many benefits as possible for its members. Later, in the second (distributive) phase, the union cooperates to distribute the benefits in an equitable manner.

Descriptive Models

The second category of models is the descriptive type. These models, relative to the normative models, take even more elements of decision making into consideration. In this regard, descriptive models are viewed as part of the interrelated facets of decision making rather than oppositional to the normative models (Slovic et al., 1977). In the poker-chips example shown earlier, individuals tend to be conservative when making judgments involving probability. Here, the tendency is to combine probabilistic information to come up with a posterior probability closer to the prior probability than that specified by Bayes' theorem. Other factors may influence the judgment of individuals. The order in which blue and white chips are sampled is not part of Bayes' theorem but could be a major influence on a decision made by individuals. When order effect was examined, Shanteau (1972) found a strong recency effect where the judgment on a given trial depended most heavily on the immediately preceding outcome. Hence, their ability to calculate probabilities and make accurate decisions was handicapped. So, probability rules in decision making assume that the position between alternatives in decisions is important.

Other researchers have also discovered that decision makers can continue to use certain information at each stage of the decision-making process, even when the information is unreliable. This is known as the cascaded inference effect. Thus, humans are not good intuitive statisticians.

Descriptive models, in contrast to normative models, incorporate the order of stimulus into their decision making. The model also considers the idea that decisions could be made through other factors (e.g., heuristic representativeness) where the similarities between events are used to make decisions.

Decision Tree

One particular descriptive model is the decision tree—which is a representation that shows the stages of responses across time. An early method of identifying the psychological process involved in decision making is the think-aloud protocol (Newell & Simon, 1972). Individuals describe their mental actions while they perform a task (think-aloud) and their responses are recorded. The responses are charted in terms of a decision-tree diagram—a representation that shows the stages of the responses across time.

Regression Analysis

Another way in which decisions are made is through regression analysis. This has the assumption that the judgmental process is an algebraic one where individual factors are identified, weighted, and combined to result in decisions. The process of combining the weights is done via regression techniques such as analysis of variance, conjoint measurement, and multiple regression.

Specifically, analysis of variance focuses on interaction of variables, conjoint measurement examines the scaling techniques for rank-ordered data, and multiple regression investigates the linear combination of variables. Also, regression techniques such as information integration (Anderson, 1974) examine the type of combination rule of variables (e.g., adding or averaging rule) while policy capturing (Hammond, Steward, Brehmer, & Steinmann, 1975) examines the relations of environmental cues and the judgment of the decision makers (e.g., alternative land use policies). The multiple cues probability learning (Slovic & Lichtenstein, 1971) examines the cue interrelationships while dynamic decision making (Rapoport, 1975; Rapoport & Burkheimer, 1971) examines the information available for later decisions based on outcomes of earlier decisions.

Development of New Methods

The focus on descriptive models resulted in the development of new methods which examined the process involved in judgment and decision making. For example, to study the multiple attributes that influence interpersonal and intergroup conflicts, computer programs were designed to accept decisional variables of the individuals and their relative importance and generate outcomes of the conflicts (Hammond, 1971; Hammond et al., 1975). Participants judged the weights (importance) of each variable, as in the study on public participation in regional impacts of alternative land use policies (Hammond et al., 1975), that examine aspects of recreation, agriculture, industry, and environment. In this way, policymakers would be in a position to examine the different viewpoints of the factions within the community by interaction and weights of the variables of each faction.

Specific programs can also be designed to follow an individual's progress and provide continuous recommendations on the next decision (Weisbrod, Davis, Freedy, & Weltman, 1975). Individuals could seek information from an information-display board and the sequence in which information was sought could be recorded (Payne, 1976). Similarly, simultaneous recording of individuals and their verbal protocols could be administered (Russo & Rosen, 1975) to track the information processing sequence.

To further describe the roles of relevant factors that lead to judgments and decisions, designs in which each of several factors are manipulated across several levels and all possible factor level combinations could be constructed. For example, if factor A has three levels and Factor B has two levels, then a complete factorial design would contain six different combinations. Analysis of variance tests would then be used to determine the relative importance of each factor on the judgment of interest.

Individuals are limited in their ability to make decisions, and they may experience cognitive overload and therefore resort to rules-of-thumb or heuristics (Tversky & Kahneman, 1974) and cognitive shortcuts (e.g., cognitive scripts, Abelson, 1976). These shortcuts in heuristics, however, contribute to a large part to the decisional errors made.

Heuristics and Their Biases

Researchers have shown that individuals rely on a few heuristic principles which reduce the complex task of decision making to simpler operations. A heuristic is a strategy for simplifying a problem; it places more emphasis on some aspects of information while ignoring others. With heuristics, individuals develop subjective operational knowledge of the world. With such a limitation, this strategy may lead to systematic errors in the decisional process.

Representativeness. In an experiment (Tversky & Kahneman, 1974), subjects were shown brief descriptions of several individuals sampled at random from a group of 100 professionals consisting of engineers and lawyers. Subjects were then asked to assess the probability of each description being that of a lawyer or an engineer. They were then told that the group consisted of 30 lawyers and 70 engineers. Another group was told the reverse, that the group consisted of 30 engineers and 70 lawyers. The assessment would then depend on the ratio of engineers and lawyers in a particular group.

With the application of Bayes' rules, the ratio of odds should be 0.3 (i.e., 30 engineers versus 70 lawyers), 0.7 (i.e., 70 engineers versus 30 lawyers), and 5.44 (i.e., ratio of both odds are [.7/.3]2 or 5.44) for each situation. The subjects, however, based their decisions on the degree to which the descriptions fit their stereotypes of engineers and lawyers, with little or no regard for the prior information. This showed that the individuals failed to recognize the prior probabilities or base rates.

In another example, North American individuals are told that "Steve is a meek, tidy man" and are then asked to select the most likely profession of Steve from a list of occupations—farmer, salesman, airline pilot, librarian, and physician. Most of the individuals chose "librarian" instead of "farmer." However, they ignored the statistics (base rate) that the United States had more farmers than librarians (Tversky & Kahneman, 1973 & 1974). Individuals evaluated the degree to which Steve's profession is similar in essential properties to its parent population, that is, similarity between events or representativeness rather than the frequency or base rates.

So, one heuristic strategy of decision making is representativeness. People connect events A and B by assessing the degree of similarity between them. The extent of the similarity depends on subjective evaluation of the important descriptive feature to be emphasized.

Problems arise when there are defects in judgment due to inattention to certain facts which should affect probability judgments. In the above examples, the subjects were not paying attention to the base rates and frequencies, and instead were making decisions based on their limited subjective view of the world. Hence, the decisions they made were in error. When there are differences between judgments made intuitively and the probabilities given by calculation or empirical evidence, the condition is said to be a heuristic bias. In some situations (e.g., the court room), the heuristic biases could have serious consequences. For example, if the defendant had a nervous twitch and jurors possessed inaccurate representations of the world, where they believed in the fallacy that "good people" are not afflicted by this disability, then there is a high probability that they would find the defendant guilty.

The second type of representative error is when the person is insensitive to sample size. In an experiment by Tversky and Kahneman (1974), an urn was filled with balls of which 2/3 were one color and 1/3 were another. Given that a first person draws 5 balls from the urn and finds that 4 are red and 1 is white, and the second individual draws 20 balls out of which 12 are red and 8 are white, the question asked then is which one would have more confidence of the fact that 2/3 of balls are one color and 1/3 are of the other. The odds should be 8:1 for the first individual and 16:1 for the second person. However, most subjects would choose the first individual as being more confident. The size of the sample (4:1 and 12:8) was ignored. Thus, the urn example is another limitation of the representative heuristic which leads to an incorrect judgment.

The third type of representative heuristic bias is the misconception of chance. People often expect that a small sequence of events can predict or generate enough facts to draw conclusions. To illustrate, Tversky and Kahneman (1974) considered the number of heads or tails scored in the tossing of a coin. People would regard the sequence of H-T-H-T-H-T to be more likely than a sequence of T-T-T-T-T-T or a sequence of T-T-T-H-H-H. The last two sequences do not seem to appear in a random manner. This is the chance or "luck" factor which many individuals believe to be self-corrective. That is, a deviation in one direction would eventually result in another, in order to restore equilibrium. It follows another fallacy, known as the law of small numbers, where small samples are believed to be representative of the population from which they came.

The fourth representative heuristic bias is the insensitivity to predictability. People often make predictions and are unaffected by the reliability of the information on which the prediction rests. An example of this is when individuals predict the future earnings of a company based on a description of how well it is doing. If the description of the company is favorable, then the prediction will also be favorable. However, the reliability of the description is seldom questioned even though it may not be accurate.

A fifth representative heuristic bias is the illusion of validity; this is related to the fourth bias. Here, individuals predict outcomes that are most representative of the input. However, they seem to have a degree of confidence in the input with little regard to the factors which limit predictability. The confidence is based on the goodness of fit between the predicted outcome and the input information. This is the illusion of validity, and sometimes, even if individuals are aware of the limitations, the illusion still persists. An example of this is when subjects are given descriptions of individuals as an experiment (Tversky & Kahneman, 1974). The stereotype which one holds concerning behavior and personality of others is obtained through cultural factors, but is also partly idiosyncratic. It is untested and unconfirmed and hence should also be false.

Availability. There are two other basic types of heuristics: (a) availability and (b) anchoring and adjustments. Availability heuristic is where individuals judge the frequency of an event based on how quickly they can recall that particular experience or known experiences. For example, if individuals were asked to judge the rate of abortions, they would do so based on the availability of related experiences or knowledge of abortions. If in the past few months when individuals heard or had a friend who had an abortion, they would predict that the rate of abortion was high.

Similar to representative heuristics, availability also has a set of biases; these problems are those related to the retrieval of instances. As mentioned, judgment is often based on the ease of retrievability of a particular event. For example, a list of well-known personalities of both sexes were read out to a group of subjects. They were then asked to judge whether the list contained more male or female names. By varying the number of famous personalities in either sex, the subjects consistently judged that the list with the more famous personalities was longer (Tversky & Kahneman, 1974).

The second heuristic problem that is associated with the availability heuristic is salience. This is a problem which affects the retrievability condition. For example, the impact of seeing a house burn down is greater and more vivid than if a subject simply read about it in a book. Hence, recall of actually witnessing the event is greater than reading about the it (Tversky & Kahneman, 1974). (Of note also is that recent occurrences would be more available in recall than earlier occurrences.)

The difficulty in getting certain types of data is part of the problem of availability, that is, difficulty in accessing the search sets. The search sets that most individuals have are not flexible. As in word recall, suppose one is asked to think of words that have the letter "r" as the third letter. Most individuals begin by recalling words that begin with "r." Since it is much easier to access words that begin with "r" rather than end with the letter, most would conclude that there are more words that begin with "r" than those that end with "r." So, different tasks elicit different search modes and individuals are generally rigid in their search set, hence limiting the availability of information for predictive purposes.

A fourth type of availability error is related to imaginability. Sometimes, people generate predictions even when there is no information available. In such situations, one generates instances or imagines the event and then evaluates the probability based on the ease with which one imagined. The calculated risk (probabilities) involved in certain events done through this technique is then usually inaccurate.

Adjustment and anchoring. The last of the three major heuristics is adjustment and anchoring. Individuals usually predict by starting off from an initial value that is adjusted in order to yield the most accurate prediction. They fail to consider that different individuals would be at different initial points. Furthermore, individuals' set of initial values would be biased by a process called anchoring. When predicting quantities based on incomplete computation, anchoring will occur regardless of whether a person is told of the initial value or whether the initial value is elicited from the person.

An experiment on multiplication (Tversky & Kahneman, 1974) showed the effects of anchoring and failure to adjust. Two groups of high school students were asked to estimate the products: 8 x 7 x 6 x 5 x 4 x 3 x 2 x 1 and 1 x 2 x 3 x 4 x 5 x 6 x 7 x 8. The first sequence led groups to anchor their predictions along a high scale, while the other example which started with "1" led to lower predictions. The median estimate for the ascending order was 512 and for the descending order was 2,259; the correct answer, however, was 40,320. The students also could not adjust, and the final reported answers are underestimations of the correct answer.

Related situations sensitive to the heuristic biases are observed in the evaluation of conjunctive and disjunctive events. In such a case, there are three types of events. The first is the simple event—which is similar to drawing a red marble from a bag of 50% red and 50% white marbles. The second is the conjunctive event—which is like drawing a red marble 7 times in a row from a bag containing 90% red and 10% white. The last type of event is the disjunctive event; in this situation, one draws a red marble at least 7 times out of a bag of 10% red and 90% white. In a study by Bar-Hillel (1973), subjects were given the opportunity to bet on two events, with the three situations. The majority of the students preferred to bet on the conjunctive event rather than on the simple and even less on the disjunctive event. This is against the mathematical probabilities whereby the event with the highest probability is the disjunctive event (52%).

A Recent Approach

In the beginning of the present review, we stated that there may sometimes be a level of uncertainty in decisions. As such, decision makers often approach decisions using a limited amount of knowledge. The limitations are due to the many causes and determinants and humans' limitations in the collection of facts. This distinction is not merely tautological; because many factors go into a decision, each of these factors needs to be considered when examining the process of decision making. As a result, most models are limited in that they do not allow for a large number of causes and determinants.

One of the strongest criticisms launched at research on models based on the normative procedure is offered by Anderson (1986). He questioned the whole gamut of research, starting with the biases of conservatism of Bayesian theory. He stated that "by focusing on biases, the normative conceptualization has retarded cognitive analysis" (Anderson, 1986). Specifically, Anderson (1986) criticizes Tversky and Kahneman (1973 & 1974) for their explanations of heuristics as part of the decision-making process. To understand Anderson's criticisms, an overview of his ideas are discussed in the following section.

Information Integration Theory

In line with the normative view, Anderson (1986) proposed the theory of information integration which focuses on information integration by way of a cognitive algebra. However, in accordance with the descriptive view, the subjective view was necessary for decision making. In sum, the algebraic way was good as a method of measurement, but studies needed to consider the individual/subjective view.

The integration theory is functional as it focuses on the goal-directed quality of thought and action. This is because processing of information is dependent on its function in goal attainment and hence, leads to the idea that thought and action are contextual and constructive. This brings us to focus on knowledge systems as the basis of thought and action. This is more general than the schema concepts of cognitive psychology, especially with the inclusion of motivation and affect as basic in this system (Anderson, 1986).

The conceptual foundation of the integration theory involved analysis of response patterns rather than normative inaccuracy in normative studies. Hence, instead of focusing on errors relative to a normative criterion, as in the normative approach, the integration theory focused on internal regularity or pattern among a set of responses. Anderson (1986) found that there were two useful patterns, that of parallelism and linear fan. The first is the diagnostic sign of an adding-type model and the second is the diagnostic sign of a multiplying model. Functional measurement via the multiplication rule could solve the problems of measurement related to subjective probability and utility of the utility theory, which the normative approach failed to explain (Anderson, 1986).

In the above, we have already mentioned that there are many factors which can come into play when a decision has to be taken. One problem which arises in normative research has been the question of subjective probabilities. The consideration of more general weight parameters, under certain conditions, solves measurement problems associated with models of decision making (Shanteau & Anderson, 1972). Most research used some measure of weighting for each of the factors which seemed to be related to the process of decision making. However, for most cases, these weights have been assigned in an arbitrary manner. In contrast, the integration theory employs a differential weighting system, and it provides a validational criterion of developing a general methodology of self-estimated parameters (Anderson, 1981b). This substitution of more general weight parameters for the subjective probabilities, although open to some criticisms, is in keeping with the "decision weights" idea used by Kahneman and Tversky (1979).

In the integration theory, two weight parameters are given to beliefs about an object. One parameter is the scale value which refers to the quantitative position of the belief on the judgment dimension. Scale value allows for a common denominator for integration as well as the different dimensions that a belief may have. Kaplan (1986) illustrates this with reference to Sigall and Ostrove's (1975) research on defendant's attractiveness. Attractiveness affected higher scale values for complicity in a confidence swindle than for a burglary charge. The other parameter is the weight or relative importance of the judgment. It is related to the amount of information the fact contributes to a particular judgment. Together, the scale value and the weight give rise to the process of valuation and integration. In valuation, a scale value is given to each piece of information, while in the integration process, the scale values and the weight are integrated into the overall judgment (Kaplan, 1986).

One of the strengths of the integration theory is its use of the averaging principle rather than the additive idea which is prescribed by normative theorists. The averaging effect with its functional measurement of weights allows for decisions taken when there is missing information (Anderson 1986; Levin, Johnson & Faraone, 1984; Singh, 1990). Averaging is also important in attitudes research when an estimation of weights of qualitatively different attributes in a common scale ratio is necessary. Such a comparison unconfounded by the scale value is hence possible with integration theory. As a comparison, the regression weights were confounded with scale units and, therefore were not properly comparable across different predictor variables. They also provided a validational criterion of developing a general methodology of self-estimated parameters (Anderson, 1981b).

An illustration of the way in which the averaging principle is useful is in decisions whereby there are more than one attribute related to the decision in question. For example, when one is deciding which product of washing detergent to buy, Brand X may remove dirt, lessen static, and be hypoallergenic tested whereas Brand Y may have the first two similar strengths but not the last. Standard utility theory would predict that adding a positive attribute would increase the preference value for the consumer. However, findings have consistently shown that in such attitude research (Anderson, 1981b) and consumer goods research (Shanteau & Ptacek, 1983), an averaging effect is governing preference. So, additional facts may not necessarily increase preference for an object.

There is however a bias produced by the averaging process, which differs from the normative model, whereby information for zero or near-zero values may reduce the polarity of responses to that of neutral information even though the zero value may have a non-zero weight (Anderson, 1986). This explains instances of the Bayesian two-urn inference task (Shanteau, 1975), whereby random but equal sampling of red and white beads caused a neutral 50:50 response. This is a competing explanation to that which is offered by the anchoring and adjustment heuristic.

Basically, Anderson (1986) states that normative research views "errors" as a phenomenon that needs explanation. Instead, these "errors" should be viewed as part of the decision-making reality. Thus, normative research is invalid and, therefore, any research which follows this tradition is also invalid.

Directions in Research

Following the above review of current models in judgment and decision-making research, we now consider several issues which tend to arise in all research particularly in cognition.

The goal of research is to discover ways in which humans can understand (describe), explain, and predict behavior. At any one time, we can find competing theories about any one behavior. The general question is "which is right?". There is always a tendency to attempt to find one absolute answer and to embrace the theory which seems most plausible, rejecting all others. In some situations, as in the perennial battle between behaviorism and genetics (nurture versus nature), there may not be an answer.

Perhaps one view is that the two theories examine the problem at different levels. The idea of "levels" itself can be interpreted in more than one way. Any behavior can be interpreted on either the neurological level, the biochemistry level, or by a functional/ethological level. It can also be interpreted or theorized at the familiar behavioral, cognitive, or even philosophical level.

Also, there is the other level of research, different mainly in purpose. As G. F. Pitz (1987) puts it in his book review *Advances in Decision Research*, there are those who express their ideas as formal models and those experimentalists who test hypotheses through rigorous experiments. There are also those who seek the truth through daily experience with decisions and decision makers. As none of these categories are mutually exclusive, any researcher can attempt to combine more than one of these methods. All these do not, however, preclude the possibility that some theories are more appropriate than others. However, the point here is that we should not dismiss any theory too readily, without thinking of ways in which it has its uses.

In lieu of this and with specific reference to the research on judgment and decision making, Anderson's (1986) point that Kahneman and Tversky's ideas are "seriously incorrect" is too extreme a judgment. Perhaps we would gain more from viewing them as those researchers who work more through seeking truth from daily experience with decisions and decision makers. The integration theory, in contrast, can be viewed as a more formal approach to this question of decision making. In this way, the study of judgment and decision making (and in any other research) can be obtained from a breadth of knowledge rather than be limited to any particular way. Anderson (1986) acknowledges this in the last few pages of the cited paper.

Some Final Notes

We have shown that judgment and decision-making research is heading in the direction where the factors which could affect a decision are being studied through the use of limited information processing models. The assumption taken in most research is that judgment is decomposed into several sub-processes and due to the limitations of the immediate memory, only limited information can be processed at one time. As such, there has also been much emphasis in decision studies on how one acquires information, how evaluation is made, how learning occurs and how the feedback of information is used in decision making. (Einhorn & Hogarth, 1981). Also, researchers are interested in what and how the interactions between cognition and affect could affect decision making (Pitz & Sachs, 1984). In addition, the type of culture may interact with the psychological components to influence decisions, thus adding to the many facets in a decision.

Another view is that judgment is considered a developmental one, whereby it is an organization of thought processes at a particular stage of development similar to Kohlberg's (1979) moral stage of development. The errors that occur are due to the fact that one does not possess the appropriate decision-making skills at the time. Furthermore, complex decisions may require access to techniques which are located in organizations across different stages.

With numerous models and theories, researchers may lose focus of the objectives of the research in judgment and decision making. In the end, the primary objective of research is to achieve an understanding of its applicational value, leading to results that are useful to society.

References

Abelson, R.P. (1976). Script processing in attitude formation and decision making. In J.S. Carroll and J.W. Payne (Eds.), *Cognition and Social Behavior.* Hillsdale, N.J.: Erlbaum.

Anderson, J.R. (1985). *Cognitive Psychology and Its Implications. (2nd Ed.).* San Francisco: Freeman.

Anderson, N.H. (1974). Algebraic models in perception. In E.C. Carterette and M.P. Friedman (Eds.), *Handbook of Perception,* (pp. 215-298). New York: Academic Press.

Anderson, N. H. (1974). Information integration theory: A brief survey. In D.H. Krantz, R. C. Atkinson, R.D. Luce and P. Suppes (Eds.), *Measurement, Psychophysics, and Neural Information Processing, (Vol. 2, 236-305).* San Francisco: Freeman.

Anderson, N.H. (1981a). *Foundations of Information Integration Theory.* New York: Academic Press.

Anderson, N.H. (1981b). Integration theory applied to cognitive responses and attitudes. In R.E. Petty, T.M. Ostrom, and T.C. Brock (Eds.), *Cognitive Responses in Persuasion.* Hillsdale, N.J.: Erlbaum.

Anderson, N.H. (1982). *Methods of Information Integration Theory.* New York: Academic Press.

Anderson, N.H. (1986). A cognitive theory of judgment and decision. In B. Brehme, H. Jungemann, P. Lourens & G. Sevon (Eds.), *New Directions in Research on Decision Making.* The Netherlands: North-Holland.

Bar-Hillel, M. (1973). *Organizational Behavioral and Human Performance, 9,* 396.

Bazerman, M.H. (1986). *Judgment in Managerial Decision Making.* New York: John Wiley and Sons.

Edwards, W. (1961). Behavioral decision theory. *Annual Review of Psychology,* 12, 473-498.

Edwards, W. (1962). Dynamic decision theory and probabilistic information processing. *Human Factors, 4,* 59-73.

Einhorn, H.J. and Hogarth, R.M. (1981). Behavioral decision theory: Processes of judgment and choice. *Annual Review of Psychology, 32,* 53-88.

Flood, M.M. (1954). Environmental nonstationarity in a sequential decision-making experiment. In R.M. Thrall, C.H. Coombs, and R.L. Davis (Eds.), *Decision Processes*. New York: John Wiley and Sons.

Flood, M.M. (1955). Game learning theory and some decision-making experiments. In R.M. Thrall, C.H.Coombs, and R.L. Davis (Eds.), *Decision Processes*. New York: John Wiley and Sons.

Hammond, K.R. (1971). Computer graphics as an aid to learning. *Science, 172,* 903-908.

Hammond, K.R., Stewart, T.R., Alderman, L., and Wascoe, N.E. (1975). *Report to the Denver city council and mayor regarding the choice of handgun ammunition for the Denver police department. Progress Research for Human Judgment Society Interaction Report 179.* Boulder: Institute of Behavioral Science, University of Colorado, USA.

Hammond, K.R., Stewart, T.R., Brehmer, B., and Steinmann, D.O. (1975). Social judgment theory. In M.F. Kaplan and S. Schwartz (Eds.), *Human Judgment and Decision Processes.* New York: Academic Press.

Hoffman, P., Festinger, L., and Lawrence, D. (1954). Tendencies toward group comparability in competitive bargaining. In R.M. Thrall, C.H. Coombs, and R.L. Davis (Eds.), *Decision Processes.* New York: John Wiley and Sons.

Kahneman, D. and Tversky, A. (1974). Prospect theory: An analysis of decision under risk. *Econometrica, 47,* 263-291.

Kaplan, M.F. (1986). Judgment by juries. In H.R. Arkes and K.R. Hammond (Eds.), *Judgment and Decision Making: An Interdisciplinary Reader.* New York: Cambridge University Press.

Kohlberg, L. (1979). *The Meaning and Measurement of Moral Development.* Clark Lectures, Clark University.

Levin, I.P., Johnson, R.D., and Faraone, A.V. (1984). Information integration in price-quality tradeoffs: The effects of missing information. *Memory and Cognition, 12,* 96-102.

Luce, R.D. (1959). *Individual Choice Behavior.* New York: John Wiley and Sons.

Luce, R.D. and Raiffa, H. (1957). *Games and Decisions: Introduction and Critical Survey.* New York: John Wiley and Sons.

Newell, A. and Simon, H.A. (1972). *Human Problem Solving.* Englewood Cliffs, N. J.: Prentice-Hall.

Payne, J. W. (1976). Task complexity and contingent processing in decision making: An information search and protocol analysis. *Organizational Behavior and Human Performance, 16,* 366-387.

Pitz, G.F. (1987). Advances in Decision Research. *Society for study of subjective probability and utility and decision making.* Bulletin No. 12, p. 7.

Pitz, G.F. and Sachs, N. J. (1984). Judgment and decision: Theory and application. *Annual Review of Psychology, 35,* 139-163.

Rapoport, A. and Burkheimer, G.J. (1971). Models for deferred decision making. *Journal of Mathematical Psychology, 8,* 508-538.

Rapoport, A. (1975). Research paradigms for studying dynamic decision behavior. In D. Wendt and C.A.J. Vlek (Eds.), *Utility, Probability and Human Decision Making,* (pp.

349-369). Dordrecht, The Netherlands: Reidel.

Russo, J.E. and Rosen, L.D. (1975). An eye fixation analysis of multialternative choice. *Memory and Cognition, 3,* 267-276.

Scodel, A., Minas, J.S., Ratoosh, P., and Lipetz, M. (1959). Some descriptive aspects of two-person non-zero-sum games. *Journal of Conflict Resolution, 3,* 114-119.

Shanteau, J. (1972). Descriptive versus normative models of sequential inference judgment. *Journal of Experimental Psychology, 93,* 63-68.

Shanteau, J. (1975). An information-integration analysis of risky decision making. In M.F. Kaplan and S. Schwartz (Ed.), *Human Judgment and Decision Processes,* pp. 110-134. New York: Academic Press.

Shanteau, J. and Anderson, N.H. (1972). Intergraph theory applied to judgment of the value of information. *Journal of Experimental Psychology, 92,* 266-275.

Shanteau, J. and Ptacek, C.H. (1983). Role and implications of averaging processes in advertising. In L. Perry and A. Woodside, *Advertising and Consumer.* New York: Lexington.

Sigall, H. and Ostrove, N. (1975). Beautiful but dangerous: Effects of offender attractiveness and the nature of the crime on juridic judgments. *Journal of Personality and Psychology, 31,* 410-414.

Simon, H.A. (1957). *Models of Man.* New York: John Wiley and Sons.

Singh, R. (1990). Two problems in cognitive algebra: Imputations and averaging versus multiplying. In N.H. Anderson (Ed.), *Contributions to Information Integration Theory (Vol. II).* New York: Academic Press.

Slovic, P. and Lichtenstein, S. (1971). Comparison of Bayesian and regression approaches to the study of information processing in judgment. *Organizational Behavior and Human Performance, 6,* 649-744.

Slovic, P., Fischhoff, B. and Lichtenstein, S. (1977). Behavioral decision theory. *Annual Review of Psychology, 28,* 1-39.

Tversky, A. and Kahneman, D. (1973). Availability: A heuristic for judging frequency and probability. *Cognitive Psychology, 5,* 207-232.

Tversky, A. and Kahneman, D. (1974). Judgment under uncertainty: Heuristics and biases. *Science, 185,* 1124-1131.

Weisbrod, R.L., Davis, K.B., Freedy, A., Weltman, G. (1975). Adaptive computer aiding in dynamic decision processes: An initial study in dynamic convergence and decision aiding. *Catalog of Selected Documents in Psychology, 5,* 263-264.

Notes

Part of this text is from Loke, W.H. (1989). *Human Judgment and Decision Making: Models and Applications.* Educational Research International Committee (ERIC), U.S.A. Document Reproduction Service No. ED 305 558. Ms. Bernadette Sim has been of assistance in writing the section on Information Integration Theory.

CONTEMPORARY APPLICATIONS OF RESEARCH ON JUDGMENT AND DECISION MAKING

Irwin P. Levin and Carla J. Reicks

A number of studies are described which apply recent developments in the psychology of decision making to real-life situations.
These developments consist of methods and models for describing individual and group decisions, including analyses of the
roles of decision biases and heuristics, assessments of risk, and
contextual effects such as information framing. Areas of application include medical decision making, consumer judgments,
educational evaluations, the formation of public policy, and
negotiations in industrial and government settings. The interplay
between theory, methodology and application is stressed.

Much of the early work in the area of human judgment and decision making was
concerned with tests of normative models such as utility theory and Bayes' theorem
(Edwards, 1971). There has, however, been a marked shift in emphasis to test
descriptive models that attempt to uncover psychological processes affecting judgments and decisions (Einhorn & Hogarth, 1981). More recent research has stressed
the use of judgmental heuristics, subjective valuation and weighting processes in
information integration, the assessment of risks implicit in various judgments and
decisions, and contextual effects such as the manner in which information is presented
or "framed."

The insights produced by such research have applied and theoretical significance.
The present paper will provide selected contemporary applications of some of these
newly developed insights. Areas of application include consumer behavior, negotiations in business and government organizations, decisions concerning environmental
issues, medical decisions, and educational placement decisions. The presented
examples will not only illustrate the usefulness of theory development and methodology for understanding real-world decisions, but will also demonstrate support for the
generality of laboratory-derived research principles across a wide variety of content
areas.

The Effects of Information Framing

Many of the judgments and decisions we make in our everyday lives are influenced
by factors which can alternatively be labeled in positive or negative terms. Levin,
Johnson, Russo, and Deldin (1985) showed that purchases of ground beef were judged
more favorably when the beef was described in terms of its "% lean" rather than its

"% fat," gambles were rated as more attractive when described in terms of "chances of winning" instead of "chances of losing," and student performance was rated higher when scores were expressed in terms of "% correct" rather than "% incorrect." Levin (1987) explained these results in terms of a model in which judgments were mediated by positive or negative associations evoked by stimulus labels.

In a recent study Levin and Gaeth (1988) extended this line of investigation to a more naturalistic consumer task where consumers had information provided by both external sources and by personal experience. Subjects were given a sample taste of ground beef that was labeled as either "75% lean" or "25% fat" and were asked to rate the meat on scales such as good tasting-bad tasting, greasy-greaseless, and high quality-low quality. Ratings on these scales were more favorable toward the beef labeled "75% lean" than that labeled "25% fat." More importantly, the magnitude of the information-framing effect lessened when consumers actually tasted the meat compared to when they did not. This result can be described by an averaging model of information integration (Anderson, 1986) in which the effects of personal experi-ence and outside sources of information (e.g., advertisements) are balanced when arriving at an overall evaluation. Support for an averaging model here is consistent with earlier work by Troutman and Shanteau (1976) who showed that consumers evaluate products by averaging attribute information.

Framing effects extend to other domains, including decisions that affect our health and well being. For example, McNeil, Pauker, Sox, and Tversky (1982) investigated how people use statistical information regarding the possible outcomes of alternative therapies for treating lung cancer. Subjects—including patients with chronic medical problems, physicians, and a group of graduate students—were asked to choose between surgery and radiation therapy on the basis of simple descriptions of their possible consequences. For half the subjects the probability of surviving for a fixed period of time after surgery was given (e.g., 68% chance of living for more than one year) and for the other half the probability of dying was given (32% chance of dying by the end of one year). Surgery was found to be less attractive in the mortality frame (probability of dying) than in the survival frame (probability of living). Radiation therapy was preferred to surgery 42% of the time in the mortality frame and 25% of the time in the survival frame.

In a similar vein, Meyerowitz and Chaiken (1987) showed an effect of message framing on breast self-examination in college women. Subjects were given a pamphlet on breast self-exam (BSE) where information was framed positively or negatively as follows:

By [not] doing BSE now, you (can) [will not] learn what your normal, healthy breasts feel like so that you will be (better) [ill] prepared to notice any small, abnormal changes that might occur as you get older. Research shows that women who do [do not] BSE have (an increased) [a decreased] chance of finding a tumor in the early, more treatable stage of the disease. You can (gain) [lose] several potential health benefits by (spending) [failing to spend] only

5 minutes each month doing BSE. (Take) [Don't fail to take] advantage of this opportunity.

Immediately following distribution of the pamphlet, subjects who received the loss pamphlet expressed more positive attitudes toward BSE than did subjects who received the gain pamphlet. More importantly, the validity of this effect was demonstrated four months later when subjects in the loss condition reported a larger number of times they actually performed BSE than did subjects in the gain condition. The negative framing condition was thus particularly potent in demonstrating the need for breast self-examination.

The next section describes some medical decision-making tasks designed specifically to examine how information-framing affects risk-taking behavior when choosing between treatment options.

Frame of Reference and Risk Taking in Medical Decisions

Tversky and Kahneman (1981) developed a paradigm for studying risk-taking behavior as a function of the manner in which choice options are framed. Subjects were asked to choose between two programs for dealing with the outbreak of an "unusual Asian disease that is expected to kill 600 people." In the positive framing condition the options were described in terms of lives saved. One option was said to lead to a sure saving of 200 lives. The other ("risky") option was said to lead to a one-third probability of saving all 600 lives and a two-thirds probability of saving no lives. In the negative framing condition the same options were described in terms of lives lost. One option was said to lead to 400 lives lost and the other option was said to lead to a one-third probability that none will die and a two-thirds probability that 600 will die.

Tversky and Kahneman (1981) found a "preference reversal" where subjects in the positive framing condition tended to choose the "sure-thing" option over the "risky" option while subjects in the negative framing condition tended to choose the risky option over the sure-thing option. According to Kahneman and Tversky (1984), the framing manipulation serves to shift the subject's reference point from a state of affairs in which the disease is allowed to take its toll of 600 lives, thus making a sure saving of 200 lives the more attractive option, to a reference state in which no one dies of the disease, thus making a sure loss of 400 lives the less attractive option. At a more formal level, prospect theory (Kahneman & Tversky, 1979) accounts for the framing effect by assuming an S-shaped value function which is concave in the domain of gains and convex in the domain of losses. Thus, the value of a sure saving of 200 lives is higher than one-third the value of a saving of 600 lives, and the value of a sure loss of 400 lives is lower (more negative) than two-thirds the value of a loss of 600 lives.

In a recent extension of this study Levin and Chapman (1990) developed a forced-choice version of the Tversky and Kahneman task designed to examine reactions to different groups of victims of the AIDS disease. Subjects were told that the U.S. is preparing for the outbreak of a new strain of AIDS which is expected to kill 600 people in each of two separate communities. The communities were described as one consisting of illegal intravenous drug users and one consisting of hemophiliacs and others needing blood transfusions. Pilot work had shown that the first group was rated as less likable and more responsible for disease contraction than the second group.

In the positively framed version of the task, subjects were instructed to select one of the following program options for one group and the other option for the other group:

Program A: 200 people will be saved.
Program B: 1/3 probability that 600 people will be saved and 2/3 probability that no people will be saved.

The negatively framed version substituted the appropriate "number die" for "number saved."

In the positive framing condition, 80% of the subjects assigned the "sure saving of lives" option to the hemophiliac group and 20% assigned that option to the drug user group. In the negative framing condition, 70% of the subjects assigned the "1/3 probability that 0 will die" option to the hemophiliac group and 30% assigned that option to the drug user group. In other words, the usual pattern of choosing the sure-thing option in the positive framing condition and the risky option in the negative framing condition was the pattern of choice for hemophiliacs but not for intravenous drug users. These results are consistent with the basic assumption of prospect theory that the value function is concave in the domain of gains and convex in the domain of losses if we make the further assumption that the value function is flatter for the less desirable group. Because the slope of the value function at any given point represents the change in subjective value for a given number of lives saved or lost, these results can be explained by inferring that the subject's perception of the "value" of a life differs for different groups of AIDS victims. Only by the development of suitable tasks and models could such an inference be made.

Social Judgments and Policy Decisions

Social Judgment Theory (SJT) is an important and useful technique for under-standing human judgment, aiding or improving judgment decisions, and resolving conflicts. It is particularly useful for the formation of social policy, but can be applied in many other areas as well. In SJT, judgments about social values are integrated with judgments about scientific or technical facts to form the final policy decision. It is applicable in situations where two or more groups, representing differing and perhaps conflicting interests, are attempting to make a policy decision.

For example, Hammond, Rohrbaugh, Mumpower, and Adelman (1977) used SJT to help the Denver, Colorado police department select the type of bullets for its officers to use. Some bullets may be quite effective in incapacitating a criminal but create excessive injury and threat to innocent bystanders. Other bullets may be safer but less effective in stopping criminals. The policy question is then one of selecting a bullet that meets the needs of the police force without endangering the citizenry. Social values were assessed by surveying policymakers and other interested people as to the relative importance they place on three functional characteristics (cues) of bullets: their level of stopping effectiveness, injury, and threat to bystanders. Several different factions of people were identified. For example, some placed greatest weight on stopping effectiveness and some placed greatest weight on threat to bystanders. Compromise was achieved by adopting a policy that assigned equal importance to the three cues. Ballistic experts were brought in to assess the facts; they made independent judgments about the potential stopping effectiveness, injury, and threat to bystanders of 80 different bullets. Thus, to this point, the assessment of facts had been completely separated from the assessment of social values. The last step was to integrate values and facts. This was accomplished for each bullet by multiplying the weight of the compromise social policy by the mean ratings of the technical experts for that bullet on each of the three dimensions, and then summing over dimensions. The bullet with the highest resulting value was chosen as the official ammunition of the Denver Police Department.

An important advantage of SJT is that it examines judgments within the context or environment in which they are made. For example, Hendrickson et al. (1974, cited in Furby, Slovic, Fischhoff, & Gregory, 1988) applied SJT to the problem of siting electric power transmission lines in which citizens' interests conflicted with those of government regulators. After identifying criteria, or cues, which influence people's evaluations of the siting of the lines (e.g., property value effects, human safety, environmental impact), representatives of the public rated various viewscapes showing different transmission line routings. These viewscapes represented the entire environment for which the judgment was to be made, thus preserving the external validity of the ratings made by the citizens. Through regression analysis, the importance, or weight, of each of the cues in the viewscapes was found for the sample of citizens. Technical experts then judged the impact of each of the alternate routes for each cue. The weights (value judgments) and the experts' judgments (facts) were then combined into a rating score for each route. Thus both technical and public judgment were used to resolve the conflict.

Preservation of the natural context of the situation is important in SJT because often people do not know or cannot express explicitly their own weighting of the cues. However, by analyzing a series of judgments by an individual or group through regression techniques, the weights can be externalized and then used in the final decision. In addition, providing cognitive feedback to individuals and groups about their decision process (their weighting of the cues) can lead to adjustments in this process and thus better future decisions.

Cooksey, Freebody, and Davidson (1986), for example, examined teacher expectations for vocabulary development and reading comprehension for kindergarten students using SJT. This is an important area for analysis and understanding because the expectations of teachers about a student's potential for academic success can act as a self-fulfilling prophecy, affecting that child's actual future achievement.

In this study, teachers-in-training were presented with beginning-of-year profiles of 118 kindergarten children. The profiles consisted of five cues, selected on the basis of previous research, which are relevant to the prediction of early reading achievement (e.g., type of reading instructional program, socio-economic status of the family, scores on knowledge and ability tests). From this information the teachers estimated the score they felt each child would obtain on two criterion measures (word knowledge and reading comprehension) at the end of the school year. They were also asked to rank order the cues according to how important they were as prediction criteria. The teachers' estimated scores for each student were then compared to that student's actual score obtained at the end of the year.

Though on an aggregate level teachers performed adequately, there were large individual differences between the teachers and weighting discrepancies within individual teacher's judgments. This study also found that often the process of judging students and developing expectancies for them cannot be articulated by the teacher though the judgment may have large observable effects. Indeed, for the criteria used, the rank order of weights objectively derived through regression analysis did not often agree with what teachers subjectively reported as their order of importance. Thus, SJT can make explicit the covert expectation policies of teachers and can provide information through cognitive feedback regarding the appropriateness of certain expectation policies in the classroom.

Negotiations in Business and Government Settings

Negotiation is the process of resolving conflict between two or more parties to reach a final decision. The negotiation process has been found to be significantly affected by cognitive shortcuts, or heuristics, people use to reduce the amount of information when making decisions. Bazerman (1983) has identified several of these heuristics which can bias decision processes and affect negotiator judgment.

The way a problem and potential solution are worded, or framed, can affect the tactics used by a negotiator and the outcome of the negotiation. Neale and Bazerman (1985) give an illustrative example in the realm of labor/management negotiations. If labor claims they need a pay raise to $12/hour and anything less would be a loss, while management claims they cannot pay more than $10/hour and anything more would be a loss to the company, a negotiated settlement is needed. Given that both sides view the other's demand as a loss, prospect theory predicts that both will respond in a risk-seeking manner and will likely choose arbitration to settle the dispute. However, if the conflict can be framed in terms of a gain, rather than a loss, both sides would more likely respond in a risk averse manner and would more readily reach compromise. Thus, if labor views anything above $10/hour as a gain and management views anything under $12/hour as a gain, the problem is put in a positive frame and settlement is likely. In general, a risk-seeking orientation invoked by a negative frame will more likely lead to an impasse and failure of negotiation, while a risk averse orientation invoked by a positive frame will more likely lead to compromise and resolution of the conflict.

Neale and Bazerman also found that negotiator overconfidence biased their decision-making behavior. People who were overly confident that their judgments were correct showed less concessionary behavior in the negotiation process than did realistically confident negotiators. Also, the outcomes obtained by the realistically confident negotiators were superior to those obtained by those who were overconfident.

The realm of politics provides an example of how a heuristic called the "fixed-pie" bias can impede negotiations. In the "fixed-pie" bias, each party assumes that there is a fixed amount of gain available and in order to get what is wanted the other party must lose it. Pruitt and Rubin (1986) give the example of the Camp David talks between Israel and Egypt in 1978. Both countries wanted possession of the Sinai Peninsula and it appeared they were at an impasse in negotiations. However, it was eventually realized that whereas Egypt wanted control of the land, Israel was primarily interested in the security it provided. Thus, once this bias was discovered, a mutually agreeable decision could then be reached.

The escalation of commitment while negotiations are underway is another negative consequence of heuristics and biases that affect negotiation behavior. Both sides in a bargaining situation make demands and perhaps incur a loss if agreement is not reached. This is because negotiators believe they have too much invested (in the form of time, money, or ego) to give up any of their demands and thus refuse to compromise. For example, the Professional Air Traffic Controllers Organization (PATCO) went on strike in the United States in 1981, thus investing the loss of pay during the strike in order to obtain its demands. Even when faced with an unyielding administration and weak bargaining position, the union refused to reduce their demands or go back to work. Eventually, its members were fired. Thus, the union had increased its commitment to the strike in order to justify the original expense of starting it. Bazerman (1986) calls this phenomenon "reminiscent of the Vietnam War and other international and industrial failures in which both competitors get trapped by their previous commitments."

The identification of the biases that affect negotiators allows for steps to be taken to avoid them and thus results in more successful negotiations and superior outcomes. To avoid the overconfidence bias, negotiators may obtain objective assessments from experts. Presenting suggestions or compromises in a positive frame to both sides may increase chances of a settlement. Opponents' actions may be better anticipated if negotiators are aware of the biases that may be affecting the negotiation process. In general, awareness of the limitations that may prevent optimal decisions can lead to strategies to improve the process and thus improve the quality of decisions.

Risk Assessment in a Complex Society

The perception and assessment of risk in certain situations often have a profound effect on subsequent information processing and decision making. In an increasingly technological world, there is a growing awareness of the risks involved in new and potentially hazardous technologies. Conflict between the general public and industry or government can occur as a result of lack of information about these technologies and poor decision-making processes. The way such conflicts are resolved may have far-reaching effects on the technologies themselves, the societies in which they function, and perhaps even a more global impact.

Informing the public about potential risks of such things as radiation hazards, medicinal side effects, occupational hazards, food contaminants, and airplane accidents is an important step in preventing or resolving problems associated with risk assessment. However, messages and information given to the public about risks and safety must be carefully presented and explained to avoid confusion due to the information processing limitations of the human cognitive system.

Complex technical information that is clouded by uncertainty must be presented in a manner so as not to frighten or mislead people. Psychological research has shown that people's preconceptions may and often do cause them to distort information to fit those preconceptions. Often risks are presented in the form of probabilities. However, people have difficulty judging probabilities and dealing with uncertainty and will rely on judgmental heuristics to reduce the judgment task to a simpler one. Slovic, Fischhoff, and Lichtenstein (1984) have identified several problems facing attempts to inform the public about risks.

The "availability" heuristic causes an event to be judged as likely or frequent if it is easy to imagine or recall instances of that event. Air travel to certain parts of the world, for example, often decreases dramatically immediately following a well-publicized hijacking incident. People overestimate the probability of dying from dramatic or sensational causes such as accidents, homicide, or tornadoes while underestimating the probability of dying from less sensational ones such as asthma or diabetes.

Other biases in risk assessment have been identified: the tendency to consider oneself immune to hazards, difficulty in making the distinction between what is only remotely possible and what is probable, especially if the hazard is highly imaginable, and attempts to reduce anxiety due to uncertainty by denying the uncertainty and therefore denying the risk. Also, as we have already described in other contexts, small differences in the way risk information is presented (how it is framed) can greatly affect perceptions of that risk. For example, Slovic, Fischhoff and Lichtenstein (1978) manipulated the time frame in which people evaluated the usefulness of automobile seat belts. Subjects induced to consider a lifetime perspective where the odds are about 1 in 3 of being in a serious auto accident responded more favorably toward the use of seat belts than did subjects asked to consider a trip-by-trip perspective where the odds of being in a serious accident are only about 1 in 100,000.

Research on risk perception can be used to make recommendations about ways to inform the public about risks such as radiation exposure. In 1978, a White House task force, formed to coordinate research on the health effects of radiation exposure, completed a report on the development of a public information program. As Slovic, Fischhoff, and Lichtenstein (1981) point out, while the report recommended describing the risks of radiation in statistical terms along with the scientific bases for risk estimates, they did not consider that perceptions and attitudes are determined not only by statistics and probabilities, but also by characteristics of hazards such as uncertainty, controllability, catastrophic potential, equity, and threat to future generations. Because such subtle aspects of information presentation and interpretation can significantly affect people's responses to the information, findings from decision-making research can and should be used in designing public information programs.

Slovic et al. (1984) reported that their investigation led to the development of safety goals for the nuclear industry. This was possible because the techniques of measuring risk have advanced greatly and so more interest has developed in determining how safe nuclear reactors are and should be. The authors conclude that acceptable-risk problems are decision-making problems and the method chosen for decision making is a political and social issue which affects and is affected by the power and expertise in a society.

Summary and Conclusions

The illustrations provided here were not meant to be exhaustive of the potential applications of recent breakthroughs in judgment and decision-making research. Perhaps they are not even representative. (For further examples, see recent books by Arkes & Hammond, 1986 and Dawes, 1988.) We chose our examples according to several criteria: our judgment of their intrinsic interest to readers of varied backgrounds, the extent to which they illustrate recent developments in theory and methodology, and most importantly, the extent to which they represent the unique contribution that can be made when a study rich in content area is firmly grounded in basic research.

In all honesty, however, we must admit that oftentimes practitioners appear to be several steps ahead of theorists. Thus, before we published our first paper on framing of ground beef purchases (Levin et al., 1985), our local supermarkets changed the labeling of packages of ground beef from "% fat" to "% lean." Where theory and experimental design come into play is in directing future research aimed at understanding the reasons for a phenomenon such as the framing effect, delineating its boundary conditions, and identifying factors which augment or diminish it. So, based on support for an averaging model in the Levin and Gaeth (1988) study, we are now undertaking an expanded investigation of the interactive effects of personal consumptive experience and advertising. The Levin and Gaeth study as well as many of its predecessors in applied areas (see Levin, Louviere, Schepanski, & Norman, 1983) were guided by Anderson's (1986) development of methods and models for describing information integration processes.

Similarly, prospect theory (Kahneman & Tversky, 1979) played a major role in guiding Bazerman's (1983) work on negotiator behavior and Levin and Chapman's

(1990) work on the effects of victim characteristics on medical decisions. The abstract notion of the "value" of a life saved or lost took on operational meaning when related to the value function of prospect theory. This is particularly important in dealing with issues for which decision makers cannot accurately articulate the reasons for their choices.

Social Judgment Theory (Hammond et al., 1977), by virtue of its methodology for separating facts and values, has motivated a great deal of research with direct policy implications. Notably, much of this research has used the actual decision makers involved in forming public policy. Furthermore, this approach can be prescribed as a decision aid in future applications.

Studies of judgmental biases and heuristics, especially as they apply to the assessment of risk, have great potential significance for understanding important real-world decisions. Besides the examples provided earlier, a recent dramatic example illustrates this point. Several judgment and decision-making researchers were brought in to provide expert testimony in a hearing conducted by the United States House Armed Services Committee concerning the accidental downing in July 1988 of an Iranian domestic airplane by the U.S. Navy ship, *Vincennes*. In the excitement of the moment, the aircraft was mistaken for an attacking fighter plane. The researchers related the decision faced by the ship's captain to the type of inference task so often studied in the laboratory. In particular, they pointed to results of various studies showing that unaided diagnostic judgments are seriously deficient because of the inability to weigh and integrate information of less than perfect validity. Various biases were suggested as possible in this case, including an "expectancy bias" in which the data at hand were distorted to fit expectations. Of course, not everyone was convinced by this line of reasoning. Nevertheless, further studies of decision-making processes—especially in this example, under conditions of stress—were recommended to increase our understanding of events that affect us as individuals and as members of society.

References

Anderson, N.H. (1986). A cognitive theory of judgment and decision. In B. Brehmer, et al. (Eds.), *New Directions in Research on Decision Making*. The Netherlands: North-Holland

Arkes, H.R. and Hammond, K.R. (1986). *Judgment and Decision Making*. Cambridge: Cambridge University Press.

Bazerman, M. (1983). Negotiator judgment. *American Behavioral Scientist, 27,* 221-228.

Bazerman, M. (1986). Why negotiations go wrong. *Psychology Today, 20,* 54-58.

Cooksey, R.S., Freebody, P., and Davidson, G.R. (1986). Teachers' predictions of children's early reading achievement: An application of social judgment theory. *American Educational Research Journal, 23* , 41-64.

Dawes, R.M. (1988). *Rational Choice in an Uncertain World*. San Diego: Harcourt Brace

Jovanovich.

Edwards, W. (1971). Bayesian and regression models of human information processing: A myopic perspective. *Organizational Behavior and Human Performance, 6*, 639-648.

Einhorn, H.J. and Hogarth, R.M. (1981). Behavioral decision theory: Processes of judgment and choice. *Annual Review of Psychology, 32*, 53-88.

Furby, L., Slovic, P., Fischhoff, B., and Gregory, R. (1988). Public perceptions of electric power transmission lines. *Journal of Environmental Psychology, 8*, 19-43.

Hammond, K.R., Rohrbaugh, J., Mumpower, J., and Adelman, L. (1977). Social judgment theory: Applications in policy formation. In M. Kaplan and S. Schwartz (Eds.), *Human Judgment and Decision Processes in Applied Settings.* New York: Academic Press.

Kahneman, D. and Tversky, A. (1979). Prospect theory: An analysis of decision under risk. *Econometrica, 47*, 263-291.

Kahneman, D. and Tversky, A. (1984). Choices, values, and frames. *American Psychologist, 39*, 341-350.

Levin, I.P. (1987). Associative effects of information framing. *Bulletin of the Psychonomic Society, 25*, 85-86.

Levin, I.P. and Chapman, D.P. (1990). Risk taking, frame of reference and characterization of victim groups in AIDS treatment decisions. *Journal of Experimental Social Psychology*, in press.

Levin, I.P., and Gaeth, G.J. (1988). How consumers are affected by the framing of attribute information before and after consuming the product. *Journal of Consumer Research, 15*, 374- 378.

Levin, I.P., Johnson, R.D., Russo, C.P., and Deldin, P.J. (1985). Framing effects in judgment tasks with varying amounts of information. *Organizational Behavior and Human Decision Processes, 36*, 362-377.

Levin, I.P., Louviere, J.J., Schepanski, A.A., and Norman, K.L. (1983). External validity tests of laboratory studies of information integration. *Organizational Behavior and Human Performance, 31*, 173-193.

McNeil, B.J., Pauker, S.G., Sox, H.C., and Tversky, A. (1982). On the elicitation of preferences for alternative therapies. *New England Journal of Medicine, 306,* 1259-1262.

Meyerowitz, B.E. and Chaiken, S. (1987). The effect of message framing on breast self-examination attitudes, intentions, and behavior. *Journal of Personality and Social Psychology, 52*, 500-510.

Neale, M. and Bazerman, M. (1985). Perspectives for understanding negotiation. *Journal of Conflict Resolution, 29*, 33-55.

Pruitt, D. and Rubin, J. (1986). *Social Conflict: Escalation, Stalemate, and Settlement.* New York: Random House.

Slovic, P., Fischhoff, B., and Lichtenstein, S. (1978). Accident probabilities and seat belt usage: A psychological perspective. *Accident Analysis and Prevention, 10,* 281- 285.

Slovic, P., Fischhoff, B., and Lichtenstein, S. (1981). Informing the public about the risks from ionizing radiation. *Health Physics, 41,* 589-598.

Slovic, P., Fischhoff, B., and Lichtenstein, S. (1984). Behavioral decision theory perspectives on risk and safety. *Acta Psychologica, 56,* 183-203.

Troutman, C.M. and Shanteau, J. (1976). Do consumers evaluate products by adding or averaging attribute information? *Journal of Consumer Research, 3,* 101-106.

Tversky, A. and Kahneman, D. (1981). The framing of decisions and the psychology of choice. *Science, 211,* 453-458.

Note

A reduced version of this article appeared in *Commentary,* Vol 8, No 3 & 4, June1990 (published by the National University of Singapore Society).

SOCIAL COGNITION, REALITY, AND JOB PERCEPTION

Jack Feldman

Job perception is construed as the outcome of an active constructive process in which environmental "signals" are interpreted via chronic or temporarily accessible processing structures, including value systems. The degree of elaboration and
chronic accessibility of these structures, and the strength and
consistency of social influence are postulated to be elements of
a reciprocal causal relationship influencing, and being influenced
by, perception, affect, and behavior. It is concluded that both the
job characteristics and social information processing approaches
represent segments of the overall process.

The question of precisely how people come to perceive their jobs in terms of certain attributes, and the degree to which these perceptions reflect objective job character-istics, has created two opposing camps. I believe the champions of each camp, like the legendary blind scholars, are examining different parts of the elephant. As will become apparent, though, the bulk of the beast lies somewhere in between.

Job Characteristics and Job Perceptions—Two Views

Adherents of the first, or "Job Characteristics" camp, postulate that people accurately perceive and report attributes of their jobs—not only the actual activities, as in various forms of job analysis, but inferred (or perceived) attributes such as skill variety, task identity and significance, autonomy, and feedback. That such attributes are regarded as objective job characteristics is explicit in Hackman and Oldham (1976, 1980), though earlier work (Hackman & Lawler, 1971) takes a clearly perceptual viewpoint. While research testing the original Job Characteristics Model has been subject to criticism (Roberts & Glick, 1981), and a variety of studies have questioned the underlying dimensionality of job perceptions (e.g., Dunham, 1977; Dunham, Aldag & Brief, 1977; Stone & Guetal, 1985), the assumption remains (and indeed is consistent with studies such as Dunham, 1977, showing "enriched" jobs to be more difficult).

A second assumption of the Job Characteristics camp is that job attributes are associated with affect and behavior via a need satisfaction model (Stone, 1987). A finite number of needs (which may or may not be fundamental and/or fixed) or values (likewise) are assumed to drive perceptions, evaluations, and preference judgments in roughly the same way for all individuals. These, when satisfied by attributes of jobs, result in positive affect (job satisfaction). Unstated is the equally strong assumption that need or value structures exist in roughly the same form in all people, promoting reliable and cross-situationally consistent judgments of job attributes and concomitant affect.

The second, or "Social Information Processing" camp, holds that judgments of the nature of the world are ultimately social constructions, based on stimulus features made salient by, and processing structures made accessible via, social cues and interpersonal influence. Since these cues and influence sources must first be interpreted by the person, however, we are left with a theory that says that reality is as one constructs it, and that agreement between individuals is a function of common history, culture, and situational exposure. This view is supported by scores of experiments showing that perceptions, judgments and choices may be influenced by priming, framing, social pressure, and the like (e.g., Wyer & Srull, 1986; Kahneman, Slovic, & Tversky, 1982; Fischhoff, Slovic, & Lichtenstein, 1980).

Results of studies by proponents of each camp are consistent with theoretical predictions from the other. Dunham et al. (1977), for example, show that the structure of job perceptions may well be different across situations, while Thomas and Griffin's (1983) review of social cues research shows a strong and consistent effect of both "objective" (i.e., manipulated) task characteristics and social cues on perceptions. Finally, affect is involved. In addition to the many studies (see Stone, 1987) showing the influence of job attributes on satisfaction, other studies show an influence of satisfaction on perception (Adler, Skov, & Salvemini, 1985; Isen, 1984). Additionally, James and James (1980) and James and Tetrick (1986) make a strong case for reciprocal causality, in which each influences the other, as in stress and depression (Alloy & Tabachnik, 1984; Leventhal & Nerez, 1988).

The present stage of conceptualization may be likened to an impasse over whether the job characteristics glass is half-full, or the social information processing glass is half-empty. In such cases, it may be useful to approach the problem from a different direction. I believe that neither camp has seriously examined the relevant cognitive processes. If we expand our horizons beyond an immediate, "practical" concern with jobs, we may make substantial gains in both parsimony and utility.

The following is not intended to provide an alternative to Griffin's (1987) integrative review. Rather, its purpose is to point out the processes by which such models may operate, and thus provide an additional, micro-level approach to their specification and testing.

Taking Cognition Seriously

The social judgment and perception literature has long been concerned with biases and errors of various sorts, because the conditions under which perceptions and judgments depart from some normative model are informative about the cognitive processes themselves. As both Funder (1987) and Christensen-Szalanski and Beach (1984) note, however, these results tell us very little about the degree to which judgments are veridical in "real life." This research is relevant to job perception, because the "Job Characteristics" approach has focused on an *"accuracy"* question— the extent to which people's judgments, affect, and behavior are influenced by independently defined situational variation. In contrast, the "Social Information" proponents ask a *"constructive"* question—the degree to which perception, affect, and behavior are structured by internal processing mechanisms, which social cognition theory suggests may be made differentially accessible via social influence. Such influence includes communication of the "meaning" others attach to stimuli such as specific task requirements and "job context" features. Both miss the point, so well stated by Funder (see also Feldman, 1981), that precisely the same mechanisms must account for both phenomena. Funder (p. 79) notes that the same processes producing visual illusions account for accurate perception of the real world. Further, people less susceptible to "cognitive illusions" (e.g., attribution biases) may be less, rather than better, able to manage their social relationships (p. 86).

Glaser (1984) observed that formally incorrect rules can produce a high rate of accurate judgments as well as "errors," supporting the utility of approximate heuristics. In the same vein, Gould (1985) points out that evolution works with what is available, on a satisfying model, and maladaptive or irrelevant characteristics are carried along with attributes promoting survival. The point is, simply, that in order for people to function at all, perceptions must be correlated with environmental demands. But there is no reason to expect that people's perceptions will, or need to be, identical, allowing variability across people, situations and times.

In the present case, we should expect substantial variability in perception because the "normative model" for judgments of motivationally relevant task attributes is defined only within a given cognitive structure, which is certainly not universally shared. Lord's (1985) signal detection model is relevant. Those job attributes which send the strongest "signals"— for example, whether or not one must carry a hundred-pound sack of cement up a ladder—are accurately perceived. Whether this attribute is a "challenge" or drudgery depends on other factors that both define the "signal" and determine its interpretation. The subjective meaning of objective task and contextual attributes is the essence of "psychological climate" (James & James, 1980; James & Tetrick, 1986). The same processes occur in memory, which is relevant here because perception—under the name of "encoding"—and schematic organization are both important influences on memory. The evidence is clear—memory is not entirely schematic or reconstructive (Alba & Hasher, 1983); people can distinguish between what has been experienced and what they've constructed (Johnson & Raye, 1981), but only with effort. In the absence of effort, schematic intrusions can easily occur (Slusher & Anderson, 1987). Furthermore, "perspective" at encoding can influence organization in memory; perspective taken at recall can also influence organization, especially if the material itself presents no strong organizing cues or if a chronically accessible schema does not exist. If such effects occur, they can influence not only later memory-based judgments, but "on-line" or spontaneous judgments as well.

How much effort is consciously exerted, and how many alternative perspectives are deliberately taken, when an employee completes a "Job Characteristics" rating? It is likely that the answers are "not much" and "none," respectively. Prior judgments and affective responses (which may be elicited automatically; Fazio, Sanbonmatsu, Powell, & Kardes, 1986) are likely to be used to generate answers. These have been formed based on the cues most salient in the environment and processing structures made accessible by either habits of use (e.g., value systems) or environmental input. When coupled with the facts that the actual jobs themselves vary between persons (see e.g., Graen's VDL model, 1976) and that jobs are often ambiguous stimulus packages, these processes allow for both "accuracy" and "construction," for intraindividual and interindividual, temporal, and situational variability on various dimensions (see e.g., Pulakos & Schmitt, 1983).

These effects cannot be avoided by the use of similarity judgments, as in multidimensional scaling studies. Tversky (1977) has shown how such judgments may be altered by shifts in context, while Murphy and Medin (1985) and Glucksberg (1987) show how the concept of similarity itself depends on internal and accessible theories.

A note on the concept of need. Because we observe constancy in judgments of and affective responses to particular circumstances, as well as relatively intense affect related to "important" behaviors such as job change, it is tempting to postulate "needs" as causal entities. Whether thought of in hierarchies or not, needs seem to "fit" our observations well. This is an illusion, a version of the "magical thinking" (Schweder, 1977) pervading everyday perceptions. "Big" motives are unnecessary to account for "big" effects. The concept of "need" (e.g., Stone, 1987) has a major drawback.

If we postulate a fixed, unchanging set of human needs, the only way to account for the observed variation in behavior is to specify precisely how activation of a given need (or set of needs) and the level of each is related to equally well-specified classes of behavior. Without such specificity, we may be left with a proliferation of "needs" (as in earlier "instinct" and "drive" theories) that quickly become circular, or with multiple manifestations of needs, which just as quickly become untestable.

While "cognitive structures and strategies" are every bit as hypothetical as needs, researchers have developed at least a preliminary theory of their activation and operation (e.g., in terms of constructs such as accessibility, automaticity, and elaboration, using operations such as priming and the measurement of memory organization). Need theories, to remain viable, must be developed along similar lines and provide alternative, testable, hypotheses. Until such development occurs, I propose to go somewhat beyond Locke (1976) and apply "need" only to things the individual will die without, like air and vitamins. Value systems, conceptualized as types of cognitive structures, are capable of development, change, and the production of very intense affect through well-specified and testable mechanisms. If need theories cannot do the same, the concept is simply not useful at this level of explanation.

Judgment construction and retrieval. The distinction between construction and retrieval process is fundamental in the study of cognition (Lingle, Altom, & Medin, 1984). As noted by Fischhoff et al. (1980) and others, evaluative and descriptive judgments typically are not made until a reason exists for doing so. In case they have been made, they are stored until needed (Anderson & Hubert, 1963); if they have not been stored, they must be constructed when a salient environmental demand (including a researcher's question) occurs. Lichtenstein and Srull (1985) illustrate this process with a consumer's response to the question "Is a Buick Regal a luxury car?" If the answer exists (and is accessible) in memory, it is retrieved for subsequent use, for example in answering questions like "Are power windows standard in the Buick Regal?"

If the answer is not accessible, it may be constructed by recalling examples of Buick Regals and comparing them to one's category representation. It is at this point that social influence may occur, by influencing the category representation (Barsalou, -1987), the set of examplars recalled for comparison (Alba & Hutchinson, 1987), stimulus features attended to, for example in similarity judgments (Tversky, 1977), and the contents of the category constructed (or retrieved) for comparison (Barsalou, 1982). These social influences are, of course, moderated by the strength of the "signal" produced by the stimulus, which has accessibility-enhancing effects of its own (Taylor & Fiske, 1978), and the degree to which chronically accessible categories and other processing structures exist (Bargh, 1984; Fishhoff, Slovic, & Lichtenstein, 1978) as will be seen below.

The nature of the constructive process itself may be influenced by environmental and individual difference factors. As Petty and Cacioppo (1986) have detailed, either chronic involvement (due to enduring value systems and affective relevance) or temporary involvement (due to the temporary personal consequences of an issue) produces "central" processing, with greater attention to arguments and details of the stimulus. Elaboration of beliefs, greater persistence of changed/constructed attitudes, and resistance to counterargument also occur. "Peripheral" processing, found in low-involvement situations, produces change due to credibility, self-perception, and other "social cueing" effects; though attitude judgments may be as polarized, they are not as long-lasting or resistant to counterargument, due to lesser elaboration. Similar effects are produced by personal experience, which increases both elaboration and attitude accessibility (Fazio & Zanna, 1981). People who habitually engage in cognitive elaboration behave as do highly involved and experienced people.

Furthermore, judgments tend to be self-maintaining. Ross, McFarland, Conway and Zanna (1983) demonstrated the enhancing effect of newly formed attitudes on recall of attitude-consistent behaviors; such rehearsal tends to strengthen the attitude. Darley and Gross (1983) demonstrated selective attention to impression-confirming information; Kulik (1983) showed that situational attributions are invoked to explain expectation-discrepant behavior. Einhorn and Hogarth (1978) discussed the "illusion of validity" produced by people's tendency to infer covariation on the basis of the simple frequency of "jointly positive outcomes"; Alloy and Tabachnik (1984) showed that covariation perception (or its behavioral counterpart) depends on both environmental information and the strength of existing schemata. The fact that "illusory correlation" is maintained despite nonsupportive personal experience (Chapman & Chapman, 1982) testifies that experience and involvement are not enough, in and of themselves, to guarantee responsiveness to "objective reality," especially when neither the dimension of judgment nor the stimulus is unambiguous.

Spontaneity and the content of judgments. Hastie and Park (1986), in discussing memory-based and on-line processing, note that people tend to make spontaneous judgments. Indeed, elaborate manipulations are typically required to prevent judgment (e.g., Lichtenstein & Srull, 1987). However, saying that judgments are spontaneous says nothing about their direction or content.

Many spontaneous judgments have an affective component (Hastie & Park, 1986, p. 262). Since the evaluative dimension is ubiquitous in human experience (Osgood, Suci, & Tannenbaum, 1957), this is hardly surprising. Belief judgments frequently accompany affect, either as cause or as consequence (Feldman & Lynch, 1988), and consideration of their source will illuminate the process of job perception and its relationship to satisfaction and motivation.

Fiske and Pavelchak (1986) discuss two ways in which affect may be experienced. The first, category-based, is the counterpart to automaticity in person perception. When a stimulus "fits" an accessible category representation, both the characteristics of category members and affect associated with that category are associated with the stimulus. This is experienced as a perceptual event; whether cognition precedes or follows affect, or whether the two are independent, is irrelevant.

In cases where no category is accessible, "piecemeal" or thoughtful processing takes place. The individual is aware that a judgment is being made, though he or she may not be aware of all of the influences on that judgment (Bargh, 1984; Nisbett & Wilson, 1977). An affective response is formed based on salient stimulus attributes and their interpretation, including whatever causal attributions occur. Both category-based and piecemeal judgments depend, in a reciprocal fashion, on stimulus attributes, their relative salience, and accessible processing structures. Importantly, the "Job Characteristics" perspective places its major emphasis on stimulus attributes and "need" or value-based structures—and deals only with piecemeal processing—while the "Social Information Processing" viewpoint places major emphasis on environmentally induced accessibility and on categorical processing. Neither allows for both, nor for reciprocity between affect and cognition.

Value Systems as an Integrating Device

Integration of these viewpoints can be achieved by regarding an individual's "value system" as a highly elaborated cognitive structure or associative network developed in response to the events and contingencies of one's life, not necessarily consciously or intentionally (e.g., Lewiki, Czyzewska, & Hoffman, 1987). Individuals differ in the domains in which their values are elaborated, so that people are differentially "schematic." Simply put, not everyone has the same values to the same degree even within a common culture, although values can also be defined at the aggregate (e.g., cultural) level (Fischhoff et al., 1980; Triandis, Bontempo, Villareal, Asai, & Lucca, 1988). These individual cognitive structures have greater or lesser degrees of affect associated with them, affect being imperfectly correlated with elaboration. (The relation may be curvilinear at the extreme). They also contain processing "strategies" which may be elicited; these are highly accessible, unitized or automated production systems (Anderson, 1987; Hayes-Roth, 1977) that guide category formation (Barsalou, 1987), memory encoding and organization, and judgment/choice processes. They act like expert systems because they are precisely the same as expert systems (e.g., Alba & Hutchinson, 1987). Like expert systems, they guide encoding, organization, and storage of memory and spontaneous, sometimes automatic, responses to judgment and decision problems; they contain precomputed and highly rehearsed judgments and behavioral scripts; they are domain-specific, rendering social influence, framing and priming manipulations less effective only within their domain of application (Bettman & Sujan, 1987; Anderson, 1987; Alba & Hutchinson, 1987; Feldman & Lynch, 1988); and, finally, they are not totally immune to environmental manipulation, including both accessibility effects and social influence (Fischhoff et al., 1978; Schwartz & Inbar-Saban, 1988).

Cross-cultural research illustrates the variability of value systems. At the extreme, values reflected in one culture's work and social life may have no counterpart in another's. The Japanese concept of amae or "indulgent love" is one example. Amae is a feeling that one may not only completely trust another on whom one is dependent, but that one can "presume upon the indulgence" of the other. Such trust is necessary to interpersonal and business relationships, especially the superior-subordinate, and is a concept that non-Japanese find difficult to understand because they do not have the associative structure or affective responses to support it (DeMente, 1981).

The point is not that culture produces uniformity; individual differences are both obvious and important (Triandis et al., 1988). The point is that the structures guiding perceptions, affect, and behavior vary widely as a function of one's social environment, and these must influence job perceptions as well if parsimony is to have any meaning at all. It is not a case of bias or of misperception, but of an inherently subjective "social reality" differing between people.

When value systems are not elaborated in a particular domain, and when environmentally induced accessibility effects and signals from the stimulus are particularly strong, the constructive processes described earlier will occur. Their influence on judgment, affect, and behavior depends on the accessibility and strength of precomputed responses and/or habitually used (chronically accessible) processing mechanisms. It should not be supposed that environmental influences apply only to relatively trivial issues. Not only have Fischhoff et al. (1978) shown that framing can influence the use of expert knowledge, but Higgins (1987) has shown that relatively simple questioning manipulations can influence perceptions of and affect toward the self, hardly a construct of little concern or elaboration to most people.

Furthermore, it should not be supposed that the affect produced from such sources is (or remains) relatively low-level. Once a judgment is made, rehearsal tends to further polarize it (Tesser, 1978), especially when a supportive structure exists (Chaiken & Yates, 1985). Any emotion-arousing event associated with one's self, and which is elaborated, tends to be experienced more strongly. People differ reliably in their tendency to personalize and elaborate experience (Larsen, Diener, & Cropanzano, 1987), but any external inducement to do so should have similar effects. Over time and repeated experience, and with reflection, a highly polarized affect may develop.

Ultimately, job perception is a part of the process of three-way reciprocal causation. As information from any source(s) is absent, conflicting, or ambiguous, perception and affect are structured from the remaining sources. The responses thus formed in turn change the structures, and the behavior generated on their basis changes the effective environment (e.g., Einhorn & Hogarth, 1978; Feldman, 1986; Snyder, Tanke, & Berscheid, 1977). Statistically speaking, reciprocal interactions cannot be decomposed into components of variance attributable to each source (L.R. James, personal communication). Theoretically, we can understand why this is so. A given behavior arises only from unique combinations of individual and environmental states or events, and all are jointly sufficient. Furthermore, once the event has occurred both the person and the situation are changed, and cannot be returned to their former states.

Social Influence in Real Life

I believe it is reasonable to assume that the processes whose small effects can be studied with relatively weak laboratory manipulations are capable of generating the large effects we see in "real life." It remains to examine the kinds of "manipulations" that people may experience in their everyday lives and their effects on cognition and behavior. The present focus is both broader and narrower than that of Ferris and Mitchell (1987). It is broader in that I will consider anecdotal but suggestive descriptions of influence settings; narrower, in that I consider a more restricted range of social influence data.

Allen (1965, 1975) has reviewed the situational factors promoting both social influence and resistance to it. In conformity studies done twenty-five or more years ago, relatively long-term change in perception, belief, and attitude was found to occur when the stimulus situation was ambiguous (e.g., on autokinetic tasks or opinion items), when the source of influence had credibility (due to expertise or group unanimity and size), when prior judgments were not formed, and when social support was absent. It is noteworthy that when (for instance) unambiguous stimuli were presented, behavioral conformity occurred, but private change did not; it is also noteworthy that some private change occurred following compliance even on strongly held opinions, as a result of exposure to unanimous group pressure. Social support however, markedly decreased both compliance and true change.

These results are consistent with the persuasion/construction model discussed above, in which information integration and cognitive elaboration induced by situational factors is guided by knowledge and processing structures chronically or temporarily accessible. It is also consistent with Bem's (1972) self-perception theory, Anderson and Graesser's (1976) model of information integration in groups, the group polarization phenomenon in general (Isenberg, 1986), and "minority influence" (Nemeth, 1986).

The strength of such effects are seen in many places. Milgram's (1965) destructive obedience studies can be analyzed in terms of situational factors promoting compliance: public responding, prior commitment, gradual escalation of demands by a credible source, a morally ambiguous task (am I contributing to science or hurting someone?) not strongly connected to the individual's value structure, the absence of previously formed judgments or intentions, a lack of opportunity to consider alternative constructions of the task, and so forth. Even when a bogus group of "subjects" provided the pressure, instead of the experimenter, compliance was maintained, although increasing the salience of the victim's suffering did reduce it. Both results are consistent with a judgment-construction model of the meaning of the behavior.

Consider also Schein's (1956) description of life in a Korean War POW camp. Young men were segregated by rank and race so as to reduce exposure to military norms and authority figures who could structure the decision situation; completely dependent on their captors, they were induced in gradual steps to "cooperate" by listening to lectures and signing seemingly innocuous statements; without well-formed values or scripts of behavior, constantly exposed to propaganda and prevented from forming cohesive support/escape groups by mutual suspicion, they were induced to "collaborate" in unprecedented numbers. I submit that their perception of the situation, and of the behaviors in question, was influenced by the same constructive processes discussed above.

Finally, consider organizational socialization. According to *Fortune* magazine (Pascale, 1984), many firms subject new trainees to a process that begins with rigorous and stressful interview procedures, eliciting high commitment; once hired, trainees are put into a program requiring long hours of difficult, tedious work with other trainees, effectively restricting social contacts; the firm requires mastery of the "company way" of doing business and rewards value-consistent behavior and performance; it also provides explicit statements of value, folklore, and a credible, affectively positive "mentor." Furthermore, a trainee is often thousands of miles away from family and friends; is unlikely to speak critically of the firm to coworkers; is unlikely to have elaborated a job-relevant value system; and is likely to perceive the organization as a valued in-group. The result is a very powerful engine of social influence. As Walton and Hackman (1986) have said: "Groups create social reality (by their interpretations of 'objective' reality and by constructing a new social reality), transmit it (making sure all members comprehend 'how things are here'), and provide a setting in which groups can firm up their self-perceptions... These activities are critical... because 'objective' reality is usually difficult to determine in constantly changing social systems." (p. 193).

An Application: Job Design in Singapore

Singapore, a rapidly growing business environment with a multicultural workforce and a mixture of high technology and traditional occupations, is a natural arena in which to apply job design concepts. Previously assured annual wage increments may no longer be feasible, and many firms are seeking to tie wage incentives to productivity (Tsung, 1986). There is increased concern that firms will be unable to attract and retain the most skilled and valuable employees (Anonymous, 1987a, b; Neo, 1987; Seow, 1988). Without such skilled employees, the recent drive to improve the quality and image of Singaporean goods may well falter (Tsung, 1988).

While wage and other incentives are debated (Anonymous, 1987c), the more educated and skilled workers appear to value more than simply economic outcomes (Anonymous, 1987d). Ming (1987a) reports that university students placed "interesting work" first when evaluating jobs. Opportunities for training and experience and promotion prospects were valued as or more highly than salaries, benefits and working conditions.

These statements suggest that work redesign along lines suggested by the Job Characteristics Model may be a viable means of attracting and retaining employees where they are most needed. It should be pointed out, however, that survey responses cannot be taken as unequivocal evidence of people's work values (Feldman & Lynch, 1988). Especially in a multicultural setting, and where female employees' numbers are growing, careful experimental studies of job designs and other work outcome manipulations will be required. Furthermore, jobs "enriched" according to Job Characteristics Model principles inevitably differ on other dimensions as well (Campion, 1988) and may require higher wages. This will put a premium on the accurate selection of highly skilled employees, already a matter of controversy (Huat, 1987). Training initiatives will likewise be required (Ming, 1987b; Tho, 1987; Teo, 1987). Almost certainly, the methods and techniques of work redesign must be adapted to a generally Asian and specifically Singaporean cultural context. The features that make a job interesting and involving to a European, or that lead an American to be highly committed to an organization, cannot be assumed to be the same for a Singaporean.

Perception and Reality: Conclusions

This discussion has ranged far from the specifics of job perception. In a sense, that captures the central theme and leads directly to my conclusion: jobs are inherently social objects, and cognitive and affective responses to them are determined by the same factors that govern responses to any social objects. The physical and mental demands of jobs are "reality," just as are the physical attributes and behaviors of persons. These are, however, apprehended via processing structures developed largely through social interaction, and these determine "reality" as it is experienced.

We can now appreciate both the benefits and the drawbacks of each of the positions sketched earlier. The "Job Characteristics" view stresses the effects of the job's requirements and the powerful influence of strongly held, affect-laden value systems. It does not, however, give enough weight to the social environment as the source of these values or to its role in changing them. The "Social Information Processing" view recognizes but exaggerates the power of the social environment, both to direct attention and determine the contents of the processing that creates affect and belief. Both the strength of the environmental "signal" and the characteristics of the "receiver" are given too little weight, in favor of emphasis on the tuning mechanism.

Experiments demonstrating that social cues may influence perception and affect in new and ambiguous situations capture part of the process but miss its major impact, which occurs through the very powerful mechanisms of organizational and cultural socialization (e.g., Walton & Hackman, 1986, p. 193). Studies showing the benefit of "enriched" work and the effect of actual job demands on perception and affect capture another part of the process but likewise miss the impact of social factors, which do not vary enough within a given setting to make their influence known. What is needed are experiments that illuminate basic processes and theoretically guided field studies and experiments in a wide range of jobs and social contexts, including multiple cultures.

The final, and fundamental, point is that the processes of social perception are neither sources of error nor windows to some external reality. Both "accuracy" and "bias," as they have been used in the job perception literature, are somewhat misleading concepts. Job perceptions, and responses to job design, reflect the processes that define social worlds and shape values, determine one's sense of what is, and what is good. Understanding the fundamentals of perception, motivation and attitude requires both greater theoretical rigor and an intimate understanding of specific situations and cultures. This seems to be the best kind of problem for applied researchers to undertake, no matter which part of the elephant one favors.

References

Adler, S., Skov, R.B., and Salvemini, N.J. (1985). Job characteristics and job satisfaction: When cause becomes consequence. *Organizational Behavior and Human Decision Processes, 35,* 266-278.

Alba, J.W., Chromiak, W., Hasher, L., and Attig, M.S. (1980). Automatic encoding of category size information. *Journal of Experimental Psychology: Human Learning and Memory, 6,* 370-378.

Alba, J.W. and Hasher, L. (1983). Is memory schematic? *Psychological Bulletin, 93,* 203-231.

Alba, J.W. and Hutchinson, J.W. (1987). Dimensions of consumer expertise. *Journal of Consumer Research, 13,* 411-454.

Allen, V.L. (1965). Situational factors in conformity. In L. Berkowitz (Ed.), *Advances in Experimental Social Psychology (Vol. 2).* New York: Academic Press.

Allen, V.L. (1975). Social support for nonconformity. In L. Berkowitz (Ed.), *Advances in Experimental Social Psychology (Vol. 8)*. New York: Academic Press.

Alloy, L.B. and Tabachnik, N. (1984). Assessment of covariation by humans and animals: The joint influence of prior expectations and current situational information. *Psychological Review, 91*, 112-149.

Anderson, J.R. (1987). Skill acquisition: Compilation of weak-method problem solutions. *Psychological Review, 94*, 192-210.

Anderson, N.H. and Graesser, C.C. (1976). An information-integration analysis of attitude change in group discussion. *Journal of Personality and Social Psychology, 34*, 210-222.

Anderson, N.H. and Hubert, S. (1963). Effects of concomitant verbal recall on order effects in personality impression formation. *Journal of Verbal Learning and Verbal Behavior, 2*, 379-391.

Anonymous. (1987a, Feb. 10). Young job-hoppers will hurt investment climate. *Straits Times*, p. 26.

Anonymous. (1987b, Feb. 7). Low labour turnover is good for investors. *Straits Times*, p.15.

Anonymous. (1987c, Feb. 5). To pay or not to pay for unused sick leave. *Straits Times*, p.17.

Anonymous. (1987d, Oct. 22). Our country, our home. *Straits Times*, p.16.

Bargh, J.A. (1984). Automatic and conscious processing of social information. In R.S. Wyer & T.K. Srull (Eds.), *Handbook of Social Cognition (Vol. 3)*. Hillsdale, NJ: Erlbaum.

Barsalou, L.W. (1982). Context-independent information in concepts. *Memory and Cognition, 10*, 82-93.

Barsalou, L.W. (1987). The instability of graded structure: Implications for the nature of concepts. In U. Neisser (Ed.), *Concepts Reconsidered: The Ecological and Intellectual Basis of Categories*. Cambridge: Cambridge University Press.

Bem, D.J. (1972). Self-perception theory. In L. Berkowitz (Ed.), *Advances in Experimental Social Psychology (Vol. 6)*. New York: Academic Press.

Bettman, J.R. and Sujan, M. (1987). Effects of framing on evaluation of comparable and noncomparable alternatives by novice and expert consumers. *Journal of Consumer Research, 14*, 141-154.

Campion, M. (1988). Interdisciplinary approaches to job design: A constructive replication with extensions. *Journal of Applied Psychology, 73*, 467-481.

Chaiken, S. and Yates, S. (1985). Affective-cognitive consistency and thought-induced attitude polarization. *Journal of Personality and Social Psychology, 49*, 1470-1481.

Chapman, L.J. and Chapman, J.P. (1982). Test results are what you think they are. In D. Kahneman, P. Slovic, & A. Tversky (Eds.), *Judgment Under Uncertainty: Heuristics and Biases*. Cambridge: Cambridge University Press.

Christensen-Szalanski, J.J.J., and Beach, L.R. (1984). The citation bias: Fad and fashion in the judgment and decision literature [Comment]. *American Psychologist, 39*, 75-78.

Darley, J.M. and Gross, P.H. (1983). A hypothesis-confirming bias in labelling effects. *Journal of Personality and Social Psychology, 44*, 20-33.

DeMente, B. (1981). *The Japanese Way of Doing Business*. Englewood Cliffs, NJ: Prentice-Hall.

Dunham, R.B. (1977). Relationship of perceived job design characteristics to job ability requirements and job value. *Journal of Applied Psychology, 62,* 760-763.

Dunham, R.B., Aldag, R.J., and Brief, A.P. (1977). Dimensionality of task design as measured by the job diagnostic survey. *Academy of Management Journal, 20,* 209-223.

Einhorn, H.J. and Hogarth, R.M. (1978). Confidence in judgment: Persistence of the illusion of validity. *Psychological Review, 85,* 395-416.

Fazio, R.H., Sanbonmatsu, D.M., Powell, M.C., and Kardes, F.R. (1986). On the automatic activation of attitudes. *Journal of Personality and Social Psychology, 50,* 229-238.

Fazio, R.H. and Zanna, M.P. (1981). Direct experience and attitude-behavior consistency. In L. Berkowitz (Ed.), *Advances in Experimental Social Psychology (Vol. 14).* New York: Academic Press.

Feldman, J.M. (1981). Beyond attribution theory: Cognitive processes in performance appraisal. *Journal of Applied Psychology, 66,* 127-148.

Feldman, J.M. (1986). A note on the statistical correction of halo error. *Journal of Applied Psychology, 71,* 173-176.

Feldman, J.M. and Lynch, J.G., Jr. (1988). Self-generated validity and other influences of measurement on belief, attitude, intention and behavior. *Journal of Applied Psychology, 73,* 421-435.

Ferris, G.R. and Mitchell, T.R. (1987). The components of social influence and their importance for human resources research. In K.M. Rowland and G.R. Ferris (Eds.), *Research in Personnel and Human Resources Management (Vol. 5).* Greenwich, CT: JAI Press.

Fischhoff, B., Slovic, P., and Lichtenstein, S. (1978). Fault trees: Sensitivity of estimated failure probabilities to problem representation. *Journal of Experimental Psychology: Human Perception and Performance, 4,* 330-344.

Fischhoff, B., Slovic, P., and Lichtenstein, S. (1980). Knowing what you want: Measuring labile values. In T. Wallsten (Ed.), *Cognitive Processes in Choice and Decision Behavior.* Hillsdale, NJ: Erlbaum.

Fiske, S.T. and Pavelchak, N.A. (1986). Category-based versus piecemeal affective responses: Developments in schema-triggered affect. In R.M. Sorrentino & E.T. Higgins (Eds.), *The Handbook of Motivation and Cognition: Foundations of Social Behavior.* New York: Guilford Press.

Funder, D.C. (1987). Errors and mistakes: Evaluating the accuracy of social judgment. *Psychological Bulletin, 101,* 75-90.

Glaser, R. (1984). Education and thinking. *American Psychologist, 39,* 93-104.

Glucksberg, S.(1987). *Understanding Metaphors: Beyond Similarity.* Unpublished manuscript. Princeton University.

Gould, S.J. (1985). *The Flamingo's Smile.* New York: W.W. Norton.

Graen, G. (1976). Role-making processes within complex organizations. In M. Dunnette (Ed.), *Handbook of Industrial and Organizational Psychology.* Chicago: Rand McNally.

Griffin, R.W. (1987). Toward an integrated theory of task design. In B.M. Staw & L.L. Cummings (Eds.), *Research in Organizational Behavior (Vol. 9).* Greenwich, CT: JAI Press.

Hackman, J.R. and Lawler, E.E., III (1971). Employee reactions to job characteristics. *Journal of Applied Psychology, 55,* 259-286.

Hackman, J.R. and Oldham, G.R. (1976). Motivation through the design of work: Test of a theory. *Organizational Behavior and Human Performance, 16,* 250-279.

Hackman, J.R. and Oldham, G.R. (1980). *Work Redesign.* Reading, MA: Addison-Wesley.

Hastie, R. and Park, B. (1986). The relationship between memory and judgment depends on whether the judgment is memory-based or on-line. *Psychological Review, 93,* 258-268.

Hayes-Roth, B. (1977). Evolution of cognitive structures and processes. *Psychological Review, 84,* 260-278.

Higgins, A. (1987). Self-discrepancy: A theory relating self and affect. *Psychological Review, 94,* 319-340.

Huat, T.T. (1987, Aug. 19). Tougher road to some new jobs. *Straits Times,* p.13.

Isen, A.M. (1984). Toward understanding the role of affect in cognition. In R.S. Wyer & T.K. Srull (Eds.), *Handbook of Social Cognition (Vol. 3).* Hillsdale, NJ: Erlbaum.

Isenberg, D.J. (1986). Group polarization: A critical review and meta-analysis. *Journal of Personality and Social Psychology, 50,* 114-115.

James, L.R. and James, A.P. (1980). Perceived job characteristics and job satisfaction: An examination of reciprocal causation. *Personnel Psychology, 33,* 97-135.

James, L.R. and Tetrick, L.E. (1986). Confirmatory analytic tests of three causal models relating job perceptions to job satisfaction. *Journal of Applied Psychology, 71,* 77-82.

Johnson, M.K. and Raye, C.L. (1981). Reality monitoring. *Psychological Review, 88,* 67-85.

Kahneman, D., Slovic, P., and Tversky, A. (1982). *Judgment Under Uncertainty: Heuristics and Biases.* Cambridge, MA: Cambridge University Press.

Kulik, J.A. (1983). Confirmatory attribution and the perpetuation of social beliefs. *Journal of Personality and Social Psychology, 44,* 1171-1181.

Larsen, R.J., Diener, E., and Cropanzano, R.S. (1987). Cognitive operations associated with individual differences in affect intensity. *Journal of Personality and Social Psychology, 53,* 767-774.

Leventhal, H. and Nerez, D. (1988). Representations of threat and the control of stress. In D. Meichenbaum & M. Jaremko (Eds.), *Stress Prevention and Management: A Cognitive Behavioral Approach.* New York: Plenum.

Lewicki, P., Czyzewska, M., and Hoffman, H. (1987). Unconscious acquisition of complex procedural knowledge. *Journal of Experimental Psychology: Learning, Memory, and Cognition,* 13, 523-530.

Lichtenstein, M. and Srull, T.K. (1985). Conceptual and methodological issues in examining the relationship between consumer memory and judgment. In L. Alwitt & A. Mitchell (Eds.), *Psychological Processes and Advertising Effects: Theory, Research and Application.* Hillsdale, NJ: Erlbaum.

Lichtenstein, M. and Srull, T.K. (1987). Processing objectives as a determinant of the relationship between judgment and recall. *Journal of Experimental Social Psychology, 23,* 93-118.

Lingle, J.H., Altom, M.W., and Medin, D.L. (1984). Of cabbages and kings: Assessing the extendability of natural object concept models to social things. In R.S. Wyer & T.K. Srull (Eds.), *Handbook of Social Cognition (Vol. 1)*. Hillsdale, NJ: Erlbaum.

Locke, E.A. (1976). The nature and causes of job satisfaction. In M. Dunnette (Ed.), *Handbook of Industrial and Organizational Psychology*. Chicago: Rand McNally.

Lord, R.B. (1985). Accuracy in behavioral measurement: An alternative definition based on rater's cognitive schema and signal detection theory. *Journal of Applied Psychology, 70,* 66-71.

Milgram, S. (1965). Some conditions of obedience and disobedience to authority. *Human Relations, 18,* 57-76.

Ming, C.P. (1987a, July 15). Interesting jobs valued more than security, survey says. *Business Times,* p.18.

Ming, C.P. (1987b, July 10). Upgrade skills to stay number one. *Business Times,* p. 2.

Murphy, G.L. and Medin, D.L. (1985). The role of theories in conceptual coherence. *Psychological Review, 92,* 289-316.

Nemeth, C.J. (1986). Differential contributions of majority and minority influence. *Psychological Review, 93,* 25-32.

Neo, L.S. (1987, Jan. 3). SIA looks abroad for top flight crew. *Business Times,* p.1.

Nisbett, R.E. and Wilson, T.D. (1977). Telling more than we can know: Verbal reports on mental processes. *Psychological Review, 84,* 231-259.

Osgood, C.E., Suci, G.J., and Tannenbaum, P.H. (1957). *The Measurement of Meaning.* Urbana, IL: University of Illinois Press.

Pascale, R. (1984). Fitting new employees into corporate culture. *Fortune, 109 (May 28),* 28-43.

Petty, R.E. and Cacioppo, J.T. (1986). The elaboration likelihood model of persuasion. In L. Berkowitz (Ed.), *Advances in Experimental Social Psychology (Vol. 19).* New York: Academic Press.

Pulakos, E.D. and Schmitt, N. (1983). A longitudinal study of a valence model approach for the prediction of job satisfaction of new employees. *Journal of Applied Psychology, 68,* 307-312.

Roberts, K.H. and Glick, W. (1981). The job characteristics approach to task design: A critical review. *Journal of Applied Psychology, 66,* 193-217.

Ross, M., McFarland, C., Conway, M., and Zanna, M.P. (1983). Reciprocal relation between attitudes and behavior recall: Committing people to newly formed attitudes. *Journal of Personality and Social Psychology, 45,* 257-267.

Schein, E.H. (1956). The Chinese indoctrination program for prisoners of war: A study of attempted "brainwashing." *Psychiatry, 14,* 149-172.

Schwartz, S.H. and Inbar-Saban, N. (1988). Value self-confrontation as a method to aid in weight loss. *Journal of Personality and Social Psychology, 54,* 396-404.

Schweder, R.A. (1977). Likeness and likelihood in everyday thought: Magical thinking in judgments about personality. *Current Anthropology, 18,* 637-658.

Seow, S. (1988, Aug. 3). Skills-intensive industries the key to growth, says EDB. *Straits Times,* p. 15.

Slusher, M.P. and Anderson, C.A. (1987). When reality monitoring fails: The role of imagination in stereotype maintenance. *Journal of Personality and Social Psychology, 52,* 653-662.

Snyder, M., Tanke, E.D., and Berscheid, E. (1977). Social perception and interpersonal behavior: On the self-fulfilling nature of social stereotypes. *Journal of Personality and Social Psychology, 35,* 656-666.

Stone, E.F. (1987). Further consideration of the supposed invalidity of need-satisfaction models of job design and job attitudes. *Paper presented at the Bowling Green Conference: Job Satisfaction: Advances in Theory, Research and Application,* October 1987.

Stone, E.F. and Guetal, H. (1985). An empirical derivation of the dimensions along which jobs are perceived. *Academy of Management Journal, 28,* 376-396.

Taylor, S.E. and Fiske, S.T. (1978). Salience, attention, and attribution: Top of the head phenomena. In L. Berkowitz (Ed.), *Advances in Experimental Social Psychology (Vol. 11).* New York: Academic Press.

Teo, A. (1987, July 8). NPC proposes moves to upgrade labour. *Business Times,* p. 18.

Tesser, A. (1978). Self-generated attitude change. In L.Berkowitz (Ed.), *Advances in Experimental Social Psychology (Vol. 11).* New York: Academic Press.

Tho, T.Y. (1987, July 8). Strategy to boost skills. *Straits Times,* p.13.

Thomas, J. and Griffin, R. (1983). The social information processing model of task design: A review of the literature. *Academy of Management Review, 8,* 672-682.

Triandis, H.C. (1972). *The Analysis of Subjective Culture.* New York: Wiley-Interscience.

Triandis, H.C., Bontempo, R., Villareal, M.J., Asai, M., and Lucca, N. (1988). Individualism and collectivism: Cross-cultural perspectives on self-ingroup relationships. *Journal of Personality and Social Psychology, 54,* 323-338.

Tsung, J. (1988, Mar. 8). Good designs to be rewarded. *Business Times,* p. 7.

Tversky, A. (1977). Features of similarity. *Psychological Review, 84,* 327-352.

Walton, R.E. and Hackman, J.R. (1986). Groups under contrasting management strategies. In P.S. Goodman (Ed.), *Designing Effective Work Groups.* San Francisco: Jossey-Bass.

Wyer, R.S. and Srull, T.K. (1986). Human cognition in its social context. *Psychological Review, 93,* 322-359.

Notes

Thanks are due to Larry James, Michael Campion, Eugene Stone, and Harry C. Triandis for their many helpful comments. Request for reprints should be addressed to Jack Feldman, School of Psychology, Georgia Institute of Technology, Atlanta, GA 30332, U.S.A. This paper was originally presented at a symposium entitled "New directions in job design: Expanding predictors, criteria, and theory" (M. Campion, chair), at the Third Annual Conference of the Society for Industrial-Organizational Psychology, Dallas, TX, April 1988.

SECTION B
Cross-Cultural Factors and Decision Making

CULTURE AND ITS EFFECTS ON DECISION MAKING

Mark H. B. Radford

Decision making is an important everyday behavior. As a field of study, it has been the subject of an array of theoretical models and empirical research (for reviews, see Abelson & Levi, 1985; Slovic, Fischhoff, & Lichtenstein, 1977). Decision making has attracted the attention of scholars from many different disciplines, especially from economics, mathematics and psychology. While theories differ in both their approach and content, most assume a universal decision maker. With the exception of decision making in organizations (e.g., Misumi, 1984), the role of culture is often ignored or given only a passing consideration. In this paper, the importance of cross-cultural research in decision making is outlined, current research on decision making in different cultures is discussed, and a theoretical framework for future research is presented.

Most decision research has dealt with the "prescriptive" aspects of decision making, that is, with how an individual estimates the utility (attractiveness) and probability (of occurrence) values for a given range of options (or alternatives) and arrives at a choice (e.g., Beach & Beach, 1982; Jaccard & Wan, 1986). With the work of Tversky and Kahneman (1974) on biases and limitations in human judgment and information processing, classic decision-making theory research came under criticism for failing to describe how decisions are made, or to account for poor decisions being made when optimal conditions for good decision making existed (Janis & Mann, 1977). Recently, there has been an increase in research into the descriptive aspects of decision making. By understanding how decisions are made, one is not only better able to understand the decision-making process itself, but also to improve deficient decision-making behavior.

Studying the effect that culture has upon decision making is an important extension of research on descriptive aspects of the decision-making process. The fact that culture does influence decision making can be seen in the research into organizational decision making. Important differences between Japanese and American (United States of America) corporate decision making has been the subject of much recent treatment (e.g., Misumi, 1984; Ouchi, 1981). Decision making in American corporations tends to be the responsibility of an individual, or a small, clearly defined senior management group with little, if any, participation of those outside the management elite. Japanese organizational decision making, however, often involves senior, middle, and sometimes junior management. Through both *I memawashi* (groundwork or "lobbying") and *ringii* (consensus seeking), Japanese organizations seek consensus in the decisions made, by most of those concerned. While American organizational decision making is relatively quick, it fails to directly involve those outside the management group. Japanese decison making, on the other hand, is slow but is considered to have strong support and commitment at all levels. These differences in behavior have often been cited as important factors in the dramatic growth of Japanese economic dominance over the last several decades (e.g., Hirokawa, 1981; Masatsugu, 1982).

Just as organizational decision making may vary as a function of culture, so too may individual decision making. Understanding the way in which culture influences individual decision-making behavior allows greater understanding, communication and cooperation in both cross-cultural studies involving descriptive aspects of decision making are discussed.

Current Cross-Cultural Research in Decision Making

Most current research on descriptive aspects has developed from the conflict theory of Janis and Mann (1977). Drawing heavily on the psychological aspects of stress, Janis and Mann developed a theory based on the assumption that making decisions of consequence is stressful. Simply stated, the model identifies five major coping patterns that can be adopted to resolve the stress (decisional conflict) aroused by having to make a decision: (1) "Unconflicted adherence" (complacency—no change in behavior: little or no stress); (2) "Unconflicted change" (complacency—adopts most salient course of action: little or no stress); (3) "defensive avoidance" (escapes stress by procrastinating, buck-passing, or rationalization: high stress); (4) "hypervigilance" (full range of alternatives are ignored because of extreme emotional arousal, perseveration and limited attention: high stress); and (5) "vigilance" (careful, unbiased search, assimilation and evaluation of alternatives: moderate stress). According to the conflict theory an ideal decision maker is the "vigilant decision maker." Such a person has high self-esteem, carefully canvasses alternatives, searches and assimilates information, chooses and implements the best option, and subsequently evaluates the outcome.

In a study designed to test the validity of the Decision-Making Questionnaires (D.M.Q. I & II), a self-report measure based on the conflict model (Mann, 1982; Radford, Mann, & Kalucy, 1986), Mann and his colleagues collected data from undergraduate university students in several Eastern (Japan, Singapore and Taiwan) and Western societies (Australia, New Zealand and the United States) (Mann, Radford, Nakamura, Vaughan, Taylor, Burnett, & Yang, 1989). This study reported higher levels of decision self-esteem in students from Western societies than those from Eastern society. No differences were reported in the use of the "vigilant" decision response style, although Japanese and Taiwanese students tended to be higher than other students in their reported use of the "maladaptive coping patterns"—"defensive avoidance," "procrastination," "rationalization," "buck-passing," and "hypervigilance." The pattern of Singaporean students was more similar to that of the Western students.

In a separate research program and using slightly different measures, data from both Japanese and Australian university student samples (Radford, Mann, Ohta & Nakane, 1989) was collected. A questionnaire (different from the study reported above) containing descriptive measures of decision making, based on the conflict theory of Janis and Mann (1977), was administered to 156 Japanese and 94 undergraduate students as part of a general questionnaire battery examining the relationship between culture, personality and decision making. The summarized results are presented in Table 1.

TABLE 1

Decisional self-esteem, stress and response styles in Japanese (n=156) and Australian (n=94) university students (Adapted from Radford et al., 1989).

Variables	Japanese Mean	S.D.	Australian Mean	S.D.	F(df=1)
Decisional Self-Esteem	10.36	3.0	13.77	2.9	36.29 **
Decisional Stress	11.30	4.5	7.98	3.9	28.46 **
Decision Response Styles					
1. Complacency	5.53	2.3	2.70	2.0	60.96 **
2. Avoidance	5.84	3.0	3.86	2.7	31.70 **
3. Hypervigilance	6.78	3.2	4.83	3.0	22.09 **
4. Choice	9.77	2.8	11.98	2.9	23.12 **

** $p < 0.001$

The results of the above study showed that high self-esteem as a decision maker was positively correlated with a "choice" or vigilance (equivalent patterns) decision response style, and negatively correlated with stress aroused by having to make a decision and maladaptive patterns of decision making (e.g., "defensive avoidance" and "hypervigilance"). Initial interpretation of these results (including those reported by Mann et al., 1989) provides empirical support for the basic tenets of the conflict theory of decision making as described by Janis and Mann (1977), using different cultural samples.

While the nature of relationships between variables is similar across cultures, significant differences between cultures were found. In comparison with similar Western samples (using the same measures), non-Western students (especially

Japanese and Taiwanese) had significantly lower decisional self-esteem, higher decisional stress, higher use of maladaptive decision response styles and lower use of the "choice" decision response style. A strict interpretation of the results according to Janis and Mann's theory would suggest that non-Western decision makers are more likely to use non-vigilant or maladaptive decision behavior patterns than Western decision makers, and by implication are not as effective decision makers (cf. Janis & Mann, 1977).

The two important questions which arise from these studies are simple: (1) Are non-Western individuals less efficient decision makers than Western individuals? (2) If not, are current theories of decision making culturally specific—in other words do they rely too heavily on "emic" assumptions and concepts? If so, can such theories account for decision making in non-Western societies? A simple examination of the long history and achievements of non-Western cultures indicates that non-Western decision makers have not been disadvantaged in terms of their progress by their decision-making style. In fact, in many cases the opposite can be said to be true (e.g., economic growth in Japan).

The answer to the first question is that, in terms of the outcome of their decisions, non-Western decision makers are not necessarily less efficient than their Western counterparts. By extension, the answer to the second question is—"yes," current theories of decision making are culturally specific and therefore cannot adequately account for decision making outside Western cultures. Attention is drawn to two important considerations.

First, the assumption that the goal of decision making is to reduce conflict (Janis & Mann, 1977) may simply reflect an underlying cultural ethos of a particular Western society (e.g., Horney, 1964; Janis & Mann, 1977; Kraus, Rohlen, & Steinhoff, 1984; Stewart, 1985). The underlying cultural ethos of many non-Western cultures, such as China, Japan and Singapore, is said to be one of promoting and maintaining group and social harmony (e.g., Hasegawa, 1966, Nakamura, 1964). In such cases, the aim of decision making may be to promote harmony—not to avoid or reduce conflict.

Second, any consideration of decision-making behavior (or any behavior for that matter) needs to be considered in relation to the culturally accepted patterns of behavior of the particular society in which the decision is being made. Much has been written concerning the social and group orientation of Eastern (especially Japanese) behavior, as compared to the mostly self-centered, individualistic behavior of Western, and particularly North American, behavior (e.g., Caudill, 1973; Christopher, 1983; Draguns, 1980; Marsella, Devos, & Hsu, 1985; Masatsugu, 1982; Nakamura, 1964; Nakane, 1973; Stewart, 1972). Several writers have proposed an "individualism-collectivism" dimension to differentiate cultures (cf. Hofstede, 1980; Sampson, 1975). Collectivism, or the emphasis on social group, entails a belief in the importance of maintaining group harmony and interests above the interests of particular individuals. Indeed, in some cases, the needs of the individual are subsumed by the maintenance of group harmony, although one is not necessarily separable from the other. In collectivist cultures, the group (e.g., family, friends, company) is the most important focus of personal identity. The individual functions in terms of his social context. In terms of decision-making this means a greater concern by and participation in the decision-making process by others. The group allows for a sharing of resources and responsibility, with the role of individual ability not being so important (Doi, 1973; Lebra, 1974, 1976).

Individualism, on the other hand, places a greater importance on the individual—on individual attributes, rights and rewards. In the West this is especially character-ized by the emphasis on the importance of the development of "self" (cf. Draguns, 1980; Kimura, 1965, 1967; Stewart, 1972). The result of this is a self-centeredness that is so apparent that at least one writer believes it is now a universal value in itself (e.g., Rogers, 1964). According to some writers, "individualism" and "harmony" are not compatible. In terms of decision making, it is the individual who is confronted by a decision, is affected by the decision, and who is responsible for making the decision and its subsequent consequences (Janis & Mann, 1977; Stewart, 1972). Decisions are therefore made in relation to how they are perceived to affect the "self."

Mann, Radford, and Kanagawa (1985), in one of the few studies which has examined differences in "functional decision making" between Japanese and Western societies, found that 12-year-old children when confronting majority and minority groups involved in a decision conflict reacted in different ways. Western children (in this case Australian) were found to be more self-centered and individualistic in their decisions than Japanese children who were more concerned about the group as a whole. Australian children tended to make decisions according to how it affected them personally as members of the majority or minority, while Japanese children were more concerned about how the decision might affect the entire group, both majority and minority.

Thus, it appears that Western theories of decision-making may not, in their present form, account for decision-making behavior in non-Western societies or, more cautiously, it cannot be safely assumed that they account for non-Western decision making. In order to learn about decision-making behavior in non-Western cultures, we need to develop a framework within which such behavior can be investigated.

Both the factors mentioned above suggest that there is a need for a theoretical framework of decision making which allows for the role of culture. In the next section, an outline of such a framework is suggested. Before this presentation, however, it is important to note that there are three general types of decision making: (1) functional, (2) organizational, and (3) logical.

"Functional decision making" refers to decisions which have to be made in order for a society simply to exist and function (e.g., clothes to wear, food to eat, marriage, employment, etc.). "Organizational decision making" refers to the procedures and practices (bureaucratic or otherwise) developed to allow organizations to function. Sometimes these procedures or practices may be similar to those used in "functional decision making." If culture does affect decision making, then it is likely to do so in both the "functional" and "organizational" forms, as both involve a subjective experience of the culture by its members, which in turn is influenced by that society's values and traditions. Finally, "logical decision making" refers to the development of specific "tree-type" paradigms to facilitate and standardize decision-making behavior. Such paradigms allow the decision maker to work through a series of questions (or steps) and consequently arrive at a decision. Examples of this type of decision making can be readily found in medicine with such procedures as the "Present State Examination" (Wing, Cooper, & Sartorius, 1974). "Logical decision making," because of the way it is designed, rarely differs from one culture to another. These paradigms are usually designed for a specific purpose, often to reduce the great differences that can occur when different people (within one culture as well as between cultures) use non-standardized or different methods to arrive at a conclusion or decision. This chapter is mainly concerned with "functional decision making" with some reference to "organizational decision making."

A Framework for Studying Decision-Making Behavior

The fundamental assumption that underlies the following approach is that basic cognitive abilities (e.g., abstraction, classification, etc.) exist in all cultures (cf. Cole & Scribner, 1974). Decision making can be regarded as a *functional cognitive system* which combines perception, memory, thinking, judgment and values in a way that allows for and governs action (cf. Cole & Scribner, 1974; Stewart, 1985). Cultural variations in thinking and behavior occur at the level of the functional cognitive system and are due to different cultural experiences which yield differences in world views, values, traditions, forms and so on, and in turn govern the nature and type of behavior

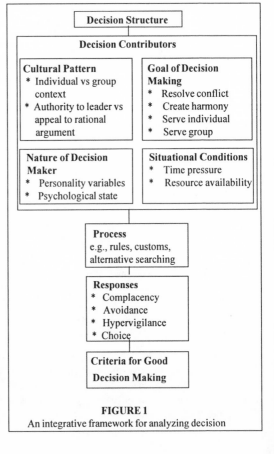

FIGURE 1
An integrative framework for analyzing decision

that is exhibited in any given situation (cf. Cole & Scribner, 1974). As a behavior, decision making is influenced and governed by a number of cultural, social and individual factors. These factors include: the nature of the problem (e.g., important versus inconsequential decisions); reasons for making the decision; cultural pattern, behavior and expectations (e.g., role of the group versus the individual); nature of the decision maker (e.g., personality characteristics, psychological adjustment/impairment, information processing capacity and capability, tolerance for uncertainty and for dealing with conflicting options for action); and situational conditions (e.g., time constraints, competing demands). These factors in turn determine what processes or behaviors are important and used in making a particular decision (e.g., the manner in which information is gathered, processed and evaluated), and the way in which the decision is actually made. The relationship between these factors is illustrated in Figure 1.

Decision Stimulus

The "decision stimulus" refers to any situation which requires a decision to be made. Without such a stimulus, decision making as a behavior is unnecessary or becomes superfluous. The decision stimulus may be a warning, threat or an opportunity. It can relate to any sphere of life—personal (e.g., choice of occupation, medical treatment), interpersonal (e.g., marriage), societal (e.g., laws), and international (e.g., establishment of treaties, diplomatic relations with another country).

The decision situation can be influenced by the importance and the complexity of the task. Tasks which are more important (i.e., have greater risks) are more likely to require more attention in order to find a satisfactory solution (cf. Highbee & Lafferty, 1972; Irwin & Smith, 1957; Janis & Mann, 1977). Further, the more complex a task, the more likely that it will require greater attention, or in some situations be ignored (cf. Streufert & Schroder, 1965).

Decision Contributors

Decision Contributors refers to four inter-related factors that have direct influence on the decision maker: Cultural pattern, nature of the decision maker, goal of decision making and situational conditions.

I. Cultural Pattern

The nature and orientation of a culture plays an important role in how an individual of that culture develops (i.e., psychologically), how he/she approaches a decision situation, the processes that he/she uses to solve that situation, the reasons why he/she uses the processes that he/she does, and what criteria he/she and others use to determine whether the decision made is a good one or not (see Radford et al., 1989). Further, culture can determine the age at which a person is given the right to make decisions for himself/herself or to participate in family/group decisions.

"Cultural pattern" can be represented by the concept of "individualism" (Candis et al., 1986). Such a concept is an important starting point in the examination of the way in which culture influences decision-making behavior (Mann, Radford, & Kanagawa, 1985; Sampson, 1975). An "individual orientation" (or "individualism") within a society is characterized by an emphasis on the individual as the instigator of a decision, on his/her personal attributes and personality, and on the importance of considering the consequences of a decision for the self. This orientation is character-istic of Western societies, especially North America and Australia (cf. Hofstede, 1980; Janis & Mann, 1977; Stewart, 1972, 1985).

A "group orientation" (or "collectivism") is characterized by a greater concern by the individual with the interests and maintenance of the social group (e.g., family, company, etc.). It also involves a greater emphasis on group decisions as a means of regulating and solving personal problems. Decisions are made with respect to how they affect the group as a whole (e.g., maintenance of social harmony, group cohesion, etc.). In this situation the needs of the individual are satisfied within the context of the group. Individual identity is not lost, but is preserved within the group structure. This orientation is said to be an essential characteristic of Japanese society (cf. Doi, 1973; Lebra, 1976; Nakamura, 1964; Nakane, 1973), but can also reflect any society where the group rather than the individual is used as the prime reference point by the individual (e.g., the Samoans, see Goodenough, 1963).

It is important to emphasize that "group orientation" refers to orientation towards one's own group within a society or culture, and not necessarily towards the society or culture as a whole. This point is especially important in the consideration of Japanese behavior[1].

Finally, culture can also influence decision making through authority figures who traditionally make or authorize decisions (e.g., tribal chiefs, the elders, the priest, etc.) and those who are called on to provide expertise and advice on what to choose (e.g., economists and witch doctors).

II. Nature of the Decision Maker

The nature of the individual, his or her personality and psychological state, are also important in helping to determine how the decision maker views and approaches a decision problem (cf. Janis & Mann, 1977; Radford, Mann & Kalucy, 1986). Personality and related motive systems (e.g., for status, independence, achievement) can vary both within cultures and between cultures. Different people have different personality characteristics and different levels of psychological impairment or adjust-ment (e.g., levels of anxiety, neuroticism, psychoticism, depression, etc.). They also have different motive systems such as the need for autonomy, for respect and social recognition, for acceptance and for self-esteem, all of which can affect how decisions are made.

In individual-orientated societies, high self-esteem as a decision maker may be important for attempting and making "good" decisions (Janis & Mann, 1977). When individuals in Western societies become depressed and their self-esteem is lowered, they are more likely than non-depressed people to use maladaptive decision-making styles and make "poor" decisions (Janis & Mann, 1977; Radford et al., 1986).

In group-oriented societies, the level of self-esteem may not have the same influence on decision making as it does in individual-oriented societies. Because of the importance of the group and the role of the individual in relation to that group, the role of personal self-esteem is reduced. As primary social groups play an important part in the decision-making process, both in initiating and bearing responsibility for decisions, they may provide the necessary support to assist individuals to make decisions and to protect their self-esteem even if the decision turns out badly. Thus, although depression (or some form of psychoneurotic disturbance) may affect an individual's self-esteem, because decision making is essentially a social process in group-oriented cultures, the depressed person's decision making is less likely to be affected than it would be in individual-oriented cultures.

III. Goal of Decision Making

The goal of decision making is related to the cultural pattern of the society in which the decision maker lives and to which he or she relates. As mentioned earlier, decision making in Western society is regarded primarily as an activity influenced by motives to resolve conflict or uncertainty (Janis & Mann, 1977; Idemitsu, 1975). Thus, the goal of decision making may be to resolve a conflict facing an individual, and thereby to serve the individual's purpose. In group-orientated cultures, such as Japan, the goal is to create and preserve harmony and prevent intra-group conflict (Idemitsu, 1975; Lebra, 1976). As in Western societies, personal decision making in Japan can serve the purposes of the individual, but in comparison to Western societies there is greater focus on the effects of decision making on others and consideration for the group (Lebra, 1976).

IV. Situational Conditions

Janis and Mann (1977) have described the importance of situational factors in decision making, especially those related to time pressure and information or resource availability. If there are time pressures involved in a decision situation, then there is a greater likelihood that a decision maker may not have the time to adequately prepare him or herself to make the best decision possible. On the other hand, if there is too much time, the decision maker may keep postponing resolution of the problem. Availability of information and resources also play an important role. If there is a lack of relevant information, then poor decisions can be made as a result of ignorance. Similarly, too much information may result in only irrelevant information being considered.

These four "decision contributors"—cultural pattern, nature of the decision maker, goal of decision making and situational conditions—are inter-related. Each affects the other, and in turn influences the way in which the decision maker responds to the decision stimulus (i.e., what processes or behaviors are used, and the final response style which is adopted).

Decision Processes

Many psychological processes and rules may be used in making a decision. Often the use of a particular process or set of processes will depend on culturally determined and acceptable behavior. An investigation of the literature has identified a number of processes or behaviors that can be and are used by different cultural groups (Radford, 1989). These include: collection and importance of facts; role of feelings/emotions, intuition, and past experiences; use of rules, traditions/customs, precedents, universal or situational laws; impression of self in the eyes of others; problem definition; practicality of solutions; acceptance of behavior by others; role of significant others (e.g., parents, teachers, leaders) and group in the decision-making process; use of established bureaucratic procedures; consideration of all possible alternatives; conception of time restraints; importance of implementing the decision once it has been made; role of values; role of authority figures; evaluation of utilities and probabilities; use of "non-rational" aids (e.g., dice, cards); and evaluation of decision outcome itself (especially Christopher, 1983; Doktor, 1982; Janis & Mann, 1977; Lebra, 1976; Masatsugu, 1982; Nakane, 1973; Nakamura, 1964; Stewart, 1972, 1985). Different cultures may use different processes. For example, the combination of processes that Western decision makers use may well be different from the combination used by non-Western decision makers.

Decision Responses

There are several possible coping responses that can be used in resolving decision problems (cf. Janis & Mann, 1977; Radford et al., 1989). These responses may be adaptive (appropriate) or maladaptive (inappropriate) depending upon the nature of the decision and the cultural norms that govern decision behavior. These coping responses include: (1) When faced with a challenge or decision situation, a person may ignore that challenge and adhere to his or her present course of action (i.e., "complacency"); (2) A person may respond to a challenge or decision situation and change to or adopt the first alternative course of action that presents itself (i.e., "complacency"); (3) When faced with a decision situation, a person may adopt an avoidance strategy such as buck-passing, procrastination or rationalization (i.e., "avoidance"); (4) Under extreme circumstances such as severe time pressures, a person may panic and make a hasty, ill-conceived decision, without consideration of possible alternatives (i.e., "hypervigilance"); and (5) When faced with a decision situation, a person may think through the various alternatives carefully and then make a choice (i.e., "choice"[2]). The choice response may take one of three forms: (i) individual choice; (ii) choice by individual and others; and (iii) choice by others (i.e., group choice).

Criteria for Good Decision Making

After a decision has been made, it may be evaluated in terms of to what extent it has achieved its intended goal(s). As mentioned earlier, responses in a decision-making situation may be regarded as either adaptive or maladaptive depending on the decision itself and the behavioral norms within the culture in which the decision is made.

There are many criteria that determine the soundness and acceptability of a decision. In some cultures, a good decision is one that has been made using the relevant considerations and following a set of traditional rules. In another culture, it may be that for a decision to be considered as appropriate it needs to be implemented as well. In this case, the idea of making a decision and that of implementing that decision are independent (Stewart, 1985). Decisions may be thought of as appropriate if the individual feels satisfied and has no regret (especially in individual-orientated cultures). Finally, decisions may be defined as "sound" if they cater for long-term goals (versus short-term goals), or perhaps if they return a profit (be it monetary or social), or perhaps a decision is "good" if it produces social or group cohesion and harmony. The use of particular criteria relates to the nature of the decision, and the cultural pattern of the society in which the decision is made.

Summary

In this section a framework has been presented in which decision making in different cultures can be examined. This framework has allowed some of the major components important in the decision-making process to be identified. In the next section, this framework will be used to present a cultural theory of decision making which takes into account the role of culture.

A Theory of Decision Making Taking into Account Culture

In the following analysis, four roles or styles of decision making will be identified.[3] Each role involves a corresponding set of behaviors and processes from each of the seven components mentioned in the preceding section. The four roles and their corresponding "ideal" behavior are presented in Table 2.

Three roles—"individual," "collateral," and "lineal" are based on concepts proposed by Kluckhohn and Strodtbeck (1961), and refer to or contrast with the PRIMARY GROUP (i.e., the main group to which the individual identifies). The *individual* orientation refers to the emphasis placed on self as source, instigator and beneficiary of decision making. The *collateral* orientation refers to sibling-type relationships within the family and group-type relationships outside the family. Finally, the *lineal* orientation refers to parent-child relationships within the family and hierarchical relationships outside the family. The nature of these orientations is best illustrated by using an example presented by Caudill and Scarr (1974) concerning "help in case of misfortune."

> "A man had a crop failure or let us say, had lost most of his cattle. He and his family had to have help from someone if they were going to get through the winter. There are different ways of getting help, as in the following.
>
> [Collateral] Would it be best if he depended on his brothers and sisters or other relatives to help him out as much as each one could?
>
> [Individual] Would it be best for him to try to raise money on his own, without depending upon anybody?

TABLE 2

Cultural Theory of Decision Making: Decision Making Roles and Associated Process

	INDIVIDUAL INDIVIDUAL (Enhancement)	PRIMARY GROUP		ORGANIZATION BUREAUCRATIC (Routine/formal)
		COLLATERAL (Harmony)	LINEAL (Social Order)	
I. CULTURAL PATTERN	Individual orientated	Group orientated	Group orientated	
II. NATURE OF DECISION MAKER	Emphasis on self, high self-esteem, personal ability & responsibility	Self in relation to group, group responsibility & dependency	Self in relation to group & leader, role (e.g. leader, deity, parent) decides	Committee makes decision (e.g. work group, policymakers)
III. GOAL OF DECISION MAKING	Resolve conflict, serve interests of individual decision maker	Promote harmony, serve interests of self in relation to group	Promotes interests of group	Promotes interests of group
IV. PROCESS 1. General Considerations	Facts, rules, past experience	Facts, experience, opinions of others, emotions, actions	Observations, dicta, theories	Raw data, rules, precedents, experience

Table 2 *continued*

| | INDIVIDUAL | PRIMARY GROUP | | ORGANIZATION |
	INDIVIDUAL (Enhancement)	COLLATERAL (Harmony)	LINEAL (Social Order)	BUREAUCRATIC (Routine/formal)
2. Situation Considerations	Problem definition, time, importance, losses & gains, abstract ideas, use of logical & sequential connections	Form, traditions, demands of social group, concrete perceptions, reliance on sensory data, intuition, situation	Values, rules, set procedures, classification system, traditions, situation	Plans, systems, policy considerations, anticipated consequences, group processes
3. Action	Choice, conceptual decision	Imitation, adaptation, historical & projected response	Follows precedents, acts of classification	Group decision, procedural
V. POSSIBLE RESPONSES	Choice, complacency avoidance, hypervigilance	Avoidance, choice, complacency, hypervigilance	Choice, complacency avoidance, hypervigilance	Choice, complacency, avoidance, hypervigilance

[Lineal] Would it be best for him to go to a boss or to his head house ("honke"), and ask for help until things got better?"

As a result of general differences in decision-making behavior in different cultures, it is possible at the *most general level* to associate each role with a particular cultural group. For example, the *individual* role can be identified with Western and, in particular, North American societies; the collateral role can be identified with Japanese society; while the lineal role with certain "tribal" societies (e.g., Ibans of Sarawak, East Malaysia).

The fourth role—*bureaucratic*, refers to ORGANIZATIONS, and organized committee procedures, which characterize many of the major business companies, and governmental and private organizations throughout the world. Often these organizations function in a way that crosses national and cultural boundaries. As the primary interest of this research is "functional decision making," discussion of the bureaucratic role will be limited.

Decision Roles: I. Individual

The *individual* role of decision making is usually associated with individually orientated (or individualistic) societies, such as North America and Australia. It is in this role that the individual is seen as being responsible for initiating and making a decision. He is also responsible for its consequences. The success of the decision depends on the decision maker's personal ability to make the best one possible. In such cultures, the mode of thinking is often an "analytical" one.

The goal of decision making is to resolve conflict that can arise as a result of a choice situation. Further, the aim of the decision, in many cases, is to further the interests of the decision maker, and reduce possible losses to him or herself. When making a decision, the decision maker relies on past experiences, factual information, and sometimes a set of decision rules (e.g., maximization of utilities, cf. Edwards, 1961). When making the decision, the decision maker defines the nature of the problem, takes account of time constraints, and possible losses and gains (material and social). He often uses abstract ideas and concepts to make logical and sequential connections between considerations (e.g., "if this happens, then this must follow"). Action involves making a conceptual choice (i.e., a decision) even though the decision-making process may be largely subconscious.

Once pre-decisional behavior has been completed, one of several possible responses may occur—"choice" (the implementation of a considered course of action); "complacency" (ignoring the decision challenge by adhering to the present course of action, or by simply changing to the most obvious alternative); "avoidance" (avoiding making a decision oneself); or "hypervigilance" (leaving a decision to the last minute and then panicking, choosing on the spur of the moment).

For the decision maker, the "best" decision is the one that is the most attractive (often in the short-term), the most practical and produces self-satisfaction or an absence of regret. Often implementation of the decision is quick.

Decision Roles: II. Collateral

The *collateral* role of decision making is associated with group-orientated (or collectivistic) societies, such as Japan or Samoa (e.g., Goodenough, 1963; Mann et al., 1989). The decision maker has a strong sense of self in relation to his or her social group. Decisions are made with reference to the group, and are sometimes made by the group itself. The individual feels a sense of obligation towards the group. The group allows for a sharing of responsibility for making decisions and encourages a degree of dependency. Because the group shares resources, individual ability is not so important. The goal of decision making in collateral decision making is to preserve group harmony. Unlike the "individual role" the interests of the group member are looked after in terms of the interests of the group.

In making a decision, the decision maker not only takes into account facts and past experiences, but also the opinions and interests of others within his/her social context. He takes into account the traditions and requirements of the social group. He relies on sensory data and concrete perceptions as well as intuition and emotions. Further, the nature or context of the decision situation is also considered.

As with the "individual role" the responses to a decision situation are "choice," "complacency," "avoidance," or "hypervigilance." These responses are common to all styles, as they represent *possible responses*, not necessarily what is done. An efficient decision is one that is attractive (usually in the long-term), and which benefits the whole group (thereby benefiting the individual). It is made within the immediate social network, and often as a result of the group reaching consensus. Decisions are often a long time in preparation.

Decision Roles: III. Lineal

The *lineal* decision role is also characteristic of collectivistic societies. Sometimes it is also characteristic of Japanese decision making, especially in the past when it was the parents who often decided their child's marriage partner. Like the "collateral" role, the individual perceives him or herself in relation to his or her group. The actual decision maker (i.e., parent, teacher, leader, deity who decides) is in a position higher to the individual.

The goal of the decision maker is to promote the interests of the group, but unlike the "collateral" role, it is not necessarily the interests of the individual, but rather the group's head, leader, or authority on behalf of the individual and/or group.

When making a decision, certain dicta (or theories) are used. Recognition of precedents, the wishes of authority, leaders and elders is important. Observation of environment and the situation is important, with cultural values and norms playing an important part in how a decision is seen and made. Depending on the nature of the decision and sometimes the context in which it is being made, particular systems (i.e., classificational, for example "augury") and set procedures can be used.

Action is often taken on the basis of a system of classification, which is known to a select group of "experts" such as the leader or soothsayer (e.g., in the Iban society of East Malaysia, a decision could depend on which direction a bird flew after being released). The decision is often given over to an "invested authority" (e.g., parent or headman) and is often evaluated by the authority in terms of how well it fits the desired goal of maintaining the social order.

Decision Roles: IV. Bureaucratic

The *bureaucratic* decision role can be found in most societies in which organized committees exist (e.g., businesses, political parties, etc.). The people responsible for making a decision are the work group or policymakers designated to do that task. The goal of decision making is to promote the interests and aims of the group or organization making the decision, which has been formed expressly for the purpose of making decisions or policy that will serve the group.

When making a decision, raw data, past experiences, precedents and rules may all be considered. Policy considerations, intergroup processes, formulated plans, and anticipated consequences all play an important part. Action is usually procedural (i.e., follows a particular formal pattern). Decisions usually depend on majority vote, although not always (sometimes consensus is used). A good decision is one that meets the aims of the group and is usually the most attractive (in terms of utilities) alternative. Often decisions made by such groups are prepared in great detail and are carefully implemented (Pfeffer, 1985).

In summary, the above discussion has outlined four kinds of decision-making roles—"individual," "collateral," "lineal," and "bureaucratic." It does not claim to account for all variations that may occur in decision making. Its main purpose is to provide a conceptual framework in which decision-making behavior and the influence of cultures can be studied and discussed. Before examining research support for the theory presented above, two important cautionary notes are needed. The first refers to the concept of "social relativism" versus "social absolutism." The second to the role of cultural dynamism.

"Social Relativism" versus "Social Absolutism"

In many situations, generalizations (such as those made above) may be valid, but some cultures (e.g., Japanese culture) may alternate between the roles depending on the issues involved. Although it is suggested that the *collateral* role is the role most often adopted by the Japanese, it may not be exclusively so. Two concepts often used to describe and explain Japanese behavior are "social relativism" (Lebra, 1976) and "situationalism" or "situation ethic" (Hamaguchi, 1966, 1970). Both concepts describe the Japanese tendency to react in seemingly contradictory (according to Western perceptions) ways. In essence these concepts refer to the notion that behavior cannot be removed from the immediate social context. Thus, for a behavior to be carried out, it must conform to situational requirements, to logistical, environmental and social restraints. Behavior must be considered in relation to the immediate context or situation. "Social relativism" serves the purpose of Japanese society because it maintains group harmony. It allows a degree of individual freedom within the confines of group structure.

As the concept of "social relativism" may seem obscure, an illustration is offered. During the Second World War, Japanese war prisoners were faced with a challenge to their strong sense of social responsibility and their failure to fight to the end. "Some men asked to be killed, 'but if your customs do not permit this, I will be a model prisoner'" (Benedict, 1946/1974, p. 41). This is an example of a decision made contrary to wish, but with respect to situational considerations. Action sometimes involves adaptation (as above), imitation, or adherence to historical and projected social responses (cf. decision to take one's life because it is "bushi-do," or the way of the samurai).

Cultural Dynamism

Another point which must be considered is that cultures and societies are not static. They change over time—as a result of outside influences, internal movements and ideas and so on. Any consideration of specific cultural modes of operation needs to take account of the time factor. Thus, what may be true of a culture in 1889 may not be true in 1989. Age and generational differences (e.g., 15 to 19 year olds versus 35 to 40 year olds) within one decade and over several decades are important considerations. Similarly, behavior in a city with much intercultural contact and fusion may be quite different from more conservative rural communities in the same country. Even a time span of one generation can change what a society does and what it values.

Current and Future Research

In the previous section, a theoretical framework for studying decision making was outlined. Currently, our research group is conducting a program of studies examining the role of culture in decision-making behavior taking into account personality and psychological state in three cultures—Australia, China and Japan. Results to date with Japanese and Australian university students have found that, while for both cultural groups decisional self-esteem was positively correlated with the "choice" style of decision making, and was negatively correlated with decisional stress and the "complacency," "avoidance," and "hypervigilance" coping styles in personal decision making, cultural differences do exist. Japanese students are lower than Australian students on decisional self-esteem, higher on decisonal stress, and higher on "complacency," "avoidance," and "hypervigilance" coping styles (Radford et al., 1989, 1990a). However, in an analysis of what processes and behaviors were regarded as important and were reported as being used in decision making, Japanese students reported greater use of decision behaviors associated with the involvement and influence of others ("collateral role"), while Australian students reported greater use of decision processes associated with self-reliance and personal ability ("individual role"; Radford et al., 1990b).

To date, we have concentrated on developing a descriptive understanding of the nature of relationships. Our measures have been based on self-report questionnaire type formats. Future work needs to include other cultural samples and objective measures to examine the decision-making process. The methodological difficulties involved in developing decision tasks that are both relevant and meaningful in different cultures are great, however, until this is done, only half the story is told.

Conclusion

The area of cross-cultural research into decision making is a very important one. It has both theoretical as well as applied implications. Through such studies we not only extend our knowledge of an important cognitive function, but we also extend our understanding of how culture affects the manifestation of that function. By understanding the process in different cultures, we can understand the process in our own cultures.

Finally, decision-making research needs to be applied to real-life (world) problems (Pitz & Sachs, 1984). Theoretical research without (actual or potential) meaningful application has limited value. In a world which is becoming increasingly small, greater knowledge and awareness of the behavior of ourselves and others is essential for better communication and interaction as well as for peaceful coexistence. Social scientists have an important role to play in this area.

Footnotes

1. Although Japanese culture is examined as a point of departure, it is emphasized that Japanese culture does not reflect all non-Western cultures. Likewise, the same is true in relation to Western cultures—North American or Australian cultures do not necessarily reflect all Western cultures and societies.

2. In Janis and Mann's (1977) original conflict theory of decision making the choice response was called "vigilance." In this framework I have decided against using this term, as "vigilance" is more of a prescriptive pattern of decision making, which if followed will more likely produce a decision with which the decision maker is satisfied (Janis & Mann, 1977). A vigilant pattern of decision making may be followed but the decision itself may never be implemented (i.e., because of the use of an "avoidance" style). Thus, I have distinguished the decision-making response (*choice*) from the Western ideal set of decision-making processes (*vigilance*).

3. For another theory of decision making taking into account the role of culture but using a different theoretical foundation (a "structural" model rather than a "process model," cf. Abelson & Levi, 1985), the reader is referred to Stewart (1985). While both models were developed independently there are many similarities, and the author acknowledges the development of several ideas suggested by Stewart's analysis.

References

Abelson, R.P. and Levi, A. (1985). Decision making and decision theory. In G. Lindzey and

E. Aronson (Eds.), *Handbook of Social Psychology (Vol. 1) (3rd ed.)*. New York: Random.

Beach, B.H. and Beach, L.R. (1982). Expectancy-based decisions schemes: Sidesteps toward applications. In N.T. Feather (Ed.), *Expectations and Actions: Expectancy-value Models in Psychology*. Hillsdale, NJ: Lawrence Erlbaum Associates.

Benedict, R. (1974). *The Chrysanthemum and the Sword: Patterns of Japanese Culture*. Tokyo: Tuttle. (Original work published 1946).

Caudill, W.A. (1973). The influence of social structure and culture on human behavior in modern Japan. *Journal of Nervous and Mental Disease, 157*, 240-257.

Caudill, W.A. and Scarr, H.A. (1974). Japanese value orientations and culture change. In T.S. Lebra and W.P. Lebra (Eds.), *Japanese Culture and Behavior: Selected Readings*. Honolulu: University of Hawaii Press.

Christopher, R.C. (1983). *The Japanese Mind*. London: Pan Books.

Cole, M. and Scribner, S. (1974). *Culture and Thought*. New York: John Wiley & Sons.

Doi, T. (1973). *The Anatomy of Dependence (J. Bester, Trans.)*. Tokyo: Kodansha International. (Original work published 1971).

Doktor, R. (1982). A cognitive approach to culturally appropriate HRD programs. *Training and Development Journal, 36*, 32-36.

Draguns, J.G. (1980). Psychological disorders of clinical severity. In H.C. Triandis and J.G. Draguns (Eds.), *Handbook of Cross-cultural Psychology (Vol. 6)*. Boston: Allyn and Bacon.

Edwards, W. (1961). Behavioral decision theory. *Annual Review of Psychology, 12*, 473-498.

Goodenough, W.H. (1963). *Cooperation in Change*. New York: Russell Sage Foundation.

Hamaguchi, E. (1966). *"Jokyoteki" koi no genri [On the principle of "situational" behavior]*. Shakaigakai Hyoron, 16, 51-74.

Hamaguchi, E. (1970). Hihonjin no mararu shisutemu [The Japanese moral system]. In T. Shigematsu (Ed.), *Hendoki no Shakai to Kyoiku [Society and Education in Our Changing Times]*. Tokyo: Reimei Shobo.

Hasegawa, N. (1966). *The Japanese Character: A Cultural Profile (J. Bester, Trans.)*. Tokyo: Kodansha International. (Original work published 1938).

Highbee, K. and Lafferty, T. (1972). Relationship among risk preferences, importance and control. *Journal of Psychology, 81*, 249-251.

Hirokawa, R. (1981). Improving intra-organizational communication: A lesson from Japanese management. *Communication Quarterly, 30*, 38.

Hofstede, G. (1980). *Culture's Consequences: International Differences in Work-related Values*. Beverly Hills: Sage.

Horney, K. (1964). *The Neurotic Personality of Our Time*. New York: W.W. Norton.

Idemitsu, S. (1975). *The Eternal Japan: Conversations with Sazo Idemitsu*. Tokyo: Idemitsu Kosan.

Irwin, F.W. and Smith, W.A.S. (1957). Values and cost of decision on hand and amount of information demanded by subjects and his confidence in his decision. *Journal of Experimental Psychology, 54*, 229-232.

Jaccard, J. and Wan, C.K. (1986). Cross-cultural methods for the study of behavioral decision theory. *Journal of Cross-Cultural Psychology, 17,* 123-149.

Janis, I.L. and Mann, L. (1977). *Decision making: A Psychological Analysis of Conflict, Choice, and Commitment.* New York: Free Press.

Kimura, B. (1965). Vergleichende Untersuchungen uber depressive Erkrankungen in Japan und in Deutschland. *Fortschritte der Psychiatrie und Neurologie, 33,* 202-215.

Kimura, B. (1967). Phanomenologie des Schulderlebnisses in einder vergleichenden psychitrischen Sicht. *Aktuelle Fragen der Psychiatrie und Neurologie, 6,* 54-65.

Kluckhohn, F.R. and Strodtbeck, F.L. (1961). *Variations in Value Orientations.* New York: Row and Peterson.

Kraus, E.S., Rohlen, T.P., and Steinhoff, P.G. (Eds.). (1984). *Conflict in Japan.* Honolulu: University of Hawaii Press.

Lebra, T.S. (1974). Reciprocity and the asymmetric principle: An analytical reappraisal of the Japanese concept of "on." In T.S. Lebra and W.P. Lebra (Eds.), *Japanese Culture and Behavior: Selected Readings.* Honolulu: University of Hawaii Press.

Lebra, T.S. (1976). *Japanese Patterns of Behavior.* Honolulu: University of Hawaii Press.

Mann, L. (1982). *Decision Making Questionnaires I and II.* Flinders Decision Workshops, The Flinders University of South Australia.

Mann, L., Radford, M., and Kanagawa, C. (1985). Cross-cultural differences in children's use of decision rules: A comparison between Japan and Australia. *Journal of Personality and Social Psychology, 49,* 1557-1564.

Mann, L., Radford, M., Nakamura, H., Vaughan, G., Taylor, K., Burnett, P., and Yang, K.S. (1989). *Cross-cultural and gender differences in self-reported decision making styles and confidence.* Paper presented to the Second Regional Conference of the International Association of Cross-Cultural Psychology, Amsterdam, June 27-June 1.

Marsella, A.J., Devos, G., and Hsu, F.L.K. (Eds.). (1985). *Culture and Self: Asian and Western Perspectives.* New York: Tavistock.

Masatsugu, M. (1982). *The Modern Samurai: Duty and Dependence in Contemporary Japan.* New York: AMACOM.

Misumi, J. (1984). Decision-making in Japanese groups and organizations. In B. Wilpert and A. Sorge (Eds.), *International Perspectives on Organizational Democracy.* New York: John Wiley & Sons.

Nakamura, H. (1964). *Ways of Thinking of Eastern Peoples: India, China, Tibet, Japan.* Honolulu: East-West Center Press.

Nakane, C. (1973). *Japanese Society.* Harmondsworth, Middlesex: Penguin Books.

Ouchi, W. (1981). *Theory Z: How American Business Can Meet the Japanese Challenge.* Reading, MA: Addison-Wesley.

Pfeffer, J. (1985). Organizations and organizational theory. In G. Lindzey and E. Aronson (Eds.), *Handbook of Social Psychology (Vol. 1) (3rd ed.).* New York: Random.

Pitz, G.F. and Sachs, N.J. (1984). Judgment and decision: Theory and application. *Annual Review of Psychology, 35,* 139-163.

Radford, M.H.B. (1989). *Culture, Depression and Decision Making Behavior: A Study With Japanese and Australian Clinical and Non-clinical Populations.* Unpublished Ph.D thesis, The Flinders University of South Australia.

Radford, M.H.B., Mann, L., and Kalucy, R.S. (1986). Psychiatric disturbance and decision making. *Australian and New Zealand Journal of Psychiatry, 20*, 210-217.

Radford, M., Mann, L., Ohta, Y., and Nakane, Y. (1989). Kojin no ishiketteliko to jinkaku tokusei [Individual decision-making behavior and personality: A preliminary study using a Japanese university sample]. *Japanese Journal of Experimental Social Psychology, 28*, 21-28. (In Japanese).

Radford, M., Mann, L., Ohta, Y., and Nakane, Y. (1990a). *Differences between Australian and Japanese students in decisional self-esteem, decisional stress and coping styles.* Submitted for publication.

Radford, M., Mann, L., Ohta, Y., and Nakane, Y. (1990b). *Differences between Australian and Japanese students in reported use of decision processes.* Submitted for publication.

Rogers, C. (1964). Towards a modern approach to values. *Journal of Abnormal and Social Psychology, 68*, 160-167.

Sampson, E.E. (1975). On justice as equality. *Journal of Social Issues, 31*, 45-64.

Slovic, P., Fischhoff, B., and Lichtenstein, S. (1977). Behavioral decision theory. *Annual Review of Psychology, 28*, 1-39.

Stewart, E.C. P(1972). *American Cultural Patterns: A Cross-Cultural Perspective*. Chicago, Illinois: Intercultural Press.

Stewart, E.C.P. (1985). Culture and decision making. In W.B. Gudykunst, L.P. Stewart, and S. Ting-Toomey (Eds.), *Communication, Cultural and Organizational Processes.* Beverly Hills: Sage.

Streufert, S. and Schroder, H.M. (1965). Conceptual structure, environmental complexity and task performance. *Journal of Experimental Research in Personality, 1*, 132-137.

Triandis, H.C., Bontempo, R., Betancourt, H., Bond, M., Leung, K., Brenes, A., Georgas, J., Hui, C.H., Marin, G., Setiadi, B., Sinha, J.B.P., Verma, J., Spangenberg, J., Touzard, H., and de Montmollin, G. (1986). The measurement of the etic aspects of individualism and collectivism across cultures. *Australian Journal of Psychology, 38*, 257-267.

Tversky, A. and Kahneman, D. (1974). Judgment under uncertainty: Heuristics and biases. *Science, 185*, 1124-1131.

Wing, J.K., Cooper, J.E., and Sartorius, N. (1974). *The Measurement and Classification of Psychiatric Symptoms*. Cambridge, MA: Cambridge University Press.

Notes

The framework and model presented in this chapter are based on a model described in the author's doctoral thesis (Radford, 1989). Papers from the research program examining the relationship between culture and decision making reported in this paper are currently being prepared for publication. Any correspondence should be addressed to the author. The cooperation, collaboration, and advice of Professor Leon Mann of The Flinders University of South Australia, and Professors Yoshibumi Nakane and Yasuyuki Ohta of Nagasaki University are gratefully acknowledged.

A COMPARISON OF CHINESE AND U.S.A. CONSUMERS' DECISION MAKING: SOME EMPIRICAL EVIDENCE

Richard Ettenson and Janet Wagner

The conversion of the People's Republic of China (PRC) to a system of market socialism has been referred to as "the largest field experiment in consumer behavior ever undertaken." One manifestation of market socialism is the emergence of a growing number of privately owned retail establishments. Kindel's (1983) model of Chinese consumer behavior was used to develop research hypotheses concerning differences in the evaluation and selection of retail stores by Chinese and American (United States of America, USA) consumers. Conjoint analysis was employed to model the decision making of both groups. Consistent with Kindel's model, the Chinese were found to place greater emphasis than USA consumers on convenience of location and salesperson's manner, and less emphasis on the store's return policy. Contrary to expectations, USA consumers were more concerned than the Chinese with merchandise quality.

International marketing has grown dramatically in the last 25 years. Unfortunately, there has not been a commensurate increase in cross-cultural research on consumer decision making. Such research has been hampered by both limited access to subjects and lack of an appropriate theory to guide the formulation of research questions.

The most serious dearth of information involves consumer decision making in developing countries (Belk, 1989), such as the People's Republic of China (PRC). The PRC is of particular interest to researchers because of its commitment to market socialism, a system of economic reform that has been described as "...the largest field experiment in consumer behavior ever undertaken" (Belk, 1989, p. 6). Under market socialism, market forces, including individual entrepreneurship and competition among firms, are allowed to operate within the context of a centrally planned economy. Although state-run stores continue to dominate the distribution of goods and services, Chinese consumers are reported to be dissatisfied with many of their merchandising policies (Thorelli, Fu, & Sentell, 1985). One manifestation of this has been a proliferation of privately owned retail enterprises (Salisbury & Swarts, 1986).

Since access to samples of Chinese consumers has been severely constrained, most information on their purchasing behavior is anecdotal. Observers (e.g., Reeder, 1983; Wattel, 1989) have reported that the retail market in the PRC is characterized by poor quality products, limited merchandise assortments, lack of convenience, poor service by salespeople, and little opportunity for redress among consumers. The results of a pioneering attitude and opinion survey of 148 Chinese professionals and managers, conducted by Thorelli, Fu, and Sentell (1985), confirmed that Chinese consumers perceive these attributes to be a problem, particularly among state-run stores.

Sheth and Sethi (1977) proposed a model of cross-cultural consumer behavior that describes how consumers living in different cultures evaluate products and services. According to this model, cultures may be envisaged on a continuum of social change, ranging from the traditional to the developed. Similarly, the PRC and the United States might be envisaged on an economic continuum ranging from a socialist, planned economy, to a capitalist, market-oriented economy. Sheth and Sethi (1977) imply that consumer decision making may vary according to the position of a culture on such continua.

In order to make valid cross-cultural comparisons, it is necessary to study constructs which are "functionally equivalent" across cultures (Bhalla & Lin, 1987). A construct which would appear to be functionally equivalent in the PRC and the USA would be the selection of retail stores in which to shop. Given the increasing globalization of both marketing and retailing, the results of information comparing the decision-making processes of Chinese and American consumers should be of interest to both researchers and a wide range of multinational corporations. Consequently, the purpose of this research was to compare the evaluation and selection of retail stores by Chinese and American consumers.

The research method used in this study was conjoint analysis. The conjoint approach is often applied in research on consumers' decision making involving products. As such, it is based on the assumption that consumer decision making involves the evaluation and combination of information on multiple product attributes (Anderson, 1981; Green & Srinivason, 1978). The conjoint method is thought to be more effective than attitude and opinion surveys (e.g., Thorelli et al., 1985) in modelling the consumer's decision-making environment, because such surveys force the consumer to focus on single product attributes, in isolation from the array of attributes that typically defines a product. In this research, the conjoint method was extended to the evaluation of retail stores. As such, it was assumed that in selecting a retail store in which to shop, consumers evaluate and integrate information on an array of attributes derived from store merchandising policies. This research is believed to be the first to apply conjoint analysis in the study of consumer decision making in the PRC.

Decision Making by Chinese and USA Consumers

The Sheth and Sethi (1977) model is intended to describe the behavior of households across cultures. Kindel (1983) proposed a model of individual decision making by Chinese consumers that suggests differences between Chinese and American consumers' decision making. The Kindel model is derived from observations of traditional Chinese values, such as politeness, thrift, and saving face, as well as dimensions of the Chinese lifestyle, such as frequency and enjoyment of shopping. This model suggests that the decision-making processes of Chinese and American consumers are likely to differ with respect to convenience of location, the manner of salespersons, price, quality of merchandise, and the ability to return merchandise.

According to Kindel (1983), the Chinese are habituated to daily shopping trips, and tend to view shopping as a social occasion. Because of the frequency of their shopping trips, it was expected that Chinese consumers might be more concerned than Americans with convenience of store location. Because of the social nature of the shopping experience, Chinese consumers prefer to develop personal relationships with salespeople. Moreover, the Chinese consider politeness to be an important virtue. Consequently, it was expected that the manner of salespeople would have a stronger effect on the choice of a retail store by Chinese, as opposed to American consumers. Given their cultural emphasis on thrift, the Chinese are likely to be more price-conscious than Western consumers, particularly when purchasing items for themselves. Therefore, it was hypothesized that, in choosing a retail store, the price range of the merchandise would be more important to Chinese than to American consumers. One of the more pervasive values of Chinese culture is saving face, which may manifest itself in the retail market in two ways. First, the Chinese may be more concerned than Americans with the quality of merchandise because purchasing an unsatisfactory product may represent a loss of face. Similarly, there may be loss of face associated with having to return a defective product. Consequently, the Chinese were expected to be less concerned than USA consumers with the store's return policy.

Method

Experimental Design

The design was a 2 x 2^8 mixed fractional factorial with a full replication. One independent variable was culture, which was varied at two levels: PRC and USA. Also included were a set of eight retail store attributes, each of which was varied at two levels. The fractional design consisted of 16 profiles (Hahn & Shapiro, 1966; plan 7b), and permitted estimates of the eight main effects independent of all two-way interactions [A fractional factorial design enabled the researchers to address the research objectives without including all possible combinations of attribute levels (i.e., 256 profiles).]. To permit individual-subject analyses, the 16 profiles were fully replicated. Eight "filler" stimuli were also included to provide practice profiles and to disguise the experimental design. This brought to 40 the number of profiles evaluated by each participant.

Participants

In June 1988, a convenience sample of Chinese consumers (n = 43) was recruited from several undergraduate management courses at the North-West Institute of Textile Science and Technology in Xi'an. While students are not likely to represent the population as a whole, it was believed that they would adhere to traditional Chinese values. For purposes of comparison, a group of USA consumers (n = 55) was recruited from undergraduate courses at the University of Maryland.

Analysis of the demographic data for the Chinese consumers indicates that they were generally young (average age 21.6 years), male (55% vs 45% female), and single (93% vs 7% married). A majority of the sample (74%) was employed. To examine how often they might evaluate a retail store, the Chinese were asked how often they shopped for clothing. They reported shopping, on average, 4.3 times per year. Sixty-one percent preferred shopping in the free market, 32% in state-run stores, and 7% had no preference.

Demographics of the USA consumers indicated that they were young (average age 21.9 years), mostly female (67% vs 33% male), and single (95% vs 5% married). Most were employed (71%). As might be expected, the USA consumers reported shopping for clothing more frequently than the Chinese (over 30 times per year).

The Decision-Making Task

Both the Chinese and American consumers evaluated a series of conjoint profiles which described retail stores based on eight attributes: (1) ability to inspect the merchandise; (2) variety of merchandise; (3) prices; (4) quality of merchandise; (5) speed of checkout; (6) salesperson's manner; (7) convenience of location; and (8) return policy. The eight attributes and their corresponding levels are shown in Table 1. The attributes and levels were derived from three sources: (1) the Kindel (1983) model; (2) previous research on factors affecting store choice (e.g., Hansen &

TABLE 1

**The Eight Store Attributes and
Their Corresponding Levels**

1. ABILITY TO INSPECT MERCHANDISE
   (a) The merchandise is not easily available for you to inspect.
   (b) The merchandise is available for you to inspect.

2. VARIETY OF MERCHANDISE
   (a) The variety of goods is limited.
   (b) There is a wide variety of goods.

3. PRICE
   (a) The price of most goods is higher than average.
   (b) The price of most goods is reasonable.

4. QUALITY
   (a) The quality of the merchandise is below average.
   (b) The quality of the merchandise is above average.

5. SPEED OF CHECKOUT
   (a) One usually has to wait in line to make a purchase.
   (b) One rarely has to wait in line to make a purchase.

6. SALESPERSON'S MANNER
   (a) The salespeople are often rude.
   (b) The salespeople are always pleasant.

7. CONVENIENCE OF LOCATION
   (a) The location of the store is not convenient for you.
   (b) The location of the store is convenient for you.

8. RETURN POLICY
   (a) You may not return goods if you are not satisfied with them.
   (b) You may return goods if you are not satisfied with them.

Deutscher, 1977-78; Westbrook, 1981); and (3) consultation with a group of Chinese students studying in the USA.

In the task instructions, participants were told to imagine that they were shopping, and that they would be presented with a series of store descriptions. Participants were asked to indicate the likelihood of patronizing a given store by placing a slash along an unmarked 100 cm. continuum with ends marked "not at all likely" (scored 0) and "very likely" (scored 100). A sample store profile appears in Figure 1.

FIGURE 1
Sample Retail Store Profile
Store WPJ

1) The merchandise is not easily available for you to inspect.
2) There is a wide variety of goods.
3) The price of most goods is higher than average.
4) The quality of the merchandise is below average.
5) One usually has to wait in line to make a purchase.
6) The salespeople are always pleasant.
7) The location of the store is convenient for you.
8) You may not return goods if you are not satisfied with them.

Based on the above information, how likely is it that you would shop in this store?

NOT AT ALL   VERY
LIKELY ├───────────────────────────┼───────────────────────┤ LIKELY

The decision-making task was translated into Mandarin calligraphy and back-translated into English to ensure "linguistic equivalence" (Bhalla & Lin, 1987) between the Chinese and English versions.

Results

Chinese Consumers

Statistical significance of the store attributes. To identify the store attributes that had statistically significant effects, an individual-subject analysis of variance (ANOVA) was performed on the decisions of each of the 43 Chinese consumers. The results of these analyses are shown in the left-hand column of Table 2. As can be seen, the attributes that were significant ($p < .05$) most frequently were quality of merchandise, salesperson's manner, and convenience of location. Quality was significant for 86% of the Chinese consumers (37 of 43), followed by salesperson's manner at 72% (31 of 43) and location at 56% (24 of 43). Significance was observed less frequently for the five remaining attributes. Twenty-six percent had a significant effect for return policy, 21% for variety, 19% for ability to inspect merchandise, 14% for speed of checkout, and 12% for price.

Relative importance of the store attributes. Although two or more store attributes may significantly affect a consumer's decision making, it is unlikely that those attributes will be of equal importance. Therefore, Hays' (1973) omega squared (w^2) was used to assess the relative importance of the eight store attributes for each participant. The average of these values, presented in the right-hand column of Table 2, demonstrates that the quality of the merchandise was most important in evaluating a retail store, accounting for 22% of the explained variance in the Chinese consumers' decisions. Salesperson's manner was next in importance, accounting for 16% of the variance, followed by the store's location with 9% of the explained variance. Each of the remaining attributes accounted for 3% or less of the variance in the Chinese

TABLE 2
Chinese Consumers' Percentage of Significant Main Effects ($p < .05$) and
Average Omega Squared (w^2) Values for the
Eight Stores Attributes

		% Main Effect (n = 43)	Avg. (w^2)
1)	Ability to Inspect Merchandise	19%	.02
2)	Variety of Merchandise	21%	.02
3)	Prices	12%	.02
4)	Quality of Merchandise	86%	.22
5)	Speed of Checkout	14%	.02
6)	Salesperson's Manner	72%	.16
7)	Convenience of Location	56%	.09
8)	Return Policy	26%	.03

consumers' decision making. It appears that the overriding factors in the Chinese consumers' selections of retail stores were the availability of high-quality merchandise, whether or not the salespeople were courteous, and a convenient location; the other attributes appear to have had considerably less effect.

USA Consumers

Statistical significance of the store attributes. Individual-subject ANOVA's were performed on the store evaluation decisions of each of the USA consumers. As can be seen in the left-hand column of Table 3, quality of merchandise was, by far, the attribute used most frequently when evaluating a retail store; 95% of the USA consumers (52 of 55) had a significant effect for this attribute. This was followed by the salesperson's manner which was significant to 60% (33 of 55) of this group. The six remaining attributes were used less frequently; return policy and location were each used by 33% (18 of 55), followed by price (31%), ability to inspect merchandise (29%), variety (23%), and speed of checkout (15%).

Relative importance of the store attributes. For the USA consumers, the average omega squared (w^2) values in Table 3 indicate that, much like the Chinese, the quality of merchandise was the dominant attribute, accounting for 30% of the explained variance in the decision making of the USA consumers. Salesperson's

TABLE 3
USA Consumers' Percentage of Significant Main Effects ($p < .05$) and
Average Omega Squared (w^2) Values for the
Eight Store Attributes

		% Main Effects (n = 55)	Avg. (w^2)
1)	Ability to Inspect Merchandise	29%	.03
2)	Variety of Merchandise	23%	.01
3)	Prices	31%	.03
4)	Quality of Merchandise	95%	.30
5)	Speed of Checkout	15%	.01
6)	Salesperson's Manner	60%	.11
7)	Convenience of Location	33%	.04
8)	Return Policy	33%	.07

manner was next in importance, explaining 11% of the variance, followed by nature of the return policy which explained 7% of the variance. Convenience of location explained 4% of the variance, while price and ability to inspect the merchandise each explained 3%. Variety of merchandise and speed of checkout were the least important attributes.

Comparison of Chinese and USA consumers. Since the decision-making tasks were both functionally and linguistically equivalent (Bhalla & Lin, 1987), direct comparisons between the decision strategies of the Chinese and USA consumers were possible. Bhalla and Lin (1987) contend that "scalar equivalence" is critical to making valid statistical comparisons across cultures. Scalar equivalence is attained when it can be demonstrated that two individuals from different cultures with the same value on some variable score the same on some test. This is not likely to be an issue in the present study since individual-subject analyses are performed on the data, and the resultant omega squared (w^2) values form the basis of the cross-cultural comparisons. A 2 (culture) x 8 (attributes) ANOVA was performed on the average omega squared (w^2) values of both groups. This analysis revealed no significant effect for culture (F<1), a significant effect for attributes [F $(7, 672) = 64.62$, p < .05], and more important, a significant culture x attributes interaction [F $(6, 672) = 4.36$, p < .05]. Post-hoc Newman-Keuls analyses revealed differences in the use of some store attributes across cultures. For example, the Chinese consumers were found to place significantly greater importance (p < .05) than their American counterparts on both the salesperson's manner (16% vs 11% explained variance, respectively) and convenience of location (9% vs 4%). Quality of merchandise, which explained the greatest amount of variance for the Chinese (22%), was found to be of even greater importance for the USA consumers (30%) (p < .05). The USA consumers' greater use of return policy (7% vs 3% for the Chinese) was found to be marginally significant (Bhalla and Lin, 1987). No significant differences were found in the two groups' use of the four remaining attributes.

Discussion

The results of this study are consistent with the observations of Reeder (1983) and Wattel (1989) as well as the results of empirical work by Thorelli et al. (1985) in the Chinese market. They lend support to the Kindel (1983) model by showing that Chinese consumers evaluate retail stores in terms of multiple attributes, many of which reflect traditional Chinese values. The results are also in keeping with the Sheth and Sethi (1977) model in demonstrating that there are differences in the decision-making strategies of Chinese and American consumers.

The Evaluation of Retail Stores by Chinese Consumers

Merchandise quality dominated the evaluation of retail stores by the Chinese consumers. This result lends support to the Kindel (1983) model, which suggests that Chinese consumers are likely to be concerned with quality because of the loss of face involved in purchasing an inferior product. This attribute proved to be more important, however, to American than to Chinese consumers. A difference between the two cultures had been anticipated; however, the direction of this difference had not. The Sheth and Sethi (1977) model suggests that differences in market conditions may explain the results found here for quality. American consumers are used to operating in a buyers' market, in which the needs and wants of consumers are usually met. Consequently, Americans expect merchandise to be of good, not poor, quality. Chinese consumers, on the other hand, are used to operating in a sellers' market, which is, for the most part, unresponsive to their needs. Consequently, they may simply accept poor quality in many products

Two additional attributes—the manner of salespeople and convenience of store location—were important to the Chinese consumers. As hypothesized, these attributes were of more importance to the Chinese than to the Americans. This is consistent with the traditional Chinese value of politeness that Kindel (1983) suggests is likely to affect the behavior of Chinese consumers. To the extent that the Chinese view shopping as a social occasion, salesperson's manner is likely to continue to play a significant role in store choice decisions. Also anticipated, convenience of store location was more important to the Chinese than to the American consumers. This may reflect the frequency with which the Chinese shop, as well as the unavailability of automobile transportation in the PRC.

Thorelli et al. (1985) reported that the majority of Chinese consumers in his survey were dissatisfied with many of the things they buy. However, the Chinese placed less emphasis on the nature of a store's return policy than did their American counterparts. This result is consistent with the idea that, in China, returning defective merchandise may be tantamount to admitting a mistake, resulting in a loss of face (Kindel, 1983). This result may also reflect the fact that in a sellers' market, favorable return policies may be the exception, rather than the rule.

As suggested by Kindel (1983), the relationship between a retail store and the Chinese consumer is critical. The cultural values of loyalty and harmony (resistance to change) suggest that, once satisfied, the Chinese consumer is likely to be a loyal customer. The results of this study indicate that, in order to attract customers and cultivate loyalty, retail stores in the PRC should provide quality merchandise, foster helpfulness and congeniality among sales clerks, and offer convenient locations.

While differences were observed in the decision-making strategies of Chinese and American consumers, important similarities were noted as well. Quality of merchandise was the dominant store attribute for both groups, followed by salesperson's manner. In addition, there were four attributes—price, ability to inspect merchandise, variety of goods, and speed of checkout—that were found to play minor roles in the decision making of both Chinese and American consumers. Somewhat surprising was the fact that the Chinese consumers placed little emphasis on price in evaluating and selecting stores. Although Kindel (1983) suggests that the value of thrift, coupled with low incomes, might influence the use of price by Chinese consumers, the results do not support this idea. Apparently, the Chinese are willing to trade-off price in order to obtain higher-quality merchandise. Thorelli et al. (1985) came to a similar conclusion, in that a majority of the Chinese in his survey indicated that they believe a price-quality relationship exists for many products in the marketplace.

Future Research

The present study provides a first effort at comparing Chinese and USA consumers' decision making. However, we have only scratched the surface of this important and evolving area of cross-cultural research. A considerable number of unanswered questions remain for subsequent study. For instance, while the present study examined decision making when evaluating a retail store, it is quite possible that these strategies may vary according to store type. One possibility would be to compare stores which sell merchandise of high (e.g., food) and low (e.g., appliances) cultural content (Tan & Farley, 1987). As market socialism evolves, future studies may also wish to employ longitudinal measures to track changes in Chinese consumers' attitudes, perceptions, and decision making. In addition, the globalization of consumer markets and consumption experiences make a comparison of decision-making strategies of Chinese consumers in Hong Kong, Taiwan, and the PRC another interesting avenue to pursue (see Tse, Belk, & Zhou, 1989).

Finally, while the present study examined the decision making of individual Chinese consumers, the extended family framework may be another appropriate unit of analysis for future cross-cultural research with the Chinese. Kindel (1983) argues that many consumer purchases in the PRC are the result of group decisions made by the family. It is quite possible that the influence of others may vary by the product considered, and may be more of a concern for those products that will be consumed by the entire family (e.g., televisions, refrigerators, etc.). The psychology and marketing literatures on family decision making would provide a useful starting place for studies of this type in the PRC.

Conclusions

Kindel (1983), Sheth and Sethi (1977) and others (Tan & Farley, 1987; Thorelli et al., 1985; Tse, Belk, & Zhou, 1989) suggest that cultural values will affect the consumption patterns and behavior of individuals in different societies. Using an "ecological" approach to cross-cultural analysis (Thorelli et al., 1985), we hypothesized that consumer decision making will be influenced by contextual variables such as culture and type of marketing system (quasi-socialist vs. capitalist). While market socialism has moved China more toward a capitalist society, it was presumed that the influence of Chinese culture would have a substantial impact on the consumption experiences of Chinese consumers. The results from the present study support this idea.

References

Anderson, N.H. (1981). *Foundations of Information Integration Theory*, New York: Academic Press.

Belk, R. (1989). *The Benefits and Problems of Market Socialism for Chinese Consumers*. AMA Winter Educator's Conference Proceedings, (Eds.) Richard Bagozzi and J. Paul Peter, Marketing Theory and Practice.

Bhalla, G. and Lin, L. (1987). Cross cultural marketing research: A discussion of equivalence issues and measurement strategies. *Psychology and Marketing, 4,* 275-285.

Green, P. and Srinivason, V. (1978). Conjoint analysis in consumer research: issues and outlook. *Journal of Consumer Research, 5, (September),* 103-123.

Hahn, G. and Shapiro D. (1966). *A Catalog and Computer Program for the Design and Analysis of Orthogonal Symmetric and Asymmetric Fractional Factorial Designs, Report No. 66-C-165*, General Electric Corporation, Schenectady, NY.

Hansen, R. and Deutscher, T. (1977-78). An empirical investigation of attribute importance in retail store selection. *Journal of Retailing, 53*, 4, 59-73.

Hays, W. (1973). *Statistics.* New York: Holt, Rinehart and Winston.

Kindel, T.I. (1983). A partial theory of Chinese consumer behavior: Marketing strategy implications. *Hong Kong Journal of Business Management 1*, 97-109.

Reeder, J. (1983). A small study of a big market in the People's Republic of China—the "free market" system. *Columbia Journal of World Business*, (Winter), 74-80.

Salisbury, H. and Swarts, S. (1986). Geographic perspectives of China's contemporary free markets. *Asian Profile, 14(3)*, 195-200.

Sheth, J. and Sethi, S.P. (1977). A theory of cross-cultural buyer behavior. In A. Woodside, J. Sheth, and P. Bennett (Eds), *Consumer and Industrial Buyer Behavior.* New York: North-Holland.

Tan, C.T. and Farley, J. (1987). The impact of cultural patterns on cognition and intention in Singapore. *Journal of Consumer Research, 13*, (March), 540-544.

Thorelli, H.B., Fu, S.H., and Sentell, G. (1985). The middle class and the marketplace: The PRC, overseas Chinese and Thailand. *Advances in International Marketing, 1*, 143-178.

Tse, D., Belk, R., and Zhou, N. (1989). Becoming a consumer society: A longitudinal and cross-cultural content analysis of print advertisements from Hong Kong, the People's Republic of China, and Taiwan. *Journal of Consumer Research, 15, 4, (March)*, 457-472.

Wattel, H. (1989). The consumer in China: Adjusting to a world of Marx and Smith, *Paper presented at the 35th Annual American Council on Consumer Interests Conference*, Baltimore, Maryland (March 30).

Westbrook, R. (1981). Sources of consumer satisfaction with retail outlets. *Journal of Retailing, 57, 3, (Fall)*, 68- 85.

Acknowledgments

The authors gratefully acknowledge the kind and very patient assistance of Zhang Zhiming, Wu Yeija, and Chiu Gang, who translated the research materials into Mandarin. In addition, the cooperation of Pan Zhao Jun, Qi Yenong, and Zhang Zhe in the PRC is greatly appreciated. Without these wonderful people this research would not have been possible. Computer time was provided by the University of Maryland Computer Science Center.

THE EFFECTS OF FRAMING AND INCOMPLETE INFORMATION ON JUDGMENTS

Wing Hong Loke

Subjects indicated their likelihood of taking each of a series of gambles based on probability and/or payoff information and their confidence in each likelihood judgment. Overall, subjects who received positively framed information evaluated decision options more favorably than subjects who received the same information framed negatively. Also, subjects who produced greater likelihood to make a judgment reflect their greater confidence in their judgments. The present study showed stronger evidence than past studies that confidence level is reduced when probability information is missing. A transfer phase, where the subjects were tested in the positive-frame first and then in the negative-framed condition or vice-versa, showed that the initial frame continues to influence confidence responses of a given subject despite a subsequent change in the frame. The present study suggests a similar judgmental process for Eastern and Western subject populations and suggests further research to identify cultural factors that make judgments vary.

Judgments and decisions can be influenced by the way information is presented or framed. For example, choices between two intervention strategies for dealing with an emergency situation differed depending on whether the strategies were described in terms of likelihood of lives saved or lives lost, even though the objective information (i.e., the number of lives lost) was the same in each case (Tversky & Kahneman, 1981). According to prospect theory (Kahneman & Tversky, 1979), choices framed in terms of losses have a greater influence than those framed in terms of gains. One interpretation is that the displeasure with losses is generally greater than the pleasure associated with gains of the same amount. An alternate interpretation is that negative relationships between variables are more difficult to learn and use than are positive relationships (Slovic, 1974). For example, individuals judged more accurately the price of ground beef when the "quality" information was expressed in positive terms (percent lean) rather than in negative terms (percent fat) (Levin & Johnson, 1984).

Another consideration is that choices and decisions may vary depending on the amount of information given. In making decisions on the purchases of public securities (stocks and bonds) or consumer goods (food and clothing), individuals make purchases without all the available information. One method of making a decision is that high prices imply high quality and low prices imply low quality (Huber & McCann, 1982;

Levin, Johnson, & Faraone, 1984; Yamagishi & Hill, 1981). An alternative method is that individuals may impute a fixed value for the missing information such as they may assume average values for missing scores (Slovic & MacPhillamy, 1974) or they may assign less favorable values (Levin, Kim, & Corry, 1976; Yates, Jagacinski, Carolyn, & Faber, 1978).

The present study examined the effects of framing and incomplete information on the evaluation of a gamble situation. Subjects indicated their likelihood of taking each of a series of gambles based on both probability and payoff information or only one of these sources of information. They also rated their confidence for each likelihood judgment. The purpose is to examine whether positive information would induce more favorable responses of the decision options than the same information framed in a negative manner. Because the present study tests performance of Chinese Singaporeans, failure to show the effects of framing would suggest that there exists a separate process of judgment and decision making particular to non-Caucasians. With limited information, given that probability information reflects the degree of risk of gambles, individuals would be expected to make more extreme judgments when given probability information only than when given payoff alone.

In addition, a transfer phase was introduced where the subjects were tested twice, once in the positive-framed and once in the negative-framed condition, on separate days (48-hours apart). This phase attempts to examine the persistence of an information frame once it is established. The present study combines aspects of the Levin, Johnson, and Davis (1987) paper which included a transfer phase like the present study but did not have a 48-hour interval, and the Levin, Chapman, and Johnson (1988) paper which included confidence ratings. A gambling task was used because it is in some ways a model for risk-taking economic decisions (such as business ventures and stock investments; Levin et al., 1987) and it is a valid predictor of behavior outside the laboratory setting (Lichtenstein & Slovic, 1973).

Method

Experimental Design

Probability information used in describing gambles was framed in either probability of winning (positive condition) or probability of losing (negative condition). Each subject received both conditions: positive- and negative-framed. A total of 19 subjects completed the positive condition first and then the negative condition (positive-negative framed condition) and the other 13 subjects completed the task in the reverse order (negative-positive framed condition). They were tested in groups of eight at a time. An interval of 48 hours separated the testing of the first and second conditions.

A total of 38 gambles, each of the 19 unique gambles repeated twice (positive and negative conditions), were printed on each booklet. The positive-framed booklets contained two gambles of each combination of the probability of winning (.5, .10, .15, .20, and "blank") and the amount to be won ($100, $150, $200, and "blank"). The negative-framed booklets contained two gambles of each combination of the probability of losing (.80, .85, .90, .95, and "blank") and the amount to be won ($100, $150, $200, and "blank"). The two gambles representing the combination of "blank" probability and "blank" amount were not included in the booklets. "Blank" means no information is given on the particular dimension (probability or amount).

A typical response structure of a gamble, illustrating stimulus presentation and response scales, is shown in Table 1. This one is for a gamble in the positive framed condition with missing ("blank") payoff information. (The equivalent gamble in the negative condition substitutes "Chance of winning: 10%" for "Chance of losing: 90%").

TABLE 1

A typical response structure of a gamble illustrating stimulus presentation and response scales. A gamble in the positive framed condition with missing ("blank") payoff information is shown.

Amount of investment: $15
Amount to be won: $____
Chance of winning: 10%

Your response (check one):
--- very likely to take gamble
--- likely to take gamble
--- somewhat likely to take gamble
--- equally likely to take or refuse gamble
--- somewhat likely to refuse gamble
--- likely to refuse gamble
--- very likely to refuse gamble

Degree of confidence in your response (circle one number):

1 2 3 4 5 6 7 8 9 10 11 12 13 14 15 16 17 18 19 20
very   very
unconfident   confident

Instructions

Subjects were given two pages of instructions describing the nature of the hypothetical gambles or lotteries. They were informed that the task represents situations we sometimes face that require us to make judgments and decisions. They were informed that they would sometimes have two pieces of information on which to base a judgment and sometimes only one. Subjects were told that each gamble would suppose a $15 investment. If they decide to take a gamble, that means that they would invest the $15 to possibly win a larger amount. If they decide to refuse a gamble, that means that they would keep the $15 and not invest it. They were instructed to think through each situation carefully and to try to imagine how they would react in each case. Note that subjects were not told that they would receive different framing conditions.

Procedure

At each test session, subjects were presented with one booklet containing 38 gambles. Two gambles were printed on a page. For each gamble, following the information provided on probability and amount, subjects were asked to evaluate the likelihood of taking the gamble on a scale of "very likely to take a gamble" to "very likely to refuse a gamble" (responses are later scored from -3 to 3, correspondingly; 0 was "equally likely to take or refuse a gamble"). Then, subjects were to indicate how confident they were in each of their likelihood ratings. Subjects were told to work at their own pace. In general, they completed the booklet in about 15 minutes.

Subjects

They were 32 paid undergraduates (16 females and 16 males; mean age of 20 and standard deviation of +1.56 years) in first-year arts and social sciences courses at the National University of Singapore.

Statistics

Unequal cell analyses of variance (ANOVAs) were used to examine the two dependent measures, ratings of likelihood of taking a gamble and ratings of confidence in each likelihood judgment. The main independent variables examined were framing (positive frame—probability of win—and negative frame—probability of loss), probability of win (.05, .10, .15, and .20), probability of loss (.80, .85, .90, and .95), and amount to be won ($100, $150, and $200). Also a secondary independent variable, subjects' experience of frame order (positive-negative and negative-positive conditions), was examined.

Framing (positive versus negative frame) was examined for each of the two days of testing. Separate analyses were also done for probability of win by amount to be won and for probability of loss by amount to be won for each day. In addition, framing effect was examined for missing probabilities—positive-framed versus negative-framed gambles with "blank" probabilities—and for missing amount—positive-framed versus negative-framed gambles with "blank" amounts. Furthermore, to examine whether responses differ given probability alone versus given amount to be won alone, one-factor ANOVAs (limited information—probability [missing amount to be won] and amount to be won [missing probability]) were done for each combination of framing by day of testing.

Correlations were calculated between likelihood and confidence ratings for each combination of framing and day of testing. The analysis examined whether individuals who had high ratings of likelihood (i.e., they were very likely to take or refuse gambles) also had high ratings of confidence (i.e., they were very confident of their likelihood responses) and, correspondingly, low confidence ratings for low likelihood responses.

Significant ($p < .05$) and marginal ($.05 < p < .10$) effects were reported. Significant effects were further analyzed using the Duncan's multiple-range tests for comparison of two means.

Results and Discussion

In each of the Figures 1-4, positive and negative conditions are plotted on the left and right panels, respectively. Figures 1 and 2 show the mean likelihood to take gambles; the figures represent days 1 and 2 of testing, respectively. Figures 3 and 4 show the mean confidence ratings; the figures represent days 1 and 2 of testing ,respectively. Solid lines represent mean scores for two-attribute stimuli. Dotted lines represent mean ratings for one-attribute stimuli—where only the probability of winning (left panels) or probability of losing (right panels) is given and the amount to be won is missing.

Figure 1 shows that the solid line of .20 probability of winning (left panel) is higher than the solid line of .80 probability of losing (i.e., .20 probability of winning; right panel). The general pattern in Figures 1, 2, and 4 is that the solid lines (with identical information but framed differently, e.g., .20 probability of winning versus .80 probability of losing) have higher ratings in the positive condition than in the negative condition.

For likelihood ratings, differences in responses between positive and negative conditions were observed, although not statistically significant for day 1 of testing [$F(1, 36) = 1.15$, $p = .29$; see Figure 1] and only marginally significant for day 2 of testing [$F(1, 36) = 3.05$, $p < .10$; see Figure 2]. Although the effect of framing is weak for likelihood ratings, individuals do distinguish among the different levels of probability and amount to be won; that is, increasing the amount to be won increases the likelihood ratings. For example, individuals in the positive-framed condition on day 1 of testing showed that increasing the probability and also the amount to be won increases ratings of likelihood from "very likely to refuse a gamble" to "equally likely to take or refuse a gamble" [$F(3, 54) = 44.20$ and $F(2, 36) = 10.27$, p's < .001 for probability and amount to be won, respectively; see left panel of Figure 1]. Similar results were shown for the other conditions [$F(3, 36) = 21.52$ and $F(2, 24) = 17.21$, p's < .001 for right panel of Figure 1 for probability and amount to be won, respectively; $F(3, 33) = 22.90$ and $F(2, 22) = 8.45$, $p < .001$ and .01 for left panel of Figure 3; $F(3, 51) = 25.99$ and $F(2, 34) = 15.20$, p's < .001 for right panel of Figure 2].

Compared to likelihood ratings, the effect of frame is greater for ratings of confidence. Analyses of frame (left versus right panels; Figures 3 and 4) showed that gambles framed in a positive or negative manner alter the judgment of individuals to take gambles. Specifically, Figure 3 shows lower ratings for the positive than the negative condition [$F(1, 36) = 102.33$, $p < .001$] and Figure 4 shows the reverse effect [$F(1, 36) = 154.01$, $p < .001$].

So, the present study shows the effects of framing on responses of individuals. The effects were more pronounced for confidence ratings than for likelihood. As a comparison, the relative positions of the solid and dash lines of the present figures paralleled the positions found by Levin and colleagues (Levin et al., 1987; Levin & Johnson, 1984); the difference in ratings between the positive and negative conditions are also about the same.

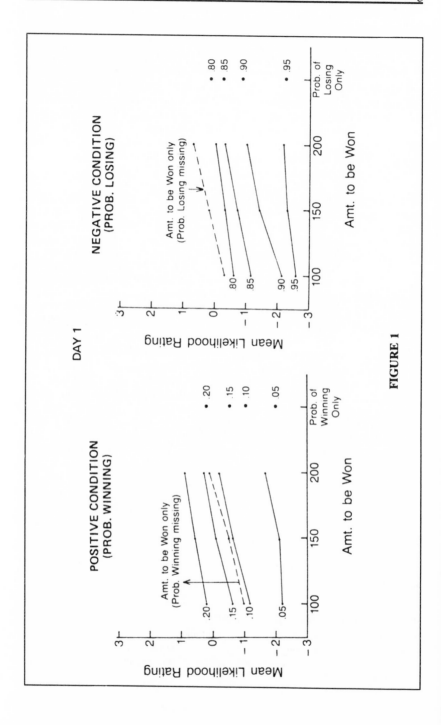

FIGURE 1

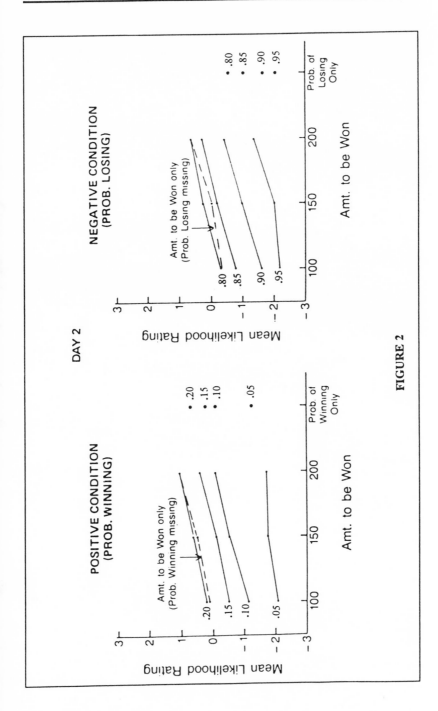

FIGURE 2

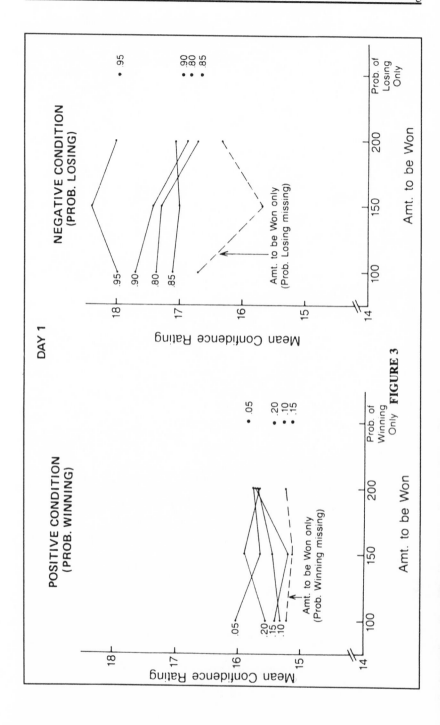

FIGURE 3

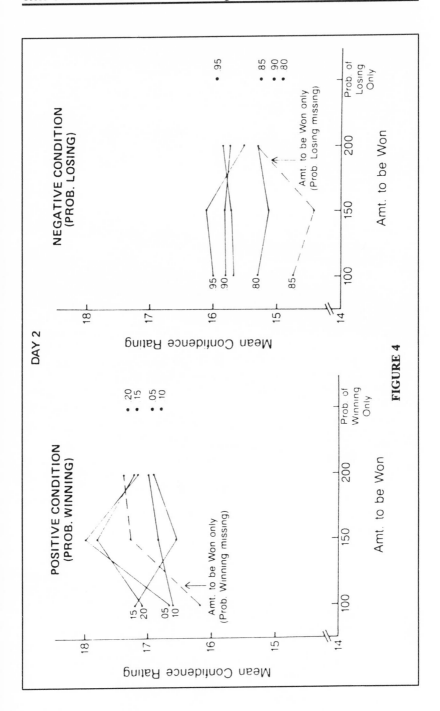

FIGURE 4

TABLE 2
The effect day of testing by frame for limited information
(probability alone or amount alone)

Condition	Probability alone	Amount alone	F(1,18)	p <
Day 1				
Positive	-0.79	-0.46	3.35	0.10
Negative	-0.03	0.64	3.44	0.01
Day 2				
Positive	-0.79	0.19	11.98	0.10
Negative	-1.31	-0.18	10.78	0.01

Of note is that on day 1 of testing, individuals in the negative condition showed more extreme confidence scores than those in the positive condition. When individuals switched framed conditions on day 2 of testing, those in the positive condition (who previously were in the negative condition) maintained high extreme scores and those in the negative condition (who previously were in the positive condition) maintained low scores. Previous researchers (Levin et al., 1987; Miller, 1958), who observed similar results, suggested that individuals attempt to be consistent in their responses even when the frame is changed. Once information is presented in a particular frame on day 1 of testing, it is difficult to reverse that frame even when the same information is framed in a different manner on day 2 of testing. The 48-hour interval between the first and second day of testing diluted the particular effect induced on day 1 of testing for likelihood responses but was not sufficient to dilute the effect for confidence ratings. Future studies are suggested to examine the magnitude of the perseverance of the initial frame by varying the interval between the transfer (positive-negative and negative-positive) phases.

In addition, whether individuals who did the positive and then the negative condition differ from those who did the reverse order of the test was examined using an ANOVA of frame (positive versus negative frame) by frame order (positive-negative versus negative-positive order of frame presentation). A significant interaction for the likelihood to take gambles [F(1, 28) = 9.68, p < .01] and a significant frame order for confidence ratings [F(1, 29) = 5.58, p <.05] were shown. For the main effect, individuals who were in the negative-positive condition were more confident of their likelihood responses (mean of 17.49) than those in the positive-negative condition (mean of 15.25). The high confidence levels in the negative condition are consistent with results from Levin et al. (1987). That is, there is a strong tendency not to take gambles in this condition and the more extreme the individuals' ratings are in the negative direction, the more confident they are. Of note is that individuals who were in the negative-positive condition were more likely to refuse positive gambles than those in the positive-negative condition, as shown by further analysis on the interaction of order and framing. Individuals who were given the negative- then the positive-framed test (negative-positive condition) were more likely to refuse positive-frame gambles (mean of -1.35) than subjects in the positive-negative condition (mean of -0.44); in contrast, similar scores were obtained for the negative-framed gambles (means of -0.73 and -0.46 for individuals in the positive-negative and negative-positive conditions, respectively). So, the presentation order of the frames appears itself to be a background framing effect. Perhaps subjects who did the positive gambles first could recognize later that the negative gambles were similar to the positive gambles (except for the reversed information).

Analyses on missing values—either probability or amount is missing—were also done. The effect of frame was significant for missing amount (probability information only) on the second day of testing; specifically, individuals were more likely to refuse gambles (mean of -1.31) when only probability of losing was given than when only probability of winning was given (mean of - 0.03; $F(1, 29) = 8.14$, $p < .05$; in Figure 2, the dots for the .80, .85, .90, and .95 probabilities of losing only [see right panel] are lower than those for the .20, .15, .10, and .05 probabilities of winning only [see left panel] respectively).

Also, the difference between probability alone (solid dots) and amount alone (dotted line) was examined for each combination of frame and day of testing. Individuals were more likely to refuse gambles when only probability was given compared to when only amount was given (see Table 2; the mean likelihood values for probability alone are more negative than for amount alone). So, with limited information individuals were more likely to make extreme judgments given probabilities alone than amounts alone. The present study with a gambling scenario suggests that individuals were more likely to refuse gambles when probability of losing information (.80, .85, .90, and .95 chance of losing) was given than when probability of winning (.20, .15, .10, and .05 chance of winning) was given. In other words, individuals were more likely to take a gamble given probability of winning. In contrast, Slovic and Lichtenstein (1968) showed that for gambles where individuals were asked to make monetary bids, they attended to information on the yield (payoff) from a win instead of the probability of its occurrence.

In addition to ANOVAs, correlations were done between likelihood and confidence responses of each combination of frame and day of testing. Significant positive correlations were obtained for (a) day 1/positive-framed [$r(17) = .84$, $p < .001$; cf. left panels of Figures 1 and 3], (b) day 2/positive-framed [$r(11) = .76$, $p < .01$; cf. left panels of Figures 2 and 4], and (c) day 2/negative-framed [$r(17) = .91$, $p < .001$; cf. right panels of Figures 2 and 4]. The day 1/negative-framed condition, however, produced a zero correlation. So, correlations between likelihood and confidence ratings for day of testing by frame showed the general pattern—that the more likely individuals were to take a gamble, the more confident they were of their judgments. Also, individuals showed consistent confidence ratings from one part of the task to the next. The individuals, however, were conservative in their use of the 20 points of the rating scale; the difference in magnitude of rating is about two units (e.g., in left-panel of Figure 4 where the ratings ranged from 16-18; also see other panels of Figures 3 and 4). The written instructions to inform individuals to use the entire range of the rating scale were not adequate.

Conclusion

In general, the present results support those of Levin and his colleagues (Levin et al., 1987, 1988). One main difference from Levin et al. (1988) is that the present study found stronger evidence that confidence level is reduced when probability information is missing. Perhaps, the difference is that the present study used Singaporeans whereas past studies tested Westerners (mostly North Americans), considering that all other comparisons of individual characteristics such as age and level of education are similar. Singh and Bhargava (1985) have shown that Indian and North American college students differ in their cultural outlook on how motivation and ability may determine performance. Future studies are suggested to examine differences in the extent of confidence between players from distinct cultures.

Overall, the present study suggests that the process of judgment and decision making for both Western and Eastern populations is similar. This suggestion, however, is limited by several considerations. The present study employed subjects who are well-versed in the English language (the average score of the Test of English as a Foreign Language [TOEFL] is 600); it did not select subjects who were educated in Chinese-medium schools. Perhaps cultural differences in the judgment and decision processes of English- and Chinese-educated individuals and cultural factors such as risk-taking propensity (or degree of conservativeness) should be investigated.

References

Anderson, N.H. (1965). Averaging versus adding as a stimulus combination rule in impression formation. *Journal of Experimental Psychology, 70*, 394-400.

Huber, J. and McCann, J. (1982). The impact of inferential beliefs on product evaluations. *Journal of Marketing Research, 19*, 324-333.

Kahneman, D. and Tversky, A. (1979). Prospect theory: An analysis of decision under risk. *Econometrika, 47*, 263-291.

Levin, I.P., Chapman, D.P., and Johnson, R.D. (1988). Confidence in judgments based on incomplete information: An investigation using both hypothetical and real gambles. *Journal of Behavioral Decision Making, 1*, 29-41.

Levin, I.P. and Johnson, R.D. (1984). Estimating price-quality tradeoffs using comparative judgments. *Journal of Consumer Research, 11*, 593-600.

Levin, I.P., Johnson, R.D., and Davis, M.L. (1987). How information frame influences risky decisions: Between-subjects and within-subject comparisons. *Journal of Economic Psychology, 8*, 43-54.

Levin, I.P., Johnson, R.D., and Faraone, S.V. (1984). Information integration in price-quality tradeoffs: The effects of missing information. *Memory and Cognition, 12*, 96-102.

Levin, I.P., Kim, K.J., and Corry, F.A. (1976). Invariance of the weight parameter in information integration. *Memory and Cognition, 4*, 43-47.

Lichtenstein, S. and Slovic, P. (1973). Response-induced reversals of preference in gambling: An extended replication in Las Vegas. *Journal of Experimental Psychology, 101*, 16-20.

Miller, G.A. (1958). Free recall of redundant strings of letters. *Journal of Experimental Psychology, 56*, 484-491.

Singh, R. and Bhargava, S. (1985). Motivation, ability, and exam performance: Tests of hypotheses of cultural difference and task difficulty. *Journal of Experimental Social Psychology, 21*, 466-479.

Slovic, P. (1974). Hypothesis testing in the learning of positive and negative linear functions. *Organizational Behavior and Human Performance, 11*, 368-376.

Slovic, P. and Lichtenstein, S. (1968). Relative importance of probabilities and payoffs in risk taking. *Journal of Experimental Psychology Monograph, 78*, (No. 3, Pt. 2, Whole).

Slovic, P. and MacPhillamy, D.J. (1974). Dimensional commensurability and cue utilization in comparative judgment. *Organizational Behavior and Human Performance, 11*, 172-194.

Tversky, A. and Kahneman, D. (1981). The framing of decisions and the psychology of choice. *Science, 211*, 453-458.

Yamagishi, T. and Hill, C.T. (1981). Adding versus averaging models revisited: A test of a path-analytic integration model. *Journal of Personality and Social Psychology, 41*, 13-25.

Yates, J.F., Jagacinski, C.M., Carolyn, M., and Faber, M.D. (1978). Evaluation of partially described multiattribute options. *Organizational Behavior and Human Performance, 21*, 240-251.

Note

The above article was published in Loke, W.H. (1989). The effects of framing and incomplete information on judgments, *Journal of Economic Psychology, 10*, 329-341. Used with permission from Elsevier Science Publishers B.V. (North Holland).

TO WAIT OR NOT TO WAIT: THE INFLUENCE OF CULTURE ON DISCOUNTING BEHAVIOR

Chwee Teck Tan and Richard D. Johnson

Patterns of discount rates as a function of the size, risk and delay associated with an anticipated gain were found not to differ between Canadian and Oriental subjects. However, Oriental subjects were significantly more risk sensitive than Canadians when choosing whether to wait for delayed gains.

Consumers are often faced with a choice between purchasing an acceptable product immediately and waiting for a more attractive product. For example, some consumers may take advantage of "no money down" finance plans because of an unwillingness to wait until they can afford to pay cash. Other consumers may choose to wait for an improved version of a product. Still others may prefer to purchase products with immediate benefits (such as instant cameras) over products whose benefits are delayed.

People may choose the immediate alternative even when the delayed alternative is lower in cost, better in features, and/or higher in quality; because future gains are discounted relative to immediate gains (Mischel, 1974; Ainslie, 1975; Strotz, 1955). This phenomenon, called "temporal myopia," is often attributed to characteristics of the consumer, such as (lack of) self-control, intelligence, and education level (Fisher, 1965; Mischel & Metzner, 1962).

Recent evidence indicates that discounting behavior is also influenced by characteristics of the alternative. Normative theories in finance and economics postulate that discount rates should either remain constant or increase when the principal amount and the delay period are increased. Strotz (1955) challenged contemporary thinking with his hypothesis that the utility of a future reward falls off quickly for relatively short delays, but that the rate of decline eases as the period of delay is lengthened. Ainslie (1975) obtained empirical evidence of an identical pattern of discounting in a series of studies of animal behavior. Johnson and Leeworthy (1988) extended the empirical evidence to human subjects and demonstrated that increasing the amount of gain, as well as the length of delay, resulted in the pattern of discounting described by Strotz and Ainslie. They suggested that the previous analyses need to be reevaluated and generalized to account for influences of non-temporal variables on discounting. Johnson and Leeworthy also pointed out that marketers who understand the relationship of discounting to product variety, price range and distribution should be able to more effectively tailor the marketing mix.

At issue in this study is whether culture interacts with product variables to influence discount rates and willingness to wait. Comparative studies of Chinese and

North American cultures highlight several distinguishing characteristics. In particular, the Chinese adopt a collective orientation, taking an intergenerational (long-term) time perspective; whereas, Americans embrace an individual orientation and a shorter time frame (Chan, 1986; Moore, 1967). Smith (1961) emphasized two primary characteristics of the Chinese, patience and perseverance, from which we generate the predictions of this study. Tse, Lee, Vertinsky, and Wehrung (1988) found that, in contrast to Canadian executives, Chinese executives highly value preservation of personal dignity, establishment of long-term relationships, and unquestioning respect for leaders; and they expressed these values in their product and market entry decisions. The authors noted an erosion of traditional Chinese values in the case of Hong Kong as a consequence of the "globalization" process and the exposure to Western culture. Other studies (McCullough, Tan, & Wong, 1986; Tan & Farley, 1987) have found similar "erosion" effects in Singaporean subjects. Tse et al. (1988) maintained that the residual influence of deeply rooted Confucian values is present despite modernization.

To the extent that patience, perseverance, and a long-term perspective are present in our Oriental subjects, cultural effects on discounting behavior and willingness to wait for delayed rewards can be expected. Patience and perseverance imply less discounting of delayed gains and greater willingness to wait for a larger-later reward. Four predictions are addressed in this study:

(a) Oriental subjects require a smaller premium for waiting, relative to Canadian subjects; although, in both cases the amounts required will be a monotonically increasing function of both the amount of principal and length of delay.

(b) Discount rates are lower for Oriental subjects than for Canadians.

(c) Discount rates decrease at a slower rate for Oriental subjects.

(d) Oriental subjects are more willing to wait for a delayed larger reward.

Method

Twenty Canadian undergraduates and twenty-one foreign undergraduates from various faculties participated in this study. The foreign students, all of Chinese descent, were from Hong Kong, Singapore, Malaysia, and Indonesia. All the subjects were tested individually at various campus locations.

Each subject was asked to imagine that s/he had won a lottery. For each of eighteen cases generated from a 3 x 3 x 2 factorial design, students were told how much money they might receive immediately ($91, $868, or $8281), how long they might be asked to wait (six months, one year, or five years), and the level of risk (low or high). In the low-risk conditions, subjects were told that the money would be placed in a trust account in a national chartered bank (any interest earned would belong to the lottery organization). High risk meant that the lottery organization—a private company—would hold the money. The cases were presented in the same random order for all subjects.

For each situation, subjects were asked to state the amount of money (the bid) that would make them indifferent between receiving the original lottery winnings immediately or the bid after a specified delay. From the bids obtained, discount rates were calculated using the Net Present Value (NPV) algorithm.

The second task was designed to ascertain whether subjects employed any systematic tie-breaking schemes when choosing between equivalent alternatives (Slovic & Lichtenstein, 1968). In each case, subjects were asked to choose between immediately receiving the original winnings and waiting for the corresponding bid they had generated in the first task. This task also allowed us to examine the influence, if any, of culture on intertemporal choices.

Finally, subjects were asked to provide demographic data, in order to distinguish the foreign subjects from their Canadian counterparts. Subjects were asked to list all the countries in which they had resided and the lengths of time spent in each country. Subjects who had been born in the Orient and had lived there until not more than four of the consecutive years just prior to the time of the survey were classified as foreign students (the typical foreign undergraduate takes about four years to complete a program in the University.). All the foreign students were of Chinese descent. All but one of the Canadian subjects had lived in Canada at least since the time they began grammar school. The exception had lived in Canada for the past ten years.

Results

The results of the first task are presented in Figure 1. As may be seen in the top panel, the mean bids increase as a monotonic function of amount, time and risk. All three effects are significant at p <.05 (see Table 1). All three factors are complements of each other; that is, the effect of each factor is greater at higher levels of the other factors.

TABLE 1

MANOVA Results for Bids and Discount Rates
F-statistic (df 1,39)

	Bids		Discount Rates	
Amount[1]	42.98	**	4.83	*
Amount2	0.05		2.05	
Time	12.61	**	18.78	**
Time2	0.16		13.74	**
Risk	6.12	*	1.78	
Culture	0.07		0.80	
Time x Amount	10.95	**	4.24	*
Time2 x Amount	0.09		3.11	
Time x Amount2	0.18		1.63	
Time2 x Amount2	0.01		1.30	
Amount x Risk	6.55	**	0.18	
Amount2 x Risk	2.17		0.53	
Time x Risk	5.84	**	1.47	
Time2 x Risk	0.13		1.19	
Time x Amount x Risk	6.27	*	0.12	
Time x Amount2 x Risk	1.07		0.50	
Time2 x Amount x Risk	0.03		0.03	
Time2 x Amount2 x Risk	0.48		0.26	
Culture x Amount	0.03		1.51	
Culture x Amount2	0.74		0.41	
Culture x Time	0.09		0.81	
Culture x Time2	0.16		1.03	
Culture x Risk	6.12	*	1.70	
Culture x Time x Amount	0.06		1.48	
Culture x Time2 x Amount	0.01		1.57	
Culture x Time x Amount2	0.22		0.45	
Culture x Time2 x Amount2	0.57		0.58	
Culture x Amount x Risk	0.35		3.07	
Culture x Amount2 x Risk	2.57		1.63	
Culture x Time x Risk	0.48		1.64	
Culture x Time2 x Risk	0.93		1.57	
Culture x Time x Amount x Risk	0.25		3.24	
Culture x Time x Amount2 x Risk	0.96		1.48	
Culture x Time2 x Amount x Risk	1.37		3.86	
Culture x Time2 x Amount2 x Risk	3.40		1.03	

* $p < 0.05$
** $p < 0.01$

[1]Unnumbered variable names signify linear components.
Variable names followed by a 2, e.g., Amount2, signify quadratic components

MANOVA confirms that the two-way interactions of Time x Amount, Time x Risk, and Amount x Risk, as well as the three-way interaction of Time x Amount x Risk are all significant at p < .05. None of the quadratic main or interaction effects proved to be significant. Contrary to the first prediction, neither the main effect nor any of the interactions involving culture were significant.

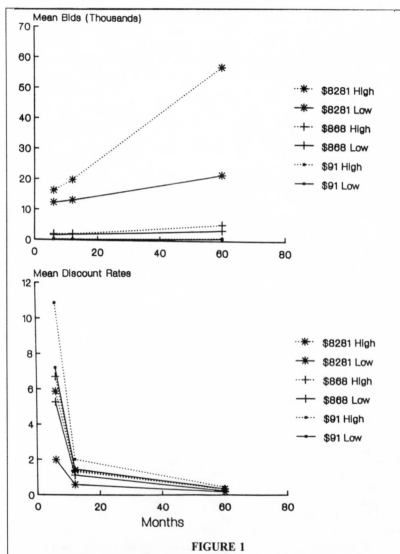

FIGURE 1

Results of the indifference judgments task. The mean bids (top panel) correspond to the amount of money subjects reported they would have to receive at a specified future time in order to be indifferent between receiving their winnings immediately and the bid later. The discount rates (bottom panel) are calculated using the formula $B=A(1+r)^d$.

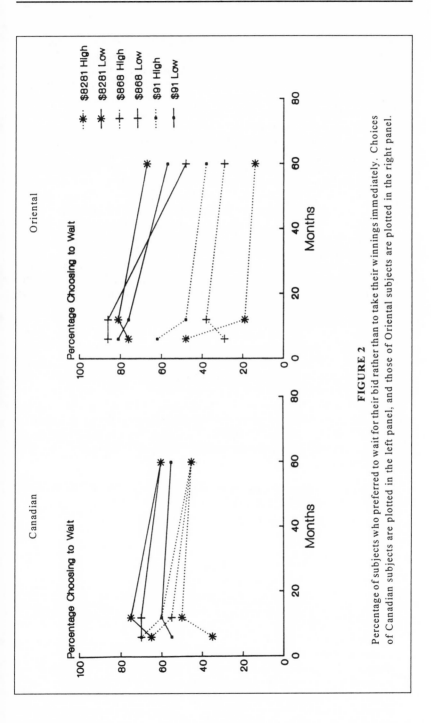

FIGURE 2

Percentage of subjects who preferred to wait for their bid rather than to take their winnings immediately. Choices of Canadian subjects are plotted in the left panel, and those of Oriental subjects are plotted in the right panel.

Mean discount rates are presented in the bottom panel of Figure 1. Both the linear and the quadratic components of the time effect were significant, thus confirming a hyperbolic curve (Strotz, 1955; Ainslie, 1975); discount rates declined as a function of delay in time, sharply for shorter delays and more gradually as the delays became longer. It was also the case that subjects discounted less as the amount was increased; but the increase was linear across the tested range. Time and amount are substitutes; that is, the length of the delay matters more when smaller amounts of money are at stake and vice versa. Risk did not influence discount rates.

Discount rates are remarkably high for the shortest delay. They drop dramatically for a one-year delay, but they begin to approach levels consistent with current financial offerings only for a five-year delay. Previous studies (e.g., Mischel, 1974; Loewenstein, 1988) that have reported extreme discounting have consistently utilized time periods on the order of days or weeks. Our results demonstrate the importance of testing the effect of long delays.

Culture did not prove to be a significant influence on discounting, either as a main effect or in interaction with other factors. The Canadians and the Orientals in our sample produced similar indifference judgments, indicating the same pattern of discount rates.

The proportions of subjects in each group that were willing to wait for the delayed reward appear in Figure 2. As may be seen in the left-hand panel, Canadian subjects were marginally less willing to wait for high-risk alternatives, longer periods of time, and larger amounts. Similar results for time and amount were obtained for the Oriental subjects (right-hand panel), but the influence of risk is much stronger than for the Canadians. Whereas, the Canadian subjects were less discriminating about high and low risks, the Oriental subjects appeared more willing to wait in the low-risk situation and less so in the high-risk case. In addition, Oriental subjects were more influenced by amount when risk is high; whereas, amount is relatively constant across levels of risk for Canadians.

Hierarchical testing of the log-linear models confirms that all the three-way relationships are significant at $p < .001$. The likelihood ratio chi-square values are reported in Table 2.

TABLE 2
Willingness to Wait for Larger Rewards

	df	L.R. Chi-Square
Culture x Amount x Risk	24	66.14
Culture x Amount x Time	18	174.83
Culture x Time x Risk	24	60.30
Amount x Time x Risk	18	69.81

Discussion

Culture was not found to be a significant factor in the observed bids and discount rates. Since the main effects of the product variables on discounting behavior were similar for the two groups, the results obtained by Johnson and Leeworthy (1988) appear to be generalizable to the Far Eastern context. In general, bids were positively related to the amount of principal, the delay period, and the level of risk; and all three factors are complements of one another. Time and amount were significantly and inversely related to the discount rates.

It is interesting to note the robustness of this non-normative pattern of discounting. Not only is it consistent across the cultures and educational programs in this study, but it is also consistent across methods of administration. The composition of our subject pool from several educational backgrounds was more representative of the general public (albeit they were all students) than was the case for Johnson and Leeworthy (1988) where all subjects were from the business faculty. In addition, Johnson and Leeworthy (1988) surveyed large groups in intact classrooms; whereas, we surveyed individuals in a number of different locations. Despite these differences in procedure, the results of the two studies are remarkably consistent.

Given that none of the effects involving culture was significant; how may the tendency of Oriental subjects, in contrast to Canadian subjects, to be more (less) willing to wait when the risk level was low (high) be explained? One interpretation arises from the fact that the two tasks are not independent, and that bids may not accurately reflect subjective discount rates. If Oriental subjects gave bids that were systematically too high in low-risk cases, then they should be more willing to wait for the bid. If their bids were systematically too low in high-risk cases, they should be less willing to wait. This interpretation depends on the Oriental subjects approaching the first task in a manner systematically different from that of the Canadian subjects; but the results on the first task were not found to differ across groups. Given the similarity of the bids, an explanation of the difference in willingness-to-wait responses based on interdependence of the tasks finds little support.

A more parsimonious interpretation is that the bids were accurate and that the two subject groups did not differ in their discounting behavior. Although the groups displayed similar patterns of discounting when setting bids; their responses diverged when they were faced with a choice between immediate gains and delayed gains that were just enough larger to make them nominally indifferent between the alternatives. The primary difference lies in the two groups' response to risk. For both groups, risk had no significant effect on discount rates in the first task. On the second task, the Canadian subjects continued to be relatively insensitive toward risk; whereas, the Oriental subjects preferred to wait for low-risk alternatives and clearly disliked high risk.

Limitations

The small sample sizes in this study were sufficient to reveal relatively large effects but lacked power to adequately test some of the higher-order effects for which apparent trends proved nonsignificant. It is not possible, on the basis of this small sample, to say with any confidence that cultural differences in discounting behavior will not be obtained with a more sensitive instrument. For example, mean discount rates for Oriental subjects in this study were lower than those for Canadian subjects, but the apparent difference was not statistically significant. Only with a larger sample will it be possible to determine with confidence whether or not Orientals discount less than Canadians. The foreign undergraduate subjects in this study may not be representative of the populations of their home countries, but this approach provides a more feasible and economical preliminary study before embarking on a full-scale international undertaking. These students are probably more Westernized than their counterparts who have not lived in Canada; consequently, our results probably underestimate actual cultural differences.

Additional factors may have influenced the results. The most likely candidate is the financial independence of the subjects. Whereas Canadian students typically take on temporary jobs to pay their educational expenses, foreign students generally depend on funding from their home countries. Typically, such funding consists of several lump-sum transactions, which have to be managed in a prudent manner. Hence, the two subject groups may differ in their attitudes toward consumption and investment.

Implications and Future Research

Several avenues might be explored in future research. First, this study should be replicated with a larger sample, taking care to control for such factors as age, financial independence, and standard of living across the two subject groups. Surveying subjects in the Far East to minimize Westernization and self-selection biases would also be indicated. A second option involves the use of non-financial products and the mapping of discount functions for different product categories, such as durables vs. non-durables. Such experiments can be extended to brand names and no-name products in order to evaluate the impact of brands on discount functions. A variety of advertising approaches, with particular emphasis on messages created for sales promotions, can be tested to determine if discount functions can be influenced through advertising.

Other strategic implications of this line of research may be considered and tested. For example, cultural impact on the preference for later-larger rewards provides a basis on which to segment consumers in the financial market and consequently affects product positioning. Financial firms should position their services in the Far East market in a manner which places relatively greater weight on the "security" attribute. In contrast, financial firms operating in North America should emphasize "high returns" in their marketing strategy.

Conclusion

When asked to choose between an immediate payment and a larger delayed payment, Oriental subjects were more likely than Canadians to wait when risk was low and not to wait when risk was high. This higher risk sensitivity on the part of Orientals for willingness-to-wait choices was observed even though the groups did not differ in patterns of discounting as measured by indifference judgments.

Discounting patterns for both cultural groups in this study replicated those reported by Johnson and Leeworthy (1988), despite important differences in procedure. Specifically, subjects heavily discounted small payments for which they were required to wait a short time; and the amount of discounting steadily decreased with increasing amounts and delays. The relationship of discount rates to length of delay in this study was consistent with that postulated by Strotz (1955) and demonstrated in animals by Ainslie (1975). The robustness of this counter-intuitive pattern of discounting merits further study and suggests interesting marketing strategic implications.

References

Ainslie, G. (1975). Specious reward: A behavioral theory of impulsiveness and impulse control. *Psychological Bulletin, 82,* 436-496.

Chan, W.T. (1986). *Chu Hsi and Neo-Confucianism.* Honolulu: University of Hawaii Press.

Fisher, I. (1965). *The Theory of Interest: As Determined by Impatience to Spend Income and Opportunity to Invest It.* New York: August M. Kelley (Originally published in 1935).

Johnson, R.D. and Leeworthy, D.M. (1988). The influence of product variables on discounting behavior. *Paper presented at the annual meeting of ORSA/TIMS,* Denver, 1988.

Loewenstein, G. (1988). Frames of mind in intertemporal choice. *Management Science, 34,* 200-214.

McCullough, J., Tan, C.T., and Wong, J.K. (1986). Effects of stereotyping in cross cultural research: Are the Chinese really Chinese? *Advances in Consumer Research, 13,* Richard Lutz (Ed.), Association for Consumer Research, 576-78.

Mischel, W. (1974). Processes in delay of gratification. In L. Berkowitz (Ed.), *Advances in Experimental Social Psychology.* New York: Academic Press, 249-292.

Mischel, W. and Metzner, R. (1962). Preference for delayed reward as a function of age, intelligence, and length of delay interval. *Journal of Abnormal and Social Psychology, 64(6),* 425-431.

Moore, C.A. (1967). *The Chinese Mind.* Honolulu: University of Hawaii Press.

Slovic, P. and Lichtenstein, S. (1968). Relative importance of probabilities and payoffs in risk taking. *Journal of Experimental Psychology Monograph, 3 (Part 2),* 1-18.

Smith, A.H. (1961). *Chinese Characteristics.* New York: Fleming H. Revell Co.

Strotz, R.H. (1955). Myopia and inconsistency in dynamic utility maximization. *Review of Economic Studies, 23*, 165-180.

Tan, C.T. and Farley, J.U. (1987). The impact of cultural patterns on cognition and intention in Singapore. *Journal of Consumer Research, 13*, 540-544.

Tse, D.K., Lee, K.H., Vertinsky, I., and Wehrung, D.A. (1988). Does culture matter? A cross-cultural study of executives' choice, decisiveness, and risk adjustment in international marketing. *Journal of Marketing, 52*, 81-95.

Note

This paper was previously published in Alain d'Astous (Ed.) *Proceedings of the Annual Conference of the Administrative Sciences Association of Canada: Marketing Division, 10*, Sherbrooke, Quebec: University of Sherbrooke, 1989, pp. 297-305.

CULTURAL DIFFERENCES IN DECISION MAKING

Robert N. Bontempo

Culture has been shown to be an important variable, affecting many aspects of the decision-making process, yet it is often overlooked in research on decision making. The current paper examines two examples of cultural differences in decision making, and proposes cultural level theoretical explanations for these differences. In the first case, cultural differences in the way individuals interpret probabilistic information is explained in terms of Uncertainty Avoidance, which reflects the ability to tolerate ambiguity. The second example examines cultural differences in the way multinational corporations decide to finance their operations; this is explained by cultural differences in Power Distance, which reflects the degree to which managers and corporate decision makers act as individuals or seek consultation with subordinates. In both cases special attention is paid to Singapore's standing on these dimensions of cultural variation, as compared to other countries.

Cross-cultural psychologists have shown that much of what we "know" about the world really depends on where we were raised; as a result, culture plays an important role in the decision-making process. The current paper will discuss some of these cultural differences in thought processes and describe some theories of cultural differentiation that may explain them. Decision-making examples will include how individuals perceive the riskiness of investments, and how organizations decide what level of operating debt is optimal. Psychologists have been aware for a long time that humans are imperfect decision makers. Our minds are limited in the amount of information we can pay attention to, store, organize, and recall. Because of these limitations we rely on mental shortcuts known as cognitive heuristics to help us. Although these heuristics are usually very useful tools, under some conditions they lead us to make systematic, predictable errors. For example, very dramatic, vivid events are easier to recall than simple, everyday events. This is why many people overestimate the danger of flying in an airplane; a very rare airline tragedy is easier to remember than the routine safe flights which occur everyday. This greater ease of recall of vivid events is known as the availability heuristic. Over the last 20 years, psychologists have investigated several heuristics, and they are discussed in detail in other articles in this volume. This article will focus on observed cultural differences in these mental shortcuts.

The Range of Cultural Differences

People are often surprised when they first find out how much their culture affects their thought processes. For example, consider the optical illusion presented in Figure 1. Most people perceive the line on top to be slightly longer than the line on the bottom. They are usually surprised, however, when they learn that this is learned as a result of the culture they were raised in, and has nothing to do with physical properties of light refraction or optics. Filipinos from rural areas are not fooled by the optical illusion,

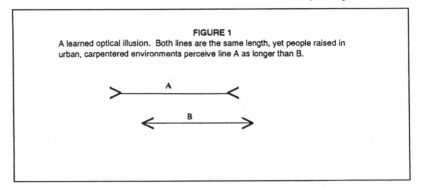

FIGURE 1
A learned optical illusion. Both lines are the same length, yet people raised in urban, carpentered environments perceive line A as longer than B.

and psychologists have explained our susceptibility to this illusion as an adaptation to growing up in a rectangular, carpentered environment.

Other researchers have documented a wide variety of cultural differences in psychological processes. For example, the language we speak plays an important role in how we perceive colors in the environment. Another example is that behavior that is considered perfectly appropriate in one culture may be defined as mental illness in another.

Also, the meanings of words have an important cultural component, even if the translation is perfect. Consider the meaning of the phrase "to be on time." In Japan, public clocks are very accurate (usually within 30 seconds of the actual time) and being "on time" means arriving within a few seconds of the appointed time. In Indonesia, public clocks are less accurate (usually within only 3 minutes of the correct time) and people are considered "on time" if they arrive within a couple minutes of the appointed time. In Brazil, a person is considered "on time" even if they arrive 30 minutes after the appointed time! (see Levine, 1988).

In addition to the way we perceive things, culture has an enormous impact on our values. For example, Leung and Bond (1984) have shown that under some conditions the Chinese prefer situations based on equality, where each member of a working group receives an identical payment regardless of input. Americans, on the other hand, tend to prefer outcomes based on equity, where each person is paid relative to their input.

The above examples are meant to provide a brief sampling of recent research in cross-cultural psychology. Because of important differences in the perception and interpretation of information, members of different cultures often come to very different conclusions, even when they are presented with identical information. Readers interested in learning more about these issues may want to consult Triandis' (1980) *Handbook of Cross-Cultural Psychology.*

Example 1: Cultural Differences in Probabilistic Reasoning

One area of decision making that has recently received attention from cross-cultural researchers concerns the way individuals use probabilistic information when evaluating uncertain or risky options. This research has important implications for a variety of financial and investment decisions, such as the way investors evaluate the components of an investment portfolio or stock market transactions. The next section of this paper will describe some of this research in detail and discuss a theory of cultural differences in probabilistic thinking.

One group of researchers (see Wright & Phillips, 1980) have reported strong cultural differences in probabilistic thinking, after studying people in Britain, Hong Kong, Indonesia, and Malaysia. One of the most important aspects of their research focuses on how well calibrated a decision maker is. Judgments are "well-calibrated" if the predictions about the frequency of events matches the actual frequency of occurrence. For example, consider a stockbroker who is evaluating 100 different stocks, each of which he or she says has a 70% chance of showing a profit over the next quarter. If the broker is perfectly calibrated, exactly 70 of these stocks will increase in value.

In this research, subjects from various countries are typically asked to answer questions such as "Is the Suez Canal over 100 miles long?" Subjects are then asked to indicate how sure of their answer they are by writing a percentage between 50 and 100. Results show large differences in calibration across cultures. British samples are less likely to give responses of "100%" than samples from Hong Kong, Indonesia, or Malaysia. Also, the British are better calibrated; their probability estimates of how likely the answer they gave was correct are more accurate. The Asian students show a strong tendency to use 100% estimates overconfidently. This occurs even though all groups give the correct answer about equally often.

Another important aspect of this research extends these findings from student samples to actual business decision makers. Wright and Phillips (1980) showed that the same pattern of findings occurs when they studied a sample of British civil servants, Hong Kong managers and Indonesian managers and company directors. Using a similar procedure results show the British sample was better calibrated than the Asian sample.

Another group of researchers (Yates, Zhu, Ronis, Wang, Shinotsuka, & Toda, 1989) employed a similar procedure with samples from Japan, the People's Republic of China (P.R.C.), and the United States. These authors again show important cultural differences in probabilistic thinking. Although the percentage of correct responses did not differ among the groups, the Japanese and American samples showed better calibration than the P.R.C. sample.

A Cultural Explanation

One of the most interesting and influential theories of cultural differences in psychology has been proposed by Geert Hofstede. In his book *Culture's Consequences* (1980) he reports his analysis of an employee survey administered by one of the largest multinational corporations in the world, where Hofstede worked as chief personnel psychologist. The data base included survey responses from 88,000 employees, whose occupational level ranged from upper management to unskilled workers. The sample was truly cross-cultural; respondents were from 66 different countries and spoke 20 different languages. Hofstede's approach relied on a technique known as factor analysis to explore cultural differences in the data. He showed that four basic dimensions of cultural variation were very useful in explaining differences in behavior across cultures. Each of these dimensions represents a continuum, along which each of the world's cultures can be placed. Knowing where a culture is located on a dimension allows us to make a wide range of predictions, including what type of management style is likely to be effective, or how an organization should be structured for maximum efficiency. Uncertainty Avoidance (UA) is the term given by Hofstede to one of the most important dimensions underlying observed cultural differences.

Uncertainty about future events is a basic fact of life which all cultures must face. Extreme uncertainty interferes with planning and problem solving, and societies try to reduce uncertainty to tolerable levels by developing technology, laws, and religious systems which provide both real and imagined control over an uncertain future.

In Hofstede's view, each culture's unique response to this fundamental issue has a profound impact on the basic thought processes of its members. Some cultures go to great lengths to minimize uncertainty in the environment; other cultures show greater tolerance for existing uncertainty. Hofstede analyzed the responses of managers from an MNC to statements and questions such as "Company rules should not be broken, even when the employee thinks it is in the company's best interest," and "How of-

TABLE 1
Uncertainty Avoidance Scores
from Hofstede (1980)

Greece	112	Thailand	64
Portugal	104	Iran	59
Belgium	94	Finland	59
Japan	92	Switzerland	58
Peru	87	Netherlands	53
France	86	Australia	51
Chile	86	Norway	50
Spain	86	South Africa	49
Argentina	86	New Zealand	49
Turkey	85	Canada	48
Mexico	82	U.S.A.	46
Israel	81	Philippines	44
Colombia	80	India	40
Venezuela	76	Great Britain	35
Brazil	76	Ireland	35
Italy	75	Hong Kong	29
Pakistan	70	Sweden	29
Austria	70	Denmark	23
Taiwan	69	Singapore	8
W. Germany	65		

ten do you feel nervous or tense at work?" Based on these responses, he was able to give each culture a UA score, and showed this correlated with observed differences for a wide variety of cultural differences in managerial decision making. For example, managers from low UA cultures tend to believe that there should be as few rules as possible, delegation to subordinates can be complete, and managers should be involved in strategy. Managers from high UA cultures tend to believe in the need for many written rules and regulations, initiative by subordinates must be kept under control, and that managers should be involved in details. A list of cultures and UA scores is presented in Table 1.

The mechanism that transmits a culture's orientation toward uncertainty is reflected in its formal institutions. For example, West Germany (which is relatively high in UA) has an extensive set of laws designed for emergencies that might occur (Notstandgesetz). In contrast, Great Britain (which is relatively low in UA) does not even have a written constitution. Hofstede further claims that a culture's orientation toward uncertainty is also reflected in its dominant religious institutions. For example, the high UA score of countries such as France, Mexico, Turkey, and Pakistan is reflected in the religion found there (Catholicism and Islam) which stresses absolute certainties regarding right and wrong (e.g., the infallibility of the Pope) and less tolerance of other religions ("Ours is the One True Faith"). This is in contrast to the religious orientation of low UA countries such as Singapore and India, whose religions (Buddhism and Hinduism) emphasize the impossibility of certainty and show greater tolerance for other beliefs.

UA and Probabilistic Reasoning

One goal of this paper is to suggest that UA may be useful in interpreting the observed cultural differences in probabilistic reasoning. Previous studies have tried to explain these differences using a variety of popular psychological variables including authoritarianism, conservatism, dogmatism, fatalism, intolerance of ambiguity, religious affiliation, occupation, and gender. None of these variables has shown any link to probabilistic reasoning. If we go back to the original papers described above and re-examine the data presented in light of UA., there is a startling result. Yates et al. (1989) report calibration scores for students from Japan, the U.S.A., and the P.R.C. Wright and Phillips present calibration scores for students from Great Britain, Hong Kong, and Malaysia. Unfortunately, Hofstede does

TABLE 2

Hit rates and UA scores for five countries. The hit rate scores for Japan and the U.S.A. are from student samples reported in Yates et al. (1989). Hit rate scores for Great Britain, Hong Kong, and Singapore are from student samples reported in Wright & Phillips (1980). UA scores are from Hofstede (1980).

COUNTRY	HIT RATE	UA SCORE
Japan	81.6	92
U.S.A.	80.8	46
Great Britain	78	35
Hong Kong	68	29
Singapore	57	8

not provide a UA score for the P.R.C., so this culture will have to be dropped from the subsequent analysis. Also, Hofstede does not provide a UA score for Malaysia, so for the following analysis, I will combine the data from Singapore (UA score) and Malaysia (calibration). Of course, this is not entirely satisfactory, although both countries share a common cultural background to some extent; they were previously integrated in the Federation of Malaysia and Singapore did not become an independent country until 1959.

To explore the relationship between UA and calibration, the data from the previous calibration studies was re-examined. Table 2 presents the hit rate scores from the 5 cultures for assessed probabilities of 1. The hit rate tells us, for questions for which individuals expressed a 100% confidence of being correct, how often they actually gave the correct answer. The UA scores are taken from Hofstede's (1980) study of managers from each country. The rank order correlation is 1.0, the Pearson correlation is .79, $p < .05$. This means that 62% of the fluctuation in probabilistic reasoning can be accounted for by changes in the UA score. The p-value means that there is less than 5 chances in 100 that this result is due to chance. The same pattern is present for hit rate scores for assessed probabilities less than 1, although the difference is not as dramatic.

These findings suggest that cultural differences in Uncertainty Avoidance may explain observed cultural differences in probabilistic reasoning. Of course, the data presented here are only a first step. The relationship between UA and cultural differences in another important decision process, risk perception, are discussed in more detail in Bontempo and Bottom (submitted for publication).

Example 2: Cultural Differences in Capital Structure

Another interesting example where cultural factors may influence decision making concerns how firms decide to finance their operations. Financial managers have reported systematic differences in the capital structures of multinational firms headquartered in different countries. This section of the paper will describe cultural differences in financial management in terms of another of Hofstede's dimensions of cultural variation, Power Distance.

The capital structure of a multinational firm is often described in terms of the debt/equity ratio. This is defined as the firm's total debt to total assets at book value. Initial

TABLE 3
Power Distance Scores from Hofstede (1980)

Philippines	94	Japan	54
Mexico	81	Italy	50
Venezuela	81	South Africa	49
India	77	Argentina	49
Singapore	74	U.S.A.	40
Brazil	69	Canada	39
Hong Hong	68	Netherlands	38
France	68	Australia	36
Turkey	68	W.Germany	35
Columbia	67	Great Britain	35
Belgium	65	Switzerland	34
Peru	64	Finland	33
Thailand	64	Norway	31
Chile	63	Sweden	31
Portugal	63	Ireland	28
Greece	60	New Zealand	22
Iran	58	Denmark	18
Taiwan	58	Israel	13
Spain	57	Austria	11
Pakistan	55		

studies tried to explain differences in capital structure in terms of the type of industry (e.g., textiles, automobiles, or steel production) but results were inconclusive. Literature reviews (Stanley, 1981; Collins and Sekely, 1983) examined several economic variables such as type of industry, domestic tax rate, domestic inflation rate, and size of country, but were unable to account for cultural differences in capital structure.

In light of the failure of researchers using economic variables to explain these differences, Sekely and Collins (1988) suggest "Given that no prior study has established a significant relationship between an economic variable and international differences in capital structure, and given the conclusions of some earlier works that cultural factors must play a role,...If some underlying relationship among countries can be shown to influence capital structure, future research should include more variables than simply economic ones in attempting to explain capital structure differences." What follows is just such an attempt.

Sekely and Collins (1988) present debt ratios for 677 companies in 9 industries from 23 countries. These firms represent the 10 largest for each industry/country combination, as reported in Moody's Industrial Manual and Moody's International Manual. Analysis revealed that the debt ratio did not vary systematically across industries; as a result, subsequent analysis is based on debt ratios averaged across industry. Table 4 presents the debt ratios for 23 countries, in increasing order of debt (Singapore is the lowest, Italy is the highest).

A Cultural Explanation

Recall that the previous section of the paper attempted to explain cultural differences in probabilistic reasoning using one of Hofstede's dimensions of cultural variation, Uncertainty Avoidance. This section will describe another of these dimensions, known as Power Distance.

Just as with uncertainty, all cultures must wrestle with the problem of the relative equality of its members. The establishment of a hierarchy among group mem-

TABLE 4

Debt Ratios and Power Distance scores for selected countries. Debt Ratio values from Sekely & Collins (1988). Power Distance values from Hofstede (1980).

COUNTRY	DEBT RATIO	POWER DISTANCE
Singapore	.34	74
Argentina	.38	49
Australia	.46	36
Chile	.46	36
Mexico	.47	81
South Africa	.50	49
Brazil	.54	69
Great Britain	.55	35
United States	.55	40
Canada	.58	39
India	.60	77
Switzerland	.60	34
W. Germany	.62	35
Denmark	.63	18
Spain	.64	57
Sweden	.68	31
France	.71	68
Finland	.72	33
Pakistan	.72	55
Norway	.74	31
Italy	.76	50

bers is one of the most fundamental functions of a society. All social creatures, from ants to chickens to baboons, have developed sophisticated means of establishing the "pecking order" among members. In some social groups, such as communes, providing all members with equal access to resources is given priority. In other cultures, such as a theocracy with a leader who is believed to be divine, preferential treatment of those in power is considered desirable. Thus, the extent to which inequality among members exists results from a basic value judgment for which societies have reached different conclusions.

Hofstede observed differences across cultures in his large sample of managers which seemed to reflect this basic value question. He found systematic cultural differences in the way managers of a multinational corporation responded to questions such as "How often are employees afraid to express disagreement with their managers?", and their expressed preferences for autocratic, democratic, or paternalistic managers. From these responses, Hofstede calculated a Power Distance (PD) score for each of the cultures in his sample. Power Distance scores for all cultures considered in this study are presented in Table 4.

Hofstede has shown that a culture's PD score is a useful predictor of a wide variety of cultural differences in managerial decision making. Managers from low PD cultures feel that super- and sub-ordinate workers are basically alike, inequality in society should be minimized, and that all people should have equal rights. Managers from high PD cultures tend to feel that super- and sub-ordinate workers are fundamentally different, that there should be an order of inequality in the world in which everyone has a rightful place, and that some individuals are entitled to privileges.

The importance of these basic value differences is often overlooked. For example, managers from low PD cultures, where a participative, consultative management style is popular, are often confused when dealing with subordinates from high PD cultures. These workers prefer an autocratic or paternalistic manager, and interpret attempts at participative or consultative management as evidence that the people at the top don't know what they're doing. This point becomes especially relevant below.

PD and Cultural Differences in the Debt Ratio

If PD has been shown to affect the type of decision-making process that managers and workers in one of the world's largest MNC's prefer, can we explain some of the results of organizational decisions in terms of PD? Specifically, can the financial decisions that account for cultural differences in debt ratios be explained in terms of PD?

Recall that recent reviews of literature suggest that several economic variables are unsatisfactory in explaining this difference. However, the correlation between the debt ratios and PD scores presented in Table 4 is -.46, $p < .05$. This means that 21 percent of the fluctuation in debt ratio can be accounted for by changes in PD. In general, the lower the Power Distance score of the country in which the MNC has its headquarters, the higher the debt/equity ratio of the firm will be. As the Power Distance score increases, the debt/equity ratio decreases. The p-value indicates that the probability that this finding is due to chance is less than 5 in 100.

Discussion

Most people who interact closely with members of other cultures quickly come to the realization that "they think differently than I do." Cross-cultural psychologists have identified a broad range of ways in which culture affects the way people think. This paper described two such areas and suggested explanations based on theories of cultural differences.

At the individual level, the way people interpret and process probabilistic information differs dramatically across cultures. Evidence for cultural differences in calibration has been gathered from both students and professionals including civil servants, business managers, and company directors. Stockbrokers and financial planners, who continuously make probabilistic assessments about uncertain information, are examples of professionals who would be especially susceptible to this problem. Yates et al. (1989) suggest that "cross-national miscommunication about uncertainty is virtually guaranteed" (p. 169).

Observed country differences in calibration may be explained by an underlying difference in culture. All societies must develop ways of responding to an inherently uncertain environment, and Hofstede (1980) suggests that the particular value judgments a culture makes in response to uncertainty has a profound effect on the way its individuals make decisions. This paper suggests that observed cultural differences in calibration are closely related to cultural differences in Hofstede's measure of Uncertainty Avoidance.

Samples from Singapore show the lowest measured Uncertainty Avoidance scores. Hong Kong is also very low. Samples from these countries also show the lowest hit rate scores and calibration rates. Subjects from Japan and the U.S.A. show both higher hit rate and higher Uncertainty Avoidance scores. Uncertainty Avoidance appears to be closely linked to cultural differences in probabilistic thinking; other attempts to explain this based on years of education, occupation, religion, and a variety of psychological variables have failed.

Hofstede (1980) has demonstrated that managers from low UA countries such as Singapore and Hong Kong are "more willing to make individual and risky decisions" (p. 187) and have "higher tolerance for ambiguity" (p. 177). This type of mind set may account for the overconfidence in probability assessment found in subjects from low UA countries. Of course, these initial results are speculative; more research is needed. A more detailed analysis of the relationship between risk perception and Uncertainty Avoidance is provided by Bontempo and Bottom (submitted for publication).

At the organizational level, cultural differences have been observed in decisions about financial management. The amount of capital organizations borrow to finance their operations varies dramatically across cultures. These decisions about the optimal debt/equity ratio seem to be independent of the type of industry involved. Furthermore, these financing decisions have not been explained by tax rates, inflation rates, or other economic variables.

The underlying dimension of cultural variation known as Power Distance may explain some of the observed cultural differences in capital structure of MNC's. Corporations based in low Power Distance countries generally have higher debt/equity ratios. Hofstede (1980) has shown that managers in low Power Distance countries express a preference for a participative decision-making style, implementing policy after consulting with employees. Managers from high Power Distance countries tend to be autocratic, and employees are less likely to raise objections to proposals from the boss.

This may be reflected in the amount of responsibility attributed to organizational decision makers. Autocratic, individual managers from high Power Distance countries may bear more responsibility for decisions made by their organizations, and so may be reluctant to borrow heavily to finance operations. In low Power Distance cultures, where organizational decision-making responsibility is more consultative and democratic, responsibility may be more diffused, allowing firms to be more heavily into debt to finance operations. Again, the results presented here are only speculative; more research is needed to more precisely identify the mechanism that links cultural differences in the debt/equity ratio and Power Distance.

References

Bontempo, R.N. and Bottom, W.P. *Cultural Differences in Risk Perception*. Submitted for publication.

Collins, J.M. and Sekely, W.S. (1983). The relationship of headquarters, country, and industry classification to financial structure. *Financial Management, Autumn:* 45-51.

Hofstede, G. (1980). *Culture's Consequences and International Differences in Work-related Values.* Beverly Hills: Sage.

Leung, K. and Bond, M. (1984). The impact of cultural collectivism on reward allocation. *Journal of Personality and Social Psychology, 4,* 793-804.

Levine, R.V. (1988). The pace of life across cultures. In J. McGrath (Ed.), *The Social Psychology of Time.* Newbury Park: Sage.

Sekely, W.S. and Collins, J.M. (1988). Cultural influences on international capital structure. *Journal of International Business Studies, Autumn,* 87-100.

Stanley, M.T. (1981). Capital structure and cost of capital for the multi-national firm. *Journal of International Business, Spring/Summer:* 103-120.

Triandis, H.C. (1980). *Handbook of Cross-Cultural Psychology.* Boston: Allyn & Bacon.

Wright, G.N. and Phillips, L.D. (1980). Cultural variation in probabilistic thinking. *International Journal of Psychology, 15*, 239-257.

Yates, F.J., Zhu, Y., Ronis, D.L., Wang, D., Shinotsuka, H., and Toda, M. (1989). Probability judgment accuracy: China, Japan, and the United States. *Organizational Behavior and Human Decision Processes, 43*, 145-171.

Note

A reduced version of this article appeared in *Commentary, Vol 8, No 3 & 4, June 1990* (published by National University of Singapore Society).

AN INTER-CULTURAL COMPARISON OF AUDITORS' RISK ASSESSMENT JUDGMENTS

Theodore J. Mock and Mary T. Washington

This paper presents the results of an inter-cultural study of the degree to which decision makers attend to differences in evidence reliability, using cascaded or hierachical inference theory as a framework. The findings are based on an audit task (experiment) using forty-nine experienced auditors. The results indicate that Norwegian auditors' judgments did differ from the the judgments of United States auditors, although none of the differences were statistically significant at traditional levels of significance. However, the judgments of both the Norwegian and United States auditors were significantly different from theoretical values computed using cascaded inference theory. Judgments of Norwegian and United States auditors receiving the higher level of evidence reliability were significantly less than theoretical values. For those auditors responding to the lower level of evidence reliability, judgments of the United States auditors were less than theoretical values, while judgments of the Norwegian auditors were greater than the theoretical values. Several of these findings differ from previous studies in judgment and decision making research. These findings raise some concerns for multinational financial statements and management audits and for judgment and decision-making research in general.

Auditors collect, evaluate and aggregate evidence from numerous sources as a basis for an opinion on a set of financial statements. The auditor usually cannot observe directly the economic actions and events that underlie financial statement assertions, so some consideration should be given to the reliability of the source of evidence the auditor evaluates.

Source reliability is an important issue to auditors because most sources of audit evidence would rarely be perfectly reliable. For example, evidence from confirmation procedures (e.g., customers confirming amounts owed to a firm being audited) was once thought to be highly reliable because it is obtained from a source independent of the firm being audited. However, empirical research has found that customers may confirm a balance without verifying its accuracy (Sorkin, 1977), or may be biased toward confirming errors in their favor (i.e., errors that understate the amount they owe; Caster, 1989).

One source of information that an auditor often relies on is evidence concerning the internal accounting control system. Most accounting systems are designed with a set of controls or checks and balances designed to help insure accurate information processing. When the auditor is evaluating evidence obtained through review of information system documentation, some consideration should be given to the reliability of the internal control system, and that evaluation should be incorporated into the auditor's assessment of the likelihood of undetected material error.

Although a number of studies have examined how the auditor evaluates system reliability (Ashton, 1974; Ashton and Kramer, 1980; Ashton and Brown, 1980; Hamilton and Wright, 1982; Kaplan and Reckers, 1984; Trotman, Yetton, and Zimmer, 1983), and the relationship between that evaluation and planned audit work (Joyce, 1976; Mock and Turner, 1981; Gaumnitz, Nunamaker, Burdick, and Thomas, 1982; Tabor, 1983; Kaplan, 1985; Srinidhi and Vasarhelyi, 1986), few studies have examined the auditor's consideration of internal control system reliability when evaluating evidence that has passed through the system.

This paper presents the results of an inter-cultural study of the degree to which auditors attend to differential internal control system reliability, using cascaded or hierarchical inference theory as a framework. Cascaded inference theory makes a clear distinction between an event or datum itself and a report of that event. When dealing with reports of events (as auditors usually do), it becomes necessary to evaluate the reliability of the information source as well as the diagnostic impact of the information itself. Considering the source's reliability introduces more uncertainty into the evidence evaluation process as Schum and DuCharme (1971, p. 112) note:

"Cascaded inference is characterized by extra aggregation or information-processing steps necessary to incorporate the additional uncertainty generated by sources of information which are less than perfectly accurate or reliable."

Whether cultural influences result in different audit judgments should also be an important issue, since multinational audits are becoming increasingly more common. This study focuses on a comparison of judgments made by Norwegian auditors with those made by United States auditors. Since Norwegian audit training is similar to that given to United States auditors (auditing courses are often taught using United States texts and auditing standards are often modeled after United States auditing standards), systematic judgment differences may be due to cultural influences.

The principal finding of this study is that Norwegian auditors' judgments of the likelihood of material error in a particular account did differ from the judgments of United States auditors, although not all differences were statistically significant at traditional levels of significance. Judgments of auditors from both countries were also compared to theoretical values computed using cascaded inference theory. There were some inter-cultural judgment difference. Although it cannot be concluded unequivocally that these judgment differences are due to cultural influences, the results reported in this paper should be of concern to those audit firms and companies with international operations. If audit opinions concerning either operations or financial statement presentation are aggregated over international operations, internal inconsistencies in assessments of material error due to cultural differences could bias such opinions.

Description of Experiment

Forty-nine auditors (35 from the United States and 14 from Norway) participated in the experiment. The Norwegian participants were graduate students with two to three years of professional (auditing and accounting) experience participating in an Advanced Auditing program at the Norwegian School of Economics and Business Administration. The United States participants (averaging 3.5 years of audit experience) were auditors attending in-firm training courses with four international audit firms. The experimental materials required participants to provide two evaluations of the likelihood that there was not a material error in a retail stereo store's inventory account, which was described as a critical or "material" audit area. The first evaluation (prior assessment) was based on background information on the client and the inventory account, evaluation of client personnel, some limited financial data, a description of the internal control system for the acquisition and payment cycle, a description of the physical controls over inventory, and details of the results of the physical inventory. The second evaluation (posterior assessment) was made after reviewing information concerning internal control system reliability and results of tests of details relating to the valuation objective. Internal control system reliability (source reliability) was the primary variable manipulated (with two levels—99% reliable versus 80% reliable) in a between-subjects design.

Hypothesis

The primary research issue was whether assessments of the likelihood of no material error would decline as internal control system reliability declined. Prior research in both psychology and auditing has found that decision makers do not always appropriately evaluate information from less than perfectly reliable sources. Psychology research has found that decision makers overvalue information from less than perfectly reliable sources (Snapper & Fryback, 1971; Schum, DuCharme & DePitts, 1973; Youssef & Peterson, 1973). Auditing research has found that decision makers will incorporate consideration of source reliability in evidence evaluation if the possibility of differential reliability is made explicit in the experimental design (Joyce & Biddle, 1981; Bamber, 1983). This particular finding is somewhat disturbing because auditors often encounter information from only one source at a time.

There is no prior research dealing specifically with whether auditors incorporate consideration of internal control system reliability in their assessments of the likelihood of material error. However, the first hypothesis is predicated on the assumption that the participants will realize the importance of attending to source reliability and, therefore, will adjust their assessments accordingly:

H1: Participants' estimates of the likelihood that there is not a material pricing error in the inventory account will decline as the reliability of the internal control system declines.

Although audit standards acknowledge that sources of audit evidence could vary in reliability, and that auditors should consider the possibility of differential source reliability in evaluating evidence, very little guidance is provided concerning precisely how the auditor should incorporate source reliability in his/her judgments. This research posits cascaded inference theory (or multi-stage Bayesian inference, Von Winterfeldt & Edwards, 1986) as a normatively correct means of incorporating source reliability in evidence evaluation. Although it is not proposed that auditors' decisions will either reflect direct application of cascaded inference theory or result in evaluations that are exactly the same as the theoretical values, the theoretical values are useful in assessing whether participants seem to overvalue or undervalue evidence from a less than perfectly reliable source.

As mentioned, psychology research using cascaded inference theory as a normative standard has found a tendency to overvalue evidence when source reliability is an issue. Based on those results, the second hypothesis concerns the accuracy of participants' judgments as compared with cascaded inference theory values:

H2: Participants' judgments of the likelihood of no material pricing error in the inventory account will be greater than the theoretical (cascaded inference) value.

The third hypothesis looks at whether inter-cultural judgment differences are apparent for these two countries and this particular task. Inter-cultural judgment consistency should be important to audit firms because, when dealing with a client with international operations, all subordinate auditor judgments will be, at some point, incorporated into the final audit opinion. To the extent that systematic cultural differences exist in judgments, systematic biases could be present in the audit opinion formulation process.

Since the Norwegian participants are exposed to many of the same educational influences as the United States participants (e.g., use of United States audit texts, training by the same international auditing firms), it is hypothesized that there will be no inter-cultural judgment differences:

H3: There will be no significant judgment differences between Norwegian participants and United States participants.

Statistical Analysis and Results

The experimental design was a 2 x 2 fixed effects factorial with two levels of internal control system reliability (99% reliable and 80% reliable) and two countries providing participants (Norway and the United States). The primary dependent variable was each participant's estimate of the likelihood of no material pricing error

TABLE 1
Summary Analysis of Variance Results
Subject Log Likelihood Ratio

SOURCE	DF	MS	F	p
Internal Control Reliability	1	.0077	0.03	.8592
Country	1	.6189	2.57	.1160
Reliability	1	.0799	0.33	.5676
Error	45	.2409		

in the inventory account after review of all information. The likelihood was calculated using the participant's prior and posterior odds of no material error. Analysis was conducted after computing the log of each of these likelihood ratios.

Table 1 contains the analysis of variance results for all subjects using the log of the subjects likelihood ratio as the dependent variable. There are no statistically significant effects at traditional levels with only the country (cultural) effect approaching significance (p = .116). A graphical comparison of mean judgments (see Figure 1) indicates that the Norwegian participants reacted differently from the United States participants.

Figure 1 seems to imply greater conservatism on the part of United States

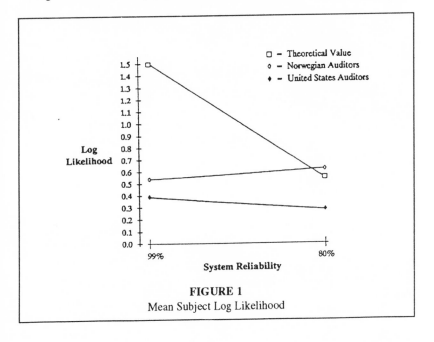

FIGURE 1
Mean Subject Log Likelihood

participants, as well as a predicted decline in log likelihood at the lower internal control system reliability level. Therefore, the graphical data support Hypothesis 1 for the United States participants, but not for the Norwegian participants. There also seems to be evidence supporting rejection of Hypothesis 3 (no inter-country differences in judgments), based on Figure 1. However, these differences were only significant at p = .12.

To test the second hypothesis, a cascaded inference theory value was calculated for

TABLE 2
Summary of Analysis of Variance Results
Subject Log Likelihood Ratio

SOURCE	DF	MS	F	R
Internal Control Reliability	1	8.3212	35.54	.0001
Country	1	0.6189	2.57	.1160
Reliability x Country	1	0.0799	0.33	.5676
Error	45	0.2409		

each of the two internal control system reliability levels (see Washington, 1989 for details concerning these calculations, and Von Winterfeldt and Edwards, 1986, pp. 163-204 or Schum and DuCharme, 1971 for derivation of the cascaded inference formula). The theoretical value (1.5 for the 99% reliability level and 0.56 for the 80%

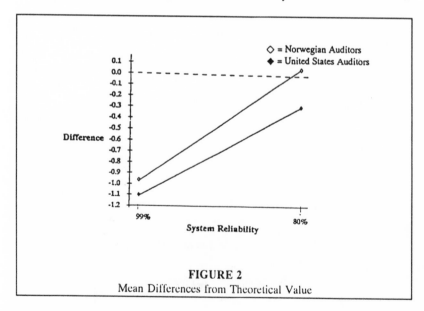

FIGURE 2
Mean Differences from Theoretical Value

reliability level) was then subtracted from each participant's log likelihood ratio, which resulted in a difference variable. Analysis of variance was used to analyze these difference scores.

Table 2 contains the results of the analysis of variance for the difference variable. The participants' significance levels on mean difference scores were $p = .0001$ for the two levels of evidence (control system) reliability and $p = .12$ for the country effects.

Graphical analysis of the mean responses (see Figure 2) illustrates that, for both United States and Norway participants, difference scores were much larger for the 99% reliability level than for the 80% reliability level. Log likelihood judgments for participants from both countries were significantly less than the theoretical value for the 99% reliability level, but tended toward the theoretical value for the 80% reliability level. As found for the log likelihood judgments, United States participants provided somewhat more conservative judgments than the Norwegian participants.

In contrast to psychology studies, which found that participant's judgments were almost always greater than the theoretical cascaded inference values, the results of this study seem to imply a tendency to undervalue information from less than perfectly reliable sources. However, the mean judgment for one of the Norwegian groups (control system reliability of 80%) was slightly greater than the theoretical cascaded inference value. The next section discusses potential implications of these results as well as limitations of the experiment.

Discussion

Most previous cascaded inference studies have employed relatively abstract judgment tasks and students as participants. Participants in this study had prior auditing experience and provided judgments in a task that mirrored a portion of an actual audit. Greater task realism may have resulted in auditors exhibiting an inherent tendency toward conservatism, resulting in a general undervaluing of evidence in most cases.

Normatively, participant judgments would be expected to be close to the theoretical values. In this experiment, however, a general tendency to undervalue audit evidence was observed (more so in the higher control system reliability groups than in the lower reliability groups). The observed undervaluing of audit evidence may have occurred because participants perceived the consequences of overvaluing audit evidence as greater than the consequences of undervaluing audit evidence. Overvaluing audit evidence may be associated with overstated audit assurance levels. Although overstated audit assurance levels are not necessarily a sufficient condition for undetected material errors, if errors do become apparent later, the auditor faces potential costs associated with loss of client fees, litigation fees if lawsuits result, and loss of firm reputation due to the likely publication of the audit failure.

Differences were also observed ($p = .12$) in judgments between participants from the two different countries. This is somewhat surprising, since education, training, professional literature and standards are similar in these particular countries. Although it is not possible to investigate the source of these judgment differences in the current study, it may be that Norwegian and United States auditors simply have different risk propensities, levels and type of experience, or that there are other cultural influences that result in different judgments.

It is also possible that there are differences in the audit environment between these two countries that may influence judgments. For example, the United States auditors were from very large audit firms in a major city. They may have been accustomed to auditing larger clients, or may have responded according to their particular firm's policies. In contrast, Norwegian participants' experience is probably based on auditing smaller clients (or smaller divisions of multinational firms). The influence of Norwegian audit firm policies is an issue for future research. However, as mentioned, to the extent that judgments of auditors from different countries will eventually be aggregated for a multinational corporation, it should be important to audit firms to become aware of possible sources of judgment differences that do not arise from differences in the audit context.

The study was a laboratory experiment dealing with evidence aggregation for one audit objective. As with most laboratory experiments, the limited scope of the experimental materials results in some limitations that should be pointed out. First, because the auditor generally collects evidence from several sources pertaining to a particular audit objective, it is difficult to determine whether responses were affected by participants' belief that other audit procedures would provide more powerful evidence concerning this audit objective. The study focused on a relatively common and important audit procedure (a pricing test) with which participants from both countries should be familiar. Future research could focus on how auditors aggregate evidence obtained from several sources using different audit procedures.

A second limitation arises from possible interpretation differences due to presenting the case materials in English to the Norwegian participants. Although this would be a potential problem in any inter-cultural study, the impact in this study was probably minimal since the Norwegian participants did not express any particular difficulty in completing the case and were attending an audit course taught in English.

Finally, there is a difference in number of subjects between the two countries (n = 14 from Norway and n = 35 from the United States). Such differences affect the power of statistical tests and imply that replicating the study with a larger Norwegian subject group might be worthwhile.

References

Ashton, R.H. (1974). An experimental study of internal control judgments. *Journal* of Accounting Research, 43-157.

Ashton, R.H. and Brown, P.R. (1980). Descriptive modeling of auditors' internal control judgments: Replications and Extension. Journal of Accounting Research, 269-277.

Ashton, R.H. and Kramer, S.L. (1980). Students as surrogates in behavioral accounting research: Some evidence. Journal of Accounting Research, 1-15.

Bamber, E.M. (1983). Expert judgment in the audit team: A source reliability approach. Journal of Accounting Research, 396-412.

Caster, P. (1989). An Empirical Study of Accounts Receivable Confirmations as Audit Evidence. Paper presented at the USC/DH&S Audit Judgment Symposium, Newport Beach.

Gaumnitz, B.R., Nunamaker, T.R., Burdick, J.J., and Thomas, M.R. (1982). Auditor consensus in internal control evaluation and audit program planning. Journal of Accounting Research, 745-755.

Hamilton, R.E. and Wright, W.F. (1982). Internal control judgments and effects of experience: Replications and extensions. Journal of Accounting Research, 756-765.

Joyce, E.J. (1976). Expert judgment in audit program planning. Journal of Accounting Research, 29-60.

Joyce, E.J. and Biddle, G.C. (1981). Are auditor's judgments sufficiently regressive? Journal of Accounting Research, 323-349.

Kaplan, S.E. (1985). An examination of the effects of environment and explicit internal control evaluation on planned audit hours. Auditing: A Journal of Practice and Theory, 12-25.

Kaplan, S.E. and Reckers, P.M.J. (1984). An empirical examination of auditors' initial planning processes. Auditing: A Journal of Practice and Theory, 1-19.

Mock, T.J., and Turner, J. (1981). Internal Accounting Control Evaluation and Auditor Judgment, American Institute of Certified Public Accountants.

Schum, D.A. and DuCharme, M. (1971). Comments on the relationship between the impact and the reliability of evidence. Organizational Behavior and Human Performance, 111-131.

Schum, D.A., DuCharme, M., and Depitts, K. (1973). Research on human multistage probabilistic inference processes. Organizational Behavior and Human Performance, 404-423.

Snapper, K.J. and Fryback, D.G. (1971). Inferences based on unreliable reports. Journal of Experimental Psychology, 401-404.

Sorkin, H.L. (1977). An Empirical Study of Three Confirmation Techniques: Desirability of Expanding the Respondent's Decision Field. Unpublished Ph. D. Dissertation (University of Minnesota).

Srinidhi, B.N. and Vasarhelyi, M.A. (1986). Auditor judgment concerning establishment of substantive tests based on internal control reliability. Auditing: A Journal of Practice and Theory, 64-76.

Tabor, R.H. (1983). Internal control evaluations and audit program revisions: Some additional evidence. Journal of Accounting Research, 348-354.

Trotman, K.T., Yetton, P.W., and Zimmer, I.R. (1983). Individual and group judgments of internal control systems. *Journal of Accounting Research*, 286-292.

Von Winterfeldt, D. and Edwards, W. (1986). *Decision Analysis and Behavioral Research*. New York: Cambridge University Press.

Washington, M.T. (1989). Incorporating internal control system reliability in audit evidence evaluation using cascaded inference theory. *Graduate School of Management Working Paper* #AC89012, University of California, Irvine.

Youssef, A. and Peterson, C. (1973). Intuitive cascaded inference. *Organizational Behavior and Human Performance*, 349-358.

Acknowledgment

Helpful comments on this paper were received from Professors Paul Caster and Karen Pincus.

EARLY CHILDHOOD TEACHER DECISION MAKING: A FOCUS ON TEACHER INVOLVEMENT IN CHILDREN'S PEER INTERACTION

Vianne McLean

An increasing volume of research is directed towards teacher thinking, but few studies have examined teacher decision making at the level of curriculum implementation. This paper reports on a study that combined interview and observation techniques to access teacher decision making and to examine the connections between teacher belief and contextual factors in everyday classroom events. The participants were four Australian early childhood teachers and the study focused on their involvement in children's peer interactions. The paper provides a methodological overview and briefly discusses findings, suggesting that the relation between a teacher's beliefs and contextual factors is an intricate, complex and multi-directional one.

"Good teaching is not, it seems, a question of right methods or behaviors, but a problem-solving matter, having to do with the teacher's unique use of self as he/she finds appropriate solutions to carry out the teacher's own and society's purposes." Combs (1978, p. 558)

The study of teaching reported in this paper (McLean, 1986) could be described as an intentionalist, constructivist or interpretive investigation (Fenstermacher, 1986; Magoon, 1982; Phillips, 1981) that set out to examine some of the ways in which a teacher's beliefs and intentions interacted with contextual factors reflexively to create a particular social reality in a preschool setting. Like other studies of its kind, it did not attempt to produce (to use Bolster's 1983, p. 305 phrase): "experimental derivation of a selected number of elements whose relationships could be replicated elsewhere," but instead used an ideographic focus to try to achieve an in-depth understanding of a small number of preschool teachers, their contexts and curricula. Schubert (1989, p. 284), in reviewing studies with a similar focus, writes:

"...we are coming closer to a description of teacher lore that embraces the commentaries and stories of teachers and reveals sources of meaning and direction in their lives and work."

Studies of real-life teaching have suggested it is a phenomenon that is often fraught with inconsistency, disequilibrium, uncertainty and ambiguity (Bolster, 1983; Good & Weinstein, 1986; Greenberg, 1969; Margolin, 1982). As Philip Jackson (1968, p. 167) wrote: "(The teacher) must be content with doing not what he knows is right, but what he thinks or feels is the most appropriate action in a particular situation." This conception is quite different from the image of teaching that is found in many pre-service teacher education texts, where the teacher is portrayed as being possessed of a calm certainty about what is going on and what will happen next.

Given the complexity of teaching, it is clear the researcher cannot hope to observe all aspects of teaching. Choices must be made about which aspects of teaching will be the focus of observation. But this initial selection must be made with great care, if it is to provide a means of accessing the underlying meanings teaching holds for the teacher.

Such penetration would seem to require an initial scope that is sufficiently narrow to allow detailed observation and recording of the surface (behavioral) interaction; yet sufficiently broad to encourage teachers to reflect upon the meanings, not only of this particular interaction, but also their connections with children in a broader sense.

In this study, it was decided to focus observations on the teacher's involvement in children's peer interactions. In early childhood education, concerns related to the child's social and emotional development are not part of a "hidden curriculum," (Combs, Avila, & Purkey, 1978; Evans, 1981; Hosford, 1980; Jackson, 1968; Overly, 1970) they are an acknowledged part of the normal curriculum.

Despite this acknowledgment, there has been little research or writing focused on early childhood teachers' actions in attempting to foster children's social development. Early childhood practitioners select their strategies for this area from a smorgasbord of theoretical models. It seems they do not feel a need to limit themselves to a particular theoretical approach. This diversity of available options suggested that for this study, the teacher's attempts to facilitate social development might provide a suitable "window" through which to access teacher decision making. A further narrowing of focus occurred to the teacher's involvement in children's peer interaction, because this aspect seemed to capture something of the complexity of early childhood education interactions, where dyadic interaction between teacher and child is only one of many types of interactional pattern.

The participants in this study were four experienced early childhood teachers of acknowledged competence. For each teacher, approximately 1,000 pages of data were accumulated during 60-65 hours of observation in each setting and approximately 7 hours of interviews with each teacher.

To provide for triangulation of data, a number of data-gathering strategies were utilized. Observations were of two major types:

(a) Event sampling was used to record detailed narrative descriptions of each occasion when the teacher became involved in children's peer interactions. These narratives were constructed using audio tapes of dialogue, supported by site notes of contextual factors and non-verbal communication.

(b) Bearing in mind Erikson and Shultz's (1981) concerns with the fragmentation and decontextualization that occurs with this type of selective observation, a "stream-of-behavior chronicle" (Le Compte & Goertz, 1984) of the entire session also was kept. This less-detailed record noted aspects of the physical environment, the number and spread of children and adults in the environment, the general atmosphere of the group and any other salient aspects of the context. In writing accounts of each session, the detailed event records were embedded in the chronicle, so that the entire session became a single narrative—often taking 50-60 typed pages to describe.

Interviews also followed two distinct formats. In the type labelled "conversations," the observational narratives were used as the basis for discussion, in a procedure Erikson and Schultz (1981), and Green and Wallat (1981) have identified as a "second-generation interview." This technique uses a record of behavior (such as videotape, audiotape, or in this case, written records) as a means of helping teachers to reflect on those events and verbalize what are usually tacit understandings (Polanyi, 1967; Williams, Neff & Finkelstein, 1981).

These sessions were called "conversations" because they were highly interactive. Often, both participants (teacher and researcher) came to the session with recollections of the observed situation to discuss and these talks became a time to put together the "outside-in perspective" of the researcher, with the "inside-out perspective" of the teacher (Yamamoto, 1984). This was also an opportunity for "member-checking" (Dawson, 1979; Lincoln & Guba, 1985; Owens, 1982) when emerging patterns or constructs could be discussed with the teacher-participant.

The other form of interview was what Massarik (1981) has described as a "depth" interview. These low-structure sessions explored the teacher's image-of-self-as-teacher, and covered such areas as the teacher's recollections of her professional biography, life experiences, and the connections perceived between her own human development and teaching activities. Much of the practical knowledge accessed during these interviews was seldom articulated and the use of multiple open-ended interviews enabled these teachers to return to their important issues again and again, as they clarified points in their own thinking.

In common with other studies of this type, categories for data coding and analysis emerged from the data itself. An extensive preliminary investigation with a single teacher had established a basic system, but new coding categories emerged, and others were collapsed or discarded as the study proceeded. For each teacher, the interview data were analyzed first, because it seemed that the conversations and interviews would suggest many categorization schemes for observations that would not be evident from the observational record alone. This decision reflected the assumption that teachers are thinking, theorizing, intentionalist creatures whose behavior cannot be understood without consideration of their own meanings (Fenstermacher, 1978, 1986; Giroux, 1985; Schubert, 1989).

As data gathering commenced, the preliminary coding system for interview data centered on three global areas:

(a) Comments on children—their competence, individual differences and the pressures they face in today's hurried life-styles.

(b) Comments on the interface that occurred when teacher and children came together in the preschool.

(c) Comments on the teacher. This was the largest category and covered such aspects as biography, teaching activities not directly involving children and professional networks.

This global framework was used throughout the data analysis, with a basic core of categories that was identical for all teachers. In order to capture the idiosyncratic differences between teachers, other categories were allowed to emerge from the data, so that the coding system for each teacher differed somewhat. For example, in the case of "Brenda," several recurrent themes appeared as she spoke of her beliefs about teaching. These were identified as: "interrelatedness," "talking things over," "it all takes time," and "being positive." These themes did not appear in the interview data from other teachers.

After much reworking of the data, the global system that eventuated for the coding of observations became one of the most concrete outcomes of the study. It provided a typology that was capable of accounting for all of the strategies observed as these four teachers attempted to facilitate children's interactions with peers. The six major categories under which strategies could be grouped were:

(a) Developing a sense of community.

(b) Helping children gain access to peer play groups.

(c) Teacher involvement in children's dramatic play.

(d) Use of social conduct rules.

(e) Resolving peer conflict situations.

(f) Arrangement of the physical environment to support peer interactions.

It should be noted, however, that the teachers differed greatly in the relative importance they placed upon these areas of involvement and the strategies they used in each area.

In addition to the macro-level coding of observations, much narrower categories of teacher behavior also were coded, and these could appear in any type of situation. (For example, "teacher observes children in interaction" and "asks information-gathering questions.") Thus, a single event record typically had multiple categories assigned to it and was cross referenced in several locations. As no statistical analysis was carried out on these data, it was not necessary to force complex examples into a single category. In this way, it was possible to honor the natural complexity, while sorting the data in ways that enabled patterns to emerge. Henry's (1971, pp. xv-xvi) statement was found to be particularly appropriate. He wrote:

"I offer no "typologies," because human phenomena do not arrange themselves obligingly in types, but rather, afford us the spectacle of endless overlapping... The less we know... the easier it is to set up categories, just as the less data we have the easier it is to write a history."

In order to maintain and protect the idiosyncratic qualities of each of these teachers throughout the study, it was decided to keep the data on each teacher separate, at least until the final chapters where commonalities and differences would be discussed. Thus, the data were treated as a series of case studies, which Emig (1983) has described as "an intense, naturalistic examination of a given individual" (p. 163).

Each case study began with a contextual description covering the physical setting; its location, environment and program. This was followed by a description of the teacher, including such aspects as speech and movement patterns, appearance, and physical contact with children.

A third section described the biography, beliefs, attitudes and philosophy as disclosed by the teacher. Because all of these aspects were found to be interrelated and bound up with the teacher's view of her place in children's lives, this section was titled: "Image-of-Self-as-Teacher."

One of the most salient sections within the "image" descriptions conveyed the teachers' accounts of the mental activities they associated with teaching. These were grouped into three phases. The first phase dealt with the mental preparation that occurred before the children's arrival. An interesting (and unanticipated) aspect of this was suggested by the teachers' responses to the question: "How do you change when that door opens at 9:00 am?" What emerged was a form of personal mental preparation ("psyching up") that each of these teachers used, in order to face the challenges of everyday teaching life with a group of very young children. The second phase dealt with their on-the-spot interpretations of classroom events and decision making about interventions. The third phase of mental activities dealt with the reflection and evaluations these teachers made after the children had gone.

In each case study, a fourth section described, in as much "thick" detail (Geertz, 1973) as possible, the teacher's involvement in children's peer interactions. The final section provided a synthesis of connections between the image-of-self-as-teacher and the observed patterns of interaction. This was where the most interesting outcomes occurred.

Studies such as this produce elaborate understandings of teaching, but such outcomes are not easily or concisely expressed. These "stories of teaching" (Schubert, 1989) require many words. Despite these difficulties, the final section of this paper will attempt to highlight some of the most interesting insights gained from this study.

Although teacher behavior could be fragmented to the point where it would have been possible to say these teachers had a common repertoire, the units of behavior were combined in ways that made each teacher's involvement in children's peer interaction unique. While several teachers had some similarities in emphasis, it was clear that these teachers had highly individualized ways of making sense of events in their classrooms and idiosyncratic patterns of involvement with children.

As an example, consider "Rhonda" and "Brenda": Rhonda believed that any teacher intervention in children's conflicts, even those aiming to teach children skills in conflict resolution, led to an undesirable level of dependency in the children. Accordingly, Rhonda tried to avoid intervening in children's peer conflicts. The frequency of peer conflict in Rhonda's preschool was very low. (During all of the hours of observation, only once was Rhonda seen to become involved in a protracted peer conflict situation.) Life in her center was governed by an extensive list of rules and consequences. The children appeared to understand these well and were observed managing peer conflicts simply by reminding each other of the appropriate rule. On the rare occasion when Rhonda intervened, she typically restated the appropriate rule, then removed one or more of the children to a less social activity.

In Brenda's preschool, rules played a much smaller part and were limited to safety and health issues. Brenda worked with aboriginal and islander children in a low-income urban area and believed it crucial for these children to gain mastery of conflict resolution skills. Unlike Rhonda, who perceived peer conflicts as something to be avoided, Brenda "read" children's peer conflicts as valuable opportunities for facilitating children's social development through the practice of conflict resolution skills. Observations showed that the frequency and nature of her interventions in children's peer interactions were in keeping with this concern.

As a means of understanding the totality of teacher-child-peer interaction in these educational environments, a conventional understanding of "teaching" as the facilita-tion of children's learning/development was found to be inadequate. A more useful conceptualization was "living together," which was conceived as incorporating two major areas of concern for these teachers: facilitating development and managing the here and now. It was suggested that the teacher's maintainance of a balance between these two concerns was capable of explaining many of the apparent inconsistencies of teacher-child interaction observed in these settings. These were complex and demand-ing environments in which management of the here-and-now had to be the fundamental concern. Only when these teachers interpreted the immediate situation as "in hand," did they engage in the types of interactional strategy commonly identified as "facilita-tive" (Katz, 1984).

These teachers interpreted classroom events in complex ways that took account of who was involved, what had happened before and what was happening elsewhere. For example, actions by one individual or group of children might be considered safe, but a similar action "read" as unsafe if a different child was involved. Having interpreted the situation in context, teachers then made decisions about what type of intervention was possible and desirable. Although complex, this decision making was extremely rapid. Brenda captured it nicely by describing it as the "quick think."

In making these interpretations of the event in its immediate context, the teacher's image-of-self-as-teacher (incorporating such aspects as perceptions of own biography and core beliefs about children and learning) was found to be highly influential, though not all-powerful. Each of these teachers made quite different sense of apparently similar contextual situations. For example, a situation one teacher would read as chaos, demanding a rapid, non-facilitative input to restore order, another would read as still permitting some prolonged attempt at facilitating conflict resolution skills.

The relationship between belief and context was found to be an intricate, complex and multi-directional one. It was clear that some beliefs had the power to virtually exclude the teacher from whole chunks of interaction. At other times, belief seemed totally overwhelmed by the pressure of contextual factors. For example, despite a firm commitment to the notion of developing children's conflict resolution skills, "Nan," when feeling pressured, sometimes swept into children's conflict situations and made a brief pronouncement that promptly ended the conflict and dispersed the children. All of these excellent teachers were observed, at some time or another, setting aside their ideals of what constituted "good teaching" as they struggled to manage the here-and-now.

Much recent work has been directed to teacher thinking (Schubert, 1989; Shulman, 1987), but comparatively few studies have yet attempted to link teacher thinking with observational studies of teacher-child interaction. This study is one of very few to explore early childhood teacher decision making at the level of curriculum implementation. As such, it does not provide definitive information, but "breaks ground" for other researchers to follow. Perhaps the most salient outcome, at least for this researcher and teacher educator, is the conviction that much remains to be understood about what it is that teachers know and do before we surrender to the urge to tell teachers what they should know and do.

References

Bolster, A.S. (1983). Toward a more effective model of research on teaching. *Harvard Educational Review, 53,* 294-308.

Combs, A.W. (1978). Teacher education: The person in the process. *Educational Leadership, 35,* 558-561.

Combs, A.W., Avila, D., and Purkey, W. (1978). Helping relationships: Basic concepts for the helping professions. Boston, MA: Allyn and Bacon.

Dawson, J.A. (1979). *Validity in Qualitative Inquiry.* Paper presented at the annual meeting of the American Research Association, San Francisco, CA.

Emig, J. (1983). Inquiry paradigms and writing. In D. Goswanni and M. Butler (Eds.), *The Web of Meaning,* (pp. 157-170). Upper Montclair, NJ: Boynton/Cook.

Erikson, F. and Schultz, J. (1981). When is a context?: Some issues and methods in the analysis of social competence, *Ethnography and Language in Educational Settings* (pp. 147-160). Norwood, NJ: Aldex.

Evans, R. (1981). Social integration of the young child: The management of change. *Early Child Development and Care, 7,* 57-82.

Fenstermacher, G.D. (1978). A philosophical consideration of recent research on teacher effectiveness. *Review of Research in Education, 6,* 157-185.

Fenstermacher, G.D. (1986). Philosophy of research on teaching: Three aspects. In M.C. Wittrock (Ed.), *Handbook of Research on Teaching (pp. 37-49), (3rd ed.).* New York: Macmillan.

Geertz, C. (1973). *The Interpretation of Cultures.* New York: Basic Books.

Giroux, H.A. (1985). Teachers as transformative intellectuals. *Social Education, 49,* 376-379.

Good, T.L. and Weinstein, R.S. (1986). Teacher expectations: A framework for exploring classrooms. In K. Zumwalt (Ed.), *Improving Teaching* (pp. 63-86). Alexandria, VA: Association for Supervision and Curriculum Development.

Green, J. and Wallat, C. (Eds.) (1981). *Ethnography and Language in Educational Settings.* Norwood, NJ: Aldex.

Greenberg, H.M. (1969). *Teaching with Feeling: Compassion and Self-Awareness in the Classroom Today.* Indianapolis, IN: Pegasus.

Henry, J. (1971). *Pathways to Madness.* New York: Random House.

Hosford, P. (1980). Improving the silent curriculum. *Theory Into Practice, 19,* 45-50.

Jackson, P.W. (1968). *Life in Classrooms.* New York: Holt, Rinehart and Winston.

Katz, L.G. (1984). The professional early childhood teacher. *Young Children, 39,* 3-10.

Le Compte, M.D. and Goertz, J.P. (1984). Ethnographic data collection in evaluation research. In D. M. Fetterman (Ed.), *Ethnography in Educational Evaluation* (pp. 37-59). Beverly Hills, CA: Sage.

Lincoln, Y.S. and Guba, E.G. (1985). *Naturalistic Inquiry.* Beverly Hills, CA: Sage.

Magoon, A.J. (1982). Constructivist approaches in educational research. *Review of Educational Research, 47,* 651-693.

Margolin, E. (1982). *Teaching Young Children at School and Home.* New York: Macmillan.

Massarik, F. (1981). The interviewing process re-examined. In P. Reason and J. Rowan (Eds.), *Human Inquiry (pp. 201- 206).* Chichester, UK: John Wiley and Sons.

McLean, S.V. (1986). *The Human Encounter: Teachers and Children Living Together in Preschools.* Unpublished doctoral dissertation, Arizona State University.

Overly, N. (Ed.) (1970). *The Unstudied Curriculum: Its Impact on Children.* Washington, DC: Association for Supervision and Curriculum Development.

Owens, R.G. (1982). Methodological perspective. *Educational Administration Quarterly, 18,* 1-21.

Phillips, D.C. (1981). Perspectives on teaching as an intentional act. *The Australian Journal of Education, 25,* 99-105.

Polanyi, M. (1967). *The Tacit Dimension.* Garden City: Doubleday.

Schubert, W.H. (1989). Teacher lore: A neglected basis for understanding curriculum and supervision. *Journal of Curriculum and Supervision, 4,* 282-285.

Shulman, L.S. (1987). Knowledge and teaching: Foundations of the new reform. *Harvard Educational Review, 57,* 1-22.

Williams, C., Neff, A., and Finkelstein, J. (1981). Theory into practice: Reconsidering the preposition. *Theory Into Practice, 20,* 93-96.

Yamamoto, K. (1984). My problems in understanding human beings. *Journal of Humanist Psychology, 24,* 65-74.

Note

An earlier version of this paper was presented at the Australian Association for Research in Education Conference, held at Armidale NSW, Australia, November-December 1988.

PECUNIARY ASPECT OF RISK TAKING: ARE SINGAPOREANS MORE RISK AVERSE THAN AMERICANS?

Tapen Sinha

There is a general belief that Singaporeans are more risk averse than their American counterparts. Using samples of students from an American university and from the National University of Singapore, it is shown that given identical contexts in well-specified experimental environments, there is no difference in risk taking between the two groups.

Are Singaporeans more risk averse than Americans? We shall attempt to answer this question. The question has a very practical economic aspect. It has been asserted by many researchers that the lack of indigenous entrepreneurship (and dominance of multinationals) in Singapore, unlike other Asian NICs, is primarily due to the lack of risk-taking character of Singaporeans. It is said that the American entrepreneurs are successful because they are willing to take risk whereas Singaporeans are not (e.g., Krause, 1987). As to why such a difference should exist, there are many explanations. One of the frequently quoted reasons is cultural. It is said that Singaporeans, being mainly ethnic Chinese, are more cautious than their Western counterparts. But this argument is rather weak. For, then, the same argument can be applied to the people from Taiwan and Hong Kong with equal force. The other argument is in the "folklore": it says that the education system in Singapore teaches the students to be risk averse and only the risk averse students succeed. Casual observations seem to be at odds with this argument: the successful products of Singaporean environment seem to thrive in the educational systems of Australia, U.K., and U.S.A. If the Singaporean system bred only risk avoiders, this observation is problematic. The purpose of our experiment is to shed some light on the alleged difference in risk taking between Americans and Singaporeans. However, to date, there has not been an explicit difference found between the two culturally different groups using a direct method.

For measuring risk, two different strands of literature have developed over the last 30 years. The first one was developed by (social) psychologists in the late 1950s. The genesis of that literature can be traced to Kogan and Wallach (1964). These researchers developed a series of 12 choice dilemmas in which subjects were asked to advise 12 different individuals in highly dissimilar settings. For example, one situation describes a prisoner of war who has two choices. The first choice is to live as a prisoner for the rest of his life where life will be very unpleasant. The second choice is a risky one. He can try to escape. This risky choice has two possible outcomes (with given probabilities). He escapes or he is caught. If he is caught, he gets executed. The subject of the experiment is asked to advise the individual at what minimum probability of success he should try the risky choice. Although the payoff for escaping is freedom, it is risky. There are several difficulties with this approach. First, the subjects may have difficulty in playing the roles of a brain surgeon/pilot/prisoner of war/concert pianist etc. in different questions as he/she might have no experience in those roles; second, alternating between roles can cause confusion and transference from one setting to the next might occur; third, typical choice dilemma questions do not have completely specified consequences. For example, a person is asked the probability of success he would require for recommending a career as a brain surgeon without being explicitly told the monetary benefits of becoming a brain surgeon. Thus, the difference in responses across individuals may solely be due to different assumptions of the respondents about these unknown consequences.

The second method is to measure risk directly. There was only one study that attempted to measure risk taking directly. This was undertaken by McCrimmon and Wehrung (1986). Their procedure to obtain the measure of risk aversion was to ask the respondent to declare an amount of money which made the respondent "indifferent" between that choice and another risky choice. The choices are essentially the same as in Figure 1. The dollar amount in choice 1 was left blank and the respondents were asked to fill it in. The disadvantage of this method is that the individual would have to be very sophisticated to comprehend the questions fully and respond appropriately as the notion of "indifference" is not obvious to naive decision makers. In our experiment, we avoid this problem by offering a series of binary choices.

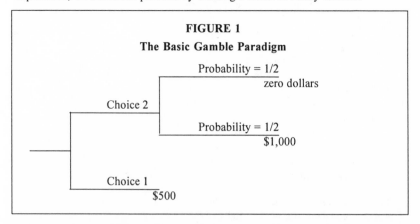

FIGURE 1

The Basic Gamble Paradigm

The aim of our experiment was to find an amount $x (in choice 1 of Figure 1) such that the individual liked (in the case of gains) or disliked (in the case of losses) the choice of $x and a risky choice of a gain of a fixed dollar amount (we chose two scenarios with $1,000 and $10,000, respectively) with a 50% chance. The experiment was designed so that the $x was revealed by a series of iterative binary choices.

Method

Subjects. We used two samples: one came from (N = 71) American students from the University of Wisconsin. These second-year University students were enrolled in the Principles of Economics course; the other was a sample of Singaporean students (N = 69; ethnic Chinese). These first-year students at the National University of Singapore were enrolled in an Elementary Statistics course in the Department of Economics and Statistics. Neither group had any previous exposure to or training in Decision Theory.

Stimuli. Stimuli were elementary lotteries (p, x), which were described verbally to the subjects as prospects of receiving or losing x dollars with probability p and nothing with probability 1- p and as the prospect of receiving x dollars with certainty in the case of p = 1. Specifically, as in Figure 1, the respondent could pick choice 1 or choice 2. Note that choice 1 was an elementary lottery with x = $500 and p = 1 and choice 2 was an elementary lottery with x = $1,000 and p = 1/2.

Procedure. There was one session with each subject. The session lasted between 10 minutes and 30 minutes. To begin with, each subject was seated in front of a computer terminal. On the screen, a situation was described verbally and diagrammatically (as in Figure 1). The first situation was described as follows:

"You are boarding an airplane with luggage worth $1,000. There is a 50% chance that the luggage will be lost forever. You have the following choices:

Choice 1. You buy an insurance policy that reimburses you the full $1,000 if the baggage is lost. But the premium for that insurance will cost you $500.

Choice 2. You do not buy the insurance policy. In this case, you have a 50% chance of losing $1,000 (conversely you have a 50% chance of losing the luggage)."

The respondent was then asked to "key in" either choice 1 or choice 2. Depending on the choice, the value of the premium was raised or lowered. A method of iteration was adopted so that the choices got "closer and closer" (in terms of the preference of the respondent). For example, if in the above situation the respondent picked choice 2, the premium in choice 1 was lowered to $400. If on the other hand, the respondent picked choice 1, the premium was raised to $600. By such manipulations, the successive difference between premia became smaller and smaller and the individual eventually became "indifferent" between the choices (this method of eliciting choice was suggested by Keeney and Raiffa (1976)).

Each respondent had to face four such situations. Two of them involved losses (of $1,000 and of $10,000) and the other two involved gains (of $1,000 and of $10,000). In each case the loss or gain probabilities were kept at the simplest level of 50% each. Each respondent also entered some background information about himself/herself (the questions asked were about age, sex, family income, family size, gambling habits).

Summary statistics of the respondents are reported in Table 1. It also provides means and standard deviations for the certainty equivalent sums for each of the four questions (the certainty equivalent for the situation with the loss of $1,000 was called L1, the certainty equivalent for the situation with the loss of $10,000 was called L10, the certainty equivalent for the situation with the gain of $1,000 was called G1, and the certainty equivalent for the situation with the gain of $10,000 was called G10).

First, we tested to see if the individuals were risk neutral on the average, that is, we tested to see if the mean for situation 1 and 3 deviated from $500 (the expected value of gambles 1 and 3 are $500 = (1/2) X 1,000 + (1/2) X 0); similarly, we tested to see if the mean for situations 2 and 4 deviated from $5,000 (the expected value of gambles 2 and 4 are $5,000 = (1/2) X 10,000 + (1/2) X 0) significantly. In all four cases, we were able to rule our risk neutrality ($p < .001$) strongly.

TABLE 1

Means (Ms) and Standard Deviations (SDs) of the Experimentally Assessed Certainty Equivalent Sums and Social-Economic Characteristics of the Subjects

Sample 1: American Students (N = 71)

Variable	Mean	SD
Age	20.48	4.12
Income	29,450.00	22,189.00
Dependents	1.92	2.01
G1	411.55	245.90
G10	3,697.18	2,449.66
L1	383.66	225.95
L10	3,309.86	1,999.23

Sample 2: Singaporean Students (N= 69)

Variable	Mean	SD
Age	21.10	2.17
Income	21,785.00	14,196.00
Dependents	1.87	1.54
G1	401.22	366.95
G10	3,702.11	2,034.19
L1	322.73	321.22
L10	3,601.46	2,555.23

The respondents, on the average, exhibited risk aversion for gains and risk-taking behavior for losses. These findings are consistent with the Prospect Theory of Kahneman and Tversky (1979). However, the correlations between the loss situations and gain situations were very low. Thus, the results are not consistent with the reflection hypothesis proposed by Kahneman and Tversky. The asymmetry of losses against gains have also been reported in the literature (e.g., Cohen, Jaffray, & Said, 1987). It should be noted that we have not made use of any behavioral model in our analysis.

Second, we carried out a one-way ANOVA test for each of the four questions by classifying them as Americans and Singaporeans. In each case, no statistically significant difference emerged (p. 25).

Third, we carried out a test for equality of means (after testing for equality of variances). None of the equality of means between the Americans and Singaporeans could be rejected (p. 25).

Finally, to check whether there was a difference in response between males and females, we carried out the ANOVA and means tests within each sample. No significant difference was found (p. 40). There is a considerable body of literature discussing male/ female difference in risk taking (Tan, 1988; Ginsburgh & Miller, 1982). There seems to be no evidence in the difference in risk taking between males and females in most age groups (except in children).

Discussion

From the tests performed it may seem that the variation within each sample may be large and therefore the statistical insignificance of all the effects discussed so far are the result of "noise in the data." However, a closer examination reveals that such a presumption is false. For example, we carried out a regression analyses of the certainty equivalent sums on the family incomes for the four situations, the results were statistically significant in all the four cases (for L1 and L10, $p < .05$ and for G1 and G10, $p < .01$). These regression results indicate that family income is an important determinant for the choices made by the respondents.

In summary, we note that we did not find any evidence to the hypothesis that risk taking among Singaporeans is any different from risk taking among Americans given the same set of choices in well-structured environments.

One potential criticism for the cross-cultural study with dollars and cents could be that one U.S. dollar is not equivalent to one Singapore dollar. Hence, our comparisons are invalid. In defense, we can provide two arguments: (a) the average family income in the two samples are quite close (of course, the U.S. sample is in U.S. dollars and the Singapore sample is in Singapore dollars); in general, per capita income in the U.S. (in U.S. dollars) was very similar to per capita income in Singapore (in Singapore dollars) in 1987; (b) casual observations tend to confirm the similarity in pricing in the two countries. For example, a can of Coca Cola costs 60 to 70 U.S. cents in Chicago and 60 to 70 Singapore cents in Singapore. There are many other comparable items similarly priced.

Therefore, we can presume that the Singapore dollar in Singapore is treated the same way as the U.S. dollar in the United States (without too much error). This can be taken as a justification for using the "dollar numbers" in the experiment without any modification.

A second question can be raised about the applicability of the method in general. Specifically, we know from the study of Hershey and Schoemaker (1985) that certainty equivalent method of eliciting preference is very context specific. Thus, the results from the above experiment may not be immediately translatable to other contexts. In other words, based on the above experiment, it would be inappropriate to declare that there is no difference in risk taking between American and Singaporean university students.

There is a third and general criticism about the incentives of telling the truth by the respondents for hypothetical gambles described above. It has been shown by Binswanger (1981) that the results typically do not alter even if actual payments are made to the subjects.

References

Binswanger, H. (1981). Experimentally determined utility function: The results from a village study in India. *Economic Journal, 93*, 612-633.

Cohen, M., Jaffray, J.Y., and Said, T. (1987). Experimental comparison of individual behavior under risk and under uncertainty for gains and for losses. *Organizational Behavior and Human Decision Processes, 39*, 1-22.

Ginsburgh, H.J. and Miller, S.M. (1982). Sex difference in children's risk taking behavior. *Child Development, 53*, 426-428.

Hershey, J. and Schoemaker, P.J.H. (1985). Probability versus certainty equivalent methods of utility measurement. *Management Science, 31*, 1213-1231.

Kahneman, D. and Tversky, A. (1979). Prospect theory: An analysis of decision under risk. *Econometrica, 47*, 263-292.

Keeney, J. and Raiffa, H. (1976). *Decision Making Under Uncertainty.* New York: John Wiley & Sons.

Kogan, N. and Wallach, M.A. (1964). *A Study in Cognition and Personality.* New York: Holt.

Krause, L. (1987). *Singapore Economy Reconsidered.* Singapore: Institute of South East Asian Studies.

McCrimmon, K.R. and Wehrung, T. (1986). *Taking Risks.* New York: Free Press.

Tan, L.C. (1988). *Sex Roles in Decision Making Under Uncertainty.* Unpublished B. Soc. Sci. (Hons) Academic Exercise, National University of Singapore.

Acknowledgment

My gratitude to Ms. Shari Due of the University of Wisconsin for the interactive program used in this paper. I am also indebted to all the participants of the experiment. This paper is dedicated to the memory of Professor Steven Johnson.

SECTION C
Medical Decision Making

PSYCHIATRIC IMPAIRMENT AND ITS EFFECTS ON DECISION MAKING

Mark H. B. Radford

Decision making is an important psychological function that is thought to provide the link between thought and action (Miller, Galanter, & Pribram, 1960). The extent to which psychiatric disturbance impairs the decision-making process is an important theoretical and clinical question. While many clinicians are used to the idea that psychiatric illness is often accompanied by an inability to make decisions (cf. Bootzin & Acocella, 1980; Klerman, 1980; Pilowsky, 1979), there is very little literature examining the relationship. This chapter outlines research concerning the relationship between both general psychiatric disturbance with specific psychiatric diagnostic categories and decision-making behavior.

In general terms, psychiatric patients are said to have problems in the area of decision making:

> Descriptions of deficits in decision making in these populations are usually presumed to reflect general impairment of performance that is associated with an excess of arousal, anxiety, tension, and panic (Radford, Mann, & Kalucy, 1986, p. 210).

Neurotic individuals have generally been described as indecisive, likely to arbitrarily limit the range of choices available, and are prone to making choices on the basis of inadequate information (Alexander & Selesnick, 1966; Broadhurst, 1976).

Radford, Mann, and Kalucy (1986) carried out a study examining the effect that general psychiatric morbidity has upon decision making. Using the Middlesex Hospital Questionnaire (Crown & Crisp, 1966) to measure the presence and severity of general psychiatric disorder, self-report measures of decision-making behavior and actual decision problems, the authors found a significant relationship between severity of psychiatric disturbance and patients' low self-esteem as decision makers, their lack of confidence in possible outcomes of their decisions, the self-reported use of maladaptive decision-making styles (e.g., "procrastination," "buck-passing" and "rationalization"), and displayed lack of rationality when making an actual decision (see Table 1). These findings are very much in keeping with the predictions made by the Janis and Mann (1977) conflict model which assumes that increased stress and arousal (characteristic of many psychiatric states) are related to an increased use of maladaptive patterns of decision making.

TABLE 1

Correlation coefficients between measures of psychiatric
disturbance and self-reported decision -coping patterns
(adapted from Radford et al., 1986).

Measures	MQ(1)	BDI(2)
Decision self-esteem	-0.79**	-0.61**
Vigilance	0.20	0.01
Defensive Avoidance	0.72**	0.55**
Hypervigilance	0.68**	0.48**

Notes

1 – Middlesex Hospital Questionnaire (Crown & Crisp, 1966).

2 – Beck Depression Inventory (Beck et al., 1961).

** – $p < 0.01$; N =35.

Although the study by Radford and colleagues is the first to systematically investigate the descriptive aspects of the relationship between decision making and psychiatric disturbance, there is a small amount of research that examines particular aspects of disordered decision making within specific diagnostic categories such as obsessive compulsive neurosis, psychotic disorders and depression.

Obsessive Compulsive Neurosis

The obsessive compulsive patient is characterized by recurrent thoughts that intrude into the conscious, without the patient being able to stop them, and repetitive acts that need to be performed despite their seemingly irrational or useless function (Christ, Brownsberger, & Solomon, 1974; Nemiah, 1980). In addition, obsessive compulsives are characterized by their need to continually check that they have done what they wanted to do (Rachman, Marks, & Hodgson, 1973).

An obsessional personality trait in non-clinical individuals involves a need to control both self and environment. The obsessive is: cautious, deliberate, thoughtful, and rational in his approach to life and its problems. He emphasizes reason and logic at the expense of feeling and intuition, and he does his best to be objective and to avoid being carried away by subjective enthusiasm (Nemiah, 1980, p. 1513).

Both the clinical characteristics as well as the non-clinical personality traits can have much bearing on decision-making behavior. Shapiro (1972) notes that one of the distinctive features of obsessional individuals is the balance between feelings.

Just at the moment when an obsessional person is at last tipping decisively in one direction, he will discover some new item that re-establishes that perfect balance (Shapiro, 1972, p. 46). The indecisiveness of the obsessive compulsive can be so extreme that it takes on a clinical status of its own.

Despite the above description, few studies have looked at the decision behavior of obsessive compulsives. Of the few that have, Milner and colleagues (Milner, Beech, & Walker, 1971), using signal detection theory, found that obsessives required more repetition of a signal than a non-obsessional group. In other words, they needed more perceptual information. Volans (1976) found that obsessional patients required more evidence concerning their decision before they made their ultimate choice than did non-obsessional patients. Thus, while it may be true that the obsessional person may display all the requirements of a vigilant decision maker (i.e., consideration of all alternatives, search for information, etc; see Janis & Mann, 1977), their inability actually to make a decision is characteristic of a decision maker whose vigilance has become maladaptive.

Psychotic Disorders

Psychotic disorders are characterized by disturbance in mood (affective disorders), thought (schizophrenic disorders), or the presence of delusions (paranoid disorders; Bootzin & Acocella, 1980). Psychotics may display either depressive symptoms (e.g., low self-esteem, retardation in behavior, etc.) or manic symptoms (e.g., inflated self-esteem, hyperactivity, etc.). A major feature of psychotic behavior is the distortion of reality and the inability to distinguish fantasy from actual experience. Although few studies have been conducted concerning "psychotic decision making," clinical case studies have shown that manic psychotics often make rash, ill-conceived choices resulting, amongst other things, in sadness and debt. These decisions are made during periods of hyperactivity, inflated self-esteem and bizarre behavior (Wolpert, 1980).

Affective Disorders (Depression)

Studies examining the relationship between personality and depression have provided a general picture of the relationship between depression and decision making. The role of dependency has been found to be very important in depression (Birtchnell, 1984). Pilowsky (1979) found that depressed individuals tended to be dependent-followers whose behavior reflected that of the group. He also found that depressives tended to depend on others to make decisions for them (cf. Chodoff, 1972; Paykel & Weissman, 1973).

Research has shown strong relationships between self-concept and depression. Although it is difficult to differentiate between cause and effect, studies have shown that depressives have low self-esteem (Battle, 1978; Beck & Beamesderfer, 1974). Beck (1972) and others (Bibring, 1953; Miller & Seligman, 1975) have suggested that depressed people are pessimistic, unable to see themselves as effective, in control, capable of achieving success, or able to get what they need and want from the environment. Nystrom and Lindegard (1975) found a strong relationship between depression and the tendency to ruminate, shyness in company and a lack of endurance. This tendency towards rumination is believed to be related to thought rigidity, a factor also found to be present in depressives.

The general picture of depressives is that they are unable to make decisions due to the lack of self-esteem and emotional control, to ruminate and display rigidity in thought processes, and to depend on others to make decisions for them; however, some personality studies have found the opposite. In a study by Dana and colleagues (1983), major depressives, despite their "depressive personality," still regarded themselves as "self-sufficient." In other words, they still believed themselves to be resourceful and able/preferred to make their own decisions (cf. Cattell, Eber, & Tatsuoka, 1970). Finally, the act of suicide or attempted suicide (often thought of as an important symptom of severe depression) can be seen as an act of decision in depressives. Both of these findings appear to be in direct contradiction to the belief of other writers who claim that one of the major characteristics of depression is the individual's inability to make decisions (e.g., Beck, 1967; Bootzin & Acocella, 1980; Klerman, 1980).

The work of Aaron Beck (1967, 1972, 1974) has provided a framework for the few studies that have examined aspects of the link between depression and decision making. Beck (1974) stated that depression could be characterized by a "negative view of the self, the outside world, and the future" (p. 17). In particular he noted that "depressed patients distorted their experience in an idiosyncratic way; they misinterpreted events in terms of personal failure, deprivation, or rejection, or they exaggerated or over-generalized the significance of events that suggested negative predictions of the future" (1974, p. 17).

Evaluation and attribution concerning the success or failure of past decision tasks is important in determining how individuals see and approach decision or choice situations in the future. Most research, however, has been largely confined to comparisons between depressed and non-depressed subjects and their attributions to, and evaluations of, the quality of their performance on set tasks. In addition, studies have examined how feedback from performance can affect the future expectation of depressives concerning their success or failure on experimental tasks. Methodology has been generally restricted to using success or failure outcomes on chance versus skilled tasks (Rotter, Chance, & Phares, 1972).

Distortions in memory and attributions relating to past events have been well documented (e.g., Klein, Fencil-Morse, & Seligman, 1976; Krantz & Hammen, 1979; Kuiper, 1978; Seligman, Abramson, Semmel, & von Baeyer, 1979). Depressives are more likely than non-depressives to recall "depressing" or negative information about themselves and their performance, and to make different causal attributions. One study (Lewinsohn, Mischel, Chaplin, & Barton, 1980), however, found that non-depressives demonstrate a positive bias in their cognitions, that is, non-depressives tend to view themselves positively, not negatively.

Studies looking at differences between depressives and non-depressives in their expectations concerning performance on future tasks have also produced inconsistent findings. Some studies have found differences between both groups in their expectations relating to tasks involving skill (e.g., Garber & Hallen, 1980; Sacco & Hokanson, 1978). Others have found differences only in those tasks involving chance (e.g., McNitt & Thornton, 1978), while still others have been unable to detect any difference at all (e.g., Smolen, 1978).

Costello (1983) has suggested that "one reason for such inconsistencies is the assumption that expectancy, or subjective probability, can be studied in isolation from other factors involved in judgment and choice: in particular that it can be measured separately from the value, worth or utility of the expected event under consideration" (p. 240). In her study, Costello investigated how depressed women integrate information about the probability and utility of choice outcomes in making decisions. She found that depressed women required much higher utility (or attractiveness) for a choice alternative before they would change from a course of action with an assured outcome (low risk) to one with an uncertain outcome (high risk). Further, contrary to expectation, Costello reported that depressed women made choices on six dilemmas which were generally more accurate and consistent in combining utilities and probabilities than non-depressed women.

To date, all the studies mentioned above have been mainly interested in what choices are made rather than how choices are made. The study by Radford and colleagues (1986), mentioned earlier, was one of the first to attempt to describe how decision making is affected by depression. Using the conflict model of decision making (Janis & Mann, 1977) as a theoretical base, Radford and colleagues administered the Beck Depression Inventory (Beck, Ward, Mendelsohn, Mock, & Erbaugh, 1961) to a group of psychiatric inpatients and obtained similar results to those reported above with the measure of presence and severity of psychiatric illness (see Table 1). In other words, the more depressed the patient, the more likely he or she was to have low self-esteem as a decision maker, low confidence in the likely outcomes of their decisions, and the greater use of maladaptive decision-making styles. They also found that the few patients diagnosed as having major depressive disorder on the DSM-III (American Psychiatric Association, 1980), who participated in the study, although reporting use of maladaptive styles, when forced to actually make a decision, tended to make rational rather than irrational decisions (i.e., were consistent in their decision making).

In summary, the overall picture regarding the nature of the relationship between depression and decision making is rather confused. Although there is some evidence to support the belief that depression may result in motivational and cognitive deficits that can be reflected in problem-solving and decision-making performance, the evidence is not conclusive. Self-reported modes of decision making may reflect maladaptive decision styles (e.g., procrastination, buck-passing, and rationalization), but when faced with having to actually make a decision, depression may help to control overconfidence and overenthusiasm, thereby reducing the chance of negative information being ignored. However, it must also be considered that the subjects who participated in the above studies may not represent the upper limits of depression. It may well be that the most severely depressed were those subjects who, because of their psychological state, failed to complete measures and therefore were treated as missing data (see Radford, Mann, & Kalucy, 1986).

In a second study, Radford and colleagues (Radford, Nakane, Ohta, Mann, & Kalucy, 1988; Radford, 1990) investigated the specific effect of depression on decision making in Australian and Japanese patients who were clinically depressed. Australian depressed patients were found to have lower decisional self-esteem and higher decisional stress, and were less likely to use their ideal style of decision making ("choice") and more likely to use a maladaptive response style ("complacency," "avoidance," or "hypervigilance") than non-depressed controls. Further, they were more likely to rely on others to aid in the decision-making process. While Japanese depressed patients revealed a similar pattern to Australian patients, the difference between Japanese depressed and non-depressed subjects was not as great. The findings from this study suggest that in Australia depression leads to a breakdown in perceived decision-making ability. The discrepancy between what is considered culturally appropriate decision-making behavior and actual decision-making behavior in Australian depressives is significant. On the other hand, the discrepancy between culturally appropriate decision-making behavior and actual decision-making behavior in Japanese depressives is much more limited. These results suggest that cultural differences can have an important influence on depression and decision making (see chapter on "Culture and its Effect on Decision Making" in this volume, and Radford et al., 1988).

The results of the above study illustrate the importance of taking into account the role of culture in the examination of behavioral (and psychological) deficits due to depression and more general psychiatric illnesses. While it may be true that a particular behavior is affected by depression, deficits in such behavior may not be as important in one culture as they are in another. Particular coping mechanisms (in this case the role of the group or family in making decisions) may come into play which help to control (or limit) the extent and importance of the deficit. This area represents an important field of future research.

Conclusion

While it is true that, in general, psychiatric illness may be accompanied by indecisiveness or by the inability to make decisions, it must also be recognized that "delayed or avoided decision-making may be adaptive, if decision-making capabilities are impaired during psychiatric illness" (Radford et al., 1986, p. 216). Avoiding a decision can help prevent complete demoralization or even suicide during long periods of deprivation or illness (Janis & Mann, 1977). Having said this, however, two important and related implications arise from the above discussion.

The first refers to the importance of determining the exact relationship between psychiatric disturbance and decision making. The lack of thought and research has prevented a real understanding of the relationship between the two variables. Decision making is an important everyday function. It is important in allowing people to simply exist (i.e., seeking treatment, moving house, taking sick leave, etc.). If individuals are unable to make decisions, even simple ones (i.e., what to eat), then "normal functioning" is difficult. The second implication refers to the need to incorporate treatment interventions that attempt to teach patients how to cope with decision-making situations. Several programs have been developed and used with some success (e.g., Mann, Beswick, Allouche, & Ivey, 1989; Cerniglia, Horenstein, & Christensen, 1978; Clark, 1974; Mann, 1985). Simple decision skills may prove to be an important aid in helping patients live day to day as well as helping in the rehabilitation of those who have returned to the community.

References

Alexander, F.G. and Selesnick, S.T. (1966). *The History of Psychiatry.* New York: Harper and Row.

American Psychiatric Association (1980). *Diagnostic and Statistical Manual of Mental Disorders (3rd ed.).* Washington, DC: American Psychiatric Association.

Battle, J. (1978). Relationship between self-esteem and depression. *Psychological Reports, 42,* 745-746.

Beck, A.T. (1967). *Depression: Clinical, Experimental, and Theoretical Aspects.* New York: Harper and Row.

Beck, A.T. (1972). *Depression: Causes and Treatment.* Philadelphia: University of Pennsylvania Press.

Beck, A.T. (1974). The development of depression: A cognitive model. In R.J. Friedman and M.M. Katz (Eds.), *The Psychology of Depression: Contemporary Theory and Research.* Washington, DC: Winston.

Beck, A.T. and Beamesderfer, A. (1974). Assessment of depression: The depression inventory. In P. Pichot (Ed.), *Psychological Measurement in Psychopharmacology: Modern Problems in Pharmoxapsychiatry (Vol. 7).* Basel, Switzerland: Karger.

Beck, A.T., Ward, C.H., Mendelsohn, M., Mock, J., and Erbaugh, J. (1961). An inventory for measuring depression. *Archives of General Psychiatry, 4,* 561-571.

Bibring, E. (1953). The mechanism of depression. In P. Greenacre (Ed.), *Affective Disorders.* New York: International Universities Press.

Birtchnell, J. (1984). Dependence and its relationship to depression. *British Journal of Medical Psychology, 57,* 215-225.

Bootzin, R.R. and Acocella, J.R. (1980). *Abnormal Psychology: Current Perspectives (3rd. ed.).* New York: Random House.

Broadhurst, A. (1976). Applications of the psychology of decisions. In M.P. Feldman and A. Broadhurst (Eds.), *Theoretical and Experimental Bases of the Behaviour Therapies.* London: Wiley.

Cattell, R.B., Eber, H.W., and Tatsuoka, M.M. (1970). *Handbook for the Sixteen Personality Factor Questionnaire (16PF).* Champaign, IL: Institute for Personality and Ability Testing.

Cerniglia, R.P., Horenstein, D., and Christensen, E.W. (1978). Group decision-making and self-management in the treatment of psychiatric patients. *Journal of Clinical Psychol-*

ogy, 34, 489-493.

Chodoff, P. (1972). The depressive personality. Archives of General Psychiatry, 27, 666-673.

Christ, J., Brownsberger, C.N., and Solomon, P. (1974). Neurosis. In P. Solomon and V.D. Patch (Eds.), Handbook of Psychiatry. Los Altos, CA: Lange Medical Publications.

Clark, D.H. (1974). Social Therapy in Psychiatry. Harmondsworth, Middlesex: Penguin.

Costello, E.J. (1983). Information processing for decision making in depressed women: A study of subjective expected utilities. Journal of Affective Disorders, 5, 239-251.

Crown, S., and Crisp, A.H. (1966). A short clinical diagnostic self-rating scale for psychoneurotic patients. British Journal of Psychiatry, 112, 917-923.

Dana, R.H., Bolton, B., and Gritzmacher, S. (1983). 16PF source traits associated with DSM-III symptoms for four diagnostic groups. Journal of Clinical Psychology, 39, 958-960.

Garber, J. and Hallen, S.D. (1980). Universal versus personal helplessness in depression: Belief in uncontrollability or incompetence? Journal of Abnormal Psychology, 89, 56-66.

Janis, I.L. and Mann, L. (1977). Decision Making: A Psychological Analysis of Conflict, Choice, and Commitment. New York: Free Press.

Klein, D.C., Fencil-Morse, E., and Seligman, M.E.P. (1976). Learned helplessness, depression and the attribution of failure. Journal of Personality and Social Psychology, 33, 508-516.

Klerman, G.L. (1980). Overview of affective disorders. In H.I. Kaplan, A.M. Freedman, and B.J. Sadock (Eds.), Comprehensive Textbook of Psychiatry (3rd ed.). Baltimore: Williams and Wilkins.

Krantz, S. and Hammen, K. (1979). Assessment of cognitive bias in depression. Journal of Abnormal Psychology, 88, 611-619.

Kuiper, N.A. (1978). Depression and causal attributions for success and failure. Journal of Personality and Social Psychology, 36, 236-246.

Lewinsohn, P.M., Mischel, W., Chaplin, W., and Barton, R. (1980). Social competence and depression: The role of illusory self-perceptions. Journal of Abnormal Psychology, 89, 203-212.

Mann, L. (1985). Decision making. In N.T. Feather (Ed.), Australian Psychology: Review of Research. Sydney: Allen and Unwin.

Mann, L., Beswick, G., Allouche, P., and Ivey, M. (1989). Decision workshops for the improvement of decision making skills and confidence. Journal of Counseling and Development, 67, 478-481.

McNitt, P.C. and Thornton, D.M. (1978). Depression and perceived reinforcement: A reconsideration. Journal of Abnormal Psychology, 87, 137-140.

Miller, G.A., Galanter, E., and Pribram, K.H. (1960). Plans and the Structure of Behavior. New York: Holt, Rhinehart & Winston.

Miller, W.R. and Seligman, M.E.P. (1975). Depression and learned helplessness in man. Journal of Abnormal Psychology, 84, 228-238.

Milner, A.D., Beech, H.R., and Walker, V.J. (1971). Decision processes and obsessional behaviour. *British Journal of Social and Clinical Psychology, 10,* 88-89.

Nemiah, J.C. (1980). Obsessive-compulsive disorder (obsessive-compulsive neurosis). In H.I. Kaplan, A.M. Freedman, and B.J. Sadock (Eds.), *Comprehensive Textbook of Psychiatry (3rd ed.).* Baltimore: Williams and Wilkins.

Nystrom, S. and Lindegard, B. (1975). Depression: Predisposing factors. *Acta Psychiatrica Scandinavica, 51,* 77-87.

Paykel, E.S. and Weissman, M.M. (1973). Social adjustment and depression. *Archives of General Psychiatry, 28,* 659-663.

Pilowsky, I. (1979). Personality and depressive illness. *Acta Psychiatrica Scandinavica, 60,* 170-176.

Rachman, S., Marks, I., and Hodgson, R. (1973). The treatment of obsessive-compulsive neurotics by modeling and flooding "in vivo." *Behaviour Research and Therapy, 11, 463-471.*

Radford, M. (1990). Utsubyo kanja ni okeru ishikettei [A review of decision making in depressed patients]. *Seishinka Shindangaku [Archives of Psychiatric Diagnostics and Clinical Evaluation], 1,* 269-277.

Radford, M.H.B., Mann, L., and Kalucy, R.S. (1986). Psychiatric disturbance and decision making. *Australian and New Zealand Journal of Psychiatry, 20,* 210-217.

Radford, M., Nakane, Y., Ohta, Y., Mann, L., and Kalucy, R. (1988). *Depression and decision making behaviour: Preliminary results from a trans-cultural study.* Paper presented at the 4th Scientific Meeting of the Pacific Rim College of Psychiatrists, Hong Kong, December.

Rotter, J.B., Chance, J.E., and Phares, E.J. (1972). *Application of a Social Learning Theory of Personality.* New York: Holt, Rinehart & Winston.

Sacco, W.P. and Hokanson, J.E. (1978). Expectations of success and anagram performance of depressives in a public and private setting. *Journal of Abnormal Psychology, 87,* 122-130.

Seligman, M.E.P., Abramson, L.Y., Semmel, A., and von Baeyer, C. (1979). Depressive attributional style. *Journal of Abnormal Psychology, 88,* 242-247.

Shapiro, D. (1972). *Neurotic Styles.* New York: Basic Books.

Smolen, R.C. (1978). Expectancies, mood and performance of depressed and nondepressed psychiatric inpatients on chance and skill tasks. *Journal of Abnormal Psychology, 87,* 91-101.

Volans, P.J. (1976). Styles of decision-making and probability appraisal in selected obsessional and phobic patients. *British Journal of Social and Clinical Psychology, 15,* 305-317.

Wolpert, E.A. (1980). Major affective disorders. In H.I. Kaplan, A.M. Freedman, and B.J. Sadock (Eds.), *Comprehensive Textbook of Psychiatry (3rd ed.).* Baltimore: Williams & Wilkins.

Notes

The research by Radford, Nakane, Ohta, Mann, and Kalucy (1988) is part of a major project on culture and decision making. The findings reported here are initial findings that were presented at the 4th Scientific Meeting of the Pacific Rim College of Psychiatrists, Hong Kong, December 1988. Any correspondence should be addressed to the author. The cooperation, collaboration and advice of Professors Leon Mann and Ross S. Kalucy of The Flinders University of South Australia, and Professors Yoshibumi Nakane and Yasuyuki Ohta of Nagasaki University are gratefully acknowledged. A reduced version of this article appeared in *Commentary, 8,* 26-30, June 1990, Singapore: National University of Singapore Society.

ACUTE RESPIRATORY TRACT INFECTIONS IN CHILDREN: DEVELOPMENT OF A DIAGNOSTIC AID

Farrokh Alemi and Janet Rice

This paper shows, by way of example, how developing countries can create decision aids that can increase the number of patients served by a group of physicians. A panel of seven American physicians practicing in New Orleans came to a consensus about the factors important in prescribing antibiotics for children with cold-like symptoms. Panelists also estimated the diagnostic value for each factor. A Bayesian probability model simulated the panel's judgment. Researchers in developing countries could use the methods described to quickly and inexpensively design similar decision aids sensitive to presentation of the disease in their locality.

Respiratory infections of children is a global health care problem (Chretien, Holland, Macklen, Murray & Woolcock, 1984). Part of the problem is the availability of antibiotics for treatment of children, but perhaps equally important is the appropriate use of available antibiotics. Recently, Sharm, Hart, and Thomas (1984) suggested a protocol for clinical evaluation of children with respiratory infections. Their system classifies children breathing more than 50 times per minute into mild, moderate, or severe pneumonia depending on varying degrees of retraction, cyanosis, or both. However, a rule-based diagnostic protocol like this oversimplifies the diagnostic problem and ignores the underlying probability relation between symptoms and the need for antibiotics. Thus it may erroneously treat patients who do not need antibiotics. In this paper, we describe a probability system, for distinguishing between appropriate and inappropriate use of antibiotics. This paper also serves as a blueprint for how researchers can create decision aids to help health care practice in their region.

System Development

The data reported here reflect how seven physicians, with extensive clinical experience, judge the presentation of respiratory infection in New Orleans, United States of America. This data may not be relevant to other locations. We recommend that other researchers should use the methods presented here but not the specific findings.

The physicians met for a two half-day conference. On the first half-day meeting, they reached a consensus about what clinical factors were relevant in deciding the need for antibiotic treatment of respiratory infection (see Table 1). On the second half-day meeting, each physician estimated the prevalence of these factors among two groups of children: one that did and one that did not need antibiotics. When their estimates widely disagreed the physicians discussed their different points of view and re-estimated their responses. For example, we asked the physicians to answer questions like:

> "Of 100 children between 6 months and five years old, who in the judgment of excellent clinicians need antibiotic therapy, how many have a fever of 101 to 104 degrees?"

> "Of 100 children between 6 months and five years old, who in the judgment of excellent clinicians do not need antibiotics, how many have a fever of 101 to 104 degrees?"

The "likelihood ratio" associated with fever between 101 and 104 degrees is the ratio of the responses to the above two questions. Questions were not presented in a random order, and physicians were allowed to back track and change their responses. Any objective data that was relevant and accessible was provided to the physicians. Physicians responded to the questions individually, discussed their answers, and re-estimated responses. This process of estimate, talk and re-estimation in our experience helps the panelist see the assumptions behind each of the other experts' estimates. Thus it leads to improved accuracy of estimates. Table 1 presents the geometric mean of the different physicians' estimates used in the analysis (the likelihood ratio for the above example is shown in the table to be 1.58).

TABLE 1

Likelihood Ratios Associated with Various Findings

Factor	Likelihood Ratio	Supports Use of Antibiotics
Age		
6 mos. – 1 yr.	1.54	Yes
1 yr. – 5 yrs.	1.00*	No
Modulating Factors		
None	0.72	No
Asthma	0.39	No
Recent Choking	0.75	No
Otitis Media	10.00**	Yes
Sickle Cell	4.22	Yes
Steroids	3.00*	Yes
Use of Antibiotics	0.88	No
Use of Cold Suppressants	1.08	Yes
Use of Antipyretics	1.38	Yes
Temperature		
< 99	0.13	No
99 – < 101	0.57	No

Table 1 (continued)

Factor	Likelihood Ratio	Supports Use of Antibiotics
101 – < 104	1.58	Yes
> 104	1.89	Yes
Duration – Improving/Not Improving		
1 day – Improving	0.87*	No
1 day – Not Improving	0.87	No
1 – 7 days – Improving	0.37	No
1 – 7 days – Not Improving	1.45	Yes
> 7 days – Improving	0.57	No
> 7 days – Not Improving	2.80	Yes
Appearance		
Alert	0.75*	No
Sleepy	2.29	Yes
Distressed	9.69	Yes
Age & Respiration Rate		
6 mos. – 1 yr., RR < 30	0.27	No
6 mos. – 1 yr., 30 > RR < 55	1.41	Yes
6 mos. – 1 yr., RR > 55	1.91	Yes
1 yr. – 5 yrs., RR < 25	0.24	No
1 yr. – 5 yrs., 25 > RR < 40	1.13	Yes
1 yr. – 5 yrs., RR > 40	3.19	Yes
Cough		
None	0.49	No
Brassy	0.37	No
Productive	1.92	Yes
Dyspnea		
Not Present	0.78	No
Present	1.82	Yes
Nasal Secretion		
None	1.00*	No
Clear	1.00*	No
Not Clear	1.00*	No
Auscultation		
Normal	0.42	No
Localized Bronchial	13.70	Yes
Localized Absent	10.80	Yes
Localized Crackles	3.73	Yes
Localized Wheezes	0.70	No
Localized Suppressed	2.55	Yes
Diffused Bronchial	4.05	Yes
Diffused Suppressed	0.62	No
Diffused Absent	2.84	Yes
Diffused Crackles	1.40	Yes
Diffused Wheezes	0.25	No
Coarse Breath Sounds	0.47	No

* Indicates that these likelihood ratios were re-estimated after second day panel by the experts.

Factors with likelihood ratios larger than one suggest that the patient may need antibiotics, smaller than one, that they do not. The closer a ratio is to one, the less useful it is as a diagnostic indicator.

Physicians also estimated that on the average one out of every 3.4 children at their offices needed antibiotics (odds of $1/3.4 = 0.29$). The Bayesian probability model uses these estimates to predict the need for antibiotics. Several researchers have successfully used this model in other diagnostic tasks (e.g., Gustafson, Greist, Strauss, Erdman, & Laughren, 1977). According to this model, the posterior odds for receiving antibiotic treatment are equal to the product of the likelihood ratios associated with the observed symptoms, times the odds of receiving antibiotic treatment.

An example will show how the Bayesian model works. Table 2 presents a patient's symptoms, each of which is associated with a likelihood ratio. First these ratios are multiplied together, then the product is multiplied by the prior odds of needing antibiotics. The result, 12.16, shows the posterior odds for needing antibiotics. The probability of needing antibiotics, calculated from the posterior odds, is 0.92, which suggests that this patient is likely to need antibiotics.

TABLE 2

Case Example Using Bayesian Model to Predict Need for Antibiotics

Factor	Description	Likelihood Ratio
Age	1 – 5 yrs.	1.00
Modulating Factors	Asthma	0.39
Rectal Temperature	More than 104	1.89
Duration	1 day improving	0.87
Appearance	Sleepy	2.30
Respiratory Rate	40	3.19
Cough	Productive cough	1.92
Dyspnea	Yes	1.82
Nasal Secretion	Absent	1.00
Auscultation	Localized suppressed sounds	2.55

Notes

Posterior Odds = Likelihood Ratios x Prior Odds
Posterior Odds = (1.00 x 0.39 x 1.89 x .87 x 2.30 x 3.19 x 1.92 x 1.82 x
          1.00 x 2.55) x 0.29 = 12.16
Need for Antibiotics = Posterior Odds/(1 + Posterior Odds) = 12.16/(1 + 12.6)
          = 0.92

System Evaluation

To evaluate the accuracy of the Bayesian predictions, the physicians on our panel described typical patients in their practice, using the symptoms in Table 1. On the first day, the physicians provided clinical factors relevant in deciding the need for antibiotic treatment. The project staff summarized, on large flip charts in front of the panel, the relevant factors the experts suggested. At the end of the session, the panelist used these factors to describe a total of 105 typical patients presented at their clinics. On the second day of the meeting, the physicians rated each case in terms of the need for antibiotics on a scale of 0 to 100. One hundred indicated a patient with a clear need and zero the reverse. Where there was substantial disagreement, the physicians discussed the case and individually rated it again. For each case, we compared the predictions of the Bayesian model with the average of the ratings of the physicians.

For each of the 105 cases, the Bayesian prediction was calculated and compared with the average rating of the physicians. Using Analysis of Variance, the Bayesian predictions explained 86 percent of the variance in the ratings of the physicians. The finding was statistically significant at alpha levels lower than 0.001, suggesting that the Bayesian model was accurately simulating the physicians' average judgments.

Discussion

The system of probabilities presented in this paper successfully simulates average judgment of seven experienced physicians. Compared with earlier research (Sharm, Hart, & Thomas, 1984), it distinguishes more carefully the need for antibiotic treatment.

Since physicians both designed and rated the cases, there might be a bias that the index is only relevant to patients presented at the clinics of these physicians. The performance of the index in another set of cases may be different. In testing a decision aid one faces a dilemma. The aid should be tested on the target population, but adherence to one makes the aid less useful to other populations. We feel that we have a representative sample of patients that typically show up at clinics in New Orleans. Researchers, who intend to use the aid in other settings, may need to modify it.

Another concern is whether the physicians' subjective ratings are an appropriate standard for testing the accuracy of the system predictions. Clinical judgments are necessarily subjective and physicians often disagree; when their judgments do agree, our confidence in their advice is increased. We therefore investigated the amount of agreement among them. Table 3 summarizes the correlation among ratings of the 105 different hypothetical patient descriptions. These correlations are high and suggest a substantial amount of agreement. In addition, analysis of the variance shows that knowing who rated the case does not provide any statistically significant information about the rating. These results suggest that the physicians agreed on the rating of the 105 cases, and it is reasonable to use these ratings to test the accuracy of the Bayesian model.

The proposed system's numerical calculations might be considered too time-consuming for practicing physicians. However, the calculations can be done by a programmable calculator or a personal computer, which are becoming widespread in clinical practice in developed countries. Or if personal computers are not widely available, an operator can use one machine to provide advice through telephone to health care providers in different clinics.

	TABLE 3					
	Correlation Between the Rating of Any Two Panelists on 105 Cases					
	EXPERT					
EXPERT	1	2	3	4	5	6
2	0.77					
3	0.82	0.72				
4	0.83	0.78	0.77			
5	0.87	0.75	0.82	0.82		
6	0.85	0.75	0.79	0.81	0.86	
7	0.88	0.77	0.80	0.84	0.87	0.79

This paper shows how a prototype advice system can be developed with ease and without substantial investment. Developers of diagnostic aids should rely on physicians familiar with the presentation of diseases among the target population. Participation of these physicians will not only improve accuracy of predictions but also enhance chances that the system may be eventually implemented and used.

References

Chretien, J., Holland, W., Macklen, P., Murray, J., and Woolcock, A. (1984). Acute respiratory infections in children: A global health problem. *New England Journal of Medicine, 310,* 615, 982-984.

Gustafson, D.H., Greist, J.H., Strauss, F.F., Erdman, H., and Laughren, T. (1977). A probability system for identifying suicide attemptors. *Computers and Biomedical Research, 10,* 1-7.

Sharm, F., Hart, K., and Thomas, D. (1984). Acute lower respiratory infections in children: Possible criteria for selection of patients for antibiotic therapy and hospital admission. *Bulletin of World Health Organization, 62,* 749-753.

Acknowledgments

The data reported here reflect judgments of Drs. Joann Gates, John Gavin, Neal Halsey, Nathan Kern, Tony Kriseman, Andrea Ruff, and William W. Waring. The Biomedical Research Support Grant PHS-2507-RR05444-23 supported this research. In addition, the authors gratefully acknowledge the help in conceptualizing the study given by Claudio Schuftan, M.D., the editorial help of Gillian F. Brown, Ph.D., and the data analysis provided by Craig Kipples, M.P.H., John Agliato, M.S.W., M.P.H., and Peter Fos, D.D.S., M.P.H.. We completed this project at Tulane University. The first author can be reached at Cleveland State University, 2121 Evelid, Rm 532, Cleveland, OH 44115, U.S.A.

Note

A reduced version of this article appeared in *Commentary, 8,* 21-25, June 1990, Singapore: National University of Singapore Society.

MEDICAL DECISION MAKING: ISSUES ON INTERPRETATION OF DIAGNOSTIC TEST RESULTS

William Chin Ling Yip, John Sin Hock Tay, and Ting Fei Ho

Medical diagnosis by logical deduction of the quantitative information obtained from a diagnostic test is no easy matter. Familiar terms to quantify the reliability of the diagnostic information, like sensitivity, specificity, positive and negative predictive values and accuracy are used commonly, but often misleadingly, in medical decision making. This article examines critically the intrinsic value of the diagnostic test and its predictive value and their interrelation. The relevant diagnostic parameters can be easily calculated by the 2 x 2 table. Selective graphs are used to illustrate the interplay of sensitivity and specificity of the diagnostic test and prevalence of the disease on the predictive values. Sensitivity and specificity are determined by the chosen diagnostic criteria. The term accuracy has little scientific meaning. With less than a perfect diagnostic test, its predictive values are affected not only by the sensitivity and specificity, but also by the prevalence of the disease. In general, positive predictive value will drop while the negative predictive value will rise with decreasing prevalence. It is therefore important to consider together all the relevant parameters of a diagnostic test before final decision making.

Medical diagnosis is frequently dependent on the results of one or more diagnostic tests. The interpretation of a diagnostic test is, however, not an easy matter. Familiar terms like sensitivity, specificity, false positive and negative rate, positive and negative predictive value and accuracy, commonly appear in the medical literature. They are unfortunately frequently misused (Phillips, Scott, & Blasczcynski, 1983). However, proper understanding of the actual meaning of all these terms is absolutely important in the correct interpretation of diagnostic information (Yip, Tay, & Wong, 1985).

The purpose of this article is not to present a comprehensive mathematical approach to medical diagnosis. This in fact has been advocated as far back as a quarter of a century ago (Warner et al., 1961). Neither is this an account of the problems or obstacles to the acceptance of clinical decision analysis. This too has been elaborately discussed recently (Balla, Elstein, & Christensen, 1989). Rather the aim is to provide the readers with a simple account on how to evaluate the reliability of a diagnostic test and how to make use of the diagnostic test to predict the presence or absence of a particular disease in a particular population with a known prevalence of that disease.

Reliability of Diagnostic Test

The relevant numerical data relating to the diagnostic test and the outcome of the disease can be represented by the simple 2 x 2 table (Table 1).

TABLE 1		
The 2 x 2 Table		
	Final Diagnosis	
	Positive	Negative
Positive	a	b
Test		
Negative	c	d
	Disease	No disease

Two simple indices to indicate the reliability of a diagnostic test are "sensitivity" and "specificity." These can be represented mathematically as follows:

Sensitivity = P (T + |D+) = a/(a+c)
Specificity = P (T - |D-) = d/(b+d)

where P, T and D represent probability, test and disease, respectively. P(T + |D+) indicates the probability of a positive test in the population with disease, while P(T - |D-) indicates the probability of a negative test in the population with no disease.

A perfect diagnostic test is one which has a perfect score for both sensitivity (= 1.0) and specificity (= 1.0). This is possible when c = 0, i.e., when there is no false negative case, and when b = 0, i.e., when there is no false positive case. Written mathematically thus, when:

False negative rate = P(D + |T-) = c/(c+d) = 0, sensitivity = 1

False positive rate = P(D - |T+) = b/(a+b) = 0, specificity = 1

Effect of Changing Diagnostic Criteria on Sensitivity and Specificity

In medical practice, a perfect diagnostic test is not only frequently difficult to come by, the reliability of the test is also influenced by the diagnostic criteria chosen. In other words, changing the diagnostic criteria may result in changes in the numerals, a, b, c, and d, in the 2 x 2 table, and thus the sensitivity and specificity of the test, even in the same sample of patients. The following hypothetical example of serum digoxin levels in 83 patients (21 with and 62 without clinical digoxin toxicity) further serves to illustrate this point (Figure 1) (Ingelfinger, Mosteller, Thibodeau, & Ware, 1987). Hence, the numericals in the 2 x 2 table (Table 2) will change if the chosen criterion for positive (digoxin level) test changes from 1.0 ng/ml to 2.0 ng/ml, resulting in different sensitivity and specificity in the same population of patients (Table 2). The sensitivity has therefore decreased from 0.86 to 0.48 (p < .01), while the specificity has increased from 0.39 to 1.00 (p < .0001).

TABLE 2

Effect of Changing Diagnostic Criterion on Sensitivity and Specificity

	Diagnostic Toxicity				Diagnostic Toxicity	
	D+	D-			D+	D-
T+	18	38		T+	10	0
Test				Test		
(>1.0 ng/ml)T-	3	24		(>1.0 ng/ml)T-	11	62

Sensitivity = 18/21 = 0.86   Sensitivity = 11/21 = 0.48
Specificity = 24/62 = 0.39   Specificity = 62/62 = 1.00

FIGURE 1

Hypothetical Example of Digoxin Level and Clinical Toxicity

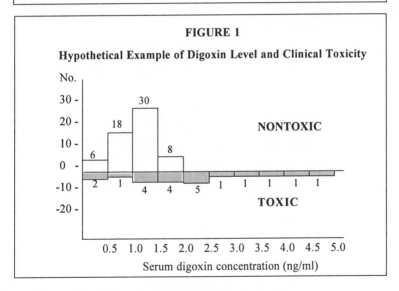

Reliability of Diagnostic Test in Different Patient Populations

One important question in the assessment of the reliability of a diagnostic test is whether the particular test is equally reliable in other patient populations, using the same diagnostic criterion. In other words, does the intrinsic value of the diagnostic test, i.e., its sensitivity and specificity, remain unchanged in different patient populations suffering from the same disease? This is frequently not so. The following examples on diagnosis of hypertrophic pyloric stenosis in infants using the recently available ultrasound technique serve to explain further (Table 3; Yip et al., 1985).

TABLE 3

Diagnostic Parameters in Infants with
Hypertrophic Pyloric Stenosis

	Sensitivity	Specificity	False Positive Rate	False Negative Rate
Strauss et al., Ventral-dorsal diameter > 1.5 cm	1.00	0.80	0.06	0
Blumhagen et al., Muscle wall thickness > 4.0 mm	0.92	1.00	0	0.09
Wilson et al., True pyloric muscle length > 2.0 cm	1.00	1.00	0	0
Wilson et al., Ventral-dorsal diameter > 1.5 cm	0.52	1.00	0	0.40

In 1981, Strauss et al. first proposed the sonographic criterion of ventral-dorsal diameter of more than 1.5 cm for the ultrasound diagnosis of infantile hypertrophic pyloric stenosis, a fairly frequent cause of severe vomiting in infants due to gastric outlet obstruction. Subsequently, two other sonographic criteria were proposed-- muscle wall thickness of more than 4.0 mm by Blumhagen and Noble (1983) and the true pyloric muscle length of more than 2.0 cm by Wilson and Vanhoutte (1984). All three diagnostic tests appeared to be equally reliable in the original series, although the true pyloric muscle length method might be marginally better as both sensitivity and specificity were 1.00 (Table 3). However, if the ventral-dorsal diameter of more than 1.5 cm were to be applied to Wilson et al.'s (1984) series of patients, the sensitivity would drop drastically from 1.00 to 0.52 with an unacceptable false negative rate of 0.40, rendering the test totally unreliable and therefore useless. Hence, it is important to remember that the reliability of a diagnostic test cannot be assumed by other workers in another group of patients. This is because the same diagnostic criterion may not "happen" to separate the disease from the non-disease so clearly in another studied patient population.

Predictive Values of a Diagnostic Test

Consideration of the reliability of a diagnostic test thus far has been centered on its intrinsic value, that is, the sensitivity and specificity. However, what is more important clinically to a physician and finally to the patient is whether the patient has or does not have the disease given a positive test or a negative test. In other words, what is the probability of the disease being present in a particular patient (positive predictive value) given a positive diagnostic test and the probability of the disease being absent in a particular patient (negative predictive value) given a negative diagnostic test?

The predictive values are usually presented by rather complicated mathematical formulae using the Bayesian theorem (Armitage & Berry, 1987). These may pose some problems in the understanding of the interrelation of the various diagnostic parameters for the uninitiated. Fortunately, the predictive values can be easily expressed by the 2 x 2 table. Hence, from Table 1:

Positive predictive value = $P(D+|T+) = a/(a+b)$

Negative predictive value = $P(D-|T-) = d/(c+d)$

In the assessment of the clinical usefulness of a diagnostic test, another frequently used index is "accuracy."

"Accuracy" = $(a+d)/(a+b+c+d)$

Thus, "accuracy" is supposed to be an overall index for positive and negative predictive values combined, since it is a measure of both the true positive (a) and true negative (d) rates. However, "accuracy" by itself has little clinical meaning, since for the physician or the patient, what is relevant is the positive and the negative predictive values separately rather than an overall figure.

Determinants of Predictive Values

It is obvious that the predictive values are determined by the intrinsic values of the diagnostic test, i.e., its sensitivity and specificity. What is commonly not realized is that the predictive values are also determined by the prevalence of the disease. This fact can be easily proven mathematically. From Table 2:

Prevalence (PREV) = $P(D+) = (a+c)/(a+b+c+d) = k1$ (1)
Sensitivity (SEN) = $P(T+|D+) = a/(a+c) = k2$ (2)
Specificity (SPE) = $P(T-|D-) = d/(b+d) = k3$ (3)

Similarly, from Table 1:

Positive predictive value (PPV) = $P(D+|T+) = a/(a+b)$ (4)
Negative predictive value (NPV) = $P(D-|T-) = d/(c+d)$ (5)
Accuracy (ACC) = $(a+d)/(a+b+c+d)$ (6)

It has been shown by simple algebra (Tay et al., 1988) that PPV, NPV and ACC can be written in terms of PREV (k1), SEN (k2) and SPE (k3) by simultaneously solving equations (1) to (6). Hence,

$$PPV = \frac{k1k2}{k1k2 + (1-k1)(1-k3)} \qquad (7)$$

$$NPV = \frac{k3(1-k1)}{k3(1-k1)+k1(1-k2)} \qquad (8)$$

$$ACC = k1k2 + k3(1-k1) \qquad (9)$$

The influence of prevalence of the disease on predictive values is illustrated by the following examples (Table 4; Yip et al., 1985).

TABLE 4

Effect of Changing Prevalence of Disease on Diagnostic Parameters

Study population	PREV	SEN	SPE	PPV	NPV	ACC
Strauss et al. (6) Ventral-dorsal	0.75	1.00	0.80	0.94	1.00	0.95
diameter > 1.5 cm	0.23	1.00	0.80	0.60	1.00	0.85
Significance of difference *	p<0.0001	-	-	p=0.017	-	p=0.17
Wilson et al. (8) Ventral-dorsal	0.58	0.97	0.86	0.90	0.95	0.92
diameter > 1.2 cm	0.12	0.97	0.86	0.48	0.99	0.87
Significance of difference *	p<0.0001	-	-	p<0.0001	-	p=0.13

ACC = Accuracy, NPV = Negative predictive value, PREV = Prevalence,
PPV = Positive predictive value, SEN = Sensitivity, SPE = Specificity.
* Fisher's exact probability test

In these examples taken from the studies of Strauss, Itzchak, and Manor (1981) and Wilson et al. (1984), the effect of lowering the prevalence of the disease (hypertrophic pyloric stenosis) results in drastically reduced positive predictive values by sonography, even though the sensitivity and specificity are kept constant. Of note is that despite the significant reduction of the positive predictive value rendering the test virtually useless for confirmation of the diagnosis of hypertrophic pyloric stenosis, the overall "accuracy" is not significantly reduced.

The complex interrelation between predictive values, prevalence and sensitivity and specificity are best illustrated by expressing equations (7) to (9) graphically (Figures 2-4; Tay et al., 1988). If the prevalence is in the region of 0.01 (Figure 2), the positive predictive value is very low despite a reasonably high sensitivity and specificity of say, 0.90. On the other hand, the negative predictive value is extremely high even though the sensitivity and specificity are as low as 0.10. "Accuracy" in this case, as an overall index, is totally inaccurate in indicating how useful is the test.

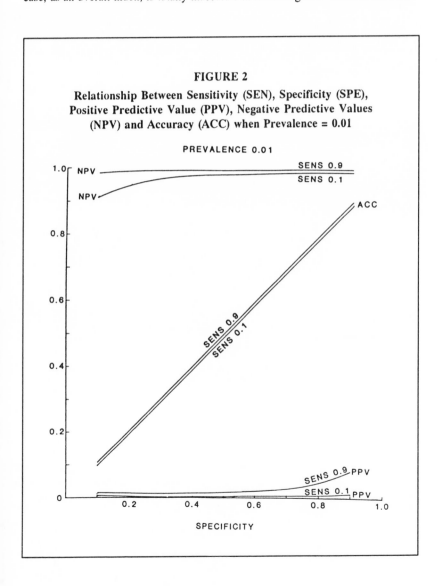

FIGURE 2

Relationship Between Sensitivity (SEN), Specificity (SPE), Positive Predictive Value (PPV), Negative Predictive Values (NPV) and Accuracy (ACC) when Prevalence = 0.01

With a prevalence of 0.1 (Figure 3), the positive predictive value starts to climb steeply if the sensitivity and specificity exceed 0.90. On the contrary, the negative predictive value gradually drops with lowering of the sensitivity and specificity. Again, "accuracy" has no useful clinical value.

In the unlikely clinical event of high prevalence of 0.9 (Figure 4), the negative predictive value is low despite high sensitivity and specificity of 0.90. The positive predictive value, on the other hand, is very high. The overall index "accuracy" does not reflect this important message given the same sensitivity and specificity.

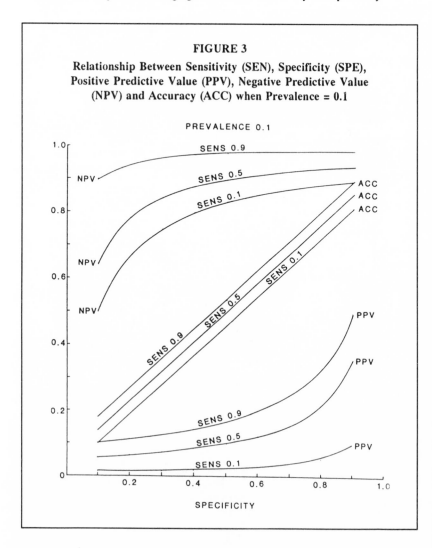

FIGURE 3

Relationship Between Sensitivity (SEN), Specificity (SPE), Positive Predictive Value (PPV), Negative Predictive Value (NPV) and Accuracy (ACC) when Prevalence = 0.1

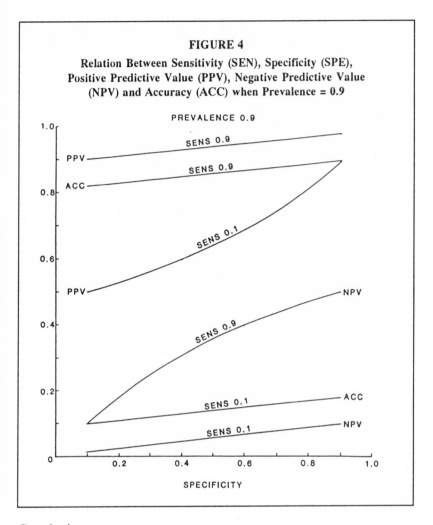

FIGURE 4

Relation Between Sensitivity (SEN), Specificity (SPE), Positive Predictive Value (PPV), Negative Predictive Value (NPV) and Accuracy (ACC) when Prevalence = 0.9

Conclusion

Correct interpretation of the results of a diagnostic test demands proper understanding of the interrelation between the intrinsic values of the test, that is, sensitivity and specificity, and the positive and negative predictive values which are influenced by the prevalence of the disease. The overall index "accuracy" has little clinical value and should be removed. In general, the positive predictive value will drop, sometimes very drastically, despite high sensitivity and specificity, if the prevalence of the disease is low. This is especially relevant in screening for rare metabolic disease in a newborn or population screening for uncommon disease. Hence, all the relevant parameters of the diagnostic test should be considered before medical decision making. These can be easily computed from the 2 x 2 table using a simple computer program (Yip, Tay, Ho, & Wong, 1986).

References

Armitage, P. and Berry, G. (1987). *Statistical Methods in Medical Research. (2nd Ed.).* Oxford: Blackwell Scientific Publications.

Balla, J.I., Elstein, A.S., and Christensen, C. (1989). Obstacles to acceptance of clinical decision analysis. *British Medical Journal, 298,* 579-582.

Blumhagen, J.D. and Noble, H.G.S. (1983). Muscle thickness in hypertrophic pyloric stenosis. *American Journal of Roentgenology, 140,* 221-223.

Ingelfinger, J.A., Mosteller, F., Thibodeau, L.A., and Ware, J.H. (1987). *Biostatistics in Clinical Medicine. (2nd Ed.).* New York: Macmillan Publishing Co., Inc.

Phillips, W.C., Scott, J.A., and Blasczcynski, G. (1983). Statistics of diagnostic procedures. I. How sensitive is "sensitivity," how specific is "specificity?" *American Journal of Roentgenology, 140,* 1265-1270.

Strauss, S., Itzchak, Y., and Manor, A., et al. (1981). Sonography of hypertrophic pyloric stenosis. *American Journal of Roentgenology, 136,* 1057-1058.

Tay, J.S.H., Yip, W.C.L., and Ho, T.F. (1988). Unpublished observation.

Warner, H.R., Toronto, A.F., Veasey, L.G., and Stephenson, R. (1961). A mathematical approach to medical diagnosis. Application to congenital heart disease. *Journal of American Medical Association, 177,* 177-183.

Wilson, D.A. and Vanhoutte, J.J. (1984). The reliable sonographic diagnosis of hypertrophic stenosis. *Journal of Clinical Ultrasound, 12,* 201-204.

Yip, W.C.L., Tay, J.S.H., Ho, T.F., and Wong, H.B. (1986). Computers in Paediatrics: 18. Medical decision making: Computer programme to calculate sensitivity, specificity, false positive and negative rates, positive and negative predictive values and accuracy of a diagnostic test. *Journal of the Singapore Paediatric Society, 28,* 74-78.

Yip, W.C.L., Tay, J.S.H., and Wong, H.B. (1985). Sonographic diagnosis of infantile hypertrophic pyloric stenosis: Critical appraisal of reliability and diagnostic criteria. *Journal of Clinical Ultrasound, 13,* 329-332.

CLINICAL DECISION MAKING: WHAT DO WE KNOW ABOUT REAL-WORLD PERFORMANCE?

Shane A. Thomas, Janet Doyle, and Colette Browning

This paper is concerned with the external validity of research in human judgment and decision making in clinical settings. A review of commonly used research tools, such as Patient Management Problems, reveals that there may be low correlations between clinician decision performance on PMOs and in the clinic. It is further argued that factors such as clinician stress and tiredness are often removed from laboratory studies, when, in fact, they are inherent features of clinical settings such as the Intensive Care Unit. It is noted that Brunswik's (1956) call for representative design principles in the construction of studies of judgment and decision making remains appropriate to this day. Much of what is known about decision-making behavior in the laboratory may not be valid in the clinic and that there is an urgent need for high-fidelity studies of clinical decision making.

Decision making in clinical settings has become of considerable interest to judgment and decision-making researchers, as well as clinicians. This high level of interest is reflected in the publication of a series of recent texts (e.g., Dowie & Elstein, 1988; Sox, Blatt, Higgins, & Marton, 1988; Turk & Salovey, 1988) and the production of journals devoted to the area such as Medical Decision Making. Fineberg (1981) has argued for the routine incorporation of judgment and decision-making principles into clinical decision making. His arguments included the necessity for systematic ways of dealing with the volume of new and complexity of information, the ability of decision principles and theory to represent knowledge across all clinical disciplines, economic pressures towards the more effective use of resources and the pressures for health consumers to participate in clinical decisions. Fineberg's arguments like many researchers in the area, revolve around the notion that clinical decision research may ultimately result in improved decision performance in the clinics, a praiseworthy objective.

What then is the evidence concerning real-world clinical decision performance? One of the landmark studies of clinical performance in real-world settings is provided by Beck, Devlin, and Lunn (1988; also see Lunn & Devlin, 1987), who investigated perioperative deaths for the Nuffield Provincial Hospitals' Trust in the United Kingdom. Over a period of 12 months, the project team collected data concerning 485,850 operations and 5,081 deaths. Each case was examined by a team of expert surgeons and anesthetists, where appropriate, to examine the quality of care. The reviews were conducted confidentially and when the analyses were complete, the data were shredded. The audit revealed that 22.2% of the reviewed deaths were classified as "avoidable." Errors of clinician judgment and decision errors were prominent as reasons for many of the deaths. The Nuffield study demonstrates convincingly that there is room for improvement in clinical performance through improved clinical decision performance. Yet aside from the Nuffield study, much of the clinical decision research has been done in the laboratory, using simulated patients and operating under conditions that do not reflect the situation in the clinic. The question that arises from these circumstances is what is really known about clinical judgment and decision making in real clinical settings?

The desirability of conducting research under realistic conditions is a basic feature of most discussions of research design (e.g., Polgar & Thomas, 1988). In the judgment and decision-making literature, Brunswik's (1956) principle of representative design, first stated over 30 years ago, emphasized the need for the use of representative and realistic tasks in the study of human judgment. More recently, Ebbesen and Konecni (1980) have raised the issue of the external validity of much decision research. By analyzing a variety of studies comparing decision-making behavior in "real" versus "simulated" situations, Ebbesen and Konecni (1980) concluded "There is considerable evidence to suggest that the external validity of decision-making research that relies on laboratory simulations of real-world decision problems is low" (p. 42). However, while Ebbesen and Konecni's work may well apply to clinical decision research, it was based on examples drawn from judicial decision making, driver behavior, and other non-clinical settings.

In the medical education literature, there has been considerable work done on the use of simulated patients and the simulated Patient Management Problem (PMP) in clinical education. The basic thrust of this work stems from the necessity for providing training and skills that will generalize into the real clinic. The simulated Patient Management Problem (PMP) was developed as a response to concerns regarding the validity of multiple choice and essay tests in assessing the clinical competence of physicians and as a method of teaching clinical skills to medical students (Goran, Williamson, & Gonnella, 1973). PMPs usually take the form of a written description of a patient's complaints together with a number of patient management options or selections, and have received widespread acceptance in the medical education community.

The content validity of the tests has rarely been questioned and most researchers agree that PMPs provide a good range of relevant subject matter and tap the cognitive skills involved in clinical decision making (Sedlacek & Nattress, 1972). However, many researchers have expressed concerns about the adequacy of the construct and criterion validity of these tests.

Newble, Hoare, and Baxter (1982) proposed that for a PMP to demonstrate good construct validity, students should show a developmental function of increasing proficiency on PMPs and that physicians should demonstrate the most proficiency on these tests. Their study indicated that physicians were less proficient (as measured by their percentage agreement with a criterion group) than senior students. It should also be noted that this trend was not verified statistically and in a reanalysis of these findings, Wolf (1984) reported only one significant effect, sixth year students were more proficient than fourth year students. Wolf (1984) concluded that the limited sample size used by Newble et al. (1982) contributed to this result. He further argued that to assess the construct validity of PMPs more rigorous designs need to be implemented, which include more difficult problems and provide more sensitive measures of differences between students and physicians of varying experience as most students and physicians may represent a fairly homogeneous group in terms of clinical competence.

The relationship between clinical decisions based on PMPs and those made by clinicians in real settings (the criterion validity) has been studied by a number of investigators. Goran et al. (1973) compared the clinical judgment of physicians assessing a urinary tract infection with their judgment on a PMP. Overall, physicians sought more history and clinical test data under the PMP condition than in the real clinical setting, and physicians who performed well on the PMP did not necessarily perform well in the clinical setting. One reason offered by the authors is that in the PMP condition, it was easier in terms of time and costs to seek out more potentially diagnostic information and order laboratory tests than in the clinical setting. The authors concluded that there are questions about the validity of PMPs in predicting physician behavior in real clinical settings.

Several authors have pointed out that because the physician has a number of management options available in written form in the PMP, he or she is cued to choose options that may not be chosen in the real setting. A common finding is that clinicians chose more options under PMP conditions (Goran et al., 1973; Page & Fielding, 1980) whereas the thoroughness of data gathering is not highly correlated with the "correctness" of the diagnosis in real clinical settings (Barrows, Neufeld, Feightner, & Norman, 1978).

In summary, most authors agree that PMPs demonstrate adequate content and construct validity but do not predict actual performance in clinical settings. Page and Fielding (1980, p. 537) concluded:

"...this result is perhaps an expression of the sad state of the art of testing clinical reasoning skills. At present there is little, if any, evidence to support the criterion validity of any technique for testing these skills."

Thus, there is evidence to suggest that some research findings about clinician judgment, that have been based on PMP tasks, may have questionable application in real clinical situations. What then is the situation in the many studies that do not employ PMPs but use other paper and pencil tasks? The use of simulated patients, paper and pencil tests and non-clinical settings is almost universal in the clinical decision literature. Even a cursory examination of the clinical decision literature reveals that most studies do not study clinical decision making in the clinic, and frequently they do not discuss the effects of the realism of the tasks in the study upon the external validity of their findings. One notable exception to this rule is the work by Elstein, Shulman, and Sprafka (1978) who provide some discussion of the level of "fidelity" or validity of the tasks they asked the physicians to perform in their studies. However, such discussion is all too rare.

There are, of course, sound logistic and methodological reasons that can be advanced for the use of laboratory settings over field settings. Laboratory settings are cheaper, ethically "safer" and more controlled. Yet perhaps it is the very level of control that may squeeze out the external validity of the research. There are many factors that may impinge upon "real-world" clinical decision making that are often removed from the laboratory context. Thus, it is all very well to permit the pure study of phenomena in the laboratory, but if these factors are profound in their level of influence, the researcher may have studied a "pure" phenomenon that is not evidenced in the clinic, or one of such small magnitude that it is overcome by the magnitude of these other effects.

It is therefore appropriate to examine factors important in real-world clinical settings that may not be represented in the simulated conditions of the research laboratory. For example, Eisenberg (1979) in a seminal review paper of the sociologic influences on clinical decisions, concluded that both clinician and patient character- istics (e.g., the patient's sex or race) have large influences on the patient outcomes and the clinicians' decision-making performance. Eisenberg has emphasized that clinical decisions are made in a social context and that this context needs to be included in explanations and descriptions of clinical decision making. Doyle and Thomas (1988) have also argued that clinical decisions are the resultants of a system including the patient, their characteristics and social context and the clinician.

Although much is known about clinician variables such as level of stress and level of arousal or tiredness and their effects on decision performance, these effects are rarely mentioned or controlled in studies of clinical decision making. For the purposes of this paper, it is proposed to examine the effects of stress and tiredness upon clinical performance, as examples of factors that are usually uncontrolled in studies of clinical decision making.

Stress and Clinical Decision Making

Stress is a concept often discussed in the health and popular literatures. Defini- tions of stress vary but Selye's (1956) definition of stress as "the non-specific physiological response of the body to any demand on it" has been widely used. Lazarus (1976) argues that stress occurs when there are demands made on a person with which he or she cannot cope, in other words, a shortfall in capacity to deal with environmental demands (see Weinman, 1987 for an introductory review of this literature).

In some areas of clinical practice, high levels of stress are inevitable. In the hospital Intensive Care Unit (ICU), the rapid changes in the health status of seriously ill patients demand that the nurse makes many decisions in a short time interval, often with partial information and a high degree of uncertainty. Further, these decisions may have a profound impact on the very life of the patient. Hay and Oken (1972) have reviewed the range of stressors in operation in the ICU but did not focus on the effects of these upon the nurse's decision performance.

A number of nursing researchers have written about the ICU experience as situations where stress can influence the quality of clinical decisions. Lippincott (1979) in a review of psychological stress factors in decision making argued that the recent advances in life support technology mean that cases with profound damage may be maintained for a protracted period whereas previously they would die without the necessity for an active decision. Lippincott (1979) argued these advances have resulted in the necessity for many more decisions to be made about termination of treatment and that these decisions are inherently stressful. Bourbonnais and Baumann (1985) have reviewed the factors in high-stress environments, such as in the ICU, that may hinder the decision-making process. They point out that much decision research has been conducted in situations without time constraints but that little work has been done in time-related high-stress situations. Bourbonnais & Baumann (1985) argue that case studies should be used in order to train critical care nurses to deal with a range of situations. They also argue that good team functioning is essential, especially in the physician-nurse relationship. Huckabay and Jagla (1979) surveyed 46 nurses working in six ICUs in the United States concerning stressful factors in the ICUs. They found that the level of workload in the ICU was perceived as highly stressful by the nurses, as was interpersonal communication with physicians. Interestingly, knowledge-based problems were not rated highly as a stressor by the nurses.

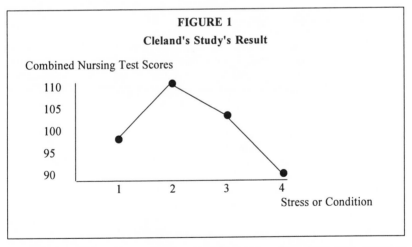

FIGURE 1
Cleland's Study's Result

Cleland (1967) is one of the few researchers to have investigated the effects of stress upon clinical thinking. She studied the reasoning of 60 nurses, of whom groups of 15 were randomly assigned to four conditions ranging from low level of stress to high level of stress, the stress being related to the level of workload and responsibility. Reasoning was measured through performance on two tests, one with items of a medical-surgical content and the other on social interaction. In the lowest stress condition nurses were given the tests, led to a quiet room and told that their nursing activities would be performed by other staff members until they were free. In the highest stress condition, the nurse functioned as charge nurse for a 40-bed unit with a large proportion of high-dependence cases and low staffing and was asked to complete the tests at the nursing station. The intermediate conditions had intermediate levels of workload. Figure 1 shows the results obtained by Cleland.

A small amount of stress improved performance on the tasks but high stress resulted in a noticeable drop in performance. This result is consistent with the inverted U-curve relationship between arousal and performance first proposed by Yerkes and Dodson (1908). The Yerkes-Dodson law proposes that arousal and performance are related such that at both low and high levels of arousal performance is poor, whereas in intermediate levels of arousal, performance is good. This finding has been repeatedly demonstrated in the research literature, and Cleland's findings reproduce this relationship. It should also be noted that the optimal arousal levels are predicted to be lower for complex tasks than for simple by the Yerkes-Dodson law. In other words, high stress levels, may in particular, adversely affect complex tasks such as decision making in the ICU. Cleland's study has the methodological problem that the task being performed may not have been viewed as seriously by the nurses who participated as the competing real jobs on the ward. Nevertheless, Cleland's study demonstrated a decline in performance to be associated with high stress levels. The question remains as to how performance of actual nursing tasks would be influenced by the stressful situations studied.

In other studies of decision makers under time pressure, it has been found that the way information is used may be adversely affected. Wright (1974) studied the effects of time pressure and distraction in a judgment task about cars. Wright allocated 210 undergraduates to six conditions, with three different levels of time pressure and three different levels of distraction. In the high time pressure condition subjects were told to proceed as quickly as possible and that other tasks awaited them. An assistant crossed off ten second intervals on the blackboard to emphasize the time pressure. In the low time pressure condition the subjects were told they had 40 seconds to make their decision and that they had to wait the full time. In the low distraction condition taped background music was played at low volume, whereas in the high distraction condition a radio quiz show was played at a high volume. Wright found that the high distraction and high time pressure groups used much less information in formulating their decisions. If these findings were translated to the clinical context, this could lead to serious decision errors through not using important information.

Thus, it is quite likely that high levels of stress can result in substantial deterioration in clinical decision performance, although there are few studies of clinicians that have investigated such deterioration in real settings. This is not surprising given the ethical difficulties in performing such studies. It is difficult to conduct such research without the risk of harm being done to patients.

Tiredness, Circadian Rhythms and Clinical Decision Performance

One of the features of centralized clinical services such as provided in hospitals is the requirement for the availability of services around the clock. This, of necessity, requires that some clinicians work shifts, often when they are tired and sleep deprived. Many clinicians will attest to the problems of "Saturday staffing" levels and full weekday workloads. Watkins (1984, p. 57) relates a quote from one nurse that is particularly relevant to the present discussion: "You never feel rested. It (rotating shifts) makes you irritable, and you make mistakes." What therefore is the impact of shiftwork and tiredness on clinical decision performance? This section is concerned with investigating this question.

The fact that humans function with a rhythmicity over day and night is well established and is the subject of study by researchers in "circadian rhythms." Many physiological variables such as body temperature, heart rate, blood pressure and the excretion of electrolytes have been shown to vary rhythmically over the daily period. Minors and Waterhouse (1985) have reported significant and regular changes in body temperature and heart rate over the daily period.

Importantly, there has also been much investigation of the changes in mental functions over the daily period. Colquhon (1971) and his team at Cambridge were concerned with studying the relationship between body temperature and mental performance. From a series of studies involving British seamen, Colquhon found a drop in performance in the early afternoon, a so-called post-lunch dip which was unrelated to body temperature changes. Colquhon interpreted the post-lunch dip as evidence of mechanisms other than body temperature affecting mental performance. Previously, variations in body temperature over the daily period had been seen as a key factor in explaining variations in performance.

It should be noted that there is other evidence to suggest that mental performance and alertness show daily variation. Industrial accident statistics reflect substantial variation in risk of accidents over the daily period.

Some research has been done on the rhythms in memory functions over the daily period. Performance on short-term memory tasks (the immediate recall of information) and long-term memory tasks (the delayed recall of information) have been shown to be quite different over the daily period. Some data collated by Monk and Folkard (1985) appear in Figure 2. These data were based on tasks involving the recall of information from written prose by university students.

It would seem that there are important changes in the effectiveness of memory over the daily period. Some memory is a significant component of decision performance. An important question is whether such changes influence decision making in the

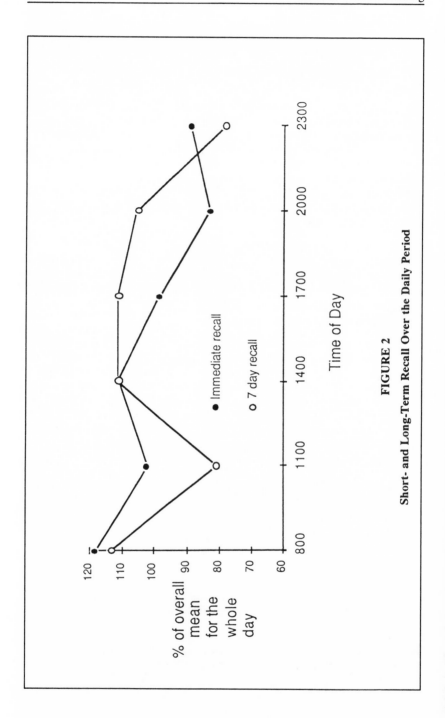

FIGURE 2

Short- and Long-Term Recall Over the Daily Period

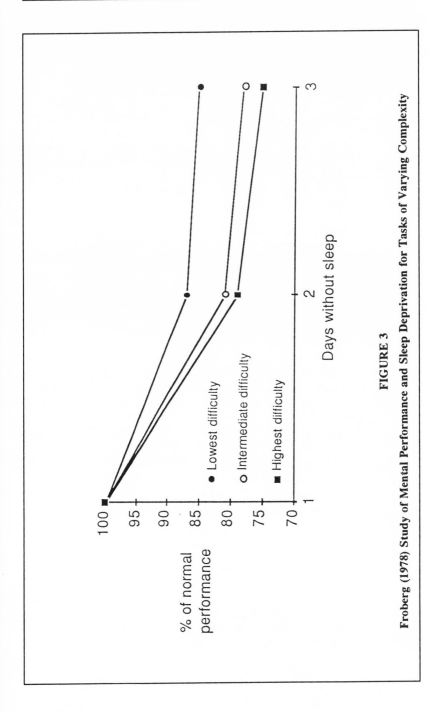

FIGURE 3

Froberg (1978) Study of Mental Performance and Sleep Deprivation for Tasks of Varying Complexity

clinic, and whether changes in memory efficiency may therefore have greater effects on decision performance, especially those involving substantial recall.

Froberg (1978) has investigated the relationship between mental performance and tiredness on tasks of varying complexity. Some of his data are presented in Figure 3.

Fifteen participants were deprived of sleep over 3 days and were required to encode varying numbers of letters into words. The more complex the task, the greater the decline in performance. Froberg (1978) also found that if extra rewards were given, the decline in performance, although substantial, was less than without special rewards. Froberg's data support the predictions made by the Yerkes-Dodson law (see section on stress) that complex tasks are more adversely affected by higher levels of stress than are simple tasks.

It should be noted that the study of circadian rhythms and the effects of sleep deprivation and shiftwork upon them is not without some difficulties. In discussing the shiftwork literature, Monk and Folkard (1985) point out that "very few researchers have been able to carry out good field studies of shiftwork." This observation particularly applies to the study of clinical decision-making performance in the shiftwork context. However, it is ethically unacceptable to place real patients at risk. Furthermore, most of the tasks that have been studied in the laboratory have been rather simple when compared with the complexity of many clinical decision tasks. Nevertheless, there is good evidence that intellectual functions are impaired by tiredness and that there are substantial variations in mental performance over the daily period. These findings are suggestive of similar impairments arising from tiredness and daily variations in levels of performance in clinical decisions, despite the lack of research in this area. This implies that decisions that have discretionary timing should be scheduled at times likely to involve peak intellectual functioning and that tired staff should not make such decisions. The combination of tiredness, stress and sub-optimal mental performance may be an explosive combination in environments demanding speedy and correct clinical decisions, such as in the ICU.

In conclusion, we tender the following observations. There is a growing body of evidence to suggest that performance on clinical decision tasks in the laboratory may not be strongly related to performance in the clinic. In seeking methodological control of extraneous variables operating in the clinic, many clinical decision researchers have constructed highly controlled but unrealistic decision environments. In the two examples of such extraneous variables reviewed in this paper, stress and tiredness, there is substantial literature to suggest that they may have large effects on decision performance. This implies that much of what is known about decision behavior in the laboratory may not be valid in the clinic, where such factors are in operation, because such factors have been eliminated or ignored in many laboratory studies. In addition, much of the judgment and decision-making literature does not draw on clinical tasks. It should also be noted that much of the work in this area has been carried out in the United States. Eisenberg's findings concerning the effects of social and cultural context upon clinical decision making imply that quite different results may be obtained in other cultural contexts. Brunswik's (1956) advice concerning the importance of representative design remains appropriate to this day. High-fidelity studies of decision-making behavior in real clinical situations are urgently required.

References

Barrows, H.S., Neufeld, V.R., Feightner, J.W., and Norman, G.R. (1978). An analysis of the clinical methods of medical students and physicians. Report to the Ontario Ministry of Health.

Beck, N., Devlin, H.B., and Lunn, J.N. (1988). *The Report of a Confidential Enquiry into Perioperative Deaths.* London: Nuffield Provincial Hospitals' Trust.

Bourbonnais, F.F. and Baumann, A. (1985). Stress and rapid decision making in nursing: An administrative challenge. *Nursing Administration Quarterly, 9,* 85-91.

Brunswik, E. (1956). *Perception and the Representative Design of Psychological Experiments (2nd ed.).* Berkeley, CA: University of California Press.

Cleland, V.S. (1967). Effects of stress on thinking. *American Journal of Nursing, 1,* 108-111.

Colquhon, W.P. (1971). Circadian variation in mental efficiency. In W.P. Colquhon (Ed.), *Biological Rhythms and Human Performance.* London: Academic, pp. 39-107.

Dowie, J. and Elstein, A. (1988). *Professional Judgment: A Reader in Clinical Decision Making.* New York: Cambridge University Press.

Doyle J. and Thomas, S.A. (1988). Clinical decision making in audiology: The case for investigating what we do. *Australian Journal of Audiology, 10,* 45-56.

Ebbesen, E.B. and Konecni, V.J. (1980). On the external validity of decision-making research: What do we know about decisions in the real world? In T.S. Wallsten (Ed.), *Cognitive Processes in Choice and Decision Behavior,* (pp. 21-45). Hillsdale, NJ: Lawrence Erlbaum Associates.

Eisenberg, J.M. (1979). Sociologic influences on decision making by clinicians. *Annals of Internal Medicine, 90,* 957-964.

Elstein, A.S., Shulman, L.S., and Sprafka, S.A. (1978). *Medical Problem Solving: An Analysis of Clinical Reasoning.* Cambridge, MA: Harvard University Press.

Fineberg, H.V. (1981). Medical decision making and the future of medical practice. *Medical Decision Making, 1,* 4-6.

Froberg, J.E. (1978). Task complexity and 24-hour performance patterns in morning and evening active subjects. *Stockholm Forsvarets Forskningsantalt FOA rapport C52001-H6.*

Goran, M.J., Williamson, J.W., and Gonnella, J.S. (1973). The validity of patient management problems. *Journal of Medical Education, 48,* 171-177.

Hay, D. and Oken, D. (1972). The psychological stresses of the intensive care unit. *Psychosomatic Medicine, 34,* 109-118.

Huckabay, L.M.D. and Jagla, B. (1979). Nurses' stress factors in the Intensive Care Unit. *Journal of Nursing Administration,* 21- 26.

Lazarus, R.S. (1976). *Patterns of Adjustment.* New York: McGraw-Hill.

Lippincott, R.C. (1979). Psychological stress factors in decision making. *Heart and Lung, 8,* 1093-1097.

Lunn, J.N. and Devlin, H.B. (1987, December). Lessons from the confidential enquiry into perioperative deaths in three NHS regions. *The Lancet,* pp. 1384-1386.

Minors, D.S. and Waterhouse, J.M. (1985). Introduction to circadian rhythms. In S. Folkard and T.H. Monk (Eds.), *Hours of Work: Temporal Factors in Work Scheduling.* Chichester: Wiley (pp. 1-14).

Monk, T.H. and Folkard, S. (1985). Circadian performance rhythms. In S. Folkard and T.H. Monk (Eds.), *Hours of Work: Temporal Factors in Work Scheduling.* Chichester: Wiley (pp. 37-52).

Newble, D.I., Hoare, J., and Baxter, A. (1982). Patient management problems: Issues of validity. *Medical Education, 16,* 137-142.

Page, G.G. and Fielding, D.W. (1980). Performance on PMPs and performance in practice: Are they related? *Journal of Medical Education, 55,* 529-537.

Polgar, S. and Thomas, S.A. (1988). *Introduction to Research in the Health Sciences.* Melbourne: Churchill Livingstone.

Sedlacek, W.E. and Nattress, L.W. (1972). A technique for determining the validity of Patient Management Problems. *Journal of Medical Education, 47,* 263-266.

Selye, J. (1956). *The Stress of Life.* New York: McGraw-Hill.

Sox, H.C., Blatt, M.A., Higgins, M.C., and Marton, K.I. (1988). *Medical Decision Making.* Boston: Butterworths.

Turk, D.C. and Salovey, P. (1988). *Reasoning, Inference and Judgment in Clinical Psychology.* New York: Free Press.

Watkins, S. (March1984). How to live with rotating shifts. *Registered Nurse,* 57-58.

Weinman, J. (1987). *An Outline of Psychology as Applied to Medicine.* Bristol: Wright.

Wolf, F.M. (1984). Validity of patient management problems reexamined. *Medical Education, 18,* 222-225.

Wright, P. (1974). The harassed decision-maker: Time pressures, distractions and the use of evidence. *Journal of Applied Psychology, 59,* 551-561.

Yerkes, R.M. and Dodson, J.D. (1908). The relation of strength of stimulus to rapidity of habit-formation. *Journal of Comparative Neurology and Psychology, 18,* 459-482.

Note

A reduced version of this article appeared in *Commentary, 8,* 31-35, June 1990, Singapore: National University of Singapore Society.

LINES OF REASONING USED BY TRIAGE NURSES IN CASES OF VARYING COMPLEXITY: A PILOT STUDY

Sheila Corcoran-Perry and Suzanne Narayan

This pilot study established the groundwork for a research program designed to investigate task characteristics which influence experienced nurses' cognitive processes, an area of investigation fundamental to other research on clinical decision making. Task analysis of telephone triage in a Senior Citizens' Clinic provided a detailed description of the nature of this particular nursing task. The key contribution of the pilot study was the confirmation that a line of reasoning (LOR) is a unit of analysis which captures nurses' cognitive processes in useful and meaningful ways.

Despite growing interest in clinical decision making in nursing, relatively little is known about nurses' decision-making processes, especially those of successful clinicians. The authors are embarking on a research program that uses information-processing theory to understand how task characteristics influence the cognitive processes of experienced nurses, and to describe such cognitive processes at a level of abstraction that is meaningful to clinicians and educators.

The initial phase of this research program focused on the task of telephone triage, a task frequently performed by nurses in health maintenance organizations, clinics, and emergency rooms. A pilot study completed during the initial phase of the research program is reported in this article. The pilot study was conducted to: (a) describe the task of telephone triage, (b) test a new unit of analysis, lines of reasoning (LOR), and (c) examine the relationship between task complexity and LOR.

Theoretical Perspective

Newell and Simon's (1972) theory of information processing, the theoretical perspective for this study, describes problem-solving behavior as an interaction between a problem solver and a task. Humans are viewed as information-processing systems operating in complex environments. A major assumption of this theory is that there are limits to the human capacity for rational thought. Despite the essentially infinite capacity of long-term memory, short-term memory is limited. There is evidence that the capacity of short-term memory is seven, plus or minus two "chunks" of information (Miller, 1956).

Research findings indicate that humans adapt to their cognitive limitations by collecting data selectively, processing data serially, and representing problems in simplified ways (Newell & Simon, 1972; Simon, 1979). Also, it has been found that information processing in decision making is contingent on the demands of particular tasks (Newell & Simon, 1972; Payne, 1976; Simon, 1979). Therefore, the nature of the task is an important variable in the study of decision making. Several task variables have been investigated, the most relevant of which is task complexity.

Related Research

Two studies which investigated task complexity operationalized it as amount of information. Payne (1976), in the task of choosing an apartment, and Gordon (1980), in a diagnostic reasoning task, found that subjects varied their information-search strategies in response to the amount of available information. In a third study Corcoran (1986) operationalized complexity by combining qualitative and quantitative elements and found that novice and expert nurses varied their approaches to planning as a function of complexity.

Although these studies indicated that complexity is an important task characteristic influencing decision making, further refinement of the variable and investigation of its relationship to cognitive processes are needed. Therefore, refinement of task complexity was an objective of the pilot study reported here.

Most investigations of decision behavior have used either units of analysis representing specific cognitive processes, such as associating a cue or set of cues with a diagnostic label, or units representing general cognitive strategies, such as information-seeking strategies. For example, Hammond, Kelly, Schneider, and Vancini (1966) and Matthew and Gaul (1979) studied discrete information units used by nurses to make clinical inferences.

General cognitive processes were used as the unit of analysis by Elstein, Shulman, and Sprafka (1978) who developed and tested a four-stage model of medical inquiry involving cue acquisition, hypothesis generation, cue interpretation, and hypothesis evaluation. Elstein et al.'s (1978) model and units of analysis were used by Tanner and associates (Putzier, Padrick, Westfall, & Tanner, 1985; Westfall, Tanner, Putzier, & Padrick, 1986) in two studies of nurses' diagnostic reasoning. Such studies generated enormous amounts of data requiring lengthy analyses, but yielded only slight support for the model.

Other general cognitive strategies were the units of analysis for three studies of decision making. Information-seeking strategies were the unit in studies by Payne (1976) and Gordon (1980). Findings from both studies indicated that subjects' patterns of search included multiple-hypotheses testing early in the process to reduce the number of alternatives being considered, and then successive testing of the remaining hypotheses. In the third study, Corcoran (1986) used the overall approach to planning as the unit of analysis, with subjects employing either opportunistic or systematic planning as general strategies; that is, they either pursued whatever seemed opportune or promising at the time, or they pursued an orderly sequence of planning.

These units of analysis involving either very specific or very general cognitive processes have not been very useful to clinicians or educators. In 1976, Payne suggested an intermediate unit, line of reasoning (LOR), but neither defined nor operationalized it. Later, Johnson and associates (Johnson, Hassebrock, Duran, & Moller, 1982) and Pechtel (1985) operationally defined LOR as "the partially or fully ordered sequence of conceptual actions or steps employed by a subject in reaching a clinical judgment" (p. 217). They represented the dynamic nature of LOR's by flow charts. In the pilot study reported here, LOR's were chosen as the unit of analysis. They were extracted from the data and shared with clinicians and educators to verify them as meaningful and useful.

Method

Repeated measures design and verbal protocol methodology were used in the pilot study. Telephone triage in a senior citizens' clinic was selected as the decision-making task because it is a complex task increasingly performed by nurses under conditions of risk and uncertainty, and it limited the data available for decision making to verbal data.

Task Description and Analysis

Task description and task analysis were completed to delineate telephone triage and to identify the knowledge and abilities necessary to perform the activity in a seniors' clinic (Davis, Alexander, & Yelon, 1974; Resnick, 1976). Initially, a task description was used to outline the sequence in which the task was performed and then a task analysis was used to identify the characteristics of the task and the knowledge and skill requirements for its performance.

In general, telephone triage begins when a patient calls the clinic with a health care problem and asks for assistance. The nurse as the triage agent collects relevant data, determines the level of threat that the patient's situation poses for his/her health or life, and arranges for further evaluation and treatment, if needed.

An analysis of the task characteristics revealed the following:

(a) the goal of telephone triage is direction of a patient to appropriate health care providers in an appropriate setting at an appropriate time;

(b) two major concerns are patient safety and efficient use of limited patient and health care resources;

(c) there are at least five possible triage options ranging from having the patient be seen immediately by a physician in the emergency room, to self care because the condition is normal and poses no health threat;

(d) triage decisions are distinct from differential diagnoses; and

(e) the time interval within which the decision must be made is short, frequently five or ten minutes.

Further, task analysis revealed that telephone triage required knowledge of:

(a) common health problems or conditions that pose varying levels of threat to health or life of elderly persons;

(b) classic signs and symptoms, as well as treatments of such problems or conditions;

(c) variations in the classic signs and symptoms which may appear in elderly persons; and

(d) services which can be offered by the health care facility.

In addition, the task analysis revealed that telephone triage requires the ability to:

(a) verbally elicit and verify relevant information;

(b) convey concern for the patient through a verbal mode;

(c) combine information to determine the level of threat to health or life; and

(d) balance concerns for patient safety with those of efficient use of patient and health care resources.

Cases

Once the task was analyzed, three hypothetical cases of varying complexity were developed. Each case was based on actual patient data and contained information about:

(a) the statement made by the patient when calling the clinic, the initial cue;

(b) written clinic care plan information for this patient; and

(c) data about the patient's current status, such as onset of the initial cue, as well as precipitating, aggravating, and relieving factors, other related symptoms, and finally, pertinent past history (Moreland & Grier, 1986).

The three initial cues given by the patients in the three cases were chest pain, shortness of breath, and black stools.

The variable of case complexity incorporated both quantitative and qualitative features. The two quantitative features were the number of levels of threat which reasonably might be considered and the number of logical triage options. The two qualitative features were the degree to which the patient presented classic symptoms of one or more health conditions, and whether the information available allowed for recall or required generation of possible associated conditions.

The least complex case involved a patient who called the clinic with the initial cue of difficulty breathing. Subjects needed to consider only two levels of threat, severe and moderate; and the triage decision for either was to bring the patient in to be seen. Also, this patient's care plan indicated a history of two conditions strongly associated with the initial cue. If subjects had reviewed the care plan, they could recall the conditions.

The case of moderate complexity involved a patient with the initial cue of black stools. In this case subjects needed to consider two levels of threat, moderate and no threat. The patient's black stools could be associated with gastrointestinal bleeding, or with the ingestion of common foods or medications. Consequently, the triage decision was about whether or not to bring the patient in to be seen. Although the patient's set of symptoms fit the classic picture of gastrointestinal bleeding, his care plan revealed no history of associated conditions. Therefore, such conditions had to be generated.

The most complex case involved a patient who called with the initial cue of chest pain. Subjects needed to consider several levels of threat and multiple triage options. While much of the patient's data could be associated with myocardial infarction, several cues did not match the classic picture and suggested other conditions. The patient had no history of health problems which would be associated with chest pain; therefore, subjects had to generate possible conditions.

Subjects

Four experienced telephone triage female nurses participated in the pilot study. Their educational background varied, including associate degree, diploma, and baccalaureate degree in preparation in nursing. Their average years of experience in professional nursing was 9.7, while their average years of experience performing telephone triage in the seniors' clinic was 4.06.

Procedure

Data collection. Data were collected from individual subjects in separate one-hour sessions. Initially, the subject was given a consent form to sign, a copy of general instructions describing the study, and an opportunity to practice the method with a sample case.

To begin the triage task, the subject was given a message that a patient had just called the clinic with a complaint (the initial cue). The subject was given an opportunity to review the patient's written care plan. Next, the subject simulated answering the phone by greeting the patient and asking questions to collect data to make a triage decision. The researcher served as the repository of information, providing the data requested about the patient. While performing the triage task, the subject thought aloud concerning the information needed, the reason the information was requested, and the influence the new information had on decision making. When the subject had completed her assessment, she wrote statements describing: (a) the judgment concerning the level of threat to the patient's health or life and (b) the decision about appropriate triage disposition of the patient according to time, place, and health professional. The entire session was tape recorded and later transcribed into a document called a verbal protocol (Ericsson & Simon, 1984). The verbal protocols along with the written statements concerning level of threat and appropriate triage disposition served as the data for the pilot study.

Although triage decisions usually are made in a short time, no time constraints were placed on the tasks because the subjects were asked to think aloud as they made their decisions, thus requiring more time than usual. All subjects made triage decisions about all cases.

Data analysis. The verbal protocols were analyzed to extract LOR's used and to identify the relationship between task complexity and LOR's. An LOR was defined as a patterned sequence of arguments leading to a conclusion, which was the triage decision.

Two levels of analyses were performed to extract LOR's from each verbal protocol. Level one involved a detailed analysis of the data which the subject elicited about the patient and the order in which it was elicited. At this level it was possible to identify the signs and symptom to which the subject was attending, the associated conditions which the subject was considering, and the order in which the conditions were considered to arrive at a judgment about level of threat and a decision about triage disposition. The second level of analysis was more global than the first and focused on translating the data into LOR's.

To identify the relationship between task complexity and LOR's, an analysis was made of subjects' LOR's within and across cases. Based on the findings of prior research, it was expected that the LOR's would vary as a function of task complexity.

Findings

Specific findings are reported for the types of LOR's extracted from the verbal protocols and for the relationship between task complexity and LOR's. An excerpt of

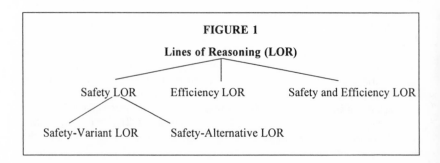

FIGURE 1

Lines of Reasoning (LOR)

Safety LOR   Efficiency LOR   Safety and Efficiency LOR

Safety-Variant LOR   Safety-Alternative LOR

a verbal protocol is presented to illustrate one LOR.

Lines of Reasoning

Data analysis revealed four different patterns of arguments used to arrive at triage decisions (see Figure 1). They involved the two major issues of concern in the context of triage, patient safety and efficient use of resources.

In the first major category, the Safety LOR, a subject consistently conveyed concern for protecting the patient from harm. Two distinct types of Safety LOR's were extracted from the data. In one, the subject initially pursued data about classic symptoms of a condition, but when encountering a piece of inconsistent data hypothesized and briefly pursued other conditions. Then the subject returned to the originally considered condition and developed an argument which incorporated the divergent data into the condition schema. This LOR was labeled Safety-Variant LOR.

In the second type of Safety LOR, the subject's pattern was similar to that just described, except that the subject did not return to the original condition considered. Instead the subject remained with the alternative condition(s) and pursued it/them until a judgment was reached. The divergent data were incorporated into a different condition rather than into a variant of the one originally considered. This LOR was labeled Safety-Alternative LOR.

In the third LOR, Efficiency LOR, a subject did not ignore patient safety, but emphasized efficient use of resources as the major argument in the pattern. The subject recognized the possibility of a threatening condition by pursuing it briefly, but then quickly pursued non-threatening conditions to be ruled in or out. Only after ruling out conditions with little or no threat, did the subject return to considering conditions which could present a threat to health or life. The implication was that efficient use of resources was the primary argument used throughout the decision-making process, even if it was not the first or even the last argument in the pattern.

In the fourth LOR, Safety and Efficiency LOR, a subject placed equal emphasis on the two arguments. This was evident as the subject moved back and forth between the argument of patient safety when considering conditions posing severe or moderate threats and the argument of efficient use of resources when considering conditions posing little or no threats.

An excerpt from one verbal protocol is used to illustrate the Safety-Variant LOR. The investigator, serving as the repository of patient data, responds as the patient to the subject's questions. "I" represents the investigator speaking as the patient, and "S" represents the subject speaking.

Introduction: The clinic secretary calls you, the clinic nurse, to say that Mrs. Olson is on the phone complaining of chest pain.

S: OK. First thing I'm going to rule out is that she has an MI in progress. Mrs.

Olson. This is Alice Abrams. I'm one of the nurses in the clinic. I understand you're having some chest pain.

I: Yes.

S: Could you describe it to me?

I: Well, it just hurts.

S: All over your chest?

I: I'd say in front, mainly in front.

S: OK. Does it feel like a squeezing kind of pain, or like something sitting on your chest?

I: It feels tight.

S: It feels tight. Are you having trouble breathing?

I: Well, it hurts when I take a deep breath.

S: It hurts when you take a deep breath. How long have you had this?

I: Well, I'd say it really started two days ago.

S: It started two days ago. Now, OK, I'm thinking she says it hurts when she takes a deep breath. I'm wondering about another condition. I still haven't completely ruled out that she has an MI in progress, but if it started two days ago, then probably she does not have an MI in progress, because she would have called before now if it were two days of this, so I am going to ask her: Has the pain been the same since you first got it or has it been getting worse, or has it changed in any way?

I: Let's see. It kind of comes and goes. It's always there. Kinda like indigestion.

S: It kind of comes and goes. The pain is always there. Kind of like indigestion. OK. So she could have an MI in progress. It just kind of comes and goes, and because of the waxing and waning, for one thing sometimes it can come and go like that and it hasn't been a steady pain the whole time. And also the indigestion can be a sign. OK. I'm convinced she needs to come in, but I'm still trying to find out whether or not she has an MI in progress. I think so. It could also be a pulmonary emboli. Whether or not I need to call the paramedics is what I'm trying to decide now. Just to be on the safe side, I am going to recommend that she come in by the paramedics. Over time, I've noticed in the elderly people, sometimes you would think that if it had been over a couple of days and it wouldn't be an MI in progress, but we have had people who have had pain for a couple of days and it still turns out to be an MI, so I really don't use the couple days as a deciding factor.

S: My judgment is that it's a serious threat, could be an MI in progress. My disposition decision is to bring her into the ER immediately to be seen by a physician.

The Safety-Variant LOR is represented in the flow chart in Figure 2. In this verbal protocol, the subject immediately associated the cue of chest pain with a condition representing a severe threat to life, a myocardial infarction (MI). Then extensive data

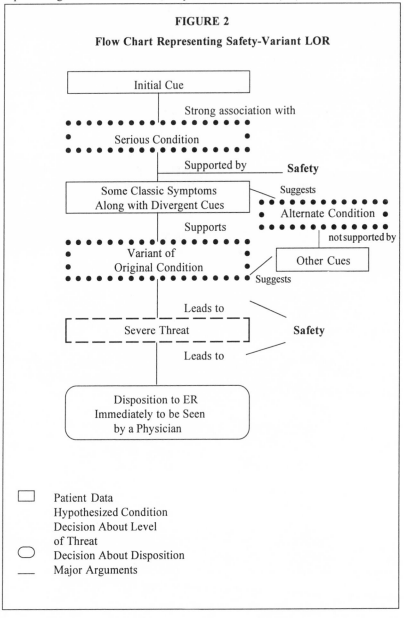

FIGURE 2

Flow Chart Representing Safety-Variant LOR

Initial Cue

Strong association with

Serious Condition

Supported by   **Safety**

Some Classic Symptoms
Along with Divergent Cues   Suggests

Alternate Condition

Supports   not supported by

Variant of
Original Condition   Other Cues

Suggests

Leads to

Severe Threat   **Safety**

Leads to

Disposition to ER
Immediately to be Seen
by a Physician

☐   Patient Data
    Hypothesized Condition
    Decision About Level
    of Threat
◯   Decision About Disposition
___ Major Arguments

were collected to rule in or out a severe threat to Mrs. Olson's life. This represented a Safety LOR. While the early data fit the classic picture of an MI, the additional datum of two days duration did not seem consistent. The subject briefly considered the possibility of a different condition, pulmonary emboli, but then generated a variant of the classic picture for an MI which incorporated the information about duration of the pain. The subject stated that she had observed this variant in other elderly patients. This line of argument, a Safety-Variant LOR, led to an accurate judgment and triage decision.

Relationship Between Task Complexity and LOR

Figure 3 shows that subjects neither used consistent LOR's across cases nor varied their LOR's as a function of task complexity. Instead the findings indicated that the subjects varied their LOR's as a function of case specific information, especially the initial cue and the association of that cue with conditions at various levels of threat to health or life. In the cases of least and most complexity, the initial cues (chest pain and difficulty breathing) were strongly associated with conditions which could pose serious threats to health or life, conditions such as MI or pulmonary emboli. In the case of moderate complexity, the initial cue was black stools which was strongly associated

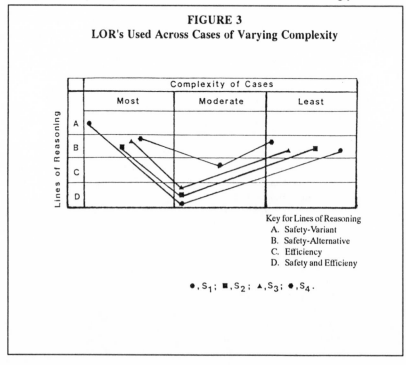

FIGURE 3
LOR's Used Across Cases of Varying Complexity

Key for Lines of Reasoning
A. Safety-Variant
B. Safety-Alternative
C. Efficiency
D. Safety and Efficieny

$\bullet, S_1; \blacksquare, S_2; \blacktriangle, S_3; \bullet, S_4$.

with normal conditions which pose no threat to life, as well as conditions which could be low or moderate threats, such as gastrointestinal bleeding. These findings indicated that when the initial cue was strongly associated with conditions that can pose serious threats to health and/or life, subjects used one of the safety LOR's. When the initial cue was strongly associated with conditions that could pose no threat to health or life, or a moderate threat that would not require immediate attention, subjects used either the Efficiency LOR or the Safety and Efficiency LOR. Therefore, the content of the case had more influence on the LOR's used than did complexity.

Discussion

This pilot study achieved the purposes of completing the task analysis and testing LOR as a unit of analysis. The task analysis revealed the knowledge and ability requirements of telephone triage, thereby contributing to an understanding of the task's information-processing demands. The task analysis was helpful to the subjects as well as the investigators. After the pilot study was completed, the task analysis results were shared with the nurses who participated in the study. They indicated that the information helped them appreciate the complexity of the triage task and enhanced their sense of competence.

LOR proved to be a useful unit of analysis. It represented the subjects' sequence of arguments leading to a decision in a concise, yet specific manner. When the results were shared with participants, they verified that the lines of reasoning accurately represented the arguments they used in the cases; however, they indicated that they would not have been able to specify those arguments, or been comfortable stating them. The subjects indicated that they would like to learn to analyze their thinking processes for LOR's and to have opportunities to share them with each other. Then they could test the LOR for accuracy in leading to appropriate triage decisions.

The finding of no relationship between task complexity and LOR's was not expected. Other studies had found that subjects varied their cognitive strategies as a function of complexity (Corcoran, 1986; Gordon, 1980; Payne, 1976). It appeared that LOR as a unit of analysis is more content dependent than are the general strategies. In retrospect, that is not surprising. The LOR's represent arguments leading to specific decisions in specific tasks. Such arguments are closely related to information available in the cases.

In subsequent phases of this research program, the authors will continue to pursue the influence of task complexity on the cognitive processes used by experienced nurses. LOR will be retained as the major unit of analysis for the cognitive processes. However, the complexity variable will be further refined. Since LOR's were found to be content dependent, all cases will be limited to a single content area, cardiovascular problems. Within this content area, the qualitative and quantitative features will be systematically varied. In particular, one qualitative feature, nature of the level of threat, will be refined and varied.

References

Corcoran, S. (1986). Task complexity and nursing expertise as factors in decision making. *Nursing Research, 36,* 107-112.

Davis, R., Alexander, L., and Yelon, S. (1974). *Learning Systems Design: An Approach to the Improvement of Instruction.* New York: McGraw-Hill.

Elstein, A., Shulman, L., and Sprafka, S. (1978). *Medical Problem Solving: An Analysis of Clinical Reasoning.* Cambridge, MA: Harvard University Press.

Ericsson, K.A. and Simon, H.A. (1984). *Protocol Analysis: Verbal Reports as Data.* Cambridge, MA: The MIT Press.

Gordon, M. (1980). Predictive strategies in diagnostic tasks. *Nursing Research, 29,* 39-45.

Hammond, K., Kelly, K., Schneider, R., and Vancini, M. (1966). Clinical inference in nursing: Information units used. *Nursing Research, 15,* 236-243.

Johnson, P., Hassebrock, F., Duran, A., and Moller, J. (1982). Multi-method study of clinical judgment. *Organizational Behavior and Human Performance, 30,* 201-230.

Matthew, C. and Gaul, A. (1979). Nursing diagnosis from the perspective of concept attainment and critical thinking. *Advances in Nursing Science, 2,* 17-26.

Miller, G. (1956). The magical number seven, plus or minus two. *Psychological Review, 63,* 81-87.

Moreland, H. and Grier, M. (1986). Use of telephone consultation in care of the older adult. *Geriatric Nursing, 7,* 28-30.

Newell, A. and Simon, H. (1972). *Human Problem Solving.* Englewood Cliffs, NJ: Prentice-Hall.

Payne, J. (1976). Task complexity and contingent processing in decision making: An information processing search and protocol analysis. *Organizational Behavior and Human Performance, 16,* 366-387.

Pechtel, B. (1985). *The Role of Experience and Specialization in Lawyer Problem Solving.* Unpublished doctoral dissertation, University of Minnesota, Minneapolis.

Putzier, D., Padrick, K., Westfall, U., and Tanner, C. (1985). Diagnostic reasoning in critical-care nursing. *Heart and Lung: The Journal of Critical Care, 14,* 430-437.

Resnick, L. (1976). Task analysis in instructional design: Some cases from mathematics. In D. Klahr (Ed.), *Cognition and Instruction.* Hillsdale, NJ: Lawrence Erlbaum Associates.

Simon, H. (1979). Information processing models of cognition. *Annual Review of Psychology, 30,* 363-396.

Westfall, U., Tanner, C., Putzier, D., and Padrick, K. (1986). Clinical inferences in nursing: A preliminary analysis of cognitive strategies. *Research in Nursing and Health, 9,* 269-277.

Acknowledgment

This study was funded in part by the Ramey-Dreves Faculty Research Award from the School of Nursing, University of Minnesota, U.S.A.

SECTION D
Decision Making in Law

A REVIEW OF THE INFLUENCE OF EXTRALEGAL FACTORS ON LEGAL DECISION MAKING

Bernadette Sim and Wing Hong Loke

A representative sample of studies on legal decision making are reviewed. Here, the importance of extralegal factors such as gender and attractiveness of individuals are discussed. The discussion focuses on three groups of individuals: defendants, lawyers, and jurors. Some concluding notes include suggestions on the definition of attractiveness and applied values of extralegal biases on the decision-making process of individuals.

Studies that focus on the characteristics of the individual or other non-law factors are known as extralegal research. In contrast, examples of legal-based research includes studies on the effects of limiting instructions on verdicts, withheld evidence on juridic decision, and effects of scientific jury selection. The basis behind research on extralegal factors initially arose from the knowledge that few decisions are made via the normative (mathematical) process (see sections on Normative and Descriptive Theories in "Models of judgment and decision making: An overview" in this volume). Research showed that most decisions incorporate subjective (extralegal) factors which affect the outcome. So, the present paper provides a review of the effects of the extralegal factors (e.g., attractiveness) of defendants, lawyers, and jurors on the process of decision making in law. The following reviews the research in regard to three groups of individuals: defendants, lawyers, and jurors.

Defendants

Research on the defendants have focused on the attractiveness component. Landy and Aronson (1969) defined attractiveness in terms of the characteristics of an individual's success in business and in community service. Unattractiveness was characterized by an unsavory past and criminal tendencies. The findings showed that when the victim involved was attractive, the defendant was sentenced more severely than when the victim was unattractive. An unattractive defendant was also sentenced more severely than a neutral or attractive individual.

Dion, Berscheid, and Walster (1972) studied the interaction of gender (male or female) and the defendant's attractiveness in terms of physical appearance (studied in terms of photographs of attractive, average attractive, and unattractive individuals). The focus was on whether both attractive males and females were assumed to possess more socially desirable personality traits than physically unattractive stimulus persons, and whether they were expected to lead better lives. Results supported the stereotype of "what is beautiful is good" where those who were viewed as attractive were treated better than unattractive. Moreover, Efran (1974) found that physically attractive defendants were evaluated with less certainty of guilt and received less severe recommended punishment than unattractive defendants. The findings were greater for the male than the female individuals.

Piehl (1977), using photographs, showed that attractive offenders were treated leniently to some extent and that attractiveness appears to have its effects according to the type of accident. The attractiveness was a positive factor compared to unattractiveness in a harmless accident case. However, in a fatal accident, physical attractiveness had a negative influence. Physical attractiveness was also examined via photographs in terms of how it affected liability in the amount of money awarded in cases of personal damage suits and was varied with the age of the plaintiff (Stephan & Tully, 1977). Results showed that attractiveness did influence the decision favorably, but not between the adult and child plaintiff.

In Michelini and Snodgrass (1980), attractiveness was defined in terms of 16 trait adjectives which varied both in personal attractiveness and its relevance in committing a traffic felony. Attractive defendants were found less guilty only when the traits were associated with the likelihood of acting in a criminal way. However, regardless of the relevance of traits, attractive defendants were given more lenient punishments than unattractive defendants.

The number of the witnesses at the crime as well as the type of motivation for the crime was also examined (Sigal & Braden, 1985). The results showed no significant effect due to attractiveness of the defendant or the number of witnesses on decisions. The authors explained the nonsignificance in terms of their manipulations. They noted that a crime of homicide might have been too serious, leading subjects to be more careful as to what influenced them in their verdict versus the crime chosen by Efran (1974). In addition, the crime chosen was not related to attractiveness versus other attractiveness-related crimes. Sigal and Braden (1985) noted that in Vidmar's (1972) study, the fewer the options or categories available to subjects the greater the percentage of defendants found not guilty. So, their options may have limited the subjects and increased the likelihood of subjects found not guilty. However, in asking for a response of guilty or not guilty, the study represents the real situation.

Lawyers
Another area of research has been on the lawyers. Villemur and Hyde (1983) studied gender effects of the attorney and juror, and the attractiveness of the victim on decisions in a rape case. Results showed that significantly more not guilty verdicts were given when the defense attorney was female than when the defense attorney was male. The jurors also attributed more fault to the victim and less to the defendant under the female defense condition. Interactions were found between the juror's gender and age of the victim, that is, female jurors attributed more fault to the defendant when his victim was old. Villemur and Hyde (1983) proposed the "talking platypus" phenomenon as an explanation of their first result; that because people find it amazing that a women can be a lawyer, they therefore inflate her abilities—the wonder which arises

if a platypus talks rather than what it might say. However, the researchers also acknowledge that the results could be due to the crime in question, whereby in having a woman argue a position which is not in the best interest of women, female attorneys then have a more persuasive effect.

In Sigal, Braden-Maguire, Hayden, and Mosley (1985), they examined the presentation style and the gender of the lawyer. The researchers defined presentation style as being passive, assertive, or aggressive. These styles differ with respects to the degree of eye contact, hesitations, speed of speech, and physical gestures. Results showed that passive defense lawyers resulted in fewer acquittal judgments than either assertive or aggressive. There was no significant difference in effectiveness for not guilty verdicts found between the assertive and aggressive style, although the aggressive lawyers were rated as more effective than assertive lawyers. No overall gender differences were found for the attorneys.

Jurors

According to Efran (1974), attractiveness had reinforcement properties, but it was not justifiable as an important influence on the jurors' decision. (Note that the Singapore courts do not use jurors and, therefore, this section is not applicable in the Singaporean environment.) More importantly, the social psychological aspects of juror's bias were examined. For example, Mills and Bohannon (1982) studied the effect of character structure of the decision maker on decision making. Character structure was conceptualized in terms of socialization, empathy, and autonomy. These were found to be significantly related to voting behavior, juror effectiveness, perception of duty, as well as outcome. Gender, race, age, and education of the decision maker were also shown to be important modifiers of the personality effect. Sealy (1981) found that younger (up to 25 years of age) and older (above 40 years) jurors tend to acquit. Of note by Sealy (1981) is that biases within the decision maker are but one of the extralegal factors that might affect legal decisions. More research is needed in other areas as "in the mode" or style of presenting the evidence as opposed to the evidence itself, the persuasiveness of the presenters and the local "climate of opinion" (Sealy, 1981, p. 189). He also criticized past studies which used only students as their subjects and often gave written synopses of invented trials.

Moran and Comfort (1982) studied how gender could be a moderator of demographic and personality predictors of an impaneled felony jury. The interest here seems to be to draw out the personality of the juror with the aid of the gender of the individuals. Twenty-three demographic/personality variables and jury verdicts, judge's predeliberation verdict, jurors' tendency to change their verdict and juror self-perceived participation and influence were studied. Results showed that conviction-prone male jurors were more interested in having families and tended to have more children and a lower income. They also had higher authoritarianism and socialization scores but lower scores on the Marlowe-Crowne Social Desirability Scale. Conviction-prone female jurors had higher scores on the Just World Scale, were high on legal authoritarianism, were more emphatic, and were less anomic.

The age of the jurors has also been studied. Ackerman, McMahon, and Fehr (1984) studied the age of the jurors, gender of the defendant, and the victim in child abuse cases. The subjects used in this experiment were undergraduates and junior high school students. Results showed that younger adolescent jurors were more punitive than older adolescent jurors. The older adolescents attributed more of the responsibility to the adult defendant in a child abuse case. The authors speculated that this might reflect that older adolescents were going through the process of reviewing the parental role of responsibility for their care-giver behaviors. As for younger adolescent jurors, they identified more closely with the child victim who may have evoked the anger and thus punishment of the parent.

MacCoun and Kerr (1988) studied how mock jury deliberations tend to have an asymmetric bias for leniency—where the proacquittal factions are more influential than proconviction factions of comparable size. The researchers wanted to see if this leniency bias was restricted to the typical college-student population versus the community mock jurors. Results, however, showed that there was no difference between the college and the community mock jurors. The researchers then hypothesized that the effect was caused by the reasonable-doubt standard. They tested this in a separate experiment and found that there was significant asymmetry in the reasonable-doubt group condition, but symmetrical verdicts for the groups in the preponderance of evidence condition.

Some Final Notes

As discussed above, the various definitions of attractiveness are dependent on the cultural context. Researchers have used that characteristic which is most descriptive for that culture example, community work, and other traits. The definition of "character" of the judge similarly changes with each research and is context dependent. As with the attractiveness variable, researchers tried to use the most salient characteristic of the decision maker, which vary across time and place. Although the context-specific approach has shown to be useful, there should also be plans to generalize the results via cross-comparison studies in context and related characteristics. Also, more standardized measures could be developed by factor analysis, item response theory, or similar psychometric methods to search for interacting variables.

As to the applied value, such studies have aided a federal district court and the court of appeals to reach a decision on the issue of whether a "death qualified" jury was more likely to convict a capital criminal defendant (Bersoff & Ogden, 1987). The issue was first raised in a case of Whitherspoon versus Illinois (1968), and later in Lockhart versus McCree (1986), and Grisby versus Marby (1980, 1983, 1985). Although these decisions were later reversed by the Supreme Court, the incidents have spurred social psychologists to consider more stringent methodologies in their analyses. This situation seemed to mark the beginning of the courts' acceptance of the social scientists as objective disseminators of information. In Singapore, research on the legal system could be initiated by building an empirical base of the various areas of legal decision making. Specifically, a worthy endeavor is to employ a behavioral science approach towards the study of legal decision making. Such an approach would account for the effects of extralegal biases on the decision-making process of individuals.

References

Ackerman, A.M., McMahon, P.M., and Fehr, L.A. (1984). Defendant characteristics and judgment behaviors of adolescent mock jurors. *Journal of Youth and Adolescence, 13*, 123-136.

Anderson, J.R. (1985). *Cognitive Psychology and Its Implications (2nd Ed.).* San Francisco: Freeman.

Bersoff, D.N. and Ogden, D.W. (1987). In the Supreme Court of the United States: Lockart v. McCree. Amicus Curiae Brief for the American Psychological Association. *American Psychologist, 42*, 59-68.

Dion, K., Berscheid, E., and Walster, E. (1972). What is beautiful is good. *Journal of Personality and Social Psychology, 24*, 285-290.

Efran, M.G. (1974). The effect of physical appearance on the judgment of guilt, interpersonal attraction, and severity of recommended punishment in a simulated jury task. *Journal of Research in Personality, 8*, 45-54.

Grisby v. Marby, 483 F. Supp. 1372 (E.D. Ark. 1980), modified and remanded, 637 F.2d 525 (8th Cir. 1980); 569 F. Supp. 1273 (E.D. Ark. 1983), aff'd, 758 F.2d 226 (8th Cir. 1985).

Landy, D. and Aronson, E. (1969). The influence of the character of the criminal and his victim on the decisions of simulated jurors. *Journal of Experimental Social Psychology, 5*, 141-152.

Lockhart v. McCree, 106 S. Ct. 1758 (1986).

MacCoun, R.J. and Kerr, N.L. (1988). Asymmetric influence in mock jury deliberation: Jurors' bias for leniency. *Journal of Personality and Social Psychology, 54*, 21-32.

Michelini, R.L. and Snodgrass, S.R. (1980). Defendant characteristics and juridic decisions. *Journal of Research in Personality, 14*, 340-345.

Mills, C. and Bohannon, W.E. (1982). Character structure and jury behavior: Conceptual and applied implications. *Journal of Personality and Social Psychology, 38*, 662-667.

Moran, G. and Comfort, J.C. (1982). Scientific juror selection: Sex as a moderator of demographic and personality predictors of impaneled felony juror behavior. *Journal of Personality and Social Psychology, 43*, 1052-1063.

Piehl, J. (1977). Integration of information in the "courts": Influence of physical attractiveness on amount of punishment for a traffic offender. *Psychological Reports, 41*, 551-556.

Sealy, A.P. (1981). Another look at social psychological aspects of juror bias. *Law and Human Behavior, 5*, 187-200.

Sigal, J. and Braden, J. (1985). The effect of attractiveness of defendant, number of witnesses, and personal motivation of defendant on jury decision-making behavior. *Psychology, A Quarterly Journal of Human Behavior, 15*, 4-10.

Sigal, J., Braden-Maguire, J., Hayden, M., and Mosley, N. (1985). The effect of presentation style and sex of lawyer on jury decision-making behavior. *Psychology, A Quarterly Journal of Human Behavior, 22*, 13-19.

Stephan, C. and Tully, J.C. (1977). The influence of physical attractiveness of a plaintiff on the decisions of simulated jurors. *Journal of Social Psychology, 101*, 149-150.

Vidmar, N. (1972). Effects of decision alternatives on the verdicts and social perceptions of simulated jurors. *Journal of Personality and Social Psychology, 22*, 211-218.

Villemur, N.K. and Hyde, J.S. (1983). Effects of sex of defense attorney, sex of juror, and age and attractiveness of the victim on mock juror decision making in a rape case. *Sex Roles, 9*, 879-889.

Whitherspoon v. Illinois, 391 US 510 (1968).

GENDER BIAS IN MOCK JURORS' DECISIONS ABOUT DAMAGE AWARDS

Marian Louise Miller

Prior research in our laboratory showed that mock jurors who heard a wrongful death case awarded lower damages when the decedent was female rather than male (Goodman, Greene, & Loftus, 1987). Two possible hypotheses can explain this finding. First, jurors may believe that the life of a female is worth less than that of a male. Second, jurors may infer that the financial needs of the female survivor of the decedent are greater than the financial needs of a male survivor. To disengage these hypotheses, two mock juror experiments were conducted. Results support the gender-based need hypothesis as opposed to the devaluation by gender hypothesis. Interestingly enough, it was females whose gender appeared to be doubly important. Jurors were more sensitive to the economic need of female spouses but female jurors awarded less money overall. A review of the relevant psychological literature on sex stereotypes in decision making is also presented.

In a case of wrongful death, mock jurors awarded less in damages when the decedent was a female than when the decedent was a male (Goodman, Greene, & Loftus, 1987). The present study examines two hypotheses to explain this finding: (a) Female decedents are awarded less because the life or expected earnings of a female, compared to those of a male, are perceived as less valuable, and (b) Jurors base their awards on the anticipated financial need of the surviving spouse, and, in the absence of sufficient data, infer that the financial needs of a female survivor are greater than those of a male survivor.

In Experiment 1, the gender of the decedent and the employment status of the survivor were varied. It was predicted that mock jurors would award more to male decedents when the employment status of the survivor was ambiguous because of the stereotypes concerning a female's lower earning capacity. No difference in rewards was expected when the survivor's status was employed. Mock jurors awarded significantly less money when the decedent was female in both conditions.

Contrast t-test for the non-significant interaction showed no differences in awards when the survivor was employed. However, marginally significant differences were found in awards when the survivor's employment was ambiguous. Since neither hypothesis was conclusively supported, a second experiment was conducted to resolve the initial question of why less money is awarded when the decedent is female.

Students read identical cases in which the decedent was either male or female, and the estate was left to (a) an employed spouse, (b) an independently wealthy spouse, or (c) the decedent was single and left the estate to charity. Results did not support the hypothesis that the life of a female is perceived as less valuable than that of a male. Students did not award less to female decedents in all conditions.

In conditions in which the survivor was employed, male decedents were nonetheless awarded slightly more than females, but a reversal of this trend was observed for conditions in which the survivor was independently wealthy and when the decedent was single. These differences were non-significant. Taken together, these results suggest that mock jurors base awards on the anticipated need of the survivor. Unless the financial security of the female survivor is underscored, mock jurors infer that the financial need of females is greater than that of males. Female subjects awarded significantly less overall than did male subjects.

This study was motivated by an observation about damage awards from prior research by Goodman, Greene, and Loftus (1987). Their investigation of possible extralegal factors that influence jurors' decisions about damage awards varied the characteristics of the plaintiff, such as the gender of the decedent in wrongful death cases. They found that mock jurors awarded significantly less in monetary damages when the decedent was a female ($409,166) than when the decedent was male ($803,189), given identical case information concerning the age, marital status, occupation, and annual income of the decedent.

Does this finding mean there is a strong gender bias operating? Jurors focusing on the decedent when awarding damages may have awarded more to male decedents because they assumed males' earning power exceeded that of female decedents. Another interpretation of this result is that the life of a female was perceived to be worth less than a male's. One problem in interpreting this finding is that it is unclear whether differential awards were attributable to the gender of the decedent or the gender of the surviving spouse. An ambiguous finding of this magnitude warrants further investigation.

The impact of sex stereotypes on human judgments can be observed in a variety of contexts (Eagly & Steffen, 1986). Examining the influence of gender stereotypes on juror decision making has obvious social importance, since the courtroom is a social context in which sex stereotypes may play a role in the comprehension of facts, in evaluation of evidence, and in the equitable distribution of rewards. Empirical research has confirmed that a variety of biases, including the gender of jurors and the gender of legal parties, affect both actual and simulated juror judgments. Most research to date has investigated juror biases in criminal cases.

Two types of gender biases can be observed in juror decision making. One is the juror's bias or initial predisposition toward the gender of the legal parties. Another is the bias of the juror which results from his or her gender. Juror gender and gender of the legal parties may also interact.

This study examines whether mock jurors' decisions are influenced by variations in gender, based on the different inferences drawn from that gender information.

Although numerous studies have addressed juror decision making, the majority of these studies have focused on how jurors decide on guilt in criminal cases (Kaplan & Miller, 1978), how jurors apportion blame (Johnson & Dronby, 1985), and how jurors decide on appropriate sentences for criminals (Kaplan & Miller, 1978). Considerably fewer empirical studies have been conducted on juror decision making in civil cases. For example, a few case studies examined juror decision making in awarding damages in civil cases (Goodman, Greene, & Loftus, 1987). There are other civil studies. The same judgmental processes and biases in jury decisions on verdicts and liability are likely to operate in decisions about damage awards.

One interpretation of the Goodman et al. (1987) finding is that mock jurors focused on the decedent when making damage awards. If the differences in the amounts mock jurors allocated to male and female decedents reflected differences in the values placed on the lives of a male versus a female decedent, then the results would suggest that a female's life is perceived as intrinsically of less worth than a male's. Simply noting that the market value for female's work is 60% of the market value of male's work, given identical performances, lends support to this interpretation of the results. Callahan-Levy and Messe's (1979) studies on sex differences and the allocation of pay also suggest that this is a plausible interpretation of the result. In these studies, the investigators examined why women receive less monetary payment than men for the same work. Subjects apportioned a sum between themselves and a partner for equal work. Variables were sex of subject and sex of partner. How was money allocated by women to women? Some hypotheses were:

1. Female tasks are usually not rewarded monetarily. The lack of relationship between female effort and financial reward generalizes to other work situations.

2. Since women usually do not provide the sole economic means of support for their families, it is acceptable for women to earn less than men.

3. Because of the connection between male work and money, males see money as a measure of their self-worth. Females may not evaluate their self-worth in terms of money because their traditional work is not monetarily rewarded.

4. Both females and males believe the social norm that women should be paid less than men (double standard).

5. Females pay themselves less because they see less connection between money and self-worth than do males.

Data supported the hypothesis that females expect less monetary reward than males for the work that they do. Female subjects always awarded less to themselves no matter who their partner was. These results have been replicated using children in first, fourth, seventh, and tenth grades, suggesting that differences in pay allocation are a product of early socialization.

Verbal responses from the Goodman et al. (1987) study, asking mock jurors to describe how they made up their minds on an appropriate sum to award, revealed that mock jurors framed their responses more frequently in terms of the survivor when the decedent was a male. When the decedent was female, mock jurors tended to focus their responses on the career of the male decedent. Factors mentioned more often when the decedent was a male were lost future wages and expected work life.

Goldberg's (1968) finding that the professional work of females is rated less favorably than the same work by a male, and Eagly and Wood's (1982) study showing that females are perceived to have lower status and are more easily influenced than males led to speculation about differences in the value placed on the lives of males and females.

An alternative interpretation of the Goodman et al. (1987) finding of lower awards to female decedents is that jurors anticipated that the financial needs of the female surviving spouse were greater than those of a male surviving spouse. Jurors might have used sex stereotypes characterizing males as competitive and independent financial providers, and females as dependent and passive homemakers (Broverman, et al. 1972; Deaux & Lewis, 1983; Eagly & Wood, 1982) to infer in the absence of contrary information that a female survivor needed more money than a male survivor.

Research supporting this view includes Callahan-Levy and Messe's (1979) work on sex differences in the allocation of pay. While females in this study consistently paid themselves less than males paid themselves for the same work, both males and females allocated more money to female individuals than to male individuals. Sex differences in reward allocation were not based on a general norm that females should be paid less by everyone, but rather that allocators were being generous to females when distributing a reward between themselves and females. This conclusion is in accord with the findings of Gruder and Cook (1971) and is congruent with the stereotypic female characteristics of passivity and dependence that implicitly assume females do not need to acquire money for their work.

The Present Study

Because it is difficult to extract clear support for either of the above hypotheses, the present study was designed to explore the issue of why mock jurors awarded less to female decedents. The degree of financial need of the surviving spouse was manipulated to discover whether mock jurors based their award on the anticipated need of the survivor. Mock jurors may have assumed that, compared with a male survivor, a female survivor was not as prepared or capable of providing for herself. Information about the financial need of the surviving spouse was conveyed either by stating explicitly that the survivor was employed, or inexplicitly by not alluding to the survivor's employment.

One possible outcome is that if subjects focus on the decedent and the life of a female is perceived to be worth less than that of a male, female decedents will receive lower damage awards notwithstanding the survivor's employment status. Alternatively, if subjects focus on the surviving spouse, higher damage awards to the male decedent will occur only when the employment status of the survivor is ambiguous. No differences in awards to male and female decedents are predicted when the survivor is securely employed.

Experiment 1

Method

Subjects.   One hundred and three undergraduates at the University of Washington participated on a voluntary basis.

Materials.   A brief written scenario described the events leading to the wrongful death of the plaintiff. The decedent, age 30, has a fatal accident driving alone when the accelerator pedal of the car malfunctions. In all conditions, the decedent was described as married, self-employed, and earning $25,000 annually at the time of the accident. The surviving spouse was the sole beneficiary of the estate. Subjects were informed that the defendant's liability had been stipulated, and that their task was to determine an appropriate sum to award in damages (see appendix).

Procedure.   Subjects were tested in groups of 5 to 20. Experimental materials included instructions, one of four case synopses, a written questionnaire to assess what strategies a subject used and what factors he or she considered in reaching a decision about the amount to award, and a brief demographic inventory. Booklets were randomly distributed.

Subjects were instructed to imagine that they had been selected to serve as jurors on the *Klemmer* case. The instructions stressed that subjects were to work independently, at their own pace, and that there were no "right" or "wrong" answers. Subjects read the case summary, deliberated on their own to reach a verdict, and answered some follow-up questions. They were debriefed at the end of the experiment.

Design.   The experiment used a 2 x 2 between-subjects design, varying gender of decedent (male or female), and the presence or absence of information concerning the employment status of the surviving spouse. Two conditions replicated the Goodman et al. (1987) study in which no information was provided regarding the status of the surviving spouse. In the two remaining conditions, subjects were informed that the spouse had been employed since he or she left college. The major dependent measure was the dollar amount each subject awarded in damages.

Results

Although 103 subjects participated in the experiment, several subjects failed to make a damage award. These subjects were excluded from the analysis, degrees of freedom were adjusted to reflect the missing data. When the decedent was male and the surviving spouse's financial status was ambiguous, the mean damage award was

$839,533 (median $753,000). When the decedent was female and the survivor's financial status ambiguous, the mean damage award was $688,851 (median $255,000). The mean damage award when the decedent was male and the survivor was employed was $697,000 (median $537,000). When the decedent was female and the survivor was employed, the mean damage award was $616,000 (median $449,000) (Table1).

Examination of within-cell variance, skewedness, and visual inspection of frequency-distributions of the dependent measure (damage award in dollars), for each of the four conditions and overall, indicated that the dependent variable was not normally distributed. Within-cell variance was high and differed between conditions justifying a log linear transformation of the dependent variable. An analysis of variance was performed on the natural log of damage awards.

TABLE 1

Mean Damage Awards by Experimental Condition:
Experiment 1

Sex of Decedent	Spouse's Financial Status	
	Ambiguous	Employed
Male	$839,533	$697,000
Female	$668,851	$616,000

A 2 x 2 x 2 analysis of variance of damages (sex of decedent by survivor's employment by sex of subject) yielded an overall main effect of gender of decedent, $F(1, 98) = 4.29, p < .05$. A borderline main effect of sex of subject was observed, $F(1, 98) = 2.87, p < .1$. The main effects of survivor's employment and the interactions were non-significant. A one-way analysis for simple effects of the non-significant interaction (a planned comparison) was performed. Results indicated that when the employment status of the survivor was ambiguous, awards to a male decedent were marginally higher than awards to a female decedent, $t(56) = -1.52, p = .06$ (1-tailed prediction). A 1-tailed p-value was used for contrasting these means because the conditions were replication of Goodman et al., using the same scenarios. A contrast t-test for differences in amount awarded to male and female decedents was not significant for conditions in which the survivor was "employed since he/she left college" ($p > .25$).

Discussion

Overall, female decedents were awarded less money than male decedents. Interpretations of the awards for cases in which the employment status of the surviving spouse was known versus unknown was more difficult. Post host t-tests indicated marginally significant differences in award allocation when the survivor's employment status was ambiguous but not when the survivor was "employed." Although knowledge of an employed spouse appeared to lessen the differences in awards to male versus female decedents, it could not be concluded from these results whether jurors based their awards on the anticipated financial need of the survivor. To determine whether differences in awards were due to assumed differences in the financial needs of the survivor, perhaps it is necessary to be more explicit about the survivor's financial security. Perhaps sex stereotypes, characterizing females as lower in status (Eagly & Wood, 1982) and more dependent (Ward & Balswick, 1978) than males, overrode information about the survivor's employment. In other words, mock jurors may have perceived female survivors as less financially stable than male survivors, even when employed. Mock jurors may have assumed that a female surviving spouse earns less or is less likely to remain employed over time than a male survivor, consistent with the female stereotype. Verbal reports from Experiment 1 suggested that this was the case. Consider some examples from mock jurors who received the case stating that the *female* survivor was employed:

> "In spite of the fact that she works, she still needs the money to live on. She is used to living on a higher salary (his and hers) and now it is cut in half. Maybe her job doesn't pay well."

> "It does not say how much Karen Klemmer earns, so I don't know how much money she makes. But if she doesn't make that much, an equivalent of $25,000 a year for 10 years until she can earn as much."

Compare these responses to those in which a *male* survivor was employed:

> "Enough money to cover funeral expenses, replace the car that was wrecked, with enough money for a mental health vacation. Money will not bring her back to life and her husband needs no extra money to survive without her income."

> "The amount stated should be enough to cover the funeral costs and any outstanding bills she may have had. Her husband is employed and could support himself with her now gone."

On the other hand, if females really were perceived as intrinsically of less worth, mock jurors would award less to female decedents regardless of the survivor's financial need. A second experiment was designed to address why mock jurors allocated more in damages when the decedent was male than when the decedent was female. To determine whether the differences in awards are due to worth of decedent or financial need of survivor, mock jurors were presented with a scenario identical to the one used in the first experiment except that the survivor was described as "independently wealthy" or there was no survivor and the decedent was described as single. Experiment 1 may not have had a strong enough manipulation to convey the idea that the survivor was not needy. Experiment 2 provides a stronger—an independently wealthy survivor—to underscore the survivor's financial stability. A single decedent condition answers the questions whether a female's life is worth less than a male's, for it compels jurors to consider the individual decedent. If higher awards are allocated to male versus female decedents, in a single decedent condition, results would suggest that the life of a female was perceived as intrinsically of less worth than a male's.

TABLE 2

Mean Damage Awards by Sex of Subject: Experiment 1				
	Sex of Subject			
	Male		Female	
Sex of Decedent	Male	Female	Male	Female
Spouse's financial status:				
Ambiguous	$720,833	$1,022,222	$869,208	$492,167
Employed	$821,111	$544,166	$660,666	$645,833
Mean award by sex of subject and sex of decedent:				
	$802,896	$905,008	$762,070	$579,590
Mean award by sex of subject:				
(Male subject) $806,000		(Female subject) $686,000		
Grand mean award: $722,800				

Experiment 2

Method

Subjects.   Subjects were 179 University of Washington undergraduates whose participation was either voluntary or for course credit.

Materials and design. This experiment utilized a 2 x 3 between-subjects design, in which the first factor was gender of decedent (male or female) and the second factor was status of the decedent's estate (surviving spouse employed since he/she left college; survivor independently wealthy; no surviving spouse, estate left to charity). The dependent measure was the dollar amount awarded in damages (see appendix).

Procedure.   Subjects were tested in groups of 20-110. Booklets containing one of six conditions were randomly distributed. The basic procedures were the same as those used in Experiment 1.

Results

Data were complete for 173 out of 179 subjects. Data from six subjects who failed to complete the experiment were excluded from the analysis. Mean damage awards when the decedent was male for conditions in which the survivor was employed, independently wealthy, or single were $587,000 (median $382,000), $587,000 (median $250,000), and $639,000 (median $504,000), respectively. Mean damage awards when the decedent was female for conditions in which the survivor was employed, independently wealthy, or single were $567,000 (median $248,000), $630,000 (median $499,000), and $659,000 (median $510,000), respectively (Table 3).

TABLE 3

Mean Damage Awards by Experimental Condition: Experiment 2		
Status of Decedent's Estate		
Employed spouse	**Rich spouse**	**No spouse**
Male $587,000	$587,000	$639,000
Female $567,000	$630,000	$659,000

Frequency distributions of the dependent measure indicated high variance within and between cells, thus, a log linear transformation of damage awards was warranted. Analyses were performed on the log of the dependent measure. A 2 x 3 x 2 ANOVA showed no significant main effect of gender of decedent. Visual inspection of cell means showed a trend similar to Experiment 1 with the male decedent receiving a slightly higher mean damage award than the female decedent for conditions with an "employed survivor." Comparison of cell means in the two conditions where the survivor was "independently wealthy" showed a reversal of this trend. Comparison of cell means in the single decedent conditions reflected the same pattern of slightly higher award allocation when the decedent was female. None of these differences was significant ($p > .25$). However, a significant main effect of gender of subject was obtained, $F(1,172 = 6.0, p = .016$. Nonparametric Mann-Whitney rank sum also indicated a significant difference in amount awarded by gender of subject, $z = 1.93$, $p = .05$.

Discussion

The main effect of sex of decedent in Experiment 1 replicating the finding of Goodman et al. (1987) that female decedents were awarded less than male decedents, especially when the employment status of the surviving spouse was ambiguous, was not obtained in Experiment 2. Although the cells comparing awards to male and female decedents failed to achieve statistical significance, the small observed differences in the "employed spouse" conditions favoring male decedents may be due to a perceived greater financial need of the female survivor. When the survivor is "independently wealthy," female and male decedents were awarded about the same amount, with the female decedent getting a slightly higher award. The "single decedent" condition answers the question raised by the Goodman et al. (1987) study: *Is a female's life worth less than a male's?* The answer is *no*. A female decedent was awarded more in damages than a male decedent in this condition.

The results of Experiment 2 indicated that gender of the mock juror influenced the amount awarded in damages, regardless of employed spouse, independently wealthy spouse, or single decedent (Table 4). Female mock jurors awarded significantly less than male mock jurors. Although this finding was neither expected nor obtained by Goodman et al. (1987) and was only marginally significant in Experiment 1, it is interesting to speculate why females allocated less in damages than males in this experiment. One empirical study by Snyder (1971) supports this finding of sex differences in award allocation. Snyder showed that the addition of females to juries resulted in significantly lower financial redress awards to the winner of a case compared to all-male juries. Callahan-Levy and Messe's (1979) study on sex differences in the allocation of pay revealed that males and females paid equal amounts when asked to apportion a sum between themselves and a partner for equal work. Female subjects allocated less to themselves than to a partner, however, female partners were paid more by both sexes. Clearly, the finding in Experiment 2, of sex of subject differences in award allocation, requires further empirical research before any solid conclusions can be drawn.

TABLE 4

Mean Damage Awards by Sex of Subject: Experiment 2				
	Sex of Subject			
	Male		Female	
Sex of decedent	Male	Female	Male	Female
Status of decedent's estate:				
Employed spouse	$661,300	$666,700	$533,000	$475,000
Rich spouse	$842,000	$735,400	$437,500	$545,700
No spouse	$900,000	$644,000	$489,300	$652,400
Mean award by sex of subject and sex of decedent:				
	$709,000	$698,000	$484,000	$569,000
Mean award by sex of subject:				
(Male subject) $735,000		(Female subject) $527,000		

Contrasting the results of Experiment 1 and 2 shows that one source of gender bias in mock jurors' decisions about damage awards stemmed from mock jurors' concern about the survivor's financial capacity. These concerns were more likely not based on sex stereotypes of female dependency on the male provider. When mock jurors had to attend to the decedent alone (as in the single decedent case), there was no evidence of gender bias in their decisions about damage awards. Similarly, informing mock jurors that the female survivor was "independently wealthy" seemed to contradict mock jurors' stereotypical assumptions about "needy widows." The subsequent equal damage awards to male and female decedent indicated this.

There was no significant main effect of the "estate status" factor in Experiment 2, nor was there a main effect of the "employment of spouse" factor in Experiment 1. Nonetheless, it is interesting to speculate why mock jurors allocated less to both male and female decedents in conditions with seemingly greater financial need. It seemed unlikely that mock jurors would show signs of bias against the decedents or their survivors of lower socioeconomic status, although socioeconomic status is a potential source of bias in jury decision making (Kalven, 1964). It was difficult to attribute the source of jurors' higher awards to single decedents. Perhaps jurors admired the philanthropic character of the decedent who "left everything he or she owned to charity."

General Discussion

The results of this study and others (Goodman et al., 1987) showed that mock jurors sometimes awarded more money in damages when the decedent was male rather than female. This appeared to occur when the financial status of the survivor was ambiguous. When the survivor had been employed since he/she left college, awards to the female decedent were only minimally lower than awards to the male decedent. When the survivor was not at all needy, absolutely no difference in awards as a function of decedent gender was detected. These results suggest that previous findings by Goodman et al. (1987) may have occurred not because a woman's life is perceived as intrinsically of less worth than a man's, but rather because jurors focused on the survivor and anticipated a greater financial need for females. These combined results provide tentative support for the hypothesis that when mock jurors know only the gender of the survivor, their subsequent awards to male and female decedents will differ. However, when there is no survivor, or when the survivor is perceptibly financially secured, mock jurors award about equal amounts to male and female decedents. The experiments show that explicit information confirming the security of the survivor's financial status diminished the worrisome pattern of higher award allocation to male decedents. This conclusion is supported by Locksley et al. (1980), showing that when information is provided which contradicts sex stereotypes that would typically serve as a basis for judgments, subsequent judgments are not biased.

Gender bias is an unwanted feature in the legal system. These results suggested that mock jurors did not perceive a female's life to be less valuable than a male's. If this was the case, mock jurors would have awarded more to the male decedent regardless of need of the surviving spouse. Instead, the results suggest that mock jurors focused on the survivor. This strategy comports with the original legislative purpose of the wrongful death statutes: to compensate the decedent's survivors. Despite the instructions given to real juries about what constitutes evidence in award allocation, jurors use their common sense to fulfill the intent of the legislature. Are jurors wrong to take extralegal factors into consideration?

References

Ashmore, R.D, and Del Boca, F.K. (1979). Sex stereotypes and implicit personality theory: Toward a cognitive-social psychological conceptualization. *Sex Roles, 5*, 219-248.

Broverman, I.K., Vogel, S.R., Broverman, D.M., Clarkson, F.E., and Rosenkrantz, P.S. (1972). Sex-role stereotypes: A current appraisal. *Journal of Social Issues, 28,* 59-78.

Callahan-Levy, C.M. and Messe, L.A. (1979). Sex differences in the allocation of pay. *Journal of Personality and Social Psychology, 37,* 433-446.

Deaux, K. and Lewis, L.L. (1983). Components of gender stereotypes. *Psychological Documents, 13,* 25 (Ms. No. 2583).

Deaux, K. and Lewis, L.L (1984). Structure of gender stereotypes: Interrelationships among components and gender labels. *Journal of Personality and Social Psychology, 46,* 991-1004.

Eagly, A.H. and Steffen, V.J. (1986). Gender and aggressive behavior: A meta-analytic review of social psychological literature. *Psychological Bulletin, 100,* 309-330.

Eagly, A.H. and Wood, W. (1982). Inferred sex differences in status as a determinant of gender stereotypes about social influence. *Journal of Personality and Social Psychology, 43,* 915-928.

Feild, H.S. (1979). Rape trials and juror decisions: A psycholegal analysis of the effects of victim, defendant, and case characteristics. *Law and Human Behavior, 3,* 261-284.

Goldberg, P. (1968). Are women prejudiced against women? *Transaction, 5,* 28-30.

Goodman, J., Greene, E., and Loftus, E.F. (1987). Jurors' cognitions about damages in complex cases. Paper presented at the 1987 Annual Meeting of the American Psychological Association, New York.

Gruder, C.L. and Cook, T.D. (1971). Sex, dependency and helping. *Journal of Personality and Social Psychology, 19,* 290-294.

Hans, V.P. and Vidar, N. (1986). *Judging the Jury.* New York: Plenum Press.

Howards, J.A. (1984). Societal influences on attribution: Blaming some victims more than others. *Journals of Personality and Social Psychology, 47,* 494-505.

Johnson, J.T. and Dronby, J. (1985). Proximity biases in the attribution of civil liability. *Journal of Personality and Social Psychology, 48,* 283-296.

Kalven, H. (1964). The dignity of the civil jury. *Virginia Law Review, 50,* 1055-1075.

Kaplan, M.F. and Miller, L.E. (1978). Reducing the effects of juror bias. *Journal of Personality and Social Psychology, 36,* 1443-1455.

Locksley, A., Borgida, E., Brekke, N., and Hepburn, C. (1980). Sex stereotypes and social judgment. *Journal of Personality and Social Psychology, 39,* 821-831.

Nagels, S. and Weitzman, L. (1972). Sex and the unbiased jury. *Judicature, 56,* 108-111.

Pennington, N. and Hastie, R. (1987). Explanation-based decision-making. Paper presented at the 9th Annual Conference of Cognitive Science Proceedings, Seattle, WA.

Snyder, E. (1971). Sex role differential and juror decisions. *Sociology and Social Research, 55,* 442-448.

Tversky, A. and Kahneman, D. (1974). Judgment under uncertainty: Heuristics and biases. *Science, 185,* 1124-1131.

Ward, D. and Balswick, J. (1978). Strong men and virtuous women: A content analysis of sex role stereotypes. *Pacific Sociological Review, 21,* 45-53.

Acknowledgments

This article is extracted from a larger M.Sc. thesis done by the present author in 1988. The author expresses sincere appreciation to Jane Goodman and Elizabeth Loftus for assistance in the preparation of the thesis and thanks to Brad Bell for his comments on the drafts. Partial support of the thesis was provided by the National Science Foundation (NSF).

SECTION E
Group Decision Making

DECISION MAKING IN ORGANIZATIONS

Wing Hong Loke and Terri Ing Fang Tan

Decision making in organizations is a multi-faceted process. Besides considering structural factors, the human variable must also be taken into account. Given the demand for low-level involvement in the decision-making process, organizations integrate human resource as part of organizational decision making. A full appreciation of decision making in organizations is achieved by examining the variables of group participation in the decision-making process of organizations.

Within an organizational structure, one of the reasons individuals or groups communicate is to make decisions. Here, organizational decision making is best considered as varying along a continuum from an entirely individual process to an entirely group process. So, decisions within an organization are points along the continuum. At each particular point, the process of decision making involves identifying a problem or opportunity and choosing from among alternative courses of action.

The current trend in perception of work and labor in a technological age has had a huge impact on decision making in organizations. In the past the image of workers, as the scientific management era perceived them, resulted in work being mechanically defined, boring, and routine. Workers were not required to think but rather they were to follow instructions. Of late, the trend is that more worker input into decisions improves satisfaction and productivity. As such, different styles of work organization need to be developed. Simon (1960) stated that Man, being a "problem-solving, skill-using, social animal," expresses a need to "apply his skills, whatever they be, to challenging tasks." Further to this, another need is to find meaningful and warm relations with other human beings. These relations include the desire of individuals to work with one another in common tasks.

Today, more employees are insisting to participate in decisions that affect them and are more involved in what they consider to be meaningful work. To meet these demands, more companies have adopted a participative management style with emphasis on feedback.

Organizational Decision Making

According to Hampton (1986, p. 89), an organization is an enduring group of people in a structured, evolving system whose coordinated efforts are meant to reach goals in a dynamic environment. As such, a decision has to be made when the organization faces a problem, when it is dissatisfied with existing conditions, or when it is given a choice. A considerable amount of managerial activity precedes the actual decision. In large organizations, these activities may be carried out by people other than the decision makers. Staff in the line organization discover problems and alternatives for decision. The actual decision is only the conclusion of a process. (Of note is that departments engaged in the most basic tasks are *line organizations* in contrast to staff organizations that provide support or are ancillary to the line organizations.)

Decisions are the outcome of a dynamic process to achieve organizational goals and objectives; it is not an end in itself. So, decisions are *organizational responses to problems*. It is a multi-phased process of which the actual choice is only one phase (see Figure 1).

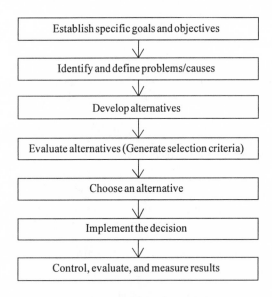

FIGURE 1
Flowchart of Decision-making Process

Features of the Decision-making Process

The following are some important features involved in the organizational decision-making process.

(a) **Setting objectives**. Establishing and defining broad organizational goals is the basic requirement for subsequent decisions to be made on a lower level. From these broad objectives, strategies and departmental goals can be set to provide the framework for decision making at lower managerial levels. However, although goals are set, problems still exist because of multiple objectives, conflicting objectives, and the hierarchical nature of the objectives.

(b) **Long-term planning**. Decision making at the various levels of management is concerned with varying degrees of the long term. Top management decisions involve longer time periods than lower level management decisions.

(c) **Sequential decision making**. Sequential decision making is the process of successively solving interrelated sub-problems which are parts of a larger complex problem. Organizations often resort to specialization of labor or breaking down the problem into many sub-problems.

(d) **Dynamic decision making**. Management decisions are usually not just a one-time event, but are successive over a time frame. Future management decisions are influenced by past decisions to some degree.

(e) **Routine and non-routine decisions**. There are two basic types of managerial decisions: routine and non-routine. Routine problems arise on a regular basis or often enough that a definite procedure can be worked out to solve them. Programmed decisions are dependent on policies, rules, and definite procedures. The procedure for admitting patients in health care services can be considered routine or programmed decision making.

Much organizational decision making involves issues that are neither important nor contested. In such cases, standard operational procedures are sufficient to get the decisions made in an inexpensive and efficient manner.

Non-routine or non-programmed decisions are novel and unstructured. There is no established procedure for handling the problem. It is specifically tailored to the situation at hand. An example is the decision to diversify into new products and markets by a business firm.

The main concern of top management should be non-programmed decisions while first-level management should be concerned with programmed decisions. The nature, frequency, and degree of certainty surrounding a problem should dictate at what level of management the decision should be made. If the top management spends too much time and effort on routine decisions, this can lead to a neglect of long-term planning. This is often the result of a lack of delegation of authority to lower level management.

(f) **Areas of decision making**. There are basically four areas that an organization encounters in decision making. They are:

(i) routine personnel functions like hiring, training, disciplining, and performance evaluation;

(ii) the nature of the work itself including task assignments, job designs, and speed (deadlines) of work;

(iii) working conditions like rest periods, hours of work, placement of equipment, and lighting; and

    (iv) company policies such as layoffs, profit sharing, capital investment, and general company-wide policies.

  (g) **The cost of decision making**. Decision making involves costs, especially the evaluation of alternatives which precedes the final choice or decision. Management must determine if the cost of the search for alternatives is worth the reduced uncertainty. A cost-benefit analysis is often conducted. In general, the cost of the search process should not exceed the benefits of improving the decision.

Though the process of decision making may seem to be performed on a unitary basis, many decisions in organizations are not the product of individual efforts. Group decision making is the norm for most levels of decision making in many organizations.

Group Decision Making

Group decision making has become an important activity of modern organizational life. Such decision is adopted based on two assumptions: (a) groups make better decisions than individuals and (b) decisions by groups are accepted more readily and are easier to implement.

In multi-part problems, especially those that are susceptible to division of labor, groups are considered to be superior to individuals. Characteristics of members, length of time in existence, heterogeneity or homogeneity of group and the size of the group will also have effects on group decisions. For example, heterogeneous groups generally performed tasks better than homogeneous groups, other things being equal. Individual differences are the major source of success of groups in decision making. Cooperation and cohesiveness are assets to the group.

Group decision making, however, has certain disadvantages. A phenomenon known as "groupthink" (Janis, 1982) occurs when a group is homogeneous or there is a high level of cohesiveness. Groupthink is characterized by a deterioration in judgment that results from in-group pressures. Decision makers (e.g., executives) abide by the decisions of the group and, sometimes, even beyond what would be justified by the value of the available information. Another is the phenomenon of the "risky shift" where more extreme than necessary decisions are made.

To be effective, organizations undertake problem identification and resolution in a group setting. This participative-group approach to problem solving requires that people will be more committed to overcoming a problem if they have helped to decide upon the strategy to be used.

For acceptance of organizations' decisions, employees and management need to discuss, negotiate, and cooperate. One device is the formulation of house unions. The feeling of togetherness by management and employees tend to bring about a climate of cooperation instead of the adversary idea of "you" versus "me."

Forms of Participation

Participation in work decisions focuses on the work itself, dealing with how it is organized, what is done, and who does what. As discussed, the role of the individual worker in the decision-making process in organizations should be emphasized. The involvement of the individual, in the context of the group, varies from organization to organization.

Consultative participation refers to situations where employees give their opinions and offer suggestions. An example would be IBM (International Business Machines Corporation) Singapore which conducts employee surveys ranging from the effectiveness of the management team to work improvement areas.

Short-term participation is of a limited duration which can range from one session to several meetings. Such arrangements are also called "ad-hoc committees" and are of a temporal nature.

Many organizations do not have formally established participatory systems or groups involved in the decision-making process. Yet, participation in decision making may occur informally through interpersonal relationships between managers and subordinates. This occurs on an ad-hoc basis and is limited to issues concerning the subordinate's work.

In *employee ownership*, employees own part of the organization. Each has a formal "right" to participate as a shareholder does. Employees can influence the decisions made by management through mechanisms like election of the board of directors and shareholders' meeting but few participate directly in decision making. The content of such participation covers any area and its level of influence is high. A good example would be Chrysler Corporation where Lee Iacocca's participative management style made the company stage a miraculous turnaround. (Of note is that Chrysler Corporation also received huge financial backing from the government.)

In *representative participation*, employees do not participate directly but through representatives elected in a council (e.g., the National Trade Union Congress in Singapore). This follows the concept of a union being an organization of workers forming a body to promote the interest of workers.

Different forms of participation are associated with different outcomes. Effectiveness in participation varies with both the form of participation in a situation and the criterion for measuring effectiveness. Certain types of participation work better in some situations than in others. For example, representative participation may not increase productivity but does increase satisfaction. Thus, situational factors play an important role in determining the feasibility of the use of participatory decision making. In organizations where the workers know very little of the subject in consideration or where the management are strongly against participation, participatory decision making will fail.

Case Studies on Participation in Decision Making
Participation and work satisfaction

A study conducted by Patchen (1967) on employee job attitudes of a cooperative program of labor-management consultation at the Tennessee Valley Authority (TVA) has implications beyond the TVA setting. The results suggested that an intensive employee participation program covering a large organizational unit can increase employee feelings of solidarity with the work organization and with management. In addition employee acceptance of work changes increased. Furthermore, the results showed that the participation program would not be maximally effective in creating favorable work groups unless employees have some chance to have their opinions heard and heeded within their immediate work groups.

The relationship between employee influence on decisions and feelings of solidarity within the organization appears to be stronger among professional engineering personnel than among skilled but non-professional workers. This finding also indicated that attitudes toward the organization are improved by participating in decision making, primarily among employees for whom such participation is seen as legitimate or as important to their occupational self-image. Increased acceptance of change is not due to improved attitudes towards management but is the product of joint labor management decision making. The employees viewed the decisions as being less imposing and more mutual solutions to common problems.

A review of the vast research in this area by Locke and Schweiger (1979) showed that in terms of actual productivity changes, participation had no effect in more than 50% of the studies. But participation did indeed have a positive impact on satisfaction for more than 60% of the time.

Obviously, no profit-oriented company exists solely to satisfy its employees' personal needs. Rather its two basic goals are to survive and to make profit. Effective use of participative management can help attain these goals and at the same time increase employee motivation. In return, such a style of management will provide a competitive edge for the company.

Tapping hidden expertise

Involving employees in identifying and solving production problems can result in improved technical solutions. Employees who face problems on a day-to-day basis often develop a clear understanding of the nature of the problems. Experts who were brought in to deal with the problems may not produce more effective solutions; the individual involved with the problem is in the position to know more about the conditions and circumstances than a senior manager. Providing a supportive environment in which employees are encouraged to express their ideas can make available to the company a reservoir of previously untapped technical expertise.

An illustration would be that of the Singapore Bus Service which began implementing ideas from its eight Quality Control Circles (QCCs) recently. A team from engineering and the supply division suggested a way to cut down the cushion replacement rate. They had noticed that slits or holes on seat cushions, if left unmended, would tempt some passengers to tear at them, therefore enlarging them. The team recommended the use of storage shelves to keep cushions removed from scrapped buses. Previously, these cushions, still in good condition when removed, could not be re-used because their quality deteriorated when left in the open. These cushions were then used to replace the removed "slits or holes" cushions; furthermore, the removed cushions were mended. The team's idea was adopted and brought substantial savings for the company.

Labor-management cooperation

Managers today realize that involving others in the decision-making process is important to many employees. In 1982, General Motors and the United Auto Workers Union agreed to encourage labor management cooperation. This contract by the management to share decision-making power with the union caused the company to remain competitive and productive. An adversarial relationship between management and non-management employees is costly and disruptive to both parties.

Within the framework of industrial capitalism, growth in labor productivity has become a joint effort between employees and management. Decisions which govern the design as well as the operation of factories have become the province of both the employer and the employee. This marks a transformation in the classic position of the two parties: management as the "order-giver" to employees who accept instructions and carry them out. The changing relation between employees and management has important effects on ways of making increased gains in industrial productivity.

Formal worker participation in Singapore

A maxim of the behavioral scientists is that creativity, imagination, and ingenuity in solving organizational problems are not the special province of the better educated and higher level elite of the organization. Instead, they are qualities found among the population. The recent trend in introducing QCCs into work organizations is an important example of the trend towards allowing employees greater participation and tapping this pool of talent. QCCs, being groups of people who meet regularly to discuss issues pertaining to work productivity and quality, provide the opportunities for workers to become involved and have influence over matters relevant to their jobs and job performance. In Singapore, 4% of the work force are involved in QCCs. The cultural diversity may be an advantage as it increases the chance for creative solutions.

Hewlett Packard (HP) Singapore, an electronics company, has 30 QCCs from its production, quality assurance, and materials departments. The company started the concept because the philosophy was similar to its management philosophy, and group discussion was seen as an important avenue through which all-round improvement to the working environment could be made.

At HP, all levels of staff are involved with the QC movement. They seek to improve the quality of their working life and upgrade skills and knowledge through group discussions. The management of HP views people as the greatest asset of the company. The basic philosophy behind all QC activities is that employees take more interest in their work when asked to contribute to decisions that affect them, and that people closest to a particular work area can best make the decisions about their work areas.

A variant of QCCs is the Work Improvement Teams (WITs). As of August 1988, there were 5,773 WITs in Singapore. Around 50,700 personnel were involved in WITs. Two complementary schemes have also been implemented by the Singapore Armed Forces (SAF). They are the Unit SAF Suggestion Scheme Management System (USMS) and the Unit WIT Management Scheme (UWMS). The aim of USMS is to get more servicemen to take part as well as to provide faster response to their suggestions. In UWMS servicemen are brought together in teams, based on their natural working groups where possible, to assist servicemen practice initiative and teamwork on a continual basis. This may lead to survival and success in the battlefield as well as in a peacetime work environment. This move not only provides a quicker response to servicemen's ideas, but also promotes mass participation which has a multiplier effect on the productivity movement as a whole.

In general, most organizations adopting the participatory approach confine decision making to the upper ranks of management and among scientific and professional employees. In goal setting, lower levels of the corporate hierarchy have neither the perspective nor the expertise to establish the long-term goals of the organization. For the setting of short-term goals, it is advantageous to include individuals who are responsible for achieving them. For these goals not only have shorter time spans, but their achievement can be more easily controlled through the effort of employees at the work group level.

Those responsible for working towards the goals may need a voice in establishing and deciding them. This, however, does not mean work groups set goals at random. Ultimately, short-term goals are established within the larger framework of long-term corporate goals. Given the need to reconcile the two, striking a balance between centralization and delegation of authority and responsibilities is a major consideration for an organization. An understanding of the nature of centralization and decentralization in organizations is crucial to a fuller appreciation of the decision-making process.

Centralization and Delegation

Centralization is the process where the top levels of an organization retain the authority to make most decisions. Control is exercised by confining decision making to a small group of senior individuals.

The power relationships at the top are influenced by factors like stock holdings and company seniority. Corporate decision making is inherently political. If the lines of responsibility are not clear, role conflict can operate to undermine top-level decision making and hinder major business decisions.

When the authority to make specified decisions is passed down to units and people at lower levels in the hierarchy, the process is known as *delegation*. Decision making is passed downwards and outwards within the formal structure, but there are strict rules imposed on the scope and type of decisions that can be made without referral upwards.

Advantages of centralization. Senior managers have a broad perspective of what is going on in the organization. They are in a better position to make decisions which are in accord with the company policies and organizational interests. Centralized control helps to keep the various functional areas like marketing, research and finance in balance with one another. Also, centralization economizes on managerial overheads by avoiding the duplication of activities or resources. It also justifies the employment of certain staff or specialist support personnel in desirable areas. If management were to be more dispersed, coordination and execution of functions like planning, legal, and personnel matters would be difficult.

Furthermore, top managers are generally proven by the time they reach senior positions. Being more experienced, they are capable of making good decisions and exercising good judgments. In time of crisis, an experienced leadership may be beneficial. Centralization focuses power, authority, and prestige onto a central key position or a senior group. Speedy decisions can also be made in reaction to unexpected crises.

Advantages of delegation. Delegation helps to relieve the burden and the organization can function more effectively if the senior managers have more time for matters of long-term consequence. Senior managers would be overburdened if they were to attend to all matters. Large-scale operations, complexity, and rapid changes all contribute to the decision-making load of the executives.

Organizations benefit by co-opting lower levels and the individual worker into participating in the decision-making process. High delegation encourages the development of the participating decision makers. Opportunities to make significant decisions enable individuals to gain skills and to advance in the company. Good decision makers involve judgment, the ability to cope with uncertainty, and other attributes which are developed through appropriate experience. Thus, workers involved in decision making are trained for promotion into positions of heavier responsibility.

Delegation permits greater flexibility at the operating levels in organizations as decisions do not have to be referred up the hierarchy, especially in bigger organizations where the hierarchies are extended and vertical communication is much harder. High delegation can also lead to a competitive climate within the organization in which managers compete on their sales records and cost-reduction performance. Semi-autonomous units can be established with operational independence or even profit responsibility. This can be a contributor to more effective controls and performance measurement in the organization. However, significant competition exists only if the individuals are given enough authority to do the things that will enable them to win.

Pico Art International, a leading exhibition firm, is recognized worldwide for its ability to stage major international events, sell its services overseas, and project Singapore as a premier exhibition venue. To get its staff to do their best, the company encourages friendly internal competition by dividing them into seven teams of thirty individuals each. Due to the delegation of authority through its team approach, Pico is able to mobilize resources faster and easier.

Business firms are becoming increasingly complex in terms of size, financial resources, manpower utilization, and product diversification. A large element of centralized decision making at the top will become inappropriate. With modern organizations, the workplace will be populated with knowledgeable workers networking to accomplish their individual tasks. Besides these workers would become experts in their fields. However, advantages of decentralization can be realized only if the units to which the decision is delegated are natural subdivisions and if the actions taken in one of them do not adversely affect that of other units. Ultimately, since hierarchy always implies some measure of decentralization, decision making in organizations is usually decentralized.

The Choice between Centralization and Delegation

The choice between centralization and delegation has to be made in the light of specific conditions and situations. Carlisle (1974) discussed thirteen variables which determine an organization's control structure:

(a)   the basic purpose and goals of the organization;

(b)   the knowledge and experience of the top-level management;

(c)   the skill, knowledge, and attitudes of subordinates;

(d)   the scale or size of the organization;

(e)   the geographical dispersion of the organization;

(f)   the scientific content or the technology of the tasks being performed;

(g)   the time frame of the decisions to be made;

(h)   the significance of the decisions to be made;

(i)   the degree to which subordinates will accept and are motivated by the decisions to be made;

(j)   the status of the organization's planning and control system;

(k)   the status of the organization's information system;

(l)   the degree of conformity and coordination required in the tasks and operations of the organization; and

(m) the status of external environmental factors such as government and trade unions.

As an organization grows, it becomes more difficult for a senior executive or top management team to have the time and knowledge to make all decisions. Moreover, these decisions would be more frequent and complex. So, large organizations are, in a way, forced to move towards delegation in order to stay efficient and competitive.

Geographical location is another contingent factor to be considered. The more scattered or dispersed an organization's operating sites, the more difficult it is for senior management to oversee the entire operation. If decisions have to be made by the senior management, the delay may involve loss of profits or opportunities for the organization.

A case in point is that of the Royal Dutch Shell's group philosophy in decentralization. The Shell companies in Singapore are free to make all but the most important decisions without referring to their parent offices in London and Hague. This means delegation and participation. The climate of the organization is that no one looks over the other's shoulder, the subordinate informs the supervisor about the essentials and consults the supervisor whenever the need for advice or guidance arises. Shell's senior management believes in training and motivating people for its high-tech operations via opportunities for delegation of authority and encourages participation in decision making. Of note, however, is that Shell selects the best applicants from the job market.

Generally, stable conditions permit a higher degree of centralization and the delegation of less authority down the hierarchy than do rapidly changing and less predictable environments. Only in the small organization does a concentration of decision-making authority in an individual makes for superior adaptation to external changes.

Both centralization and delegation are not simple dichotomies. They are strategies for maintaining control. As mentioned earlier in the present paper, there has been a movement towards decentralization over the years. Moreover, since hierarchy always implies some measure of decentralization, the question then is to what extent will the decision making in organizations be decentralized. Also, considerations must be made as to whether more decentralization is a good choice.

References

Carlisle, H.M. (1974). A contingency approach to decentralization. *Advanced Management Journal, 3*, 9-18.

Hampton, D.R. (1986). *Management (3rd Ed.)*. New York: McGraw-Hill.

Janis, I.L. (1982). *Victims of Groupthink (2nd Ed.)*. Boston: Houghton Mifflin Co.

Locke, E.A. and Schweiger, D.M. (1979). Participation in decision making: One more look. In B.M. Staw (Ed.), *Research in Organisational Behavior, 1*, 265-340. Greenwich, CT: JAI Press.

Patchen, M. (1967). Labor-management consultation at TVA: Its impact on employees.

Administrative Science Quarterly, 10, 149-174.

Simon, H.A. (1960). Decision making and organisational design. In D.S. Pugh (Ed.), *Selected Readings in Organisational Theory* (1971). Harmondsworth, UK: Penguin Books.

Note

A reduced version of this article appeared in *Commentary, 8,* 36-40, June 1990, Singapore: National University of Singapore Society.

MAKING DECISIONS IN COMMITTEES:
AN ECONOMIST'S PERSPECTIVE

Winston Teow Hock Koh

The widespread occurrence of collective decision making reflects the limitations of individual rationality. Making decisions in
a committee is an effective way to overcome judgment errors
that might be committed due to human fallibility. This paper
analyzes collective decision making in committees. Using the
Project Selection Model, some of the intuitions associated with
making decisions in committees are formalized. In particular, we
showed how the optimal size of the consensus should be related
to the decision environment. Conditions under which the majority
rule is optimal are also identified.

Despite the frequent divergence in individual interests, many of our decisions are
made collectively. It is advantageous to make collective decisions simply because
individual rationality is bounded. Indeed, the limitations of individual rationality is
a reason for the existence of economic organizations. Nonetheless, our attitudes
towards collective decision making range from the positive (two heads are better than
one) to the skeptical (too many cooks spoil the broth).

Most collective decisions are made within formal organizations, such as a firm or
the government, where members interact in a well-defined manner. With divergence
of interests, members must be motivated to act in accordance with a defined
organizational objective. This issue of incentives has been studied extensively by
economists. Among other things, the research has highlighted the tradeoff between
control and delegation in the design of organizational relationships, as well as
suggested ways to provide correct incentives through performance-based reward
schemes. By contrast, the issue of bounded rationality, and its consequences on
organizational performance, has received little attention. Even if individual interests
coincide, the quality of a collective decision depends on several factors: individual
decision-making abilities, quality and availability of relevant information, extent of
communication and the manner in which individual opinions are aggregated. Altering
any of these aspects can affect organizational performance considerably even if the
decision environment remains unchanged.

Bounded rationality exists because individuals are fallible and thus make honest
errors in information acquisition, communication and decision making. Individuals
are fallible partly because it is costly to acquire and process all the relevant
information, and partly because they have limited capacities to do so. Most of us are
often reluctant to delegate decision-making authority to a single individual because of

the implicit belief that group wisdom will avoid individual errors of judgment. With more individuals involved in the decision process, individual errors can be mitigated and decisions become more accurate. However, more time and resources have to be expended; hence, there is a tradeoff.

Human fallibility also implies that it is infeasible and undesirable for an individual to collect and process all the information. Each decision maker should specialize in only part of the relevant information. With specialization, communication becomes necessary; however, human fallibility implies that what is communicated is usually a message of much lower dimension compared with the acquired information. For instance, in a committee, members may be required only to either vote "for" or "against" a particular motion. In general, individuals can communicate information more fully, but this brings with it possibilities that information may be distorted, censored or withheld, generating further incentive problems for the organization.

The objective of this paper is to introduce an economist's perspective on collective decision making. To do so, we shall consider a popular collective decision process: the committee. First, an analytical framework is described in the following on "The Project Selection Model." Next, the subsequent sections analyze various aspects of decision making within committees. The last section provides some concluding remarks.

The Project Selection Model

Suppose a firm is presented with a project that is drawn in a random manner from a pool of available projects. It must decide whether to accept or reject a project. If the project is successful, the payoff is x_h, if unsuccessful, the payoff is $-x_l$. Potential projects are not definitely "good" or "bad," but differ in their probabilities of success p, where $0 < p < 1$. The true probability of success of individual projects cannot be observed; however, the distribution of projects is given by π (p), the density function, which is known to the firm.

The firm hires a team of managers to evaluate the project. There is no incentives problem and each manager is paid an amount Y for his services. Managers are required only to vote "Yes" or "No" regarding the acceptability of the project. Communication is thus binary and limited; this could be justified on the basis of costs, which may involve a delay in implementing a good project, if there is to be fuller communication. Delay is important in the face of market competition when the same project can be undertaken by other firms.

Each manager observes a signal r $(0 < r < 1)$ about the probability of success p of the project under review. Human fallibility implies r does not equal p with certainty; if r = p with certainty, this means managers can observe p perfectly, contradicting the human fallibility assumption. r must also be a random variable; otherwise, even though r = p, it is possible to infer p from r. However, r must be informative about p. A natural notion of informativeness, widely used in economics, is the monotone likelihood condition (MLRC). Let the density function of r conditional on p be g(r|p).

For $p_1 > p_2$ and $r_1 > r_2$, $g(r|p)$ satisfied MLRC if and only if

$$\frac{g(r_1|p_1)}{g(r_2|p_1)} > \frac{g(r_1|p_2)}{g(r_2|p_2)} \tag{1}$$

Under MLRC, it can be shown that r_1 is a more favorable signal compared with r_2, since r_1 is more likely to be generated by a project with a higher p. Consequently, the expected probability of success of a project is higher if the observed signal is higher. Each manager's strategy is therefore to choose a cutoff point $\underline{r}$ such that he/she votes in favor of the project if the observed signal is greater than $\underline{r}$. The probability of a project p being accepted by the manager is $(1 - G(\underline{r}|p))$. For a selected cutoff point, projects with higher probabilities of success are more likely to be accepted. Also, if the cutoff point is raised, evaluation becomes tighter, so that the probability of acceptance decreases.

Optimal Evaluation Standards

The objective of the firm is to maximize expected profits from each project. Suppose the rule is that a project is only accepted if k or more managers vote "yes." Let r denote $(r_1,.., r_n)$, the set of cutoff points used by managers and r_{-j} denote $(r_1,.., r_{i-1}, r_{i+1},.., r_n)$. This requires that given r_{-j}, the cutoff points of other managers, manager i chooses r_i optimally. Collective decision making thus necessitates coordination in choosing evaluation standards. Since managers are identical, there is a common optimal cutoff point r^c for every manager.

At r^c, we can write the probability of accepting a project p as such:

$$p^k_n (r^c) = \sum_{j=k}^{n} C_j [1-G)r^c|p)]^j G(r^c|p)^{n-j} \tag{2}$$

and the expected profits as such:

$$B^k_n(r^c) = \int (px_h - (1-p)x_j) \sum_{j=k}^{n} C_j [1-G(r^c|p^j]^j G(r^c|p)^{n-j} d\Pi(p) - nY \tag{3}$$

The optimality of r^c can be shown to imply that a "borderline" project earns zero expected profits. A "borderline" project is defined as one where (k-1) committee members have voted "Yes," (n-k) members have voted "No," and the last member happens to observe r^c, when the optimal cutoff point is r^c.

The quality of the project portfolio can be measured by a ratio of the payoffs, $q = x_1/(x_h+x_1)$. A larger q is due to a larger x_1 or a smaller x_h; this implies deterioration of project quality, since expected profits of every project decreases. If r^c is unchanged, the borderline project now earns negative profits. To restore profitability, r^c must be raised to tighten screening. Similarly, r^c must be raised when the committee size is increased. If r^c is unchanged, project evaluation becomes slacker since it is easier for a project to be accepted now that there are more managers. In contrast, when acceptance consensus is raised, it is more difficult for a project to be accepted; thus, r^c must be decreased to restore the optimal degree of screening tightness.

Optimal Acceptance Consensus

From the preceding discussion, it is clear evaluation standards and acceptance consensus are complementary in the sense that either or both could be adjusted to vary screening tightness. In situations where evaluation standards are set exogenously (fixed r), only the acceptance consensus may be varied. With fixed r, the managerial screening function may be written as

$$r(p) = 1-G(r|p) \tag{4}$$

The acceptance probability of a project p is therefore as

$$p^k_n(p) = \sum_{j=k}^{n} C_j r^j(p) [1-r(p)]n-j \tag{5}$$

It can be shown that $p^k_n(p)$ increases with p, so that better projects are more likely to be accepted. Furthermore, if the acceptance consensus is raised, evaluation becomes tighter, so that acceptance probability of every project decreases. By contrast, if the committee becomes larger, while the acceptance consensus is fixed, every project is more likely to be accepted.

The optimal consensus varies with the decision environment in the following ways to restore the appropriate degree of screening tightness:

(a) When q becomes larger, optimal acceptance consensus is raised, since a larger q indicates deterioration in portfolio quality.

(b) When committee size becomes larger, the optimal consensus is raised. If the acceptance consensus is unchanged, project evaluation will become slacker. More projects, including low-quality projects are accepted.

(c) The increase in optimal consensus is less than the increase in committee size. If the increase in acceptance consensus is the same as the increase in committee size, the consensus for *rejecting* a project is unchanged. A project is now rejected if the same number of managers disapprove of it, but since there are now more managers, it is easier for this to happen.

(d) An increase in the evaluation costs has a direct effect of reducing the optimal size of the committee. With a smaller committee, the optimal consensus is also smaller. However, by (c), the decrease in the optimal consensus is less than the decrease in the optimal committee size.

Majority Rule

Many decisions in committees are made on the basis of majority voting. In an election (the electorate is the committee), candidates are elected if they win by a majority; and in a trial, a defendant is to be judged by the jury via majority voting. One reason for the popularity of the majority decision rule lies in the fact that decision makers have different vested interests regarding the outcome of the voting. Another plausible reason is that the decision environment is uncertain. Majority voting may be optimal in such situations.

In the context of project selection, environmental uncertainty may arise because either portfolio quality or managerial expertise, or both, may be unknown. The uncertainty of portfolio quality can be modelled formally by assuming there are equal numbers of good projects ($p > .5$) and bad projects ($p < .5$). The uncertainty of managerial screening ability can also be modelled formally by assuming that managers are equally likely to reject a good project as to accept a bad project. In other words, the Type-I error of rejecting a project when it should be accepted and the Type-II error of accepting a project when it should be rejected are equal. Under these two conditions, it can be shown that the majority rule is optimal when $q = .5$, a condition that is satisfied when payoffs are unknown but deemed to be equal. Since the majority decision rule is commonly used to make collective decisions in uncertain situations, it is nice that this intuition can be formalized.

Furthermore, as the size of the committee increases, the optimal acceptance consensus tends to approximately half the size of the committee, regardless of the portfolio quality as measured by q. This result implies that the majority decision rule is approximately optimal when the committee size is large, regardless of portfolio quality. It confirms our intuition that the majority rule is almost efficient when there is a large number of individuals involved in the decision-making process, since individual errors of judgment will cancel out by the law of large numbers.

Managerial Expertise

With exogenous screening standards, managerial expertise can be measured by two properties of $r(p)$: level and slope. Suppose $r_o(p)$ and $r_N(p)$ represent two different screening functions ("O" for old, "N" for new). Screening is tighter under $r_N(p)$ at p if $r_N(p) < r_o(p)$; and $r_N(.)$ is locally more discriminating at p if $r_N(p) > r_o(p)$ where $r(.)$ is the slope of $r(.)$. Thus, when managerial expertise changes, it may change in either tightness or discriminating power, or both. To analyze the effects of changing managerial expertise on optimal consensus, consider an improvement in managerial expertise in the following sense: $r_N(p)$ is uniformly more discriminating compared with $r_o(p)$ if

(1) $r_N(p)$ $r_o(p)$ for all p

(2) there exists a p^* $(0,1)$ such that $r_N(p^*) = r_o(p^*)$ (6)

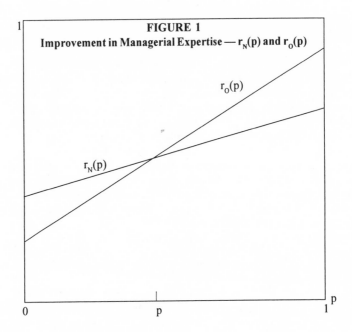

Figure 1 illustrates the two screening functions.

It can be shown that there exists a portfolio quality q^* such that for q less than q^*, optimal consensus under $r_N(p)$ is higher compared with that under $r_0(p)$. Similarly, for a portfolio whose quality is worse than q^*, optimal consensus under $r_N(p)$ is lower than that under $r_0(p)$. Managerial evaluation therefore becomes tighter/slacker for portfolios whose quality are better/worse than q^*. The direct implication of this result is that the ratio of the optimal consensus to size of committee tends to half, for all q. Hence, when managerial expertise becomes more discriminating, the optimal decision rule becomes closer to the majority rule. Thus, another circumstance when the majority rule is approximately optimal is when managerial expertise has improved.

Concluding Remarks

The analysis in this paper focused on understanding how the rules for decision making (evaluation standards, optimal acceptance consensus) within a committee should be related to the decision environment (portfolio quality, managerial expertise, evaluation costs and size of the committee). In the analysis, communication is limited to a vote of "Yes" or "No." An incentives problem arises if managers can communicate information more fully, or observe other managers' information. Each manager could save on his/her costs of gathering information and rely on other managers to furnish the relevant information. This has the effect of reducing the information content of the opinions and therefore the quality of the collective decision.

Furthermore, when the firm cannot observe a manager's actions or the information on which his/her decision is based, each manager could shirk, save on the costs of gathering information, and vote randomly. In such a situation, each manager's compensation must be made contingent on the outcome of the selection process (whether a project is selected; and if selected, whether it is successful or not) to motivate him/her to gather information. Managers' rewards should also be related to committee size and acceptance consensus: the larger the acceptance consensus, the larger should be the contract risk imposed on managers. The reasoning is straightforward: a larger acceptance consensus is optimal when the portfolio quality has deteriorated; hence, it is more important that managers should work, and not shirk and vote randomly.

References

Degroot, M.H. (1975). *Probability and Statistics.* Reading, MA: Addison-Wesley.

Holmstrom, B. (1979). Moral hazard and observability. *Bell Journal of Economics, 10,* 74-91.

Klevorick, A., Rothschild M., and Winship C., (1984). Information processing and jury decision making. *Journal of Public Economics, 23,* 245-278.

Koh, T.H. (1988). *Human Fallibility and Economic Organisations.* Unpublished Doctoral Dissertation, Princeton University.

Koh, T.H. (1989). *Human Fallibility and Sequential Decision Making: Hierarchy versus Polyarchy.* Faculty of Business Administration Working Paper, No. 89-29, National University of Singapore.

Lambert, R.A. (1986). Executive Effort and Selection of Risky Projects. *Rand Journal of Economics, 17,* 77-88.

Milgrom, P.R. (1981). Good news and bad news: Representation theorems and applications. *Bell Journal of Economics, 12,* 380-391.

Sah, R.K. and Stiglitz J.E., (1985). Human fallibility and economic organisation. *American Economic Review: Papers and Proceedings, 75,* 292-297.

Sah, R.K. and Stiglitz, J.E., (1988). Committees, hierarchies and polyarchies. *Economic Journal, June 1988.*

Note

This paper is based on Chapter 4 of the present author's doctoral thesis at Princeton University. A longer and more technical version appeared as a working paper (No. 89-30) in the Faculty of Business Administration, National University of Singapore.

SECTION F

Approaches to the Evaluation
of Decision Making

DECISION MAKING: THE VALUE OF HAVING A PROCESS

Seng Bee Keek

Most articles on decision making center around the "what," "why," "who," "when," and "where" of good decision making. This article is an attempt to uncover the "how-to" of good decision making.

Several changes in business have increased the difficulty of making good decisions. First, we are in the midst of an information explosion. Many call it information overload but others call it information pollution. Good decision makers know that insufficient information is frustrating but too much information can be equally frustrating. From 1750 to 1950 (a period of 200 years) the amount of information in the world doubled. It doubled again in the 1950s and 1960s and it tripled in the 1970s. The pace during the eighties is increasing even more rapidly. IBM is predicting that, with the advent of the personal computers and breakthroughs in telecommunications, a person in business will have seven times more information to grapple with by 1990. What this means is the increased complexity in retrieving, collecting, and organizing of relevant data. Hence, a process to help the decision maker to distinguish the relevant from the irrelevant, the historical from the hysterical data is imperative.

Second, the rate of change of technology is fast. A look at the microchip industry can frighten off many laymen. America's premier engineering school, the Massachusetts Institute of Technology has found that 50% of what an engineer acquires becomes obsolete just three years after graduation. With the increased use of technology and its almost daily improvements, one can no longer depend solely on one's experience and technical expertise to make decisions. What is happening is that more and more people are being asked to make decisions about situations of which they have little or no first-hand knowledge. Therefore, a process that cuts across all situations to arrive at good decisions cannot be overemphasized.

Third, the consequences of decisions are becoming greater. Right and wrong decisions are going to have a greater bottom-line impact. An example is the invitation by the Singapore government to the Israeli president to visit Singapore a few years ago, which caused a series of strong protests from the neighboring Muslim countries. With a process, at least the failure can be minimized if not prevented when the various risks identified are appropriately handled.

The fourth is social change. With better education and greater affluence, more people want to participate in the process of decision making. They want their objectives considered and their options debated. There is a need, therefore, for a common process of decision making that each participant involved in a decision can understand.

The Effective Decision-Making Processes

In our work with over 20,000 managers each year in 16 different countries in the past 6 years, we have been able to pin down six different processes needed in different situations to arrive at good decisions. The six are: (a) situation analysis, (b) problem analysis, (c) decision analysis, (d) potential problem analysis, (e) potential opportunity analysis, and (f) the creative process.

Each of the above processes comprises various steps that make up the respective logic paths. Just like travelling, when we have decided on the destination, the first thing we do is to look at the map and plan the appropriate route to take. Decision making involves the same process. We need a map to point us to the right direction. We call this a logic map. Let us take a critical look at each of them.

A. **Situation analysis.** The four steps are:

(a) **Situations**. Every person carries a list of issues or concerns that need to be dealt with. Some of us have a formal list. Many of us do it informally, in our heads. The first step of situation analysis is the list of daily concerns. We define a concern as any situation—threat or opportunity—that can have an impact on the results that we are trying to achieve.

(b) **Separation.** Many issues we need to address tend to be general and fuzzy in nature. We will have to apply Caesar's principle of "divide and conquer." We separate fuzzy issues until we have discrete issues, that are distinct from each other and that can be handled on an individual basis.

(c) **Set priorities**. The previous step of separation means that we now have more issues to deal with. Since individuals can only do one thing at a time, we must now set priorities on these issues. There are three elements to examine in setting priorities. First, we should look at the seriousness. What is the impact of this situation? Next, we should look at the urgency. How much time do we have? Last, we should explore the growth. If we do nothing, what will happen to the seriousness? These three components (or the SUG factors) applied to each issue will help us set priorities correctly.

(d) **Allocate**. Once we have our concerns in order of priority, the last step is to allocate each issue to the appropriate process of resolution. Three questions are used to do this:

(i) Do we want to know the cause of this situation? If the answer is "yes," then the process required for resolution is problem analysis.

(ii) Do we have a choice to make? If we answer "yes," then decision analysis is required.

(iii) Do we want to assure the success in our plan? A "yes" would lead us in the direction of potential problem analysis.

Situation analysis is the "hub" of our thinking. It is the mental compass of our logic map. It directs us to the proper analytical process in order to get issues and situations resolved successfully.

B. Problem analysis. We do problem analysis when something has gone wrong and we do not know the cause.

Let us now take a look at the skills involved in each of the steps of the problem analysis logic path.

(a) **Identification**. The first step is identification. One way of looking at a problem is to say that some obstacles are interfering with attaining some goal. Or some deviation has occurred in the expected performance, or the norm.

(b) **Description**. To properly describe a problem, there are four dimensions about which we can get information. These are identification, location, timing, and extent of the problem. The following questions would help us describe the problem exhaustively and accurately:

What is the problem unit (object)?
What could the problem unit be but is not?
What is wrong with the unit (defect)?
What else could have been wrong but is not?
Where can the problem be found (object)?
Where else can the problem be but is not?
Where is the defect on the unit?
Where else could it be, but is not?
When did the problem start (date/time)?
When else could it have happened but did not?
When is the defect/deviation seen (cycle/pattern)?
When else could it be seen but is not?
How much/big is the problem?
How much/big should it be but is not?

This "is"/"is not" dimensions are to help us make comparisons between the problem area and the non-problem area besides helping us put a boundary to our problem situation.

(c) **Analysis**. The first step of analysis is to compare the problem area to the non-problem area. In other words, the "is" to the "is not." We can compare for similarities or we can compare for differences. In looking for new and additional information, experience has shown that comparing for differences is more helpful. In particular we should examine our description to look for differences in areas where there are sharp contrasts in the information.

The next step is to examine the differences in order to identify changes that have occurred. The search for the cause must focus itself on the changes that have occurred. If no change had occurred, we would not have had a problem. To narrow our search for relevant changes, our search should limit itself to looking for relevant changes within the differences we have identified.

(d) **Hypotheses**. From our analysis of the deviation we can now formulate some hypotheses as to the possible causes of the deviation. At this stage, we list all reasonable hypotheses.

(e) **Test**. In the next step, it is important to test our possible causes to eliminate those that are not the real causes. We screen each possible cause through our description. If a possible cause cannot explain both sides of the description, that is the "is" and the "is not" then it is not likely to be the real cause. The most probable cause will be the one that best explains the description or the one with the least number of assumptions. To be 100% certain we must now verify our assumptions—quickly and inexpensively.

(f) **Action**. To address a problem, we can take three different types of action:

    (i) Interim action—to buy us time while we search out the cause of our problem. Interim action is aimed at the effects of the problem;

    (ii) Adaptive action—we decide to live with the problem or adapt ourselves to the problem; and

    (iii) Corrective action—this is the only action designed to eliminate the problem. It is aimed at the cause of the problem.

C. Decision analysis. In situations where something must be done and there are several choices or alternatives to choose from, we need to use the process of decision analysis. The following are the steps in decision analysis: (a) decision objective, (b) selection criteria, (c) compare alternatives, (d) risk evaluation, and (e) best balanced choice.

Let us now take a look at each of the steps:

(a) **Decision objective**. There are three elements of the decision objective or the decision statement that we should keep in mind. The first element is the purpose. A decision statement should be formulated in terms that represent the purpose of what the analysis is about. It should represent an end result.

From time to time we may insert in our decision statement a word which restricts the range of alternatives that will be available to us. These words are called modifiers. Without modifiers, the range of alternatives would be broader. However, by adding a modifier we restrict our range of alternatives.

The third element to consider about our decision objective or decision statement is the level of the decision. Most decisions stem from prior decisions. The higher the level of our decisions the greater the range of alternatives available to us. The lower the level, the more restricted is the range of alternatives. The level at which we start our decision dramatically changes the class of alternatives that we end up comparing.

(b) **Selection criteria.** The second step in the logic path of decision analysis is to establish some criteria for selecting the best alternative. To generate effective selection criteria, we must ask four questions. They are:

(i)   What results do we want to achieve?

(ii) What results do we want to avoid?

(iii) What resources are available to spend?

(iv) What resources do we want to preserve?

Once we have a list of selection criteria, we examine them to determine those criteria which are absolutely mandatory to the success of our decision. We classify our criteria into those that must absolutely be met and those that we want to achieve—that are desirable but not mandatory. The first criteria we list are the "must"—those that are imperative and must be met by all available alternatives. Then we take a look at the desirable criteria, or the wants, and weigh them in order of importance.

(c) **Compare alternatives**. The next step in the process of decision analysis is the step of comparing alternatives. We now filter the alternatives through the selection criteria and eliminate the alternatives that do not measure up. Because we have classified our criteria into "must" and "wants," the first filter is to screen the alternatives against the musts.

Since we have set specific limits on these "musts," we need to gather information about each alternative to see how well it meets these. By comparing the information that is available about each alternative against each "must," we can then make a "go" or "no go" decision. The purpose of "must" criteria is to quickly screen out those alternatives that violate limits which we consider to be non-negotiable and to reduce our range of alternatives.

Next, we compare the remaining alternatives against the "wants." Again, the technique is to get information about the alternative which tells us how well the alternative performs against each of our "wants." We then use our judgment in assessing the information in order to score the performance of each alternative against each "want." Using numbers to reflect our judgment we give a top score the alternative that performs the best and we give a relative score to the next best performing alternative and so forth. We then proceed to do that against each "want." By then, multiplying the weight of the "wants" by the score of the alternative we get a weighted score. We repeat the procedure for each "want." Adding the total of these weighted scores gives us an index of performance. Thus the step of comparing alternatives involves comparing our alternatives first against our "must," then scoring their performance against our "wants" and eliminating those alternatives that give us poor performance. By now, we have narrowed our choice of alternatives down to 1, 2, or possibly 3 alternatives that perform substantially better than the rest.

(d) **Risk evaluation**. The next step in the decision analysis process is the step called risk evaluation. Every alternative brings with it certain risks. Therefore in the analysis of the alternatives it is very important to evaluate the risks that are attached to each of these alternatives. The technique is simple. We take each alternative and ask: "What risks do we face if we go with this alternative?" We list those risks.

The risks will be different for each alternative, because different alternatives bring different risks. However, there are different degrees of risks. First we look at the degree of probability that any of these risks will come about. Using a scale of 1 to 10 we examine each risk and assess the probability of it occurring. The next element in determining the degree of risk is to determine the degree of seriousness should it occur. If the risk occurs, what will be the impact of our particular decision? Using the same scale, we can then assess the degree of seriousness for each risk.

(e) **Best balanced choice**. The last step of decision analysis is then making the best balanced choice. This means reviewing the risk that is represented by the probability and seriousness. The best balanced choice becomes the alternative that performs the best, or reasonably well, against our selection criteria, together with the amount of risk that we are willing to accept.

D. Potential problem analysis. This process focuses on two key actions, namely prevention and protection. Just like the earlier processes discussed, there is also a logic path for potential problem analysis.

The principle of potential problem analysis (PPA) is to help us successfully implement a chosen course of action. It is a process that helps us counter Murphy's Law (which states that if anything can go wrong, it will). Let us take a look at each of the steps in PPA:

(a) **Success statement**. We begin with a success statement. In other words, how will we know that we have achieved our goal? We try to be as specific as we can; avoiding the all too common "I want to be more successful."

(b) **Plan**. Our next step is to develop a plan and list the steps of the plan in their chronological order. At this stage it is important to identify the steps that are of critical importance to its success. The following checklist will help to identify these critical steps:

(i)   the step/s where if the potential problem/s occurs, the next step in the plan cannot take place;

(ii) the step/s where, from past experiences, potential problem/s can surface; and

(iii) step/s in the plan that is/are new to us; an unknown area.

(c) **High risks area**. Our next step is then to identify the high risks area of the plan for potential problems. The amount of risk is then identified by looking at the probability and seriousness of each potential problem.

(d) **Prevention**. We can take preventive actions that are directed at the high probable causes. We try to anticipate the likely causes of each potential problem together with the probability of each occurring. Preventive actions reduce the probability of a problem occurring and are taken in anticipation of the problem happening.

(e) **Protection**. If our preventive actions fail and the potential problems materialize (good old Murphy again!), then we need actions to protect us against the seriousness or effects of that problem. These are called contingent actions because they come into play after the problem has started. An important element of a contingent action is that it must contain a trigger to bring it to play.

(f) **Modified plan**. The last step of PPA is to take our original plan and to modify it by inserting at the appropriate steps, the best selection of preventive and contingent actions. These should reduce the potential risk to a level that is acceptable. The modified plan is the one implemented because it has a higher probability of succeeding than the original one.

The PPA process promotes proactive thinking rather than reactive thinking. Many of us are conditioned to think in terms of contingent actions instead of preventive actions. A probable reason could be that society tends to recognize and reward firefighters.

E. Potential opportunity analysis. The future, of course, not only presents us with potential problems, but also with potential opportunities. How can we position ourselves to capitalize on these opportunities? Through the process of potential opportunity analysis.

The Chinese word for "crisis" is made up of two characters: one represents danger and the other opportunity. We must be able to recognize these dangers, threats, obstacles or barriers facing us and turn them around into opportunities. The question to ask is: "How can we benefit from this situation?"

The difficulty in potential opportunity analysis is not usually a lack of opportunities; rather the difficulty lies in choosing which opportunity to pursue. In order to do this, let us look at a simple tool: that of the cost/benefit ratio or, as it is sometimes called, the risk/reward ratio. By assigning a value to the cost versus the benefit of an opportunity, we can direct our attention towards the opportunities that will produce the highest yield for us. We use the scale of high, medium, low or 1 to 10 to assign values. High yield areas are those of low cost and high benefit.

To capitalize on these opportunities, we can now do two things: First, we need to think of actions to trigger or ignite these opportunities. "What can we do to make it happen?" Second, once we have brought the opportunity about, how can we accelerate its benefits? Thus we need to think of accelerator actions to optimize the rewards.

F. The creative process. The last and final process is the creative process. The creative process spans the whole of our logic map. We have so far spoken about convergent thinking or rational thinking. The most neglected aspect of good decision making is creative thinking or sometimes known as divergent thinking.

However, many writers on creativity have emphasized divergent thinking at the expense of convergent thinking. Our experience has been that there is an interplay between divergent and convergent thinking. It is necessary therefore to combine both types of thinking to increase the probability of success in a given situation.

I wish to illustrate this with the analogy of driving a car. The rational processes are like the forward gears to move us ahead but in some specific situations we really need the reverse gear to get out of some difficult situations. Likewise, the creative process is needed when we are stuck with an unsatisfactory situation such as poor alternatives or the present way of doing things which are far from satisfactory. The five steps of the creative process are: (a) preparation, (b) generation, (c) consolidation, (d) verification, and (e) exploitation.

Let us examine each of them:

(a) **Preparation**.

    (i) Preparing information—this includes:

- establishing the end result to be achieved (establishing the objective),
- gathering information about the existing situation, searching for additional information about the situation, and
- establishing the solution criteria ("musts" and "wants").

    (ii) Preparing physical environment—this includes ensuring proper:

- room with space for people to move around,
- chairs and tables,
- writing materials like felt pens and flipcharts, and
- audio/video as "back-up," in case ideas are lost along the way.

    (iii) Preparing social environment:

- the right people to attend
- freedom from reprisal
- freedom from judgment, and
- freedom from tradition.

(b) **Generation**.

(i) Lateral thinking exercise (to illustrate self-imposed barriers to creativity so as to allow the creative juices to start flowing).

(ii) Method:

- Explain purpose and introduce background information and state clearly the objectives.

- Introduce techniques: Brainstorming, random word, reversal, etc.

(c) **Consolidation**. The result of the generation step is a large number of ideas. The purpose of the consolidation step is to collect, harvest, convert and reduce these ideas to a smaller number of alternatives which we can call super alternatives. The following are two stages of the consolidation steps:

(i) Eliminating. Check through all ideas and eliminate those that are duplicated, illegal, immoral and unethical or which are socially unacceptable.

(ii) Grouping. Collect and join together ideas which are complementary or which together form a course of action or one alternative—that is, the super alternative.

(d) **Verification**. This step is equivalent to the compare alternatives and risk evaluation steps of decision analysis.

(e) **Exploitation**. Having now chosen the best course of action, an implementation plan should be developed. Application of potential problem and potential opportunity analysis should be undertaken to maximize the benefits to be achieved while at the same time minimizing the likelihood of anything jeopardizing complete success.

Conclusion

Decision making seems simple enough but if you have the need to make major decisions, there are many aspects of the decision-making process that need thinking. Decision making is not only following one process. It is the ability to discern between the different situations that are unique to our concerns and to be able to use the different specific resolution processes appropriately. The process may seem tedious but it is best to make the right decision from the start rather than having to make it again and again.

References

Heirs, B. and Farrell, P. (1986). *The Professional Decision Thinker.* London: Sidgwick and Jackson.

Naisbitt, J. (1984). *Megatrends.* New York: Warner Books Inc.

Rawlinson, J.G. (1981). *Creative Thinking and Brainstorming.* England: Gower. [Decision Processes International (1986). *Decision Making Processes Text,* Canada.]

THE ROLE OF DECISION ANALYSIS IN URBAN POLICY EVALUATION

Alan D. Pearman

Attempts to plan changes within our major urban areas almost inevitably induce conflict between the different groups involved. In this paper, it is argued that one particular set of analytical tools, namely decision analysis, has the capacity to make a worthwhile reduction in the level of conflict which arises. This argument is developed in terms of the many important changes which have recently come about in the field of decision analysis. A number of examples from the urban public sector are given, including an assessment of likely future changes in decision analysis.

The size of the world's urban population is already numbered in hundreds, if not thousands of millions. The coming together of huge numbers of people, often from many different countries and cultures, generates a correspondingly large array of problems for the management of the cities in which they live. The theme that this paper explores is the decision-making process in urban planning and the ways in which certain techniques falling within the field of human judgment and decision making can contribute to it. In particular, it examines the potential role of decision analysis, especially in view of the rapid changes in its capabilities which are following in the wake of methodological advances and the increasingly cheap availability of computer power. Most of the illustrations are drawn from transportation and related questions about the construction and management of infrastructure, a number of them from Southeast Asia. The methodological elements, however, have a much wider range of policy applications, both potential and already implemented.

Urban Planning Projects and the Planning Process

Almost by definition, planning involves conflict. If there were no potential conflicts of interest, public planning would be for all intents and purposes redundant. Certainly in terms of their image with members of the general public, urban managers and planners are the main players of many conflicts.

The management of conflict has in recent years become a topic of academic interest to those working in the fields of human judgment and decision making. The work of Walter Isard and his colleagues is one example (see Isard & Smith, 1982). There is also increasing interest in the analysis and mathematical modelling of negotiating strategies and other examples of decision making in competitive environments (e.g.,

Raiffa, 1982). Developments of an essentially mathematical type, such as the explosion of work on game theory, and in the field of computing have been substantial. Together, they allow the formal, quantitative modelling of problems which, even twenty years ago, could only have been tackled through discursive, essentially sociological and political analysis.

Nonetheless, the topics just mentioned are still primarily issues for academic research; operational results are a considerable way off. In contrast, decision analysis has often been, and should continue to be, very much concerned with practical application. Decision analysis is effectively a set of procedures for providing formal analytical support to decision making where alternative policies have multiple dimensions of impact and where there is often significant uncertainty. It is increasingly a tool which practicing urban planners should regard as available to help diminish the conflict inherent in the planning process. Diminution is of course not the same thing as disappearance. However, it is a common experience of practitioners of decision analysis that formal, quantitative analysis of competing proposals can be a major force working for compromise and mutual understanding.

A good deal of what follows will be a discussion of methodology and developments in methodology. This emphasis, however, does not imply that the solution to the wide range of difficult and contentious urban planning problems lies simply in the adoption of the methods which will be discussed. It does not. Most people using or undertaking work in decision analysis know all too well the limited ability we have to model accurately the functioning of complex human systems. There are no clearly defined, totally accurate answers. Moreover, most urban planning problems of any consequence have a social and/or political element which makes them a legitimate subject of debate in the political arena. It would be counterproductive for proponents of decision analysis to try to usurp the role of those who have been selected, either politically or through their jobs as professional planners, to bear the responsibility of decision making. Nonetheless, the development and successful implementation of major urban plans, particularly those plans relating to infrastructure provision, is increasingly dependent on the achievement of a high level of consensus, which in turn must be based on a balance of conflicting interests. Recent and forthcoming developments in decision analysis give it the potential to make a significant contribution to achieving such a balance by providing a logically sound framework for the exploration of different policies from a variety of points of view and for demonstrating to all concerned, that proper consideration has been afforded to all aspects of the problem.

Decision Analysis

The term decision analysis is said to have been originated by Professor R. A. Howard, working in the United States in the 1960s. It grew out of the seminal work of Schlaifer, Raiffa and others at Harvard (see von Winterfeldt & Edwards, 1986, ch.

14, for a brief history). Their concern was to apply the principles of statistical decision theory to guide choice between alternative policies in real-world economic and management problems sufficiently complex to require formal analytical assistance. The basic approach is to divide the overall problem of choice into a series of relatively straightforward, interlinked sub-problems. Once the sub-problems have been adequately treated, they are recombined to specify a solution to the original overall problem. Two characteristics in particular are shared by many applications of decision analysis to public planning. First, uncertainty: it is frequently the case that the actual outcomes of choosing to implement a given policy are not known in advance with certainty. Secondly, often the impacts arising from any chosen policy occur in many different dimensions—economic, social, environmental, etc.—such that the evaluation of any single outcome is a complex, multi-dimensional balancing of different considerations. A typical decision analysis proceeds through four major phases:

Phase 1   Specify the structure of the decision/problem;

Phase 2   Assess the impact of the alternative proposals;

Phase 3   Determine the preference pattern of the decision maker;

Phase 4   Evaluate the alternatives and assess their relative performance.

The first phase involves two principal activities. The first is the generation of alternatives—the planning and design process. The second is to specify the objectives which the alternative plans are intended to achieve and the manner in which the achievement is to be measured. Often this involves the construction of a hierarchy, rather like that shown in Figure 1, which relates to a decision support system (Simon et al., 1987) to help local planning authorities decide their priorities between different possible transport improvement projects. Its use is to help guide the choice of highway projects in Hong Kong currently under consideration. At the top level of the hierarchy, the broad objectives of the authority are set out: to assess highway investment projects in terms of four principal factors, safety, traffic, environment and planning, and development impact. Working down through the hierarchy, the objectives are formulated in more detail, until, at the lowest level, they take the form of measurable attributes. To take one case, traffic impact is categorized under three headings: travel time savings, operating cost savings and delays during construction. Two of the three are then further sub-divided to yield relevant measurable attributes in terms of which a project may be assessed. Travel time savings, for example, are measured for six user groups—cars, heavy goods vehicles, light goods vehicles, public transport, cyclists and pedestrians. The 32 attributes between them describe as fully as is necessary for the decision under consideration all the different dimensions of performance of the alternative policies available.

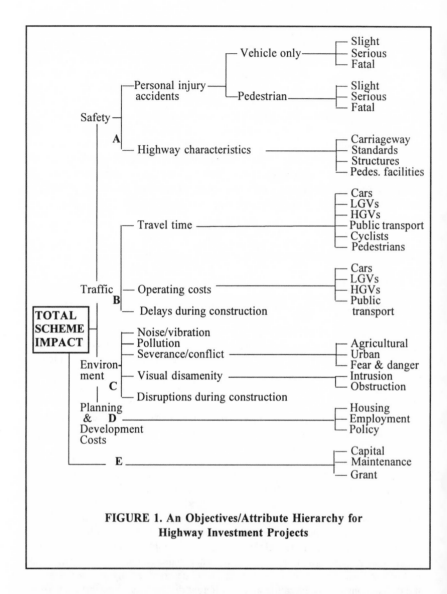

**FIGURE 1. An Objectives/Attribute Hierarchy for
Highway Investment Projects**

The second phase of a decision analysis is the mathematical modelling phase. Depending upon the particular application involved, many standard quantitative techniques may be involved—mathematical programming, simulation, queuing theory, network analysis, etc. A large proportion of the total effort of any decision analysis is likely to be associated with this phase. The main added dimension that its place as a part of a decision analysis may impart is a probabilistic element to many of the inputs and outputs, to reflect the high levels of uncertainty involved in many aspects of public planning.

The third phase of a decision analysis is independent of the alternatives under consideration. It is to derive from the decision maker trade-offs between all the different attribute dimensions which will have been specified in Phase 1, including an assessment of attitude to risk. The result is a mathematical function $U(X)$ which permits any alternative policy, characterized by a vector, X, of scores on the set of attributes, to be evaluated by a single real number. Finally, the results of Phases 2 and 3 are brought together, incorporating the inherent uncertainties, such that any alternative, A_i, may be evaluated by a score $P_j U (X_{ij})$, where P_j is the probability that a particular future set of circumstances may develop and X_{ij} summarizes the performance of plan i, should the jth set of circumstances occur and the summation is across all n of the possible future sets of circumstances that are envisaged. The higher an alternative's score, the higher it ranks.

An outline such as this of the main phases of a decision analysis often sparks one of two reactions. The first, which typically comes from people who have encountered decision analysis as part of their higher education, is to express some surprise that decision analysis could be described without reference to decision trees, the technique of analyzing decision strategies devised by Raiffa which until recently stood in many people's eyes as the key (if not the only) identifying feature of decision analysis. The second common response, often from practicing planners and decision makers, is to deny that any such process could do justice to the complexity of real-life planning and hence to dismiss decision analysis as another textbook abstraction of little value outside academia.

The two responses are not unrelated and are not without some justification. The key to understanding them lies in the rapid developments which have taken place recently in decision analysis, which have led to a quantum shift in both its nature and its capabilities. Most early decision analyses were undertaken in a business environment, where the probability-weighted monetary values of the different possible outcomes of a given strategy (expected monetary value, EMV) were an acceptable measure of its utility to the decision maker. Even for applications of this type, however, it was not entirely suitable. Expected utility replaced expected monetary value, in order to allow for risk aversion. This was followed by the recognition that many policies could not be assessed appropriately even in terms of the utility of their monetary performances. There were important dimensions to policies and plans which could not be convincingly described in the monetary dimension.

Out of this concern arose multi-attribute utility theory, the most thorough initial exploration of which is Keeney and Raiffa (1976). It is this development which links together and explains the two unbelieving responses just described. Multiattribute utility greatly changes the emphasis of decision analysis. Decision trees become just one component of a much wider array of techniques, such that decision analysis can be described in broad terms without even a mention of a decision tree. Multiattribute utility also opens up a huge range of applications of decision analysis in the public sector. The ability to begin to come to terms with the multidimensional complexity and uncertainty of policy design, evaluation and choice in the public sector is now available.

Decision Analysis and Urban Planning

The formal methodology of multiattribute utility theory has co-developed with increasing public concern about environmental and social problems which have not proved amenable to analysis by more conventional economic means, such as cost-benefit analysis, but for which some formal evaluation framework is desirable. What multiattribute utility theory and hence decision analysis has provided is not so much a prescriptive decision-making device as a framework to set down and communicate in a clear and internally consistent fashion all the relevant complexities of such problems.

For many topical public problems, the hard data which decision makers would ideally want is conspicuous by its absence. In these circumstances the best compromise is often a formal methodology for setting down and verifying subjective expert judgment as a basis for decision making in these difficult areas. Government decision makers frequently have to rely on other people's judgments, because they are often inexperienced in any particular area of decision making, unlike a businessman making a decision of comparable magnitude. A technology for transmitting judgments is therefore important, and recent developments (multiattribute utility models and multiconstituency decision analysis) have increasingly fit decision analysis for this role.

The potential value of modern decision analysis, however, is not restricted to government-level decision making on matters of national importance. There are increasingly examples of application to more local problems, one notable case being the planning of the northeast sector of the metropolitan rapid transit system in Singapore. Others include: the control of air pollution in New York (Ellis & Keeney, 1972); power station emission control policy in the UK (Watson, 1986); land use regulation for planning (Gardiner & Edwards, 1975); sewage disposal in Boston (Horgan, 1972); the transport of hazardous goods (Saccomanno, van Aerde, & Queen, 1987); and planning fire department response time policy (Keeney, 1973).

Many of the examples cited above use the multiattribute utility theory foundations developed by Keeney and Raiffa. There is, however, a separate, but important European school of work concerned with multiple criteria decision making, mostly deriving from the outranking procedures developed by the Frenchman Bernard Roy. This European work is important, not just because it has a separate methodological foundation, but also because it has found a wide range of application to urban and regional planning problems (Rietveld, 1980; Voogd, 1983; Nijkamp & Rietveld, 1986) and also a number in the transport sector (e.g., Roy & Hugonard (1982), dealing with an extension of the metro system in Paris). Although somewhat less analytically sophisticated than the multiattribute utility approach, it is more consistent in its input requirements with the type of judgments that planners and politicians are prepared to give and with the limited time which is often available for formal evaluation of public projects.

One area where formal multiple criteria evaluation methods have only limited impact is in strategic (large scale, long time horizon) infrastructure planning, say at the metropolitan scale. Recently, however, what has begun to develop is an appreciation that some formal evaluation structure can usefully and practicably be imposed on such problems. One technique which looks particularly promising is scenario analysis. This has been applied to infrastructure planning problems in a number of cities facing rather high levels of uncertainty about their development—for example Belfast (Allport et al., 1986) and Manila (Allport & von Einsiedel, 1986). The aim is not to attempt to evaluate investment strategies against all possible future developments which might unfold, but to envisage a small number of carefully differentiated but plausible and internally consistent future patterns of development (scenarios) against which individual investments and combinations of investments (infrastructure strategies) can successively be evaluated. Although inevitably the evaluations are made in a fairly broad way, experience suggests that the scenario approach to strategy choice is not only found to be helpful, but is also capable of being implemented within the time and resource constraints typically associated with real infrastructure planning exercises. It serves to concentrate attention on strategy options which are relatively robust to the very wide range of possible futures often relevant at this scale of decision making. The criterion of robustness (rather than expected value optimization) appears to be one with which, both politicians and planners are willing to accept for major long-term investments. Moreover, the creation of the scenarios themselves has been found to be a valued by-product to promote consistency in other areas of planning, only indirectly related to the problem under consideration.

Future Developments in Decision Analysis

There are developments under way in decision analysis which will further enhance its ability to help with the planning problems which face us. These are essentially developments in cognitive psychology and developments in computer power. The brief discussion which follows is set out in more detail in Pearman (1987).

The center of gravity of decision analysis has shifted recently for a number of reasons—some of which have already been touched upon. One, which is of increasing importance, is the contribution of cognitive psychology. The relationship between the descriptive and prescriptive sides of the analysis of decision making is becoming closer—witness, for example, the new journal *Judgement and Decision Making* which commenced publication in January 1988. The main thrusts of the psychologists' work (e.g., Kahneman et al., 1982) are firstly that human beings are naturally rather poor decision makers, once circumstances become at all complicated, and, secondly, that the hitherto ubiquitous maximization of subjective expected utility is not supportable, at least as a description of how people actually behave—even if it may be a good prescriptive device.

The overall implication is that the full complexity of how we interpret and make decisions is only just beginning to be understood. Although the existing formal tools, such as decision analysis, which are used to assist decision makers, may still be far from perfect, there is an increasingly large body of evidence that the unaided judgment of decision makers can be very unreliable indeed.

In terms of computers, most of the developments under way derive directly from the continuing steady decrease in the cost of computer power. With PC's increasingly available to most planners, software packages which undertake decision analysis are coming on to the market (Henrion, 1985 reviews three of them). Although such packages will not be adequate to solve some of the large scale problems touched upon earlier, they will increase the extent to which people understand and feel comfortable with the ideas of decision analysis. More effective computer graphics will also enhance the power of decision analysis as a tool for communicating some of the complexity of real-life decisions.

Another potentially interesting computer-based development is "decision conferencing." A number of companies (ICL in the UK and Decisions and Designs Inc. in the USA) are now marketing this form of "technology in the boardroom" whereby senior executives are aided in thrashing out company policy in a two- or three-day session, with a skilled analyst available to guide proceedings, but also with a significant array of computer hardware and software available to evaluate, compare and present the implication of alternative strategies.

Conclusion

What has been argued in this paper is that one of the major problems which different nations share is the planning and implementation of changes to their urban structure. Such changes contain the seeds of conflict. Examples of the confusion, unhappiness and frustration which can arise in the process are all too common throughout the world.

Decision analysis of public planning issues contributes to the minimization of conflict because of its clear logical structure and its comprehensive recognition of all types of impacts, particularly environmental and other less easily quantified impacts. It also recognizes that different people quite legitimately will have different sets of values and hence will be predisposed to prefer different types of solutions to various urban problems. Most proposals have their stronger and weaker components. By setting them down, a more balanced view of each proposal is encouraged. So too is the very important feedback loop from evaluation to design. If a proposal has some unsatisfactory features, perhaps it can be modified, rather than rejected. Increasingly this type of open, explicit decision making is sought after by members of the public. It is also increasingly the way in which conflicts are resolved and plans constructed at the international level—particularly within large multinational groups such as the European Community and the World Bank. Decision analysis cannot by any means meet all people's aspirations for changes to the planning process. However, it can make a worthwhile contribution now and in the future to the reduction of conflict in urban planning.

References

Allport, R.J. and von Einsiedel, N. (1986). An innovative approach to metropolitan management in the Philippines. *Public Administration and Development, 6,* 23-48.

Allport, R.J., Clavering, J.M., and Pearman, A.D. (1986). The use of scenario techniques to formulate transport strategy for an urban area, pp. 229-240 in *Transport Planning Methods, Proceedings of the PTRC Summer Annual Meeting,* Seminar M, PTRC, London.

Ellis, H.M. and Keeney, R.L. (1972). A rational approach for government decisions concerning air pollution In *Analysis of Public Systems.* A.W. Drake, R.L. Keeney and P.M. Morse (Eds.), Cambridge, MA: MIT Press.

Gardiner, P.C. and Edwards, W. (1975). Public Values: Multiattribute utility measurement for social decision making. In S. Schwartz and M. Kaplan (Eds.). *Human Judgement and Decision Processes.* New York: Academic Press.

Henrion, M. (1985). Software for decision analysis. *OR/MS Today, 12,* 24-29.

Horgan, D.N. (1972). *A Decision Analysis of Sewage Sludge Disposal Alternatives for Boston Harbor,* Masters Thesis, Department of Electrical Engineering, MIT.

Isard, W. and Smith, C. (1982). *Conflict Analysis and Practical Conflict Management Procedures.* Cambridge, MA: Ballinger.

Kahneman, D., Slovic, P., and Tversky, A. (1982). *Judgement under Uncertainty: Heuristics and Biases.* Cambridge, MA: Cambridge University Press.

Keeney, R.L. (1973). A utility function for the response times of engines and ladders to fires. *Urban Analysis,* 1, 209-222.

Keeney, R.L. and Raiffa, H. (1976). *Decisions with Multiple Objectives.* New York: Wiley.

Nijkamp, P. and Rietveld, P. (1986). Multiple objective decision analysis in regional economics. In P. Nijkamp (Ed.) *Handbook of Regional and Urban Economics, vol. 1.* New York: Elsevier.

Pearman, A.D. (1987). The application of decision analysis: A US/UK comparison. *Journal of the Operational Research Society, 38,* 775-783.

Raiffa, H. (1982). *The Art and Science of Negotiation.* Cambridge, MA: Harvard University Press.

Rietveld, P. (1980). *Multiple Objective Decision Methods and Regional Planning.* Amsterdam, North Holland: Elsevier Science Publishers B.V.

Roy, B. and Hugonard, J.C. (1982). Ranking of suburban line extension projects on the Paris metro system by a multicriteria method. *Transportation Research A, 16,* 301-312.

Saccomanno, F.F., Van Aerde, M., and Queen, D. (1987). Interactive selection of minimum risk routes for dangerous goods shipments. Paper presented to the 66th TRB Annual Meeting, Washington DC.

Simon, D., Mackie, P.J. May, A.D., and Pearman, A.D. (1987). Assessing local authority highway priorities, pp. 255-266. In Highway Design and Appraisal, *Proceedings of the PTRC Summer Annual Meeting, Seminar E,* PTRC, London. Vincke, P. (1986). Analysis of multicriteria decision aid in Europe. *European Journal of Operational Research, 25,* 160-168.

Von Winterfeldt, D. and Edwards, E. (1986). *Decision Analysis and Behavioral Research,* Cambridge,MA: Cambridge University Press.

Voogd, H. (1983). *Multicriteria Evaluation for Urban and Regional Planning.* London: Pion.

Watson, S.R. (1986). Modelling acid deposition for policy analysis. *Journal of the Operational Research Society, 37,* 893-900.

THE ST. PETERSBURG PARADOX: DATA, AT LAST

J. Carlos Rivero, David R. Holtgrave, Robert N. Bontempo, and William P. Bottom

The St. Petersburg Paradox has stimulated the minds of great thinkers for over two centuries. Economists and mathematicians have proposed several theoretical solutions to the paradox, but none have been subjected to experimental scrutiny. Via the development of alternative versions of the St. Petersburg game, we were able to empirically test some of these solutions. Treisman's expectation heuristic, a theory positing simple decision rules and mental shortcuts as a solution to the paradox received the most empirical support. Theoretical implications concerning a family of St. Petersburg solutions are discussed. Practical applications include evaluation of formal decision systems used by policymakers and the heuristics used by the lay public.

The St. Petersburg Paradox has stimulated the minds of great thinkers for over two centuries. Introduced to the academic community by the Swiss mathematician Daniel Bernoulli in 1738, the controversy surrounding the paradox has fueled advances in several disciplines. Indeed, elements of Malthus' treatise on population growth and Darwin's theory of biological evolution can be traced to the theme of geometric expansion underlying the puzzle (for a fascinating discussion of the puzzle's "antiquarian charms" see Samuelson, 1977). Similarly, early attempts at solving the paradox led to the development of Fechner's law, a cornerstone of modern experimental psychology. The similarity between quantitative psychophysics' law of decreasing effect and Bernoulli's law of decreasing marginal utility is "not accidental" according to Coombs, Dawes, and Tversky (1970). They add, "The logarithmic utility function proposed by Bernoulli was the one put fourth by Fechner as the form of the general psychophysical law" (p. 119).

But nowhere has the debate been so constructive as in the development of the decision sciences. Grappling with the paradox led Bernoulli to reject expected monetary value as a criterion for evaluating economic decisions in favor of expected "personal value" or utility. This shift from an objective to subjective scale paved the way for von Neumann and Morgenstern's (1944) classic exposition of utility theory and, more recently, the concept of decision frames underlying prospect theory (Kahneman & Tversky, 1979).

The paradox arises from a dramatic low probability, high consequence gamble. Offering an indefinite number of flips of a fair coin, Peter agrees to pay Paul $2 if a head appears on the first flip, $4 if it first appears on the second flip, and so on, with the potential payoff doubling on each successive flip and the game continuing until the first head appears. Thus, if a head appears on the first flip, Peter pays Paul $2 and the game is over; however, if Paul is extremely lucky and flips the coin 20 times before the first head appears, he will be $2,097,152 richer at Peter's expense.

Paul's willingness to pay for the right to play the St. Petersburg game is of great interest. At the time of the gamble's introduction, the decision rules promoted by mathematicians dictated that Paul maximize his expectation of monetary value. The expected value of the game can be determined by summing the game's outcomes, each weighted by the probability of its occurrence (in this case $\{[(1/2)*2] + [(1/4)*4] + [(1/8)*8]+...\}$). In doing so Paul would see that, mathematically, the expected value of the gamble is infinite. The paradox posed by the game is that, despite the infinite expected value, most Pauls are unwilling to pay more than a small amount for the right to play. Bernoulli's famous explanation of Paul's behavior is described below.

Solution #1: Expected Utility

Bernoulli proposed that people evaluate the game not by calculating its expected value, but its expected utility. Utility, a subjective measure, reflects the amount of pleasure associated with an outcome. In the case of monetary outcomes, utility does not correspond perfectly to dollar value. For example, the addition of a dollar to Paul's wealth is accompanied by a deposit of utility in his "psychological bank account." However, with each successive dollar, Paul's total utility grows at a slower and slower rate because, as Samuelson (1980, p. 368) points out, "his psychic ability to appreciate more of the good becomes less keen." This phenomena has been named the *law of diminishing marginal utility* and is often depicted by a "utility function," a curve describing growth in utility relative to growth in amount of goods. Depending on the characteristics of the utility function proposed, the expected utility of the St. Petersburg gamble can be a small amount.

Since Bernoulli's expected utility solution, numerous alternative explanations of Paul's behavior have been proposed. The research described in this article represents the first empirical evaluation of these solutions. Our interest in the paradox, however, is not confined to its historical significance. The principles of expected utility theory underlie many formal decision-making systems from government policy-making via cost-benefit analysis to the utility models determining organizational hiring practices (Cascio, 1982). Clearly it is important to know if the theory can solve the problem it was invented to solve. Additionally, the paradox serves as a useful paradigm for studying human interpretation of low probability, high consequence events such as nuclear plant disasters, flooding, oil-spills and other environmental risks. We will return to these practical implications below.

Solution #2: Finite Wealth

Shortly after the St. Petersburg game was introduced, the French naturalist G.L.L. Buffon cynically pointed out that by the 29th successful toss, Paul's payoff would have been so great as to bankrupt the entire Kingdom of France (see Todhunter, 1865, p.

346). Poisson (1837) turned this practical objection into a formal alternative solution to the paradox. No one could conceivably possess the infinite wealth needed to fulfill his/her obligations if Paul realized his small chance of an infinitely large win. Peter's finite resources define the maximum possible payoff, setting a limit on the expected value of the gamble and, therefore, on the amount Paul should be willing to pay. Aumann (1977) has argued that the finite wealth solution unduly emphasizes Peter's actual wealth rather than Paul's perception of Peter's wealth. In anticipation of this point, Keynes (1921) suggested that, although difficult, it is certainly not impossible for people to imagine someone with infinite resources.

Solution #3: Essentially-Zero Probability

D'Alembert proposed that at some point of the game, the probability of winning had to be considered essentially zero, thereby establishing a ceiling on expected value (see Samuelson, 1977, p. 42). Buffon (see Brito, 1975, p. 123), arguing that probabilities less than 1/10,000 were just as well considered zero, implied that Paul should expect the game to always terminate before the 15th toss. In response to Buffon's casual disregard for low likelihood events, Gibbon pointed out the distastefulness of being one of 10,000 participants in a lottery, where the grand prize is death (Keynes, 1921). More recently, Arrow (1951) has added to the debate by emphasizing the difficulty of specifying some critical number of tosses after which all probabilities are to be considered zero.

Solution #4: Expectation Heuristic

Treisman (1986) offers a novel solution to the paradox. The amount of mental effort required to calculate the expected utility of the gamble would motivate Paul to use a simplifying decision rule or judgment heuristic. Treisman identifies an "expectation heuristic" which entails breaking down a complicated problem into stages. Rather than struggling with the complexities of the entire problem, the decision maker concentrates on calculating probabilities for one manageable stage at a time. In the context of the St. Petersburg game, this would involve first figuring the expected trial on which the first head appears and then determining the value of the game based on the value of that event. In the St. Petersburg game the expected duration is 2 tosses, as most people can estimate from their experiences flipping coins (and as statisticians know from their understanding of probability theory). A game terminating on its second flip would pay $4, so Paul "should" be unwilling to pay more than that amount for the game.

Other Solutions

Lopes (1981) illustrates the need to distinguish between the infinite gambles proposed by mathematicians and the short run gambles characteristic of real life. Inasmuch as realizing the expected value of any gamble requires an extremely large number of plays, the infinite expected value of the St. Petersburg gamble is of little consequence to someone considering a single play of the game. In a single play, the St. Petersburg game has a probability of over .9 of terminating on or before the fourth toss. Following this reasoning, it makes sense that Paul is willing to pay only a small finite price to play.

Proposing yet another ceiling on a potential player's willingness to pay, Brito (1975) points out that in a finite lifetime an individual cannot enjoy an infinitely large sum of money. Aumann (1977) has countered by noting that some commodity bundle could provide infinite utility in a finite span of time.

Evaluating the Solutions

The solutions and theories described above make specific predictions about the amount of money people should be willing to pay, or bid, for the right to play the St. Petersburg game. In order to test the different solutions, we developed several versions of the game (in the spirit of Lopes, 1981) by varying the gamble's payoff. The Basic Game (B) is the traditional St. Petersburg game with a payoff of $2 raised to the number of successful tosses or (2^n). The Plus 5 game (P5) yields payoffs of (2^n) + $5. The Plus 10 game yields payoffs of (2^n) + $10. Finally, the Times 2 (T2) game yields payoffs of $2*(2^n)$. These payoffs are illustrated in Figure 1.

FIGURE 1
St. Petersburg Game Variations: Payoffs and Probabilities

Number of coin flips before first head appears	1	2	3	4	5	6	7...	20
Basic Game Payoff	$2	$4	$8	$16	$32	$64	$128	$1048576
Plus 5 Game Payoff	$7	$9	$13	$21	$37	$69	$133	$1048581
Plus 10 Game Payoff	$12	$14	$18	$26	$42	$74	$138	$1048586
Times 2 Game Payoff	$4	$8	$16	$32	$64	$128	$256	$2097152
Probability that first head will appear on that flip	1/2	1/4	1/8	1/16	1/32	1/64	1/128	1/1048576

By comparing a solution's predicted bids to the bids actually exhibited by participants in our study, we can assess the accuracy of each solution. Expected value theory (EV) predicts that people should be willing to pay very large amounts to play the four game variations. The expectation heuristic (EH) predicts that people should bid $4 for B, $9 for P5, $14 for P10, and $8 for T2. The finite wealth solution (FW) in the case of Peter possessing $1,048,576 (a case discussed by Lopes, 1981) predicts bids of $21 for B, $41 for T2, $26 for P5 and $31 for P10. The solution proposing a cutoff trial after which all probabilities are treated as essentially zero (EZ) makes specific predictions if a cutoff trial is specified. Government policy analysts in the United States suggest that probabilities less than 1/10,000 and 1/1,000,000 should be, and commonly are, ignored. Taking these probability levels as guidance, two sets of EZ predictions were constructed. First, if people consider probabilities less than 1/10,000 to be zero, then they should ignore all potential payoffs after the fourteenth toss (EZ14). This cut-off predicts the following bids: $14 for B, $28 for T2, $19 for P5 and $24 for P10. If people consider probabilities less than 1/1,000,000 to be zero, they should ignore all payoffs after the twentieth toss (EZ20). This cutoff yields the following bids: $20 for B, $40 for T2, $25 for P5 and $30 for P10.

The expected utility (EU) solution also makes specific predictions about the bids for these games if a form of the utility function is specified. We generated a set of (EU) predictions by appealing to the square root function originally described in Bernoulli's paper (1738/1954): $2.41 for B, $3.41 for T2, $3.43 for P5, and $4.16 for P10. We also tested the logarithmic function specified in Bernoulli's paper, with certain modifications to the wealth term. (This solution was not supported by our results.) These predicted bids are summarized in Figure 2.

FIGURE 2
Bid Predictions for St. Petersburg Game Variations

Game Variation	EV	EH	FW	EZ14	EZ	EUSQ
			Solution			
B	infinite	$4	$21	$14	$20	$2.41
P5	infinite	$9	$26	$19	$25	$3.43
P10	infinite	$14	$31	$24	$30	$4.16
T2	infinite	$8	$41	$28	$40	$3.41

Study #1

In an initial study (Bottom, Bontempo, & Holtgrave, 1989) we presented 47 experts (specialists in mathematics, economics and management science) and 139 undergraduate student subjects with survey forms which described the four games in detail. Subjects were instructed to imagine that they were in a sealed bid auction for the right to play and then write down their bids for each of the games.

The results of this study were strikingly clear. The median bids offered by the subjects ($4 for B, $11 for P5, $14 for P10 and $8 for T2 by experts and $4, $10, $14 and $8, respectively, by students) were remarkably similar to those predicted by the expectation heuristic and inconsistent with the bids predicted by all other solutions.

From the bidding data gathered in this study, it was determined that the expectation heuristic was the most plausible published solution to the St. Petersburg Paradox.

Study #2

As a follow-up to study #1, we presented 77 undergraduates from another university with similar survey forms and instructions to indicate their bids for the St. Petersburg games. Additionally, subjects were instructed to take on the role of the "house" and indicate the dollar value at which they would be willing to sell a single play of the various games. To explore if the willingness to buy and sell patterns observed for the St. Petersburg games were unique to complex gambles, we also had subjects fix buying and selling prices for six simpler, three-outcome gambles where all outcomes were equally likely (e.g., one in three chance of winning $10, $20, or $30).

Figure 3 shows subjects' median bids and selling prices for the games. Once again, the observed median bids for the four St. Petersburg game variations bear greatest similarity to those predicted by the expectation heuristic.

FIGURE 3						
Bids and Selling Prices for St. Petersburg and Simpler Games						
St. Petersburg **Game Variations**		**B**	**P5**	**P10**	**T2**	
Median Bid		$5	$9	$14	$9	
Median Fixed Selling Price		$5	$10	$15	$10	
Simpler Payoffs:						
Game Variations	10,20,30	2.5,5,7.5	1,20,39	1,100,199	1,5,9	50,100,150
Median Bid	$15	$4.5	$10	$40	$4	$65
Median Fixed Selling Price	$15	$5	$15	$75	$5	$80
Note Currency is in Singaporean dollars.						

A sign test (Siegel, 1956) reveals that the bid and fixed selling price distributions for the simple games are significantly different (additional information concerning the statistical analyses of this data can be obtained from the first author). The same test failed to show, however, any difference between the fixed prices and bids for the St. Petersburg games.

Discussion

We conclude that Treisman's expectation heuristic is the published theory with the most empirical support. Paul's unwillingness to pay an infinite amount of money for the St. Petersburg gamble stems from his use of a simplifying decision rule; first he predicts at which toss the game will end and, based on the expected payoff of that critical toss, he arrives at a bid.

By proposing that subjects select a critical toss, Treisman's theory suggests a whole family of St. Petersburg solutions worthy of further research. Various factors may affect the selection of a critical toss (e.g., experience, expertise) as well as the bid associated with that toss (e.g., risk aversion, risk proneness, maximum loss tolerance, aspiration level).

The similarity of buying and selling prices for the St. Petersburg game combined with the absence of such similarity for the simple gambles raises some interesting issues concerning human economic behavior. The finding for the simple games is consistent with Tversky and Kahneman's prospect theory which proposes that decision makers "frame" the expected consequences of their choices in terms of gains and losses. These decision frames are important in that people react more severely to losses than to gains. That is, the displeasure associated with a financial loss is greater than the pleasure associated with an equal financial gain. One of the more interesting aspects of Tversky and Kahneman's work is their illustration that subtle differences in the presentation of a choice can determine the decision-maker's interpretative frame, and therefore his/her behavior.

For example, it is plausible that the sellers of the simple games, focussing on their liability as the "house," frame the event as a loss. The "disutility" associated with the potential loss leads them to fix a relatively high selling price. The buyers, on the other hand, frame the gamble as a potential gain. However, since the utility of the money potentially gained is not as great as the disutility of the money the sellers stand to lose, the buyers systematically offer to pay less than the fixed selling price. It is important to keep in mind that this is the result of purely psychological processes occurring within the subject (who is both buyer and seller).

The absence of this framing effect for the St. Petersburg game bids and selling prices is not easily explained. Perhaps the lure of the fantastic payoffs possible in the St. Petersburg gamble boosts Paul's willingness to pay so that it is more in line with Peter's selling price. Our finding, however tentatively explained, contradicts Samuelson's (1977, p. 32) claim that risk averse players "will not agree to make Petersburg-like wagers with one another...what real Peters will ask, real Pauls won't pay." The observed similarity of buying and selling prices suggests that such a market might indeed exist. We are left with the troubling implication that people may willingly enter a venture which involves obligations they could never fulfill.

Practical Applications

Expected Utility Theory is a prominent model of rational thought. As such it underlies formal decision-making systems in a variety of settings. Mexico's Ministry of Public Works' use of decision analysis to evaluate alternative airport sites (Keeney & Raiffa, 1976), the U.S. government's reliance on cost/benefit analysis in policy-making (Reagan Executive Order #12291, 1981) and human resource professionals' use of utility models to determine organizational hiring practices (Cascio, 1982) are but a few present-day applications of the utility maximization principle proposed by Bernoulli. As these examples suggest, formal decision-making methods are typically reserved for complex issues involving numerous stakeholders and multiple criteria for success. One such criteria, decision acceptance, depends in part on the degree to which the agency's underlying decision philosophy is understood, valued, and shared by stakeholders.

Based on our results, however, Expected Utility Theory is not supported as a descriptive theory of human decision making. We demonstrate that, in the context of the St. Petersburg gamble, human behavior is governed more by simple decision rules than by the utility maximization principle. The implication is quite clear—there exists a great potential for conflict between policy-making agencies and the lay public due to divergent decision-making strategies. While tactics for alleviating this conflict may intervene at the level of policy-making, public interpretation of policy or somewhere in between, an important first step is building a sound descriptive theory of human decision making.

The strong support found for Treisman's claim that people rely on shortcuts and simple rules to avoid the mental calculations associated with many St. Petersburg solutions raises some interesting issues concerning the interpretation of extreme probabilities. A generalization of Treisman's heuristic suggests that, due to limits in information-processing capacity and understanding of probability theory, people interpret a probability expressed in a "1/d" format by focussing on its most salient characteristic, the denominator (d) [for a more detailed treatment of this generalization, see Holtgrave's appendix to Bottom, Bontempo, and Holtgrave (1989)]. Placing undue weight on this figure, people may incorrectly conclude that the probabilistic event will occur around the dth chance of occurrence. That is, if we say to someone that they have a 1/10,000 lifetime chance of dying from radon induced lung cancer, they may well think that were they to live 10,000 lifetimes they would get cancer once. And, this cancer would be likely to occur around the 10,000th lifetime.

People using this mental shortcut to probability interpretation surely need assistance in the proper interpretation of risk estimates. A program explaining the above random risk should help interpret a 1/10,000 cancer risk by stating that if one is exposed to 10,000 such risks in a lifetime, the probability of dying from at least one of them is .632. As Bettman, Payne, and Staelin (1987) point out in their guidelines for designing effective consumer product labels, it is crucial that the designer of an information provision program have a thorough understanding of the cognitive processes of the intended audience. The results of this paper suggest that the dominant models assumed to underlie the human decision process are inadequate; government and corporate decisions based on formal decision systems which employ these assumptions should be carefully re-evaluated.

References

Arrow, K.J. (1951). Alternate approaches to the theory of choice in risk-taking situations. *Econometrica, 19,* 404-437.

Aumann, R.J. (1977). The St. Petersburg Paradox: A discussion of some recent comments. *Journal of Economic Theory, 14,* 443-445.

Bernoulli, D. (1738). Specimen theoriae novae de mensura sortis. Commentarii Academiae Scientiarium Imperialis Petropolitanae, 6, 175-192. Translated by L. Sommer (1954). Exposition of a new theory on the measurement of risk. *Econometrica, 22,* 23-36.

Bettman, J.R., Payne, J.W., and Staelin, R. (1987). Cognitive considerations in presenting risk information. In W.K. Viscusi and W.A. Magat (Eds.), *Learning About Risk: Consumer and Worker Responses to Harzard Information.* Cambridge, MA: Harvard University Press.

Bottom, W.P, Bontempo, R.N., and Holtgrave, D.R. (1989). Experts, novices, and the St. Petersburg Paradox: Is one solution enough? *Journal of Behavioral Decision Making, 2,* 137-147.

Brito, D.L. (1975). Becker's Theory of the allocation of time and the St. Petersburg Paradox. *Journal of Economic Theory, 10,* 123-126.

Cascio, W.F. (1982). *Applied psychology in personnel management* (2nd ed.). Reston, VA: Reston Publishing Co.

Coombs, C.H., Dawes, R.M., and Tversky, A. (1970). *Mathematical Psychology.* Englewood Cliffs, NJ: Prentice Hall, 113-143.

Kahneman, D. and Tversky, A. (1979). Prospect theory: An analysis of decision under risk. *Econometrica, 47,* 263-291.

Keeney, R.L. and Raiffa, H. (1976). *Decisions with Multiple Objectives: Preferences and Value Tradeoffs.* New York: John Wiley & Sons.

Keynes, J.M. (1921). *A Treatise on Probability.* London: MacMillan.

Lopes, L.L. (1981). Decision making in the short run. *Journal of Experimental Psychology: Human Learning and Memory, 7,* 377-385.

Poisson, S.D. (1837). *Recherches sur La probabilite' Des jugements en Matiere Civile, in Precedees Des regles Generales du Calcul des Probabilites.* Paris: Bachelier.

Reagan, R. (1981). Executive Order #12291. Reprinted in: *5USC Section 601, Supplement 1988.*

Samuelson, P.A. (1977). St. Petersburg Paradoxes: Defanged, dissected, and historically described. *Economic Literature, 15,* 24-55.

Samuelson, P.A. (1980). *Economics (11th Ed.).* New York: McGraw-Hill.

Siegel, S. (1956). *Nonparametric Statistics for the Behavioral Sciences.* New York: McGraw-Hill.

Todhunter, I. (1865). *A History of the Mathematical Theory of Probability.* New York: Cambridge University Press. Reprint. New York: Chelsea, [1949] 1961.

Treisman, M. (1986). A solution to the St. Petersburg Paradox. *British Journal of Mathematical and Statistical Psychology, 36,* 224-227.

von Neumann, J. and Morgenstern, O. (1944). *Theory of Games and Economic Behavior.* New York: John Wiley & Sons.

Note

A reduced version of this article appeared in *Commentary, 8,* 46-51, June 1990, Singapore: National University of Singapore Society.

A METHOD FOR SOLVING INTRANSITIVITIES

Arne Maas

In this paper a method is presented that turns intransitive preferences between alternatives into a transitive ordering. The method has been developed for a medical situation where patients suffering from laryngeal cancer may decide which treatment they will undergo. To make a decision they first have to state preferences in a number of pair comparisons. At this stage intransitivities can be revealed. The method provides a unique solution that is easily computed, no matter how many alternatives are involved. The number of arc reversals of the solution often coincides with the minimal number of arc reversals known as Slater's i.

One crucial assumption, among others, in decision theory is transitivity. This means that if a person prefers a to b and b to c, we can conclude that he/she also will prefer a to c. So, if one prefers an apple to a banana and a banana to cherries, one will also prefer an apple to cherries. This is rather straightforward and no one will doubt the rationality of this assumption, but studies have shown that people do not always act rationally, i.e., are intransitive (inter alia, Tversky, 1969). Especially Arrow (1951) has given a boost to research on intransitivity when he stated his Impossibility Theorem. This theorem shows that a group of persons never can make a consistent choice if we assume five reasonable conditions that the persons should satisfy. One of these conditions is transitivity. The assumption of transitivity needs to be satisfied in helping people make a decision. For example, if a person prefers an apple to a banana and a banana to cherries, but also prefers cherries to an apple, the reader would have a hard time recommending the person a choice from the three fruits: banana, apple and cherries. A method to adjust someone's preferences such that they are transitive would be very useful.

The main goal of this article is to solve intransitivities. In principle, we want to keep the preferences as intact as possible. This means we want to make a minimum number of changes in preferences, or preference reversals, in order to satisfy the transitivity. The minimum number of changes is known as Slater's i (Slater, 1961). A method has been developed to search for Slater's i (Phillips, 1969). This method however, does not reckon with the intensity of preferences. The method presented here does, which is clearly an advantage. That is, if for example a person states to prefer a to b four out of five times, he/she is regarded as less consistent than a person who prefers a to b five out of five times. A second advantage of our method is that the solution is mostly unique, in contrast with Slater's i. This is important because the researcher does not have to choose between alternative solutions, as is the case when a solution on the basis of Slater's i is derived. The third advantage is that our method is much more tractable which is especially important for dealing with complex data and for programming of the method.

It should be noted that our method does not aim to satisfy theoretical conditions to make it optimal for exceptional unlikely situations. Our method aims at being tractable and natural for practice. Let us emphasize that, although the actual application of the method in this paper deals with two-dimensional stimuli, this by no means implies that intransitivities of alternatives with one, or more than two, dimensions cannot be solved by the method. The method is general and is independent of the dimensions of the alternatives.

The method will be applied to a medical situation in which patients would be able to choose. As long as medical science exists, a decision between medical treatments is determined by physicians. In many cases this decision is grounded on medical facts and is therefore clear. Sometimes, however, treatments are medically equivalent and in such cases a patient is an equally good decision maker as a physician would be. Many physicians, however, cling to their superior position or regard patients as incapable of deciding. But in general those patients make many decisions in their lives: they choose a partner, they buy a car, etc., while they do not know anything about psychology or engines. So, if patients want to decide for themselves, they should have the right to do so.

Of course, a medical decision is a difficult one. In the case of laryngeal cancer, which is the topic of study here, there are two treatments between which patients can choose. Surgery may be performed, which results in an opening in the throat, a stoma, through which patients have to breathe. They lose their voice and have to master artificial speech. Artificial speech can be attained by belching up air from the stomach, called esophageal speech, or by using an electronic device, called electrolaryngeal speech. In some cases patients remain mute. The second treatment is radiotherapy; the main disadvantage of this treatment is a decreased life expectation. The quality of voice is either normal or hoarse. So if patients choose surgery they are prepared to give in their quality of voice to preserve a longer life expectation. On the other hand, if patients choose radiotherapy, they are willing to decrease their life expectation in order to keep a better quality of voice. To help patients make their decision, a procedure has been developed to elicit their preferences (Bezembinder & Stalpers, 1988).

In the method section the application of the method of pair comparisons in this study will be illustrated and our method for solving intransitivities will be described. In the application section, a result of the method will be given. We round off with a discussion.

The Method
The method of pair comparisons: An application
The application of the method of pair comparisons to the case of laryngeal cancer

has been developed by Bezembinder and Stalpers (1988). Five levels are used for both life expectation (3, 6, 9, 12 and 15 years of living, which is clearly ordered), and quality of voice (mute, electrolaryngeal, esophageal, hoarse and normal speech, in ascending order). The latter ordering needs to be verified, since some patients, for instance, prefer esophageal to hoarse speech. We now can make a combination of two levels of the two attributes, for instance, nine years of living with esophageal speech. If we increase the quality of voice and decrease the number of years of living, we can make a second combination, for instance, six years of living with normal speech. Hence, we have created a dilemma, which is presented to a patient after proper introduction as follows:

What do you prefer?

(a) Living 9 years with esophageal speech, or

(b) Living 6 years with normal speech.

It is immediately clear that if one prefers to have normal speech, one has to contemplate giving in three years of living. (a) and (b) are examples of what will henceforth be called alternatives, and be referred to as e.g., 6N, representing 6 years with normal speech. To avoid confusion, electrolaryngeal speech will be abbreviated by EL and esophageal speech by ES.

When both attributes have five levels, the resulting number of dilemmas is 100. Patients are presented those dilemmas thrice, each time they have to decide if a better quality of voice outweighs a decrease in life years. Other combinations are possible, but those are trivial, i.e., one alternative has a better level on both attributes. Those cases are excluded because the answer is clear.

Example: It is possible that a person indicates to prefer 6N over 12ES and further prefers 12ES to 9H and 9H to 6N. If this is the case, the respondent has been intransitive in his/her answers. This example is rather straightforward but such intransitivities can occur, including more alternatives, giving a rather complex and unclear network of preferences.

Tournaments

Imagine a tournament in which ten chess players compete. In such a tournament every player plays against every other player. There are clearly three possibilities: player P beats player Q, player P loses to player Q or it is a draw. If P beats Q then it is impossible that Q beats P, because there is only one game. After the last day of playing, the tournament is complete. All relations between players are known, and each player has a certain number of points, the final score: if one has lost all games, the result is zero points, if one has won all games, the result is nine points. An ordering from the best to the worst player is possible.

However, it can occur that player P beats player Q, Q beats R but R beats P again, hence constituting intransitivity. Of course, in a tournament of chess players this often happens and it does no harm. The main point is that looking only at those three games it is not clear which of the three players is the best, or has the highest position.

Let us assume that chess players P, Q and R are alternatives as given above in the example. Like in a tournament of chess players we can count the number of times a certain alternative "beats" other alternatives. In the case of alternatives it is common sense to say that an alternative is preferred to another alternative. If we know all relations between alternatives we can compute the final score of all points. But again, it is possible that there are intransitivities and in the case of preferences this means a violation of the assumption of transitivity we made. Hence, it is necessary to correct these intransitivities and we have developed a method to do so.

A method for turning intransitive choices into transitive ones

Crucial for our method is that any patient is asked at least three times to answer all dilemmas. Moreover, the number of times needs to be odd. Each time of asking preferences is called a replication. Preferable is that there is some time between replications, though this is not always possible in practice. If a patient gives the same preference in a certain dilemma everytime, say always preferring A to B, then we say that A is absolutely preferred to B. The number of times A is preferred to B we call the value of the preference relation between A and B. The value of an absolute preference thus always equals the number of replications. Just like in the tournament of chess players, it is not possible that alternative A is preferred a majority of times to alternative B and at the same time alternative B is preferred a majority of times to alternative A. Hence, between two alternatives only one is most preferred.

If there are intransitivities, our method can be applied as follows: first we select all absolute preferences the patient has stated. In practice it is exceptional that intransitivities including only absolute preferences are present. If those intransitivities occur nevertheless, all solutions based on Slater's i may be determined and one of the possible re-orderings must be chosen, or the patients have to indicate preferences again.

If there are no intransitivities based on absolute preferences, we add all preferences that follow from transitivity. That is, if A is absolutely preferred to B and B is absolutely preferred to C, we can say that A also is preferred to C. This, of course, may also be applied to longer sequences. So, if above, C is absolutely preferred to D, then we say that A is also preferred to D. If all relations based on transitivity have been added, we check if all possible relations between all alternatives are included. If this is the case, we have a transitive tournament of alternatives; the ordering is complete, just like after the last playing day in a chess tournament.

It can very well be that the resulting number of relations does not constitute a transitive tournament. Then in our method we count the scores of all alternatives. So, if alternative A is preferred to four other alternatives, its positive score is four. On the other hand, if three alternatives are preferred to alternative A, then its negative score is three. This is comparable to a chess player who has won four games and lost three.

Next we pick out the two alternatives with the highest positive scores, comparable to the two chess players who have won the most games. We check if the relation between them has already been added, i.e., if one of the chess players has beaten the other. If not, we add the relation between those alternatives on the basis of the nonabsolute preference that is known from the data. After the addition we again check if we can add preference relations by transitivity. For example, suppose that the relation between A and C is still not added, that B is absolutely preferred to C and that the preference of A over B has been added, because A was preferred twice to B. Then we can also add the relation "A is preferred to C" on the basis of transitivity. If the relation between A and B, the alternatives with the highest and second highest positive score, already is known or has been added, we can continue the procedure for the alternatives with the highest and third highest positive score. If all relations which include the alternative with the highest positive score are known, we start again with the same procedure applied to the alternatives with the second and third highest positive scores. After each addition we add all preference relations that follow by applying transitivity. Finally we will end up with a transitive tournament.

An Application

In this section an extensive explanation will be given about applying the method. For this purpose seven alternatives are presented that include some intransitivities (see Figure 1).

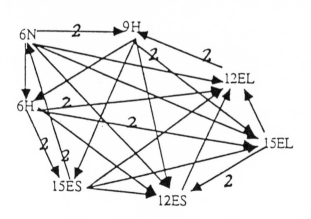

FIGURE 1

An example of an observed data matrix. The meaning of a directed arc is that the starting point is preferred to the endpoint. A number assigned to an arc means the number of times the one alternative is preferred to the other. No number means an absolute or trivial preference.

At first sight there is no unique ordering of alternatives. For instance, 6N is preferred to 6H, 6H to 15ES, but 15ES is preferred to 6N, so there is no unique ordering between these three alternatives. The first step of our method is to select all relations that have an absolute preference. The absolute preferences are represented in Figure 2.

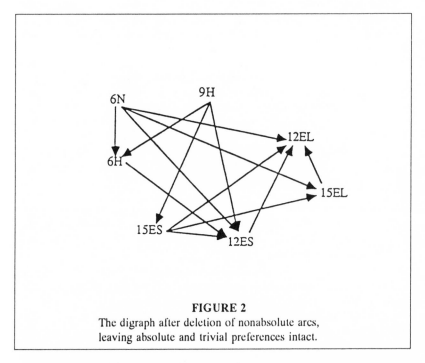

FIGURE 2
The digraph after deletion of nonabsolute arcs,
leaving absolute and trivial preferences intact.

Now, by applying the assumption of transitivity we can extend this figure. We immediately can see that 9H is preferred to 15ES, and 15ES is preferred to 15EL, so that we can add the relation "9H is preferred to 15EL" by transitivity. We may apply the same reasoning to 9H and 12EL, since 15ES is also preferred to 12EL, so we can also add "9H is preferred to 12EL." Note that in the original preferences (see Figure 1) 12EL is preferred two out of three times to 9H, so we observe that a preference reversal has taken place. A last relation we can add on the basis of transitivity is the one between 6H and 12EL, because 6H is preferred to 12ES and 12ES is preferred to 12EL. We now have established the relations as given in Figure 3.

In Figure 4 the positive and negative scores are given after each change. At stage 0 the original positive and negative scores are given; this is similar to Figure 1. Stage 1 is similar to the situation in Figure 2, stage 2 to Figure 3. We see that at stage 2, 9H and 6N have the highest and second highest positive score respectively and their relation has not been established yet in Figure 3. From the original preferences we

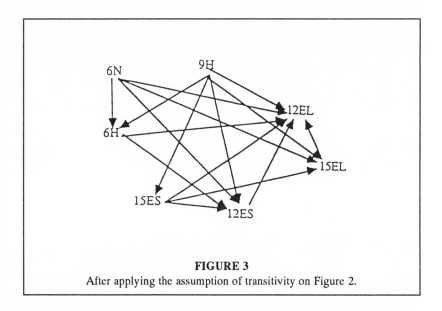

FIGURE 3
After applying the assumption of transitivity on Figure 2.

conclude that 6N is preferred to 9H two out of three times, so we add "6N is preferred to 9H." Since 9H is preferred to 15ES, this also results in "6N is preferred to 15ES," which also is the second preference reversal. At this moment all relations between 6N and all other alternatives have been established, and this also holds for 9H (stage 3 in Figure 4). This can easily be seen by adding the positive and negative score of an alternative. If this sum is equal to the number of alternatives minus 1, all relations of this alternative with others are known. We search further for the third and fourth highest positive scores, which are 6H and 15ES. 6H is preferred to 15ES two out of three times, so this relation is added. Since 15ES is preferred to 15EL, this also results in "6H is preferred to 15EL" (stage 4 in Figure 4). The last unknown relation is between 15EL and 12ES. The first is preferred twice, so "15EL is preferred to 12ES" is added (stage 5 in Figure 4). Now we have constituted a unique preference relation, in descending order 6N-9H-6H-15ES-15EL-12ES-12EL. The procedure led to two preference reversals, which is equal to Slater's i.

Discussion

We have presented a method that provides us with excellent and unique solutions. It will be very useful in practice if patients need to be helped in making a rational decision between treatments. In many cases in practice, the number of preference reversals coincides with Slater's i, which is a pro for our method. Our procedure, while reckoning more with intensities and absoluteness of preferences, did not do worse than a procedure based on Slater's i. To establish a unique preference ordering or to find a solution with a minimal number of preference reversals, was a cumbersome and

Stage	0		1		2		3		4		5	
Score	+	-	+	-	+	-	+	-	+	-	+	-
12EL	1	5	0	4	0	6	0	6	0	6	0	6
12ES	1	5	1	4	1	4	1	4	1	4	1	5
15EL	2	4	1	2	1	3	1	3	1	4	2	4
15ES	4	2	3	1	3	1	3	2	3	3	3	3
6H	4	2	1	2	2	2	2	2	4	2	4	2
9H	4	2	3	0	5	0	5	1	5	1	5	1
6N	5	1	4	0	4	0	6	0	6	0	6	0

FIGURE 4

The different stages of the method in terms of positive and negative scores.

Stage 0 represents the situation in Figure 1, stage 1 represents the situation in Figure 2, stage 2 represents the situation in Figure 3.

complex matter for previous methods. The presented method, however, gives a unique solution established in a few moments, which is an important advantage.

The method will be used in a medical setting where patients suffering from laryngeal cancer will be given the choice between two treatments. It is highly possible that, because of the difficult situation patients live in, they are insecure, hence answering inconsistently sometimes. This method will be a very useful tool in such a practical setting. It picks out the secure answers, that is those answers which are the same during a certain period of time, and tries to rely mostly on this secureness. Furthermore, our method is applicable to many situations in which decisions can or have to be made.

Of course, the advantage of the procedure based on Slater's i is that it can deal with preference relations that are asked only once. In our method we cannot start before we have three replications. However, the advantages of the presented, intuitively logical method are:

(a) Initially, the method only deals with the secure absolute preferences;

(b) The solution is easily obtained in little time and the algorithm can easily be programmed;

(c) The solution most of the time is unique; and

(d) The number of arc reversals often coincides with Slater's i.

References

Arrow, K.J. (1951). *Social Choice and Individual Values*. New York: John Wiley & Sons.

Bezembinder, Th.G.G. and Stalpers, L.J. (1988). *Trade Offs and Decisions by Additive Conjoint Measurement*. Unpublished manuscript, Department of Mathematical Psychology, University of Nijmegen.

Harary, F., Norman, R.Z., and Cartwright, D. (1965). *Structural Models: An Introduction to the Theory of Directed Graphs*. New York: John Wiley & Sons.

Moon, J.W. (1968). *Topics on Tournaments*. New York: Holt, Rinehart, and Winston.

Phillips, J.P.N. (1969). A further procedure for determining Slater's i and all nearest adjoining orders. *British Journal of Mathematical and Statistical Psychology, 22*, 97-101.

Slater, P. (1961). Inconsistencies in a schedule of paired comparisons. *Biometrika, 48*, 303-312.

Tversky, A. (1969). Intransitivity of preferences. *Psychological Review, 76,* 31-48.

Acknowledgment

I am very grateful to Dr. P. Wakker (Department of Mathematical Psychology, University of Nijmegen) for his valuable comments on an earlier draft of this paper.

DECISION-AIDING SOFTWARE FOR ALL FIELDS OF BEHAVIORAL SCIENCE

Stuart S. Nagel

This paper describes a new system of decision analysis called
Policy/Goal Percentaging (P/G%) or Best Choice. The system is
designed to process a set of (a) goals to be achieved, (b)
alternatives for achieving the goals, and (c) relations between
goals and alternatives in order to choose or explain the best
alternative, combination, allocation, or predictive decision rule.
The system is especially designed to deal with such obstacles to
systematic decision analysis as (a) multiple dimensions on
multiple goals, (b) multiple missing information, (c) multiple
alternatives that are too many to determine the effects of each
one, (d) multiple and possibly conflicting constraints, and (e) the
need for simplicity in spite of all that multiplicity. The system can
be applied to any field of knowledge that involves making
decisions, but is especially applicable to political science, economics, sociology, psychology, and their applied counterparts of
public administration, business administration, social work, and
education.

This article briefly describes a new microcomputer system called Policy/Goal
Percentaging Analysis. The system is designed to process a set of (1) goals to be
achieved, (2) alternatives for achieving the goals, and (3) relations between goals and
alternatives in order to choose the best alternative or combination for maximizing
benefits minus costs. The system is especially relevant to processing information in
order to arrive at decisions. The system is called Policy/Goal Percentaging Analysis
because it relates alternative policies to goals, and it makes use of part/whole
percentages in order to handle the problem of goals being measured on different
dimensions. The measurement units are converted into a system of percentages
showing relative achievement of each policy on each goal, rather than a system of
inches, dollars, apples, days, or other measurement scores. The abbreviated name of
the program is P/G%.

To facilitate applications of part/whole percentaging, an appropriate microcomputer program has been developed. It can be applied to any problem involving one or
more policies and one or more goals. The program is especially useful when one is
working with many policies, many goals, various measurement units, and other
constraints and conditions. The program can run on an IBM PC or an IBM-compatible
microcomputer. (This program is related to the field of multi-criteria decision
making.) That field includes such literature as Edwards and Newman (1982), Saaty

(1980), and Zeleny (1982). In comparison to those methods, the P/G% program is both simpler to use and more realistic in its procedures. The program is also related to spreadsheet analysis, but it is more focused on evaluating alternatives and informing the user as to what changes will make a difference as well as what difference they will make (see Henderson 1983).

General Aspects of the Program

A. Components of the program. The program can perform a variety of useful decision-making analyses such as (a) choosing, ranking, or allocating to alternative categories, (b) working with goals that have a common measurement unit or that are multidimensional, (c) doing what-if variations on the goals, alternatives, and relations, (d) doing a threshold or convergence analysis to indicate the scores on the goals, alternatives, or relations that will make a difference in the winning alternative or how resources are allocated, (e) adjusting results for minimums, maximums, and other constraints, and (f) comparing optimum choices with actual choices in order to reduce the gap between the actual and the optimum.

The decision-aiding system involves basically the following steps:

(a) Listing the alternatives from which a choice needs to be made, or to which an allocation needs to be made. This refers to the alternatives from which one is trying to find a best alternative, a best combination of alternatives, or a best allocation of scarce resources. The examples which follow include getting married versus staying single, or allocating cases to a trial versus an out-of-court settlement.

(b) Listing the criteria or goals which one wants to achieve and their relative importance.

(c) Scoring each alternative on each criterion with as precise or as rough a relation score as is available.

(d) Converting the scores into part/whole percentages or other scores that can show the relative relations of the alternatives on each criterion.

(e) Aggregating the relative scores for each alternative across the criteria in order to arrive at an overall score or allocation coefficient for each alternative.

(f) Drawing a conclusion as to which alternative or combination is best, or how much of a budget or a set of scarce resources should be allocated to each alternative.

(g) Changing the alternatives, criteria, relations, and other inputs to see how such changes affect the conclusion.

The computer program is divided into five parts or options covering the following:

(a) Accessing, creating, or deleting a data file of information relevant to resolving a decision problem.

(b) Inserting or changing the inputs regarding the alternatives, goals, relations, or amount of scarce resources to be allocated.

(c) The initial results based on the alternatives, goals, and relations.

(d) The post facto analysis, which include threshold analysis and convergence analysis.

(e) A provision for saving and storing data files that one might want to refer to in the future.

The post facto analyses are especially useful to aid in resolving disputes as to what the weights or relation scores should be. Threshold analysis is one option, whereby the computer shows what it would take in changing the goals-weights or the relation scores to bring the second place alternative up to first place or any alternative up to any other alternative. For example, if there is a dispute as to whether a relation score is a 2 or an 8, and the threshold value is a 10, then there should be no need to dispute the matter further since neither a 2 nor an 8 will make any difference in terms of the second place alternative moving to first place. Convergence analysis is another option whereby the computer shows at what level the weight for a goal becomes high enough to produce results that are quite close to the results that would occur if that goal were the only goal. For example, if there is a dispute as to whether a goal weight is a 5 or a 10 and the convergence value is a 3, then there should be no need to dispute that matter further.

B. General applications. The P/G% approach differs from other decision-aiding approaches by virtue of being able to deal meaningfully with all of the following decision-making situations:

(a) Multi-dimensional goals.

(b) Choosing the one best alternative.

(c) Choosing the best combination of alternatives.

(d) Making choices where risks and probabilities are involved.

(e) Making choices where doing too much or too little is undesirable.

(f) Allocating scarce resources, even where there are millions of alternative ways of allocating a given budget to a set of budget categories.

(g) Situations with multiple missing information.

(h) Situations involving public policy, law, business, medicine, or personal decision making.

(i) Situations where all the goals are measured on the same dimension.

(j) Situations involving prediction as well as prescription.

(k) Minimums or maximums on the alternatives, goals, or other constraints.

The approach also differs from other approaches by virtue of having the following characteristics:

(a) P/G% can easily go from alternatives, goals, and relations to drawing a conclusion.

(b) It has been translated into a highly user-friendly microcomputer program.

(c) It is based on mathematical justifications that relate to classical calculus optimization, especially if one views the part/whole percentages as proxies for non-linear regression coefficients.

(d) It comes with lots of illustrative applications and years of relevant experience.

(e) It is analogous to mathematical programming procedures such as linear, non-linear, integer, goal, and multi-objective programming, but without the complexity and unrealistic assumptions.

(f) The program can systematically compare optimum choices or allocations with actual choices or allocations in order to bring the optimum closer to the actual and vice versa.

Along with the program, there are a variety of computerized data files. They especially include applications from the fields of law, public policy, health care, and personal decision making. They also include applications that involve predicting decisions as well as prescribing decisions. One can easily create new applications by inserting a set of tentative alternatives, goals, and relations for various problems.

Two Examples
A. Choosing to get married. Table 1 applies the methodology to an especially simple example. The example is simple in the sense that (a) there are only two alternatives and two goals, (b) both goals are measured on the same 0-10 scale, (c) both goals are tentatively given equal weight, (d) there is no missing information on the relations, and (e) there are no constraints. The basic alternatives are to get married or to stay single. The basic goals are companionship and privacy.

On a 0-10 scale, getting married scores a 7 on companionship, but only a 3 on privacy in the eyes of the relevant decision-maker. On the other hand, staying single scores only 4 on companionship, but an 8 on privacy. If one gives equal weight to companionship and privacy, then the sum of 7 plus 3 on getting married adds to 10. The sum of 4 plus 8 on staying single adds to 12. Thus, staying single outscores getting married in the initial results by 2 points. There would be a tie if getting married could move up from a 7 to a 9 on companionship, or from a 3 to a 5 on privacy. Likewise, there would be a tie if staying single were considered to be worth only a 2 on companionship rather than a 4, or only worth a 6 on privacy rather than an 8.

	CRITERION #1	**CRITERION #2**	
	TABLE 1		
	Deciding Whether to Get Married		
	Companionship 0-10 SCALE	Privacy 0-10 SCALE	**Sum of Raw Scores**
Get Married	7 (9)	3 (5)	10
Stay Single	4 (2)	8 (6)	12
Weights	1 (1.67)	1 (.60)	

Notes

1. The numbers not in parentheses are raw scores on a 0-10 scale for companionship and a 0-10 scale for privacy.

2. The initial weights are 1.00 for both goals.

3. The numbers in parentheses are the threshold values which will cause getting married to be of equal satisfaction with staying single. They each involve adding or subtracting 2 from the raw scores since 2 is the threshold difference when summing the raw scores for both alternatives.

4. Since it may be difficult to improve on the companionship and privacy of getting married by 2 points, and it may be difficult to recalculate companionship and privacy on staying single by 2 points, the program reduces to whether the weight of companionship is more than the weight of privacy or is only as much.

5. Getting married in this context could refer to a specific person or just to the abstract idea.

The threshold analysis says that if companionship is given a weight of 1.67, then there will be a tie. It also says that if privacy is given a weight of .60 when companionship has a weight of 1, then there will be a tie. Thus, if companionship is only as valuable as privacy, then the decision maker should stay single. On the other hand, if companionship is worth at least twice as much as privacy (rounding to the nearest whole number), then he or she is better off getting married in view of the goals to be achieved, the alternatives available, and the relations between the alternatives and the goals.

Even in this simple example, one can see that the computer program can be helpful in various ways such as (1) organizing one's ideas in terms of alternatives, goals, and relations, (2) scoring the relations so as to provide consistency on each goal, (3) enabling one to see quickly the summation score for each alternative, (4) revealing the threshold value for each relation and each weight, and (5) enabling the user to make changes in the relations and weights to see how sensitive the initial conclusion is to input changes.

B. An allocation example. Tables 2 and 3 clarify further what the program involves. Table 2 provides the raw data for the problem of choosing between trials and plea bargains as the better method of resolving cases. One can also consider the problem as being one of what percent of the cases should be allocated to trials and what percent to pleas in terms of desirable target figures, rather than precise quotas. Table 2 indicates that the average trial in the sample consumes about 120 days from arrest to disposition and the average plea bargain consumes about 30 days. In a rough survey of lawyers, trials received an average score of 6 on promoting respect for the law on a 0-10 scale, whereas pleas received a score of 2. We thus have a tradeoff problem with trials doing better on respect, but pleas doing better on delay.

TABLE 2

Raw Data for Choosing Between Two Policy Alternatives

Alternatives/Criteria Scoring

	Delay	Respect
Trials	120.00	6.00
Pleas	30.00	2.00

Notes

1. Trials do better on respect than pleas with a score of 6 versus 2 on a 0-10 attitude scale. Pleas does better on delay than trials with a score of 30 days versus 120 days.

2. One cannot simply add -120 to +6 to obtain an overall score for trials to compare with -30 added to +2 to obtain an overall score for pleas.

3. One can, however, note that trials receive 76% of the sum of the 6 plus 2 scores on respect, and pleas receive only 25%. On the other hand, trials receive 80% of the 120 plus 30 scores on delay, whereas pleas receive only 20%.

4. One can more meaningfully add and subtract such part/whole percentages than one can add and subtract the raw scores, especially if one indicates how much more valuable a 1% increase is worth on one criterion versus another.

5. Thus, pleas is a better alternative than trials since it has a higher net part/whole percentage of +5% as compared to the -5% of trials. Trial, however, is a better alternative if respect is considered at least twice as important as delay.

6. Part/whole percentaging is thus a useful tool for dealing with the problem of delay, respect, or other goals being measured on two or more different dimensions.

TABLE 3

Transformed Data for Dealing with Multidimensional Goals

Weighted part/Whole %

	Delay	Respect
Trials	-80.00	150.00
Pleas	-20.00	50.00

Notes

1. The above table converts the raw scores of Table 2 into weighted part/whole percentages.

2. The original raw scores on delay were 120 and 30. They convert into part/whole percentages equal to 120/150 or 80%, and to 30/150 or 20%. Those p/w%'s are then multiplied by the weight of -1 for delay yielding -80% and -20%. The original raw scores on respect were 6 and 2. They convert into p/w%'s equal to 6/8 or 75%, and to 2/8 or 25%. These p/w%'s are then multiplied by the weight of 2 for respect yielding 150% and 50%.

3. Adding -80% to 150% gives an allocation percentage of 70%. Adding -20% to 50% gives an allocation percentage of 30%. This indicates that with the raw data from Table 2, and respect having twice the weight of delay, then the optimum allocation of cases between trials and pleas is 70% trials and 30% pleas.

4.   Part/whole percentaging is thus a useful tool for dealing with the problem of multiple alternatives. There are at least 101 alternative ways cases could be allocated to trials and pleas. One could give 100% to trials and 0% to pleas, 99% to trials and 1% to pleas, and so on to 0% to trials and 100% to pleas. There are an infinite number of alternatives if one deals with the decimal percentages and not just integer percentages. Part/whole percentaging, however, makes the allocation process quite simple and meaningful, even though the number of alternatives is infinite.

Table 3 shows how the program transforms the data so that one can give a meaningful overall score to trials and to pleas. The computer adds 120 days to 30 days and obtains 150 days. In terms of part/whole percentages, 120 is 80% of 150 and 30 is 20% of 150. The computer also adds a respect score of 6 to a respect score of 2, and obtains a total of 8. In terms of part/whole percentages for that data, 6 is 75% of 8, and 2 is 25%. The 80% and 20% are multiplied by -1 to show that delay is a negative goal like cost on which it is good to have a low score. The 75% and 25% are multiplied by 2 to show that respect is tentatively considered twice as important as delay. If we then add across each alternative row in Table 3, we obtain a 70% figure for trials and a 30% figure for pleas. Those numbers indicate trials is a more desirable alternative and they can be roughly interpreted as approximations to optimum allocation percentages.

The computer program makes all those calculations from the data given in Table 2 along with the relative weights for the goals. More important, the computer is capable of indicating what each of the inputs in Table 2 and the weights would have to change to in order to bring the second place alternative up to first place. For example, if respect were not considered twice as important as delay but only 1.2 times as important, then there would be a tie at 50% for trials and 50% for pleas. This means that if one can agree that respect is more important than delay trials comes out the winner without having to decide exactly how much more important. This kind of breakeven or threshold analysis also shows that if the respect score of pleas could be raised from 2.00 to about 3.23, then there would be a tie. Respect for plea bargains could be increased by giving more resources to both the prosecutor and the public defender so they will not be wrongly coerced into accepting a guilty plea.

Other Aspects

A. Convergence analysis. The program can also perform a convergence analysis which is another form of sensitivity analysis. It involves determining how much weight a goal needs to be given in order for the allocations to be within 5 percentage points of what they would be if that were the only goal. For example, if respect were the only goal, then 75% of the cases would be allocated to trials and 25% to pleas. That effect is virtually achieved by just giving respect a weight of 2 when delay has a weight of -1 because the allocations then become 70% to trials and 30% to pleas. Likewise, when respect has a weight of 1, delay takes over if it is given a weight of 2 because the allocations then become 15% to trials and 85% to pleas. Those allocations are within 5 percentage points of the 20% and 80% that would prevail if delay were the only goal.

B. Residual analysis. The program can also perform a residual analysis. Suppose, for example, the actual allocation to trials is 20% and 80% for pleas. That means there is a -50 residual for trials since the optimum is 70% and a +50 residual for pleas since that optimum is 30%. Those residuals are helpful in indicating that the actual decision makers and/or the researchers may be misperceiving relations or wrongly weighting goals. The program can also perform a constraint analysis. Suppose, for example, there is a constraint that says at least 10% of the cases must go to trial as a matter of basic fairness, and at least 50% must be settled through pleas in order to avoid the expense of trials. If the optimum is 70% and 30%, then the first constraint is satisfied. To satisfy the second constraint, 20 percentage points must be taken from the 70% and given to the 30%. That means the optimum constrained allocation is 50% and 50%.

C. Beyond the spreadsheet base. The program has the potential for out-performing spreadsheet programs like Lotus 1-2-3. Lotus does "what-if" analysis whereby one asks what would be the effect of a cell change on a row total, column total, or grand total. That is highly cumbersome if one has 100 cells (as one does with a 10 x 10 matrix), and each cell is reasonably capable of taking five different values. P/G% analysis instantly tells the user the threshold values of all 100 cells. For example, if the cell on row 4, column 6 has a threshold value of 89, that means any number greater than 89 will result in alternative 5 being the winner, and any number less than 89 will result in alternative 7 being the winner. One thus does not have to experiment with what would happen with a score of 95, 117, 43, or 11.

P/G% is also specifically geared toward aiding in making decisions, whereas Lotus 1-2-3 amounts to little more than a combination of columnar paper and a calculator. P/G% can be used by housewives and others on home computers, not just by business people. It can be used where columns are measured on different dimensions and with different constraints and conditions. It is both prescriptive and predictive. It clearly goes beyond spreadsheet analysis in the next generation of useful computer software.

D. Limitations. A limitation which the program currently has is the requirement that one have access to an IBM-compatible microcomputer with 192K of memory and a graphics adapter. The program is, however, being developed for running on other microcomputers. A body of experience is also being developed which will be incorporated into a booklength manual consisting mainly of various applications entitled *Evaluation Analysis with Microcomputers*. Those applications are also leading to further improvements in the versatility of the program. The program is mainly limited by the fact that the real world involves multi-dimensional goals, missing information, complex constraints and other problems, but the program seeks to handle those problems as well as can be done.

Applications to All Fields of Behavioral Science

The P/G% software was presented in a special workshop at the 1987 meeting of the American Association for the Advancement of Science. That workshop was partly designed to bring out how the decision-aiding software could be applied to natural science, behavioral science, and the humanities.

Behavioral science was divided into basic behavioral science, including political science, economics, sociology, and psychology. Behavioral science was also divided into applied behavioral science, including the counterpart fields of public administration, business administration, social work, and education. The tables which follow indicate the specific examples that were given for each of those eight fields of behavioral science.

Four examples were used for basic behavioral science. For political science, the example was evaluating democratic and undemocratic ways of relating government to the electorate (Table 4). For economics, the example was alternative ways of dealing with unemployment and inflation (Table 5). For sociology, the example was alternative public policies toward race relations (Table 6). For psychology, the example was deciding whether to take away or leave an abused child (Table 7).

Four examples were also used for applied behavioral science. For public administration, the example was allocating financial resources to the police and the courts (Table 8). For business administration, the example was assigning personnel to tasks that need to be performed (Table 9). For social work, the example was evaluating alternative policies for providing public aid, especially for dependent children (Table 10). For education, the example was evaluating alternative ways of dealing with low-income school districts (Table 11).

Further details for each example are given in (a) the tables themselves which follow, (b) the notes to the tables, and (c) the citations at the end of each set of notes which refer to journal articles or book chapters where still further details can be found.

TABLE 4

Political Science: Relating Government to the Electorate

GOALS / POLICIES	Multiple sources of ideas W= 1 (-.5)	Popular respons- iveness W = 1 (-.5)	Fast unquestioned decisions W = 1 (4)	SUM	GAP
1. No universal voting rights, and no minority political rights (dictatorship)	1 (7)	1 (7)	4 (10)	6	
2. Universal voting rights, but no minority political rights	2	4	3	9	6
3. Minority political rights, but no universal voting rights	4	1	3	8	
4. Universal voting rights, and minority political rights (democracy)	5 (-5)	5 (-1)	2 (-4)	12	

Notes

1. Democracy involves universal adult voting rights and minority political rights. Dictatorship involves the absence of both kinds of rights, or at least the absence of minority political rights.

2. Universal voting rights mean all adults have the right to vote, but only one vote per person, and candidates are chosen by majority vote. Minority political rights especially refer to the right of minority viewpoints to have access to the media in order to try to convert the majority.

3. For further details, see Nagel (1986).

	TABLE 5				
GOALS POLICIES	Reduce unemployment to 3 percent	Reduce inflation to 3 percent	Equitable distribution of unemployment and inflation	Free enter- prise	Sum
Economics: P/G% Applied to Unemployment/Inflation					
1. Doing nothing	3	3	2	4	12
2. Increase money supply Decrease interest rates	4	2	3	3	12
3. Decrease money supply Increase interest rates	2	4	3	3	12
4. Increase government spending Decrease taxes	4	2	3	3	12
5. Decrease government spending Increase taxes	2	4	3	3	12
6. Job creation Price control	4	4	4	1	13
7. Decrease taxes Decrease domestic spending	4	4	3	3	14
8. Tax breaks and subsidies Decrease defense spending	5	5	3	3	16

Notes

1. Policy 1 of doing nothing causes too much harm at least in the short run.

2. Policies 2-3 and 4-5 assume that periods of high unemployment and inflation do not occur simultaneously, which is no longer so.

3. Policy 6 is too expensive and too restrictive on marketplace incentives compared to the alternatives.

4. Policy 7 has the defect that merely decreasing taxes will not necessarily stimulate productivity without strings attached. Decreasing domestic spending may not be enough to avoid large government deficits which can stifle low interest rates needed for technological and business innovation.

5. Policy 8 presumes that tax breaks and subsidies will increase productivity which will reduce the work week and thereby make more jobs available while not reducing take-home pay. Increased productivity also means reduced inflation since workers and producers will be giving more for the increased wages and prices charged.

6. A score of 5 in a cell means the policy is highly conducive to the goal; a score of 4 means the policy is mildly conducive to the goal; a 3 means the policy is neither conducive nor adverse to the goal; a 2 means the policy is mildly adverse to the goal; and a 1 means the policy is highly adverse to the goal.

TABLE 6

Sociology: Alternative Public Policies Toward Race Relations

GOALS POLICIES	Stimulating minority advancement	Always favoring the one with the higher score	Never favoring the one who is unqualified	Sum
1. Requiring segregation or discrimination	1	1	1	3
2. Allowing discrimination (same as doing nothing)	2	2	2	6
3. Outlawing discrimination	4	4	4	12
4. Requiring affirmative action	5	4	4	13*
5. Requiring preferential hiring	4	2	4	10
6. Allowing reverse racism	2	2	2	6

Notes

1. Discrimination in this context means requiring or allowing a white with a score of 40 to be preferred over a black with a score of 60, where 50 is the minimum score for one who is qualified, or where both are qualified but the white is preferred even though the black applicant is substantially more qualified.

2. Affirmative action in this context means only hiring blacks who are qualified but actively seeking out qualified blacks through (1) advertising, (2) locating one's physical plant, (3) removing requirements that are racially correlated, but not correlated with job performance, and (4) providing on-the-job training for all, but especially to overcome the lack of training by blacks.

3. Preferential hiring means only hiring blacks who are qualified, but preferring qualified blacks over moderately less qualified whites, generally as a temporary measure to offset prior discrimination.

4. Reverse discrimination is the same as discrimination except blacks are favored.

5. The summation column tends to indicate that the optimum policy level for achieving the desired goals is to move away from discrimination to requiring affirmative action, but not to requiring preferential hiring except as a short-term remedy for prior discrimination.

TABLE 7

Psychology: Deciding Whether to Take Away or Leave an Abused Child

A.   The payoff matrix

Severe subsequent abuse
Would not occur   Would occur

	(a)	(b)
Take away	-50	+100
Leave	(c) +50	(d) -100

Benefits   Costs
(P) (100) - (1-P) (50)

B.   The P/G% approach

	Avoid abuse ($W = 2$)	Preserve family love ($W = 1$)	Save taxpayer cost ($W = 1$)	Weighted sum
Take away	4	2	2	12
Leave	2	4	4	12

Notes

1.   The cell entries are arrived at by asking the decision-makers the following questions:

   (a) Of the four possible occurrences, which ones are desirable (marked plus), and which ones are undesirable (marked minus)?

   (b) Of the undesirable occurrences, which one is the most undesirable (marked -100)?

   (c) How much more undesirable is the most undesirable occurrence in comparison to the less undesirable occurrence (marked -50) to show cell (d) is twice as bad as cell (a)?

2.   With that information, one can determine the threshold probability as follows:

   (a) At the threshold, the discounted benefits equal the discounted costs (i.e., $100P = 10-50P$).

   (b) The solution for P in that equation $P^* = d/(a+d)$ or $P^* = 100/(50 + 100) = .33$.

   (c) That means if the probability is greater than .33, there will be severe subsequent abuse, then the child should be taken away.

3.   The scoring of each alternative on each criterion is on a 1-5 scale where 5 = highly conducive to the goal, 4 = mildly conducive, 3 = neither conducive nor adverse, 2 = mildly adverse to the goal, and 1 = highly adverse. Decimal scores can be given between these numbers where appropriate.

4.   Avoiding abuse is considered to be twice as important as preserving whatever family love might exist or saving taxpayer cost.

5.   By considering multiple criteria rather than emphasizing the probability of severe subsequent abuse, the decision is a much closer decision, and more dependent on the specific facts or scores on the first two criteria than on a general threshold probability.

6.   If the criteria are given equal weight and a threshold analysis is performed, then leaving the child wins 10 points to 8 points. The threshold or tie-causing values of the weights are 2, 0, and 0. The threshold values of the relation scores are then 6,4,0,2, and 2, reading across the matrix.

7.   The advantages of the P/G% approach over a payoff-matrix include:

     (a) P/G% can explicitly consider any number of criteria such as the three shown above.

     (b) P/G% can explicitly consider any number of alternatives such as take away to an institution, take away to a foster home, take away to a relative's home, leave with counselling, or leave without counselling.

     (c) Being able to consider multiple criteria and multiple alternatives makes the P/G% approach more validly in conformance with reality, and not just a simplistic abstraction.

     (d) P/G% is also simpler with 15 scales, weighted criteria, computerized threshold analysis, and a logical way of analyzing a problem in terms of alternative, criteria, and relations.

8.   For further details, see Nagel (1987).

TABLE 8
Public Administration: Using P/G% to Allocate
Resources to Budget Categories

1A.   **The alternative budget categories and the allocation criteria**

Alternative	Criterion	Meas. Unit	Weight
1 Police	1 Crime reduction	Relative x	1.00
2 Courts	2 Fair procedure	Relative x	2.00

1B.   **The relative scoring of the alternatives on the criteria**
Alternative/Criteria scoring

	Crime re	Fair pro
Police	2.00	1.00
Courts	1.00	3.00

1C.   **Allocation percentages in light of each criterion**
Part / Whole %

	Crime re	Fair pro
Police	66.67	25.00
Courts	33.33	75.00

1D.   **Weighted allocation percentages**
(With one criterion considered twice as important)
Weighted part / Whole %

	Crime re	Fair pro
Police	66.67	50.00
Courts	33.33	150.00

1E.   **Averaging the weighted allocation percentages**

	Combined	
Alternative	Q P/ W	%
1 Police	116.67	38.89
2 Courts	183.33	61.11

1F.   **Applying the average allocation percentages to the total resource**
Total resources = 500.00

Alternative	Alloc.
1 Police	194.44
2 Courts	305.56

Note

1.   For further details, see Nagel (1990).

TABLE 9
Public Administration: Assigning People to Tasks

CASES LAWYER	CRIMINAL		CIVIL		Hours per Lawyer
	Quality Score	Hours Assigned	Quality Score	Hours Assigned	
Green	4	a	3	b	30
Brown	2	c	3	d	30
Hours per casetype		24		36	60

Notes

1. The allocation system is shown in its simplest form with two officials and two tasks. Each official is expected to put in 40 hours a week to satisfy the average total of 80 hours of working time. Processing applications constitutes 75% of the total or 60 hours, and conducting hearings constitutes 25% or 20 hours. Mr. Green received scores of 3 and 4 on the two tasks, and Ms. Brown received scores of 3 and 2.

2. A logical way to resolve the optimum allocation with this relatively simple example is to reason as follows:

   (a) Ms. Brown does a bad job on conducting hearings. Therefore, give Ms. Brown 0 hours of hearings. That means Mr. Green gets 20 hours of hearings to add down to 20 hours. That also means Ms. Brown gets 40 hours of applications in order to add across to 40 hours. Mr. Green then gets 20 hours of applications to add down to 60 and across to 40.

   (b) As an alternative, one can note Mr. Green does a good job on conducting hearings. Therefore, give Mr. Green as many hours of hearings as possible which is 20. That means Ms. Brown must then get 40 hours of applications to add across to 40. Mr. Green must also get 20 hours of applications to add across to 40 and down to 60.

   (c) Also try to minimize the number of tasks per person rather than have every person do at least a little bit of everything.

4. The optimum allocation is defined as allocating the total number of hours to each cell so as to satisfy the row constraints, the column constraints, and any cell constraints, while at the same time maximizing the sum of the products of the quality score times the hours assigned for each cell. A cell includes a quality score of a person on a task and a quantity of hours assigned to a person on a task.

5. For further details, see Nagel and Mills (1986).

TABLE 10

Social Work: Providing Public Aid, Especially For Dependent Children

GOALS / POLICIES	Low Taxpayer Burden Direct	Indirect	Encourage Recipients to Advance Themselves	Politically Feasible	No Artificial Migration	No Unconstitutional Unfairness	Sums
1. No Public Aid	5	1	2	1	3	3	15
2. The Poor House	1	2	2	1	3	2	11
3. Unreformed ADC	2	2	2	4	2	2	14
4. ADC Plus Work Incentives	2	3	4	4	2	2	17
5. The Above Plus the Working Poor	2	2	4	4	4	4	18
6. The Above Plus Due Process & NIT	2	2	4	4	4	4	20
7. Broaden Survivorship	2	4	4	1	4	4	20
8. Demogrant or Children's Allowances	1	3	2	1	4	4	15

TABLE 11
Education: Dealing with Low Income Districts

A. The alternatives and the criteria

Alternative	Previous Outcome	Criterion	Meas. unit	Weight
No equality reqd.	Yes	1 Educated pop.	1 - 3	1.00
= $ per student	No	2 Discontent		1.00
Min. $ per student	No	3 Downgrading		1.00
High $ per student	No	4 Admin. ease		1.00
Other	?	5 Consis.w/cases		1.00
		6 Expense		1.00

B. The scores of the alternatives on the criteria

	Criterion					
	1	2	3	4	5	6
No equality reqd.	1.00	1.00	3.00	3.00	2.00	3.00
= $ per student	2.00	2.00	1.00	1.00	2.00	2.00
Min. $ per student	2.00	2.00	2.00	1.00	2.00	1.50
High $ per student	3.00	3.00	2.00	1.00	1.00	1.00

C. The total scores of the alternatives

Alternative	Combined Raw Scores	Previous Outcome
No equality reqd.	13.00	Yes
= $ per student	10.00	No
Min. $ per student	10.50	No
High $ per student	11.00	No

D. What it would take to bring the second place alternative up to first place

Criterion	No equality	Min. $ per student	Weight
1	- 1.50	4.40	3.500
2	- 1.50	4.50	3.500
3	0.50	4.50	- 1.500
4	0.50	3.50	- 0.250
5	- 0.50	4.50	??
6	0.50	4.00	- 0.667

Note

1.   For further details, see Nagel (1989).

Some Conclusions

Microcomputers can be used to aid people in all fields of behavioral science in reaching decisions. Decision-aiding software is especially relevant to processing a set of goals to be achieved, alternatives for achieving them, and relations between goals and alternatives in order to choose the best alternative, combination, or allocation of scarce resources.

Decision-aiding software can be useful in dealing with such analytic problems as (a) multiple dimensions on multiple goals, (b) multiple missing information, (c) multiple alternatives that are too many to determine the effects of each one, (d) multiple and possibly conflicting constraints, and (e) the need for simplicity in view of all that multiplicity.

Using decision-aiding software can enable us to (a) avoid the drudgery of arithmetic, (b) be prompted into clarifying goals, alternatives, and relations, (c) try numerous changes to see their effects, and (d) have one's creativity stimulated in developing better explanations of why things happen the way they do and better decisions as to what should be done.

References

Edwards, W. and Newman, R. (1982). *Multi-Attribute Evaluation*. Beverly Hills: Sage Publications.

Henderson, T. (1983). *Spreadsheet Software: From VisiCalc to 1-2-3*. Indianapolis: Que.

Nagel, S. (1984). Multiple Goals and Multiple Policies. *Public Policy: Goals, Means, and Methods.*

Nagel, S. (1986). Using Microcomputers to Choose Among Government Structures. *International Political Science Review, 7,* 27-38.

Nagel, S. (1987). Multi-Criteria Versus Traditional Analysis: Microcomputer Techniques. *Social Science Journal, 24,* 115-126.

Nagel, S. (1989). Computer-Aided Advocacy. *University of Dayton Law Review.*

Nagel, S. (1990). A Theory of Rational and Feasible Budget Allocation. *International Journal of Public Administration.* New York: St. Martin's.

Nagel, S. and Mills, M. (1986). Using Management Science to Assign Judges to Casetypes. *University of Miami Law Review, 40,* 1317-1336.

Saaty, T. (1980). *The Analytic Hierarchy Process: Planning, Priority Setting, Resource Allocation.* New York: McGraw-Hill.

Zeleny, M. (1982). *Multiple Criteria Decision-Making.* New York: McGraw-Hill.

Notes

For further information concerning this multi-criteria decision-aiding tool, write or phone Stuart Nagel, 361 Lincoln Hall, University of Illinois, Urbana, Illinois 61801, U.S.A., (217) 359-8541. The microcomputer program is based on S. Nagel (1984). A copy of the program, the present manual, and periodic updates can be obtained for experimental purposes for only US$40 to cover the cost of three floppy disks, photocopying, postage, and handling. A copy of the current manuscript for the relevant book entitled *Teach Yourself Decision-Aiding Software* is also included. A reduced version of this article appeared in *Commentary, 8,* 52-55, June 1990, Singapore: National University of Singapore Society.

A LIST OF RECENT ARTICLES IN
JUDGMENT AND DECISION MAKING

Allison, S. T., Jordan, A. M., and Yeatts, C. E. (1992). A cluster-analytic approach toward indentifying the structure and content of human decision making. *Human Relations, 45(1),* 49-72.

Allison, S. T., Worth, L. T., and King, M. C. (1990). Group decisions as social inference heuristics. *Journal of Personality and Social Psychology, 58,* 801-811.

Argote, L., Devadas, R., and Melone, N. (1990). The base-rate fallacy: Contrasting processes and outcomes of group and individual judgment. *Organizational Behavior and Human Decision Processes, 46,* 296-310.

Arkes, H. R. (1989). Principles in judgment/decision making research pertinent to legal proceedings. *Behavioral Sciences and the Law, 7,* 429-456.

Artal, J. (1990). Factores determinantes de la decision de ingreso en las urgencias psiquiatricas. (Determinant factors in the decision to hospitalize psychiatric emergency patients.) *Revista de Psiquiatria de la Facultad de Medicina de Barcelona, 17,* 159-172.

Ashby, F. G., and Maddox, W. T. (1992). Complex decision rules in categorization: Contrasting novice and experienced performance. *Journal of Experimental Psychology: Human Perception and Performance, 18,* 50-71.

Baron, J. (1990). Harmful heuristics and the improvement of thinking. *Contributions to Human Development, 21,* 28-47.

Baumann, A. O., Deber, R. A., and Thompson, G. G. (1991). Overconfidence among physicians and nurses: The "micro-certainty, macro-uncertaintly" phenomenon. *Social Science and Medicine, 32,* 167-174.

Beckham, J. C., Annis, L. V., and Gustafson, D. J. (1989). Decision making and examiner bias in forensic expert recommendations for not guilty by reason of insanity. *Law and Human Behavior, 13,* 79-87.

Boreham, N. C. (1989). Modelling medical decision-making under uncertainty. *British Journal of Educational Psychology, 59,* 187-199.

Boreham, N. C., Foster, R. W., and Mawer, G. E. (1989). The Phenytoin Game: Its effect on decision skills. *Simulation and Games, 20,* 292-299.

Bradley, R. W., and Mims, G. A. (1992). Using family systems and birth order dynamics as the basis for a college career decision-making course. *Journal of Counseling and Development, 70(3),* 445-448.

Bradshaw, J. M., and Boose, H. H. (1990). Decision analysis techniques for knowledge acquisition: Combining information and preference using Aquinas and Axotl. *International Journal of Man Machine Studies, 32,* 121-186.

Chua, F. K. (1990). The processing of spatial frequency and orientation information. *Perception and Psychophysics, 47,* 79-86.

Clark, J. A., Potter, D. A., and McKinlay, J. B. (1991). Bringing social structure back into clinical decision making. *Social Science and Medicine, 32,* 853-866.

Connolly, T. J., Blackwell, B. B., and Lester, L. F. (1989). A simulator-based approach to training in aeronautical decision making. *Aviation, Space, and Environmental Medicine, 60,* 50-52.

Connor, P. E. (1992). Decision-making participation patterns: The role of organizational context. *Academy of Management Journal, 35,* 218-231.

Costanzo, M., and Costanzo, S. (1992). Jury decision making in the capital penalty phase: Legal assumptions, empirical findings, and a research agenda. *Law and Human Behavior, 16(2),* 185-201.

Dawson, N. V., and Cebul, R. D. (1990). Advances in quantitative techniques for making medical decisions: The last decade. Special issue: Reflections on research in medical problem solving. *Evaluation and the Health Professions, 13,* 37-62.

Elstein, A. S., Shulman, L. S., and Sprafka. S. A. (1990). Medical problem solving: A ten-year retrospective. Special issue: Reflections on research on medical problem solving. *Evaluation and the Health Professions, 13,* 5-36.

Engel, J. D., Wigton, R., LaDuca, A., and Blacklow, R. S. (1990). A social judgment theory perspective on clinical problem solving. Special issue: Reflection on research in medical problem solving. *Evaluation and the Health Professions, 13,* 63-78.

Erev, I., and Cohen, B. L. (1990). Verbal versus numerical probabilities: Efficiency, biases, and the preference paradox. *Organizational, Behavioral and Human Decision Processes, 45,* 1-18.

Fischhoff, B. (1990). Awards for distinguished contributions to psychology in the public interest. *American-Psychologist, 46,* 314-316.

Fitten, L. J., Lusky, R., and Hamann, C. (1990). Assessing treatment decision-making capacity of nursing home residents. *Journal of the American Geriatrics Society, 38,* 1097-1104.

Flint, D. B. (1989). Factors that influence hypothetical treatment decisions for newborns with mental retardation and an accompanying life-threatening medical disorder. *Dissertation Abstracts International, 49,* 4573.

Gibbons, P. T. (1992). Impacts of organizational evolution on leadership roles and behaviors. *Human Relations, 45(1),* 1-18.

Greer, M. L., Kirk, K. W., and Crismon, M. L. (1989). The development and pilot testing of a community-practice, clinical pharmacy decision-making assessment instrument. *Evaluation and the Health Professions, 12,* 207-232.

Guttman, L. A. (1989). The role of context and gender in moral judgment. *Dissertation Abstracts International, 50,* 764.

Hamm, V. P., and Hasher, L. (1992). Age and the availability of inferences. *Psychology and Aging, 7(1),* 56-64.

Harmon, J., and Rohrbaugh, J. (1990). Social judgment analysis and small group decision making: Cognitive feedback effects on individual and collective performance. *Organizational Behavior and Human Decision Processes, 46,* 34-54.

Heard, C. A. (1989). Factors influencing the decision making process in the substantiation of child sexual abuse cases. *Dissertation Abstracts International, 50,* 543.

Henry, S. B., LeBreck, D. B., and Holzemer, W. L. (1989). The effect of verbalization of cognitive processes on clinical decision making. *Research in Nursing and Health, 12,* 187-193.

Jacobs, J. E., and Potenza, M. (1991) The use of judgment heuristics to make social and object decisions: A developmental perspective. *Child-Development, 62*, 166-178.

Joag, S. G., Mowen, J. C., and Gentry, J. W. Risk perception in a simulated industrial purchasing task: The effects of single versus multi-play decisions. *Journal of Behavioral Decision Making, 3*, 91-108.

Josephs, R. A., Larrick, R. P., Steele, C. M., and Nisbett, R. E. (1992). Protecting the self from negative consequences of risky decisions. *Journal of Personality and Social Psychology, 62(1)*, 26-37.

Kendrick, A. J., and Mapstone, E. (1989). The chairperson of child care reviews in Scotland: Implications for the role of reviews in the decision making process. *British Journal of Social Work, 19*, 277-290.

Kilduff, M. (1992). The friendship network as a decision-making resource: Dispositional moderators of social influences on organizational choice. *Journal of Personality and Social Psychology, 62*, 168-180.

Lasher, G. C. (1990). Judgment analysis of school superintendent decision making. *Journal of Experimental Education, 59*, 87-96.

Levi, K. (1989). Expert systems should be more accurate than human experts: Evaluation procedures from human judgment and decision making. Special Issue: Perspectives in knowledge engineering. *IEEE Transactions on Systems, Man, and Cybernetics, 19*, 647-657.

Levkoff, S., and Wetle, T. (1989). Clinical decision making in the care of the aged. *Journal of Aging and Health, 1*, 83-101.

Lipe, M. G. (1990). A lens model analysis of covariation research. *Journal of Behavioral Decision Making, 3*, 45-59.

Lo, B. (1990). Assessing decision-making capacity. *Law, Medicine and Health Care, 18*, 193-201.

Longenecker, C. O., Joccoud, A. J., Sims, H. P., and Gioia, D. A. (1992). Quantitative and qualitative investigations of affect in executive judgment. *Applied Psychology: An International Review, 4*, 21-41.

Lucus, M. S. (1992). Problems expressed by career and non-career help seekers: A comparison. *Journal of Counseling and Development, 70(3)*, 417-420.

Mandes, E., and Gessner, T. (1989). The principle of additivity and its relation to clinical decision making. *Journal of Psychology, 123*, 485-490.

March, J. G., and Shapira, Z. (1992). Variable risk preferences and the focus of attention. *Psychological Review, 99(1)*, 172-183.

Marcus, B. H., and Owen, N. (1992). Motivational readiness, self-efficacy and decision-making for exercise. *Journal of Applied Social Psychology, 22(1)*, 3-16.

Margolis, C. Z., Cook, C. D., Barak, N., and Adler, A. et al. (1989). Clinical algorithms teach pediatric decision making more effectively than prose. *Medical Care, 27*, 576-592.

Marteau, T. M. (1989). Framing of information: Its influence upon decisions of doctors and patients. *British Journal of Social Psychology, 28*, 89-94.

Mattenklott, A., and Reifenberger, H. P. (1990). Anschaulichkeit und Diagnostizitat von Information in ihrer Verfugbarkeit fur die Urteilsbildung. (The effects of vividness and decision-related aspects of information on its availability for judgment formation.) *Zeitschrift fur Experimentelle und Angewandte Psychologie, 37*, 69-84.

McClane, W. E. , and Harris, W. L. (1991). Supervisor's performance attributions: A possible barrier to managerial acceptance of decision aids. *Perceptual and Motor Skills, 73(3, Pt 1)*, 971-978.

Meinhold, P. M., and Mulick, J. A. (1990). Risks, choices and behavioral treatment. *Behavioral Residential Treatment, 5*, 29-44.

Michaelson, L. K., Watson, W. E., Schwartzkopf, A., and Black, R. H. (1992). Group decision making: How you frame the question determines what you find. *Journal of Applied Psychology, 77(1)*, 106-108.

Miyamoto, J. M., and Eraker, S. A. (1989). Parametric models of the utility of survival duration: Tests of axioms in a generic utility framework. *Organizational Behavior and Human Decision Processes, 44*, 166-202.

Morgan, M. J. (1989). Perceptual decision-making: Watching neurons discriminate. *Nature, 341*, 20-21.

Munier, B. (1989). Cognition and uncertainty. Special Issue: Economic reasoning and artificial intelligence. Theory and Decision, 27, 93-106. Murdock, N. L. and Fremont, S. K. (1989). Attributional influences in counselor decision making. *Journal of Counseling Psychology, 36*, 417-422.

Nakajima, Y., and Ohta, H. (1989). Decision making with probability forecasts of rainfall. *Psychological Reports, 64*, 1051-1055.

Neisworth, J. T., and Baganato, S. J. (1992). The case against intelligence testing in early intervention. *Topics in Early Childhood Special Education, 12(1)*, 1-20.

O'Donohue, W., Fisher, J. E., Plaud, J. J., and Link, W. (1989). What is a good treatment decision? The client's perspective. *Professional Psychology: Research and Practice, 20*, 404-407.

O'Donohue, W., Fisher, J. E., Plaud, J., and Curtis, S. D. (1990). Treatment, decisions: Their nature and their justification. *Psychotherapy, 27*, 421-427.

Paese, P. W. (1989). Confidence and accuracy in concurrent and predictive judgments of performance. *Dissertation Abstracts International, 50*, 775.

Paese, P. W., and Peuer, M. A. (1991). Decisions, actions, and the appropriateness of confidence in knowledge. *Journal of Behavioral Decision Making, 4*, 1-16.

Paese, P. W., and Sniezek, J. A. (1991). Influences on the appropriateness of confidence in judgment: Practice, effort, information, and decision-making. *Organizational Behavior and Human Decision Process, 48*, 100-130.

Parker, R. J. (1990). The relationship between dogmatism, orthodox Christian beliefs, and ethical judgment. *Counselling and Values, 34*, 213-216.

Pennington, N., and Hastie, R. (1992). Explaining the evidence: Test of the Story Model for juror decision making. *Journal of Personality and Social Psychology, 62*, 189-206.

Powell, J. L. (1991). An attempt at increasing decision rule use in a judgment task. *Organizational Behavior and Human Decision Processes, 48*, 89-99.

Rather, B. C., Goldman, M. S., Roehrich, L., and Brannick, M. (1992). Empirical modeling of an alcohol expectancy memory network using multidimensional scaling. *Journal of Abnormal Psychology, 101(1)*, 174-183.

Robinson, E. J., and Mitchell, P. (1990). Children's failure to make judgments of undecidability when they are ignorant. *International Journal of Behavioral Development, 13,* 467-488.

Rothert, M., Rovner, D., Holmes, M., Schmitt, N. et al. (1990). Woman's use of information regarding hormone replacement therapy. *Research in Nursing and Health, 13,* 355-366.

Ruble, T. L., and Cosier, R. A. (1990). Effects of cognitive styles and decision setting on performance. *Organizational Behavior and Human Decision Processes, 46,* 283-295.

Sawyer, J. E. (1990). Effects of risk and ambiguity on judgments on contingency relations and behavioral resource allocation decisions. *Organizational Behavior and Human Decision Processes, 45,* 85-110.

Schkade, D. A., and Johnson, E. J. (1989). Cognitive processes in preference reversals. *Organizational Behavior and Human Decision Processes, 44,* 203-231.

Schwartz, J. P., and Norman, K. L. (1989). Separating cue relevance from cue importance within models of judgment and decision making. *Organizational Behavior and Human Decision Processes, 43,* 355-384.

Shamian, J. (1991). Effect of teaching decision analysis on student nurses' clinical intervention decision making. *Research in Nursing and Health, 14,* 59-66.

Sniezek, J. A. (1990). A comparison of techniques for judgmental forecasting by groups with common information. *Group and Organization Studies, 15,* 5-19.

Sniezek, J. A., and Henry, R. A. (1989). Accuracy and confidence in group judgment. *Organizational Behavior and Human Decision Processes, 43,* 1-28.

Sniezek, J. A., and Henry, R. A. (1990). Revision, weighting, and commitment in consensus group judgment. *Organizational Behavior and Human Decision Processes, 45,* 66-84.

Souder, S. V. (1989). The effects of mood on children's judgments of noncontingency. *Dissertation Abstracts International, 50,* 354.

Sterman, J. D. (1989). Misperceptions of feedback in dynamic decision making. *Organizational Behavior and Human Decision Processes, 43,* 301-335.

Stradling, S. G., Tuchy, A. P., and Harper, K. J. (1990). Judgmental asymmetry in the exercise of police discretion. *Applied Cognitive Psychology, 4,* 409-421.

Switzer, F. S. (1989). Judgment processes in motivation: Anchoring and adjustment effects on judgment and behavior. *Dissertation Abstracts International, 50,* 776.

Tindale, R. S., and Larson, J. R. (1992). It's not how you frame the question, it's how you interpret the results. *Journal of Applied Psychology, 77,* 109-110.

Tindale, R. S., and Larson, J. R. (1992). Assembly bonus effect or typical group performance? A comment on Michaelsen, Watson and Black (1989). *Journal of Applied Psychology, 77(1),* 102-105.

Tolbert, R. B. (1989). Decision making in psychiatric emergencies: A phenomenological analysis of gatekeeping. *Journal of Community Psychology, 17,* 47-69.

Tomlinson, T., Howe, K., Notman, M., and Rossmiller, D. (1990). An empirical study of proxy consent for elderly persons. *Gerontologist, 30,* 54-64.

Tyler, T. R. (1989). The psychology of procedural justice: A test of the group-value model. *Journal of Personality and Social Psychology, 57,* 830-838.

Van, D. K. (1991). Prijzen of misprijzen. Kanttekeningen bij 20 jaar psychologische besliskunde. (Practice or criticism: Comments on 20 years of psychological study on decision making.). *Psychology, 26,* 168-172.

Walker, D. W., and Hulecki, M. B. (1989). Is AIDS a biasing factor in teacher judgment? *Exceptional Children, 5,* 342-345.

Wanberg, C. R., and Muchinsky, P. M. (1992). A topology of career decision status: Validity extension of the vocational decision status model. *Journal of Counseling Psychology, 39(1),* 71-80.

Wang, Z. M. (1990). Information structures and cognitive strategies in decision-making on systems development. Special issue: Ergonomics in China. *Ergonomics, 33,* 907-916.

Weber, E. U., and Coskunoglu, A. (1990). Descriptive and prescriptive models of decision making: Implications for the development of decision aids. *IEEE Transactions on Systems, Man, and Cybernetics, 20,* 310-317.

Wedding, D., and Faust, D. (1989). Clinical judgment and decision making in neuropsychology. *Archives of Clinical Neuropsychology, 4,* 233-265.

Witt, L. A. (1992). Exchange ideology as a moderator of the relationships between importance of participation in decision making and job attitudes. *Human Relations, 45,* 73-85.

Wolff, N. (1989). Professional uncertainty and physician medical decision-making in a multiple treatment framework. Special Issue: Geographic variation of health care use. *Social Science and Medicine, 28,* 99-107.

Wright, A. A. (1992). Learning mechanisms in matching to sample. *Journal of Experimental Psychology: Animal Behavior Processes, 18,* 67-79.

Wright, W. F., and Anderson, U. (1989). Effects of situation familiarity and financial incentives on use of the anchoring and adjustment heuristic for probability assessment. *Organizational Behavior and Human Decision Processes, 44,* 68-82.

Zuber, J. A., Crott, H. W., and Werner, J. (1992). Choice shift and group polarization: An analysis of the status arguments and social decisions schemes. *Journal of Personality and Social Psychology, 62,* 50-61.

Zygmond, M. J., and Boorhem, H. (1989). Ethical decision making in family therapy. *Family Process, 28,* 269-280.

CONTRIBUTORS

FARROKH ALEMI received his Ph.D. from the University of Wisconsin, Madison, in decision analysis. He is the Director of Research for Jefferson Medical College's Center for Research in Medical Education and Health Care. He is the co-author of an upcoming book on analysis of health care policy.

ROBERT N. BONTEMPO received his Ph.D. from the University of Illinois, where he specialized in cross-cultural psychology. He is Assistant Professor of International Business at Columbia University in New York City. His research interests include international management, international negotiations, and cultural factors in international economic policy.

WILLIAM P. BOTTOM is Assistant Professor of Organizational Behavior in the John M. Olin School of Business at Washington University. His current interests include decision making and negotiation.

COLETTE BROWNING is a lecturer in the Department of Behavioral Health Sciences in the Lincoln School of Health Sciences at La Trobe University. She holds an M.Sc. in Psychology from Monash University and is presently pursuing her Ph.D. studies in the effects of aging upon problem-solving and decision making performance.

SHEILA CORCORAN-PERRY received her Ph.D. in Educational Psychology and Philosophy from the University of Minnesota in 1983. She is Associate Professor in the School of Nursing, University of Minnesota. She worked as a qualified nurse, and also has held various teaching positions. She had published on education and nursing, with current interest in clinical decision making by nurses.

JANET DOYLE is Senior Lecturer in the Department of Communication Disorders in the Lincoln School of Health Sciences at La Trobe University. She holds an M.App.Sci. in Health Sciences and is completing a Ph.D. in the decision making of audiologists in real-world settings, as well as being a practicing audiologist.

RICHARD ETTENSON is a cognitive research psychologist whose research areas include consumer decision making and human judgment. He is Assistant Professor in the Department of Textiles and Consumer Economics at the University of Maryland. He received his Ph.D. in Experimental Psychology from Kansas State University.

JACK FELDMAN has a Ph.D. in industrial/organizational psychology at the University of Illinois. He was Chairman of the Department of Management, University of Texas at Arlington and is now a Professor of Psychology and Management, Georgia Institute of Technology. His research concerns the effects of measurement operations on the constructs and behavior measured, the role of rationality in decision processes, and the design and implementation of performance appraisal systems in organization.

TING FEI HO, MMed, MD, is Senior Lecturer of the Department of Physiology, National University of Singapore and Visiting Specialist of the Department of Paediatrics, National University Hospital. Her current research interest is in childhood obesity, lung function testing in children, and national blood pressure studies in children.

DAVID R. HOLTGRAVE received his Ph.D. in Quantitative Psychology from the University of Illinois in 1988 and spent the next one and a half years as a research fellow at Harvard's School of Public Health. He is now Assistant Professor of Family Medicine (Clinical Decision Analysis Unit) at the University of Oklahoma Health Science Center. His primary research interests are in the areas of risky choice, risk perception, and health applications.

RICHARD D. JOHNSON is Assistant Professor of Marketing and Economic Analysis at the University of Alberta. He received his Ph.D. in psychology at the University of Iowa in 1985 and a post-doctoral fellowship at the University of Chicago in 1986. His research interests concern a number of facets of human judgment and decision making like decisions based on incomplete information, interactions of memory and judgment, probability estimation, and influences on subjective discount rates.

SENG BEE KEEK received his B.Soc.Sc. (Hons) from the National University of Singapore and is a consultant at Hay Management Consultants, Malaysia. He was previously a partner of Decision Processes International (DPI), Singapore. His current interest is on how the local successful innovative and entrepreneurial companies are being managed.

WINSTON TEOW HOCK KOH is a lecturer of the Department of Business Policy, Faculty of Business Administration, National University of Singapore. He read Economics at the University of Cambridge on a Singapore Government Scholarship (1982-1985) and obtained his B.A. (Double First-Class) in 1985. He was awarded a Princeton University Fellowship to do his Ph.D. under Joseph Stiglitz and received his doctoral degree in 1988.

IRWIN P. LEVIN is Professor of Psychology and Honors Director at the University of Iowa. He has been on the faculty at the University of Iowa since receiving his Ph.D. from U.C.L.A. in 1965. He is a member of the Judgment and Decision Making Society and is on the editorial board of Organizational Behavior of Human Decision Processes. His recent research includes studies of inferential processes in information integration and development of models of information framing effects.

WING HONG LOKE is a tenured Senior Lecturer of Psychology at the Department of Social Work and Psychology, and was previously also the Sub-Dean of the Faculty of Arts and Social Sciences, National University of Singapore. He received his M.A. and Ph.D. in experimental/cognitive psychology from the University of Iowa and M.Sc. in human resource management from Rutgers, The State University of New Jersey. His current research is in the effects of personality and culture on decision making. His recent publications are *A Guide to Journals in Psychology and Education* (Scarecrow, 1990) and *Human Resource Management (Commentary: Journal of the National University of Singapore, 1991)*.

ARNE MAAS has studied psychology at the University of Leiden and is working in the field of preferences since 1986. Now he is doing research at the University of Nijmegen on patients suffering from laryngeal cancer, who have problems deciding which medical therapy to follow. His research interests are decision theory and measurement theory.

VIANNE MCLEAN is Head of the Department of Care and Education within the School of Early Childhood Studies at the Queensland University of Technology. She gained her Ph.D. from Arizona State University in 1986. Her current research is examining the use of case study material and "stories of teaching" in pre-service teacher education programs.

MARIAN LOUISE MILLER is a final-year graduate student in clinical psychology at the University of Washington. Her research interests include psychotherapist job stress and burnout, community psychology, and borderline personality disorder.

THEODORE J. MOCK is the Arthur Andersen Alumni Professor of Accounting and Director, Center for Accounting Research within the School of Accounting at the University of Southern California (USC). He has a doctorate in business administration from the University of California at Berkeley. He was the first audit research fellow at Peat Marwick Mitchell (now KPMG) in New York City and was Director of Research of the American Accounting Association (AAA).

STUART S. NAGEL is Professor of Political Science at the University of Illinois. He is the secretary-treasurer and publications coordinator of the Policy Studies Organization. He holds a Ph.D. in political science from Northwestern University (1961) and a J.D. in law, also from Northwestern (1958). His recent books are *Policy Studies: Integration and Evaluation* (Praeger, 1988) and *Evaluation Analysis with Microcomputers* (JAI Press, 1989).

SUZANNE NARAYAN is an Assistant Professor in the Nursing Program, Metropolitan State University. She holds a MSN (Nursing) from Case Western Reserve University in 1976 and is pursuing her Ph.D. in Metropolitan State University. She worked as a qualified nurse and instructor since 1973 and her current research interest is in clinical decision making by nurses.

ALAN PEARMAN gained a doctorate in transport economics and planning from the University of Leeds. He is now senior lecturer in the School of Business and Economic Studies, University of Leeds and holds an associate post in the Institute for Transport Studies. He has published in the fields of multicriteria decision analysis and decision making under uncertainty and is concerned with the application of formal decision-making techniques to public sector problems.

MARK H. B. RADFORD is a lecturer in the Department of Behavioral Science, Bungakubu, Hokkaido University. He was a Japanese Government (Monbusho) Research Fellow in the Department of Neuropsychiatry, Nagasaki University School of Medicine. He received his Ph.D. from the School of Medicine, The Flinders University of South Australia. His research areas are social psychology and social psychiatry, with particular interests in the role of culture on human behavior, decision making, and international communication and interaction.

CARLA J. REICKS is completing her Ph.D. program in psychology at the University of Iowa. She has conducted research with Professors Irwin Levin and Gary Gaeth on marketing applications of judgment and decision-making models.

JANET RICE teaches bio-statistics at Tulane School of Public Health. She received her doctorate in Educational Research from Purdue University. She has published in health care and statistical journals.

J. CARLOS RIVERO is a doctoral candidate in the Department of Psychology at New York University. He is also an internal consultant in training and professional development at Goldman Sachs & Co., New York. His current research interests include dynamic decision making and models of investor choice.

BERNADETTE SIM is an honors graduate in Psychology at the National University of Singapore in 1990. Her thesis was on decision making in the legal area. Her research interest is in the effects of extralegal factors on legal decisions.

TAPEN SINHA is currently an Assistant Professor of Insurance in the School of Business of Bond University, Queensland, Australia. He obtained his Ph.D. in Economics from the University of Minnesota. He was a lecturer at the National University of Singapore, Department of Economics and Statistics (1987-1989). His current research interests are decision making under uncertainty and economics of insurance.

CHWEE TECK TAN is a graduate student in marketing at the University of Alberta. A native of Singapore, he worked in sales and marketing for five years, most recently as a product manager of Gillette Singapore for two years before continuing his education. His research interests are in international marketing and marketing strategy.

TERRI ING FANG TAN is a graduate in Psychology and Social Work from the National University of Singapore in 1989. She is presently working as a bank officer and intends to do research in the area of customer service.

JOHN SIN HOCK TAY, MD, FRACP, is currently Professor of Paediatrics and Acting Head of the Department of Paediatrics, National University of Singapore. His current research interest is in molecular genetics, clinical paediatric cardiology, and medical statistics.

SHANE A. THOMAS is a lecturer in the Department of Behavioral Health Sciences in the Lincoln School of Health Sciences at La Trobe University. He holds a Ph.D. in psychology from the University of Melbourne and is pursuing a research program in clinical decision making and health psychology.

JANET WAGNER received her Ph.D. in Textile Marketing from Kansas State University. She currently is an Assistant Professor in the Department of Textiles and Consumer Economics at the University of Maryland. Her research areas include consumer decision making and retail buyer behavior.

MARY T. WASHINGTON received her Ph.D. from the University of Southern California in 1987. She is currently an Assistant Professor at the University of California, Irvine, and is a Certified Public Accountant in the state of Ohio. She was the recipient of an Arthur Andersen Dissertation Fellowship and a Richard D. Irwin Dissertation Fellowship. Her research interests are in the areas of audit decision making and human information processing.

WILLIAM CHIN LING YIP, MD, FRCP (Edinburg), is a Consultant Paediatrician and Paediatric Cardiologist in private practice at the Gleneagles Medical Center, a Visiting Consultant at the National University Hospital, and a Clinical Teacher in the Department of Paediatrics, National University of Singapore. His research interest is in Doppler color flow mapping and exercise physiology in children with heart disease, paediatric sonography, and application of computer in medical research.